OCCULT SECRETS
Of The Thrid Reich

**Timothy Green Beckley, Sean Casteel, Tim Swartz,
Olav Phillips, Hercules Invictus, Tim Cridland,
Albrecht Giddings, Peter Moon,
Brad Steiger, Téodoro Rampalé**

Conspiracy Journal
PRODUCTIONS

Occult Secrets Of The Third Reich

Published in the United States of America By
Global Communications/Conspiracy Journal
Box 753 · New Brunswick, NJ 08903

Staff Members
Timothy G. Beckley, Publisher
Carol Ann Rodriguez, Assistant to the Publisher
Sean Casteel, General Associate Editor
Tim R. Swartz, Graphics and Editorial Consultant
William Kern, Editorial and Art Consultant

Sign Up On The Web For Our Free Weekly Newsletter
and Mail Order Version of Conspiracy Journal
and Bizarre Bazaar
www.ConspiracyJournal.com

Order Hot Line: 1-732-602-3407
PayPal: MrUFO8@hotmail.com

CONTENTS

CAVEAT

Noun:
1. A Warning Or Proviso Of Specific Stipulations,
Conditions Or Limitations.

There are many things you will see and read in this book that seem astonishing.

And truly they are!

It is important to take an open-minded, but critical, view of the material covered within the pages of this work, especially when it comes to the depiction of Nazi UFOs in the air and on the ground. There are those who maintain that these photos have been propagated for propaganda purposes by neo-Nazi groups active around the world or are part of a massive disinformation campaign waged by some possible Fourth Reich positioned at the South Pole. I find it amazing that there are more "good" photos of Nazi UFOs – all looking very "plush and polished," and many done before Photoshop existed – than the UFO groups or even YouTube submitters can supply us with. They look "authentic" but are in many cases staged. The question is: who is putting up the financing to accomplish this task with the hope of possibly fooling the world?

Maybe you have an answer. We welcome feedback at mrufo8@hotmail.com

Conspiracy Journal
PRODUCTIONS

OCCULT SECRETS OF THE THIRD REICH

THE WAR IS OVER – OR IS IT?
By Timothy Green Beckley

Everyone knows that the Allies were victorious over the Axis powers.

The U.S. and Great Britain formed an alliance with troops from all over the world to defeat a godless foe who would lay waste to a major part of Europe in a burnt earth policy that left millions dead in its wake. Furthermore, it tried to exterminate the whole of European Jewry because the Jews did not live up to the Nazis' racially "superior" belief system.

Hitler is considered to have been one of the most evil individuals who ever walked amongst us. Some see him as a spawn of Satan himself. Someone who tapped into an energy so dark and heinous as to defy human expression.

Though the war is long since over, many who lived through those days of darkness cannot shake the horrible memories from their minds. To those who served, it seems like the monster may still be hiding in the closet, ready to pounce at any given moment, if we ever lose our sense of reason and responsibility in matters of personal and global civility.

There are even those who dwell upon the continuing perceived powers of Hitler and his storm troopers. One of the most popular TV series in the last few years has been produced by Amazon.com and is based on a science fiction novel by Philip K. Dick in which there is a reversal of history and the Nazis have won the war. "The Man in the High Castle" explores what it would be like if the Allied Powers had lost WWII, and Japan and Germany ruled the United States, keeping us as virtual prisoners, enslaved in vast concentration camps throughout North America.

As part of this fascination with all things Nazi, there is a belief that Hitler was very much into – and connected with – sinister aspects of the occult, making friends with supernatural forces willing to collaborate in an attempt to debase humanity and leave behind its cruel footsteps in the sands of time. This book attempts neither to prove or disprove such a connection, but provides a vessel for delivering the flow of information provided by assimilators of the vast network of knowledge on the topic of Occultism and the Nazi offensive – which some say may still result in a forthcoming Fourth Reich that could sweep the world should we not heed the various signs that warn us that such a monstrous conspiratorial group is in hiding and ready to strike when given the opportunity.

HITLER'S OCCULT WARRIOR MONKS: THE AHNENERBE
By Olav Phillips

History, as we know it, is a pervasively malleable thing and, as time has shown us, history has often been used as an ideological tool to support a philosophical or political agenda. World history is ripe with examples of historical tampering, such as the near deletion of World War Two Japanese aggression in modern Japanese text books, or the downplaying of our own aggression, such as the bombing of dresden or the use of nuclear devices in combat. In the United States, we have removed historic references to our own atrocities, like the Tuskegee Syphilis Experiments, or covered up government projects such as Operation Midnight Climax and the LSD experimentation done in San Francisco. But perhaps the most interesting and sinister use of revisionism belongs to the Warrior Historians of the Third Reich, the Ahnenerbe.

So who are the Ahnenerbe and what exactly did they do? More importantly, how was Ahnenerbe research leveraged by the Nazi political machine to create a broader mythology? A mythology, which when leveraged by the Nazi propaganda machine, galvanized the German people behind the sinister beliefs of the upper tier Nazi organization.

Our story starts in January of 1929 with Henrich Himmler, leader of the fledgling Schutzstaffel or SS. At the time of its creation, the SS numbered some 300 individuals, but Himmler quickly realized that to fully realize his vision of the SS he needed to establish a powerful Nordic mythos which would propel the SS from a bodyguard of around 300 to a power political engine of nearly 10,000 members by 1931. To achieve his fully realized agenda and aggressively recruit, he knew that the SS must be transformed into an elite organization of Nordic men and women with some sort of historical precedent. It was a precedent derived from theosophy and the deeply occult advisors to the then German leaders.

An example of this can clearly be seen later in Leni Rienfenstahl's Nazi epic film "Triumph of the Will," which portrayed the SS as knights riding into the Nuremberg rally on horseback sporting chainmail armor and shields sporting the swastika. Banners fluttering in the wind as the "volk," or German people, stand besides these modern Nazi nights. It was an image which forever reinforced the vision of the SS as the knights of the Third Reich.

OCCULT SECRETS OF THE THIRD REICH

But we need to get back to our story. As an avid student of history, Himmler fundamentally knew he needed to establish a divine providence in order to perpetuate this myth and chose to do this by fashioning the SS after his mythological interpretation of the Teutonic Knights, but that required reeducation and research. It also required historic precedent. So, in 1931, Himmler tasked SS-Obergrupenfuher Ruchard Darre to form the "Race and Settlement Office of the SS." The formation of this office resulted in new SS recruits being trained, or re-educated, by Darre's office and their senior officers as well as a publication called "SS-Leitheft," which again reinforced this mythos of the SS as modern Nordic Teutonic Knights protecting the motherland and most importantly the volk or peasant population.

The project and Darre's contribution was seen as highly successful, and in 1935 Himmler again met with Darre as well as Herman Wirth, who at the time was seen as one of Nazi Germany's preeminent pre-historians, as well several other "racial" experts with the intent to form a think tank to provide ongoing research and support of the Nazi's racial superiority as well as supporting the constructed history and pre-history of the German people.

What came out of that meeting was the "Deutsches Ahnenerbe—Studiengesellschaft für Geistesurgeschichte" or translated as "German Ancestral Heritage—Society for the Study of the History of Primeval Ideas." Long title, but short story. This was the very think tank and research arm the SS needed to perpetuate their philosophy and contrived history.

Wirth was given the role of president of the organization with Wolfram Sievers as the General Secretary functioning as the head of Ahnenerbe operations. An operational portfolio which was as vast as it was damaging, especially long term.

Sievers, Wirth and later Dr. Walther Wurst, former dean of Ludwig Maximillians University, set about to fashion the Ahnenerbe as a research organization and filled it largely with academics whose pedigree was used to reinforce the legitimacy of the Ahnenerbe findings, no matter how insane it was. Because at the end of the day those findings were legitimized by the state. So it was presented and staffed as a legitimate SS research organization, which sought to prove the racial claims of the Third Reich. They did it with PhD's and experts, which is a pretty scary notion. It is historical manipulation on a mass scale and implemented by the very academics who were supposed to be in search of actual history, but instead leveraged their skills to perpetuate an ideology.

OK, so you mentioned the Ahenerbe was a research group. So what kinds of things did they research?

Financed by a SS budget line (which was massive to say the least), and beholden only to Heinrich Himmler directly, the Ahnenerbe began to spread out across the world in search of scientific proof of Aryan superiority, which also included some interesting side trips in search of historical Christian relics and other strangeness.

What follows is a partial list of some of the Ahnenerbe research excursions:

Karelia: In 1935 Himmler commissioned an expedition led by Yrjo Von

OCCULT SECRETS OF THE THIRD REICH

Gronhagen to journey through the Karelia area of Finland in search of Nordic pagan practices, including the use of witches and sorcerers in hopes of not only using their skills to perpetuate the thousand year Reich but also to foresee the outcomes of battles. The expedition got underway in June of 1938 and resulted in the capturing of a ritual performed by a soothsayer named Miron-Aku, who was convinced to perform a ritual on camera. Miron-Aku then proceeded to contact the ancient ancestors to divine future events after informing the Ahnenerbe team they were expected.

Bohuslan: In August of 1936 a new expedition was commissioned under the control of Wurst but managed by Sievers to explore ancient petroglyphs of the Bohuslan region of Sweden. On the island of Rugen, Wurth believed he found symbols representing an ancient archaic Aryan alphabet, and he interpreted the symbols to represent "the Son of God" due in part to a petroglyph of a man with raised arms. This was taken to show that ancient Aryan's mastered, even early on, an alphabet and demonstrated their advanced intellectual superiority.

Val Camonica: In 1937 the Ahenenerbe expedition led by Dr. Franz Altheim, a lecturer at the University of Frankfurt, journeyed to Val Camonica, again in search of petroglyphs which they believed showed that Rome and by proxy the Romans were of Nordic descent.

Middle East: In 1938 based on his perceived success at Val Camonia, Altheim led an expedition that moved throughout the Middle East in search of evidence of war fought between the Nordic Roman Empire and the Semitic peoples of the area. This expedition took Altheim from Romania to Istanbul, Athens, Lebanon, Iraq and eventually ending in Saudi Arabia.

New Swabia: In 1938 through 1939 the Ahnenerbe were again out in search of pre-historic archeological finds. This time in Antarctica, and led by noted explorer Capt. Alfred Ritsher. The Antarctic expedition was partially to explore the Antarctic continent but the team also had a secondary objective of locating the lost continent of Atlantis, which some had hypothesized resided in Antarctica. What is notable about this expedition is that it also laid the groundwork for the Nazi Antarctic survival mythos and the ideas around Base 211. Some readers may remember that a site which was supposedly found during the expedition and later extended by elements of the Navy and Army to serve as Base 211 or a hidden long term fortress from which the dying (at that point) Third Reich could continue their movement.

Germany: Starting early on in the history of the Ahnenerbe several major operations were undertaken a little closer to home in both the Murg valley where Ahnenerbe teams excavated a ancient fortress as well as the burial mounds in Tumulus. Perhaps their largest discovery came in Jura Mountains where R.R. Schmidt discovered the use of red ochre pigment used by Cro-magnon artists. Additionally they found other artifacts such as pendants, spears and a wooly mammoth skeleton, which Dr. Assien Bohmers interpreted to show that the site had been used by the earliest Cro-Magnon in the world who were not only amazing artists but also the predecessors to the Aryans.

OCCULT SECRETS OF THE THIRD REICH

Meanwhile, in France, two separate Ahnenerbe team members were dispatched to recover the Bayeux Tapestry which purported to show long lost Germanic heroes defeating their enemies. The mission was a failure but again demonstrates the Ahnenerbe's interest in all things Heroic and Germanic.

Tibet: Perhaps one of the most famous Ahnenerbe missions was one led by Dr. Ernst Schafer, a zoologist by training. Dr. Schafer lead the expedition in 1938 to journey to Tibet and show a clear link between the Tibetans and the mythological Germanic heroes especially interesting to the Ahnenerbe scholars because of the Tibetian use of the Swastika. The mission was also tasked with finding the mystical cities of Shambala and Agarti and to make contact with their mythical populations to secure their support and gain access to the high tech weaponry they were believed to possess. More modern appraisals of the mission have also pointed to Dr. Schafer performing scouting for a base from which the Nazi's could harass or attack India. It is also believed that Dr. Schafer brought back a group of Tibetan monks who took up residence in Berlin and were later found after the occupation having committed ritual suicide.

Poland: Shortly after the invasion of Poland, Sievers secured an Ahnenerbe mission to Poland to retrieve the Viet Stoss altar as well as the general looting of the museums in Krakow and other major cities in search of records of Germanic conquest.

Crimea: In July of 1942 Dr. Herbert Jankuhn was sent to the Crimea to loot several museums in search of Germanic and Gothic artifacts denoting Germanic ancestry. After conferring with the local Einsatzkommando unit, the museums were located and with the cover of the 5th SS Panzer unit Jankuhn was able to enter the museum, only to find that the artifacts had been relocated.

This represents just a fraction of the missions carried out by the Ahnenerbe over the course of their existence, and serves as a snapshot into the minds of the Ahenenerbe program managers and their selection criteria. Most notably the ongoing scientific justification for the Nazi mythos, and by proxy the justification for their ongoing programs of atrocity based on that mythos.

Even while these explorations, and others, were underway, including missions to locate Atlantis and Ultima Thule in both the Antarctic and the Arctic, as well as Scandinavia, another more sinister pattern was also starting to emerge.

It's long been known that many members of the Nazi regime were occultists, and by proxy many of their decisions were driven by their firm belief in things like the occult and theosophy. But what is not generally known is their dedicated programs to recover, for some unknown purpose, Christian religious artifacts.

A case in point is the mission of Otto Rahn. Rahn, who, while studying at the University of Giessen as a medievalist, came into contact with a professor named Baron von Gall. That contact lead Rahn to become fascinated with the Cathar Heresy and the Massacre at Monsegur where in the final battle of the Albigensian Crusade the crusader forces defeated the last Cathar stronghold and slaughtered all if its occupants.

Rahn, fascinated by the Cathar heresy and the Albigensian Crusade, began to do research and at some point became convinced that the Holy Grail was to be found in the Pyrenees region of southern France and was somehow related to the Heresy. Aided by Wolfram Von Eschenbach's Perzival as well as Antonin Gadall, Rahn sought to link the Cathars, who he believed to be the guards of the Holy Grail, which he also believed to have been housed at the castle of Montsegur, to druids who had apparently converted to Gnostic Manichaeism.

Rahn held firmly to the belief that the Druids in Britain formed the foundation of the later Celtic Christian Church and that in the culture of the medieval Cathars there was a strong resemblance to the beliefs of the ancient Druids. He equated the Druidic priests to the Cathar Parfaits and believed strongly that the Cathar Mystery School was being preserved by the Troubadours, a type of the traveling poet and entertainer of the medieval courts of France.

In researching the Grail mystery, Rahn developed the idea that the Cathers, as the Grail Guardians, had hidden the Grail at Monsegur, and, as impending defeat approached, had moved it to some other location in the Languedoc region by sending small teams of men over the walls to rappel down the sides of the fortress with the Grail in hand.

Shortly after the publications of his books, Otto Rahn's research came to the attention of Himmler, who requested an audience and later convinced Rahn to join the SS as a non-commissioned officer. Rahn's joining the SS gave Himmler the ability, through the Ahnenerbe, to bankroll Rahn's research.

Rahn's quest took him from Southern France to Iceland and all points in-between. But at some point during his research and travels, Rahn became disillusioned with the SS, the Ahnenerbe and Himmler's questions and eventually sought to leave the SS. This repudiation of the SS and Ahnenerbe lead to Rahn being punished, and sent to be a guard at Dachau until his eventual dismissal from the SS in 1939. Shortly after, he was found frozen to death in the Tyrolean Mountains.

At the time, Rahn's death was ruled suicide, but many have hypothesized that Rahn had been privy to some sort of larger Nazi plan and was murdered to close the loop.

Rumors still abound, despite his denial, that he actually did discover the Holy Grail and transferred it to the SS/Himmler and was then washed out and murdered to bury the secret. According to this theory, the Grail, Spear of Destiny and the Ark of the Covenant were taken into protective custody by the United States Government at the end of the war, having been recovered during previous Ahenenerbe expeditions.

The larger question that needs to now be taken on is Himmler and by proxy the Nazi's interest in Christian artifacts. Why would an organization that is fundamentally occult search out and stockpile artifacts of a competing religion? On the surface it seems like a very simple equation. The Nazis who sought total societal domination were seeking to suppress non-state sponsored occult practices but at the same time the Nazi party enjoyed some level of support, as well as ongoing support, by the Catholic Church. So we face a conundrum – why would a fundamentally occult state fund operations to recover Christian artifacts?

For the answer to this we must look again look at the Ahenenerbe and the SS as an organization as a whole. For example, shortly after looting the "Spear of Destiny" from an Austrian museum, looted by elite SS commandos, it has been reported by various authors that the spear was presented to Hitler by Himmler and at that point early in the Nazi odyssey that the Nazis started to overtake vast chunks of Western Europe. It was also reported that while rebuilding Wewelsburg Castle there was a design on the books for a main hall, whose design was inspired to be the earth bound representation of the Spear of Destiny and by leveraging that design invoking the spear's power for the SS and its conquests.

The Nazi party, or at least the leaders, obviously believed that these objects contain some sort of ritual power, which they could leverage for continued success. In the case of the Spear of Destiny it's believed it was carried during early SS engagements during World War Two. But it is clear that the Nazis were after religious artifacts, they were deep occultists, and they believed at multiple levels in the power those objects wielded.

There is also another option. In conspiracy theory many times we seek as researchers to establish links to a Luciferian agenda. In some ways, it seems to be a catchall for the bad. We as humans can't believe that we would do such things to each other, so we evoke a kind of evasion tactic and blame the Devil/Lucifer. In this case, though, especially given the obvious occult agenda, it might be a situation where these very same artifacts captured by the Ahnenerbe could have been used in occult rites to summon or to invoke. At some level that would make sense; it's uncomfortable but it would answer a lot of unknowns about why.

The investigations by the Ahnenerbe to establish the Aryan/Nazi mythos make sense. The leadership had so much invested in this type of propaganda and used Ahnenerbe findings to bolster their claims. It's the obsession with Christian artifacts that is puzzling, and can really only be attributable to some larger occult agenda that was in play. The higher echelon certainly believed in the occult agenda and attempted to leverage it throughout their reign of power not only to inspire the volk as they put it but also in their daily dealings. So it really does make sense that if they could find these Christian artifacts they would utilize them in their occult dealings as well as leveraging the power which they are purported to contain.

One final note on the Ahnenerbe, which is also very interesting. When the Germans were defeated, a great many things and people went missing. Priceless artifacts, paintings, money and people disappeared through the ratlines. Billions of dollars disappeared into banks, and it is believed a massive loot of gold was dumped into a lake in northern Germany.

One thing that did not go missing is the Ahnenerbe research archive. As Germany was falling in those final days, soldiers were sent to round up documents and preserve them and prevent them from being destroyed. While they didn't gather all the documents, and I'm sure some were inevitably destroyed, someone somewhere placed a great significance on the preservation of the Ahnenerbe archives. Some of them can be found today in the United States Archive, if you know where to look. What's missing we'll never know, but what is there is significant. Their protection and presence adds an interesting final note on the Ahnenerbe.

Why would a fringe occultish organization have such significant information as to be protected at that level? We can only wonder what they really did find and what is suppressed. Did they succeed in tracking down the Holy Grail, the Ark, or the Spear of Destiny? Possibly. And, just as in the closing to "Raiders of the Lost Ark," are those items stored in a warehouse somewhere? It makes you wonder.

ABOUT OLAV PHILLIPS

Olav Phillips is a Conspiracy Researcher, specializing in the Secret Space Program, Exotic Aircraft, High Technology, Foreign Policy, Pre-History and Mysterious Civilizations. He is a regular contributor to "Paranoia Magazine" and "ConspiracyHQ."

He has also written for "Mysteries Magazine" and served as Executive Producer and Principle Researcher for Ground Zero Radio with Clyde Lewis (Nationally Syndicated by Premiere Radio Networks). Olav has also appeared on many popular radio shows as well as television presentations including: The Outer Edge, The Higher Side Chats, ConspiracyHQ TV, and more.

SUGGESTED READING BY OLAV PHILLIPS

THE SECRET SPACE PROGRAM

THE SECRET COLD WAR IN SPACE

PARANOIA MAGAZINE

THE SAUCERS SPEAK

OCCULT SECRETS OF THE THIRD REICH

HITLER CONFRONTS THE "SUPERMAN" – AND HE IS PURE EVIL!

By Timothy Green Beckley and Sean Casteel

The popularization of occultism as related to Hitler and the National Socialist movement has propelled itself in the last few years into popular American culture.

This popularization, it seems, started several decades ago with the release of the books "Morning of the Magicians" and "The Spear of Destiny," books which increased this fascination among the public until it reached a fever pitch with the release of "Indiana Jones and the Raiders of the Lost Ark." It didn't quite matter how reliable this information was or how much of it was based upon historical fact. What was important was its shock value and its "romantic" appeal.

During a particularly "lucid moment" – whether drug-induced or not – Hitler was said to have seen "the man of tomorrow," and he was fearful of this "Superman."

Hitler's motives for world conquest and his ascension to power are no doubt varied and more complex than we can hope to understand. But when combined with this near hysteria about occultism and the SS – real or imagined – one can almost understand the will for conquest, for domination, and how a concept or a theory can be propelled such that it takes on a life almost all its own.

We address many of the issues involving Hitler, the SS and occultism through the voices of those who have researched the subject.

******

There is a wide body of science fiction literature, conspiracy theory and stories and claims circulating linking UFOs to Nazi Germany. These theories describe supposedly successful attempts to develop an advanced aircraft or spacecraft prior to and during World War II, and further claim that these craft survived into the postwar world in secret underground bases in Antarctica, South America and the United States, along with their creators.

In effect, there is a sort of a flying saucer mythos that has grown up that encompasses Hitler, the Nazis, a belief in a hollow earth and German-staffed bases at the Poles and on the dark side of the moon.

THE STORY OF IRON SKY

"Towards the end of World War II, the Nazi scientists made a significant break-

9

through in anti-gravity. From a secret base built in the Antarctic, the first Nazi space-ships were launched in late '45 to found the military base Schwarze Sonne (Black Sun) on the dark side of the Moon. This base was designed to build a powerful invasion fleet and return to take over the Earth once the time was right.

"Now its 2018, and it's the time for the first American Moon landing since the 70s. Meanwhile the Nazi invasion, that has been over 70 years in the making, is on its way, and the world is goose-stepping towards its doom."

The above is a "propaganda quote" from a media kit for a film that was a long time in the making, had a limited theatrical release and now can be found streaming online. A much hyped sci-fi thriller produced entirely with private funding, this huge-looking cinema epic from Finland, IRON SKY, could well be the "Dr. Strangelove" for the current generation.

Rife with special effects that depict the Nazi flying saucer program, this epic has done its share to provoke controversy over the notion that WWII German scientists put humankind on the moon much earlier than it has been generally believed.

There are some points where German UFO literature conforms largely to documented history. For example, it is true that the German Third Reich claimed the territory of New Swabia in Antarctica, sent an expedition there in 1938, and planned others. It is also true that the German Third Reich conducted research into advanced propulsion technology, including rocketry. A scientist named Viktor Schauberger did a great deal of research into developing flying winged craft and circular winged aircraft. In addition, some UFO sightings during World War II, particularly those known as "foo fighters," were thought by the allies to be prototype enemy aircraft designed to harass Allied aircraft through electromagnetic disruption, a technology similar to today's electromagnetic pulse (EMP) weapons.

THE STUFF OF LEGENDS

From there, the story grows stranger. In 1950, a former minister of the National Economy under the Mussolini regime named Professor Giuseppe Belluzzo claimed in a newspaper article that "types of flying discs were designed and studied in Germany and Italy as early as 1942." Belluzo also said that "some great power is launching discs to study them."

The Bell UFO was among the first flying objects to be connected with the Nazis. It apparently had occult markings on it and was said to be similar to a vertical takeoff craft described in a Wehrmacht document. One should note that a bell-shaped UFO crashed in Kecksburg, Pennsylvania, on December 9, 1965. The same month, a German engineer named Rudolph Schriever gave an interview to a German newsmagazine in which he claimed that he had designed a craft powered by a circular plane of rotating turbine blades. He said he had worked on the project with his team at BMW's Prague works until April, 1945, when he fled Czechoslovakia. His designs were later stolen from his workshop in Bremerhaven-Lehe in 1948, and he was convinced that Czech agents had built his craft for "a foreign power."

German engineer Georg Klein claimed in 1953 that the Third Reich had developed two types of flying discs. First, a non-rotating disc that was developed at Breslau by V-2 rocket engineer Richard Miethe, which was captured by the Soviets. Klein also spoke of a disc developed by Rudolph Schriever and others at Prague, which consisted of a ring of moving turbine blades around a fixed cockpit. Klein claimed to have witnessed this craft's first manned flight in February of 1945, when it managed to climb to 40,000 feet in three minutes, and attained a speed of 1,400 mph in level flight.

Aeronautical engineer Roy Fedden would later comment that the only craft that could approach the capabilities attributed to flying saucers were those being designed by the Germans toward the end of the war. Fedden had earlier stated that, "I have seen enough of their designs and production plans to realize that if the Germans had managed to prolong the war some months longer, we would have been confronted with a set of entirely new and deadly developments in air warfare."

A similar comment was made in 1959 by Captain Edward Ruppelt, the editor of the US Air Force's Project Blue Book. "When WWII ended," he said, "the Germans had several radical types of aircraft and guided missiles under development. The majority were in the most preliminary stages, but they were the only known craft that could even approach the performance of objects reported by UFO observers."

THE ACCUSATIONS FLY

Beyond the hard science and history related to the alleged German UFOs, what was the real driving force behind Hitler's push to create new aeronautical wonders? In an online posting called "The Nazi-UFO Connection," an unidentified writer says, "Following the war, there is more than enough evidence to conclude that American corporate fascists secreted literally thousands of hardcore Nazis into the USA, shuffling them into the various levels of the military-industrial-intelligence fraternity. In recent years, men like Vladimir Terziski have exposed a literal 'vast right wing conspiracy' involving fascist military-industrial fraternities in Germany, the United States AND in Antarctica, of all places . . . from where hardcore fascists who still believe that Adolph Hitler was a god continue to advance the dark technology which began in the underground bases and concentration camps of World War II Germany.

"S.S. 'pure bred' scientists within the alleged Nazi base in Antarctica, codenamed the 'New Berlin,' have been carrying out, in addition to mind control and biogenetic experimentation, continuous research and development in the field of Antigravity propulsion, at least to a ten-fold degree over and beyond the research efforts that were carried out by Nazi scientists during World War II."

The writer goes on to point out that the American moon program was basically founded on the research of one Nazi "rocket scientist" named Wernher von Braun, and that rocket propulsion and antigravity propulsion were both an integral part of the Nazi space projects. The writer even asks, "Could the Nazis have gone to the moon prior to the USA? There are even reports of Nazi space bases on the moon, and also of massive Nazi bases under the mountains of Neu Schwabenland, Antarctica. And these reports just keep coming."

OCCULT SECRETS OF THE THIRD REICH

HITLER UNDER THE INFLUENCE

"It is a known fact," the writer continues, "that Adolph Hitler read a book by Rosicrucian Grandmaster E. Bulwer Lytton, titled 'The Coming Race,' about a subterranean race which possessed supernatural technology and who, according to the novel, were intent on one day claiming the surface world for their own. Probably due to his fascination for occult legendary and mystic tales – such as the Buddhist's traditions of a vast underground world called Agharti and the Hindu legends of a reptilian cavern world called Patalas, etc. – Hitler became obsessed with the novel and was apparently fanatical over the prospect of an imminent underground invasion of the surface world in the future, and wanted to make alliances with these underground races so that once they emerged he could rule the earth in joint capacity."

Some have offered the theory that these underground beings consist of three main types: humanlike sorcerers, reptilian humanoids who are apparently a branch off from the ancient raptor-type bipedal saurian species who bypassed extinction by escaping into an underground cavern realm, and also short, grayish cybernetic drones.

There are underground bases rumored to exist around the world. For example, there are reports of a Nazi-alien connection/collaboration operating in a massive underground base near or under the Denver International Airport in Colorado. Also, a major control center for Nazi-reptilian collaboration is reported to exist beneath the Gizeh plateau of Egypt, in a strange scenario that seems similar to a cross between the movies "Stargate" and "Raiders of the Lost Ark."

Another rumor about a Nazi underground base claims that the Nazis have infiltrated en masse the cavern systems and ancient tunnel networks left by the Lemurians and the Atlanteans, which exist below the western United States. The Nazis may also be part of the horror show said to exist underground in Dulce, New Mexico, which is familiar to UFO believers as a joint human-alien operation where genetic experiments are carried out and where attempts to reverse-engineer UFO technology may be taking place, with or without alien help.

"Incidentally," the posting continues, "some abductees have been taken to underground bases where they have seen swastikas on the walls, or have seen UFO craft with the same symbol. There are many sources that tend to confirm the Nazi-UFO connection."

The writer refers to the alien that early abductee Barney Hill encountered along with his wife Betty in 1961. Under regressive hypnosis, Barney is quoted as making the following statement: "Another figure has an evil face. He looks like a German Nazi. His eyes! His eyes! I've never seen eyes like that before."

WHERE DID THIS KNOWLEDGE COME FROM?

There is of course the question of where this Nazi-inspired UFO technology might have come from. Certainly it's a valid question if one is to entertain the notion that Hitler's rocketry henchmen had a bit more under their V-2 sleeves than we are led to believe.

12

OCCULT SECRETS OF THE THIRD REICH

"Abducted by Aliens" author Chuck Weiss has researched the Nazi occult conspiracy extensively and observes that, as a young man, "Hitler came under the influence of Germany's darkest occultists, members of the Thule Society and its inner circle of Black Magicians called 'The Luminous Lodge,' although amongst themselves these Magicians referred to their order as the 'Vril Society.'"

This, says Weiss, was the beginning of the twentieth century's "great struggle between the Light and the Dark, when Adolph Hitler rose to absolute power in Germany and almost succeeded in his attempt to dominate the world. What only a few people understood at the time, and what was never publicly acknowledged, was the fact that the Nazi hierarchy, including Hitler himself, was deeply involved in the practice of Black Magic." In fact, Hitler himself claimed to have met the "superman" and stated that he was evil beyond belief!

Did this "superman" originate on another world or did he pop in from another dimension?

THE BEAUTIFUL MEDIUMS OF THE VRIL

In our earlier published work, ROUND TRIP TO HELL IN A FLYING SAUCER, we approached this subject and put forward a somewhat startling scenario.

They were utterly fetching.

Almost beautiful beyond belief.

A true Aryan's Dream.

Even the top-ranking officer of the SS, Rudolf Hess, was smitten, so much so that he listened enraptured as the young mediums formed a séance circle and began to channel communications from an unknown race far removed from the bunkers of Berlin.

Artist and historical architect Jim Nichols of Tucson has examined the role of UFOs and ETs in the formation and development of Nazi Germany, noting: "The medium Maria Orsic was leader of the Vrilerinnen, the beautiful young ladies of the Vril Gesellschaft. Characteristically they all wore their hair in long horsetails, contrary to the popular short bobbed fashion of their day, claiming their long hair acted as cosmic antennas that helped facilitate their contact with extraterrestrials beings from beyond."

And furthermore, says Nichols, "According to the legend of the German Vril Society, a fateful meeting was held in 1919 at an old hunting lodge near Berchtesgaden, where Maria Orsic presented, to a small group assembled from the Thule, Vril and Black Sun Societies, telepathic messages she claimed to have received from an extraterrestrial civilization existing in the distant Aldebaran solar system, sixty-eight light years away, in the Constellation of Taurus. One set of Maria's channeled transmissions was found to be in a secret German Templar script unknown to her." When translated, these transmissions held the key to constructing a circular flying craft capable of traveling around the world at great speed as well as exiting the Earth's uppermost atmospheric levels.

13

OCCULT SECRETS OF THE THIRD REICH

The Vril Society was an occult "Luminous Lodge" that was a sort of inner circle for the Thule society that was in close contact with an English-based group called the Hermetic Order of the Golden Dawn, a magical cabal that had great influence on western occultism throughout the 18th and 19th centuries. The members of the Golden Dawn were Rosecrucians and Masons and it is said they conjured up many an obstinate spirit. The Vril ladies claimed their group was formed as a meditation and mystical society meant to awaken the Vril force or "prana," as many would come to call this invisible mystical cosmic force today. Any of the ancillary benefits such as contacting extraterrestrials would come as a bonus . . . a bonus that Hitler and his henchmen became fascinated with as it offered up a potential power comparable – perhaps surpassing – anything being developed by the Allies.

The Vril mediums were perplexed by the content of the messages from off world. One of their order, a psychic known as Sigrun (named after one of the nine daughters of Wotan of Norse mythology), joined the gallery and began to decipher the images being channeled via automatic writing. It is generally thought that the transmissions were strikingly similar to ancient Sumerian.

The Nazi connection to UFOs and alien abduction remains unproven, of course, but we would venture to say that it is a concept that is growing increasingly more popular every day. But it still staggers the mind even to contemplate the evidence of the monstrous Third Reich having such radically advanced science, a technology that continues to lurk in the shadows of the UFO mystery. But if true, some of the signs and symbols of their mastery might already be visible to the naked eye and by looking up at the moon through a telescope. A frightful sight indeed!

THE NAZIS AND TIBET

No less a news source than the New York Times has commented on the Nazis and their fascination with Tibet and its mysticism.

"The Nazis were obsessed by Central Asia," writes columnist Karl E. Meyer, "as evident in the swastika, a symbol they purloined variously from ancient India, Persia and Tibet. According to their ethnic pseudo-science, Asia was the ancestral cradle of the Aryan race. By virtue of their isolation, Tibetans were deemed racially 'pure,' and hidden somewhere in their mountains was Shambhala, an earthly paradise.

"All of this was of peculiar interest to Heinrich Himmler," Meyer continues, "the SS Reichsfuhrer, a devotee of the occult. Himmler recruited Dr. Ernest Schafer, an SS major who had in 1934 led a Tibetan expedition sponsored by a science academy in Philadelphia. Dr. Schafer returned to Tibet in 1938 as head of an SS team."

Dr. Schafer's team filmed and measured Tibetans while also preparing maps and surveying passes for possible use of Tibet as a staging ground for guerrilla attacks on British India. Most accounts of Dr. Schafer's SS expedition to Tibet downplay the role of the occult in the venture, opting to focus more on the hard science aspects of the affair.

But researcher and author Alan Baker, whose work is so crucial to the book you are now reading, is prone to a little more of what is sometimes called "magical thinking," or the idea that the paranormal is to some extent real. Baker begins his own examination of the Nazi/Tibetan connection like this:

"The legends surrounding the realms of Aghartha and Shambhala," Baker writes, "are confusing, to say the least, and their frequently contradictory nature does nothing to help in an understanding of their possible influence on the hideous philosophy of the Third Reich. As we have seen, some writers claim that Aghartha and Shambhala are physical places, cities lying miles underground with houses, palaces, streets and millions of inhabitants. Others maintain that they are altogether more rarified places, existing on some other level of reality but apparently coterminous [of a common select group] with our physical world."

Baker cites well-known scholars in the field who say the celebrated paradise Shambhala may be to the north of Lhasa, possibly in the Gobi Desert. Others place it somewhere in Mongolia or else in northern Tibet. Meanwhile, Aghartha is said to be south of Lhasa, perhaps near the Shigatse Monastery or even in northwest Nepal or somewhere in Sri Lanka. Both have been located inside the hollow earth. Adding to this confusion is the idea that one or the other represents goodness and light while the other expresses evil and darkness. Rumors of practitioners of black magic in the region are numerous. Although the evil sorcerers are outlawed by Tibetan Buddhists, they are said to continue their activities in secret.

A writer named Theodore Illion spent the mid-1930s traveling through Tibet. He claimed to have gained access to a subterranean city inhabited by monks that he later found to be "black yogis" planning to control the world through telepathy and astral projection. When he discovered the food he was being given contained human flesh, he decided to make a break for it and fled across Tibet with several of the monks after him. After several weeks on the run, he managed to escape from Tibet and returned to the West with his bizarre and frightening tale.

It is said that the Nazi interest in Tibet was actually inspired by a desire to contact the black adepts of Shambhala or Aghartha and to enlist their aid in the conquest of the world. In his desire to contact the dark occult groups described by Illion, Hitler sent the expedition headed by Dr. Schafer, though its true mission was kept obscure and vague and never completely revealed.

Also, it is claimed that, as a result of the expedition, Hitler made the acquaintance of a mysterious Tibetan monk who told him Germany could conquer the world by forging an alliance with the "Lords of Creation." Another story posits that Hitler fled Berlin at the end of the war to rendezvous with a U-boat that would take him to either Argentina or Antarctic – or possibly Tibet!

Hitler was said to be hidden there by those same mysterious Tibetans whose alliance he had sought. Nazi henchman Martin Bormann told a magazine in 1950 that Hitler was still alive in a Tibetan monastery and that one day he would be back in power in Germany.

This kind of historical reckoning is often called "crypto-history," or "hidden" history, and by definition it mostly remains unproven. Nevertheless, the stories surrounding Hitler, Nazi occultism and Tibet offer a tantalizing but incredible vision of world events from that time. Did Hitler and his inner circle really harness Tibetan black magic and use it to their own demonic ends? And can those demons still be summoned in our own age by the enemies of mankind?

Such are among the questions that linger as you delve into this examination of the evil face of a murderous fascism and the maniacal supernatural ambitions that drove it.

HITLER'S FASCINATION WITH ANCIENT ARTIFACTS

Highly acclaimed paranormal researcher Nick Redfern is a knowledgeable historian. His research takes in the breadth and scope of more than just modern revelations. He is a high-profile figure on paranormal podcasts and has written a vast array of books on what we would term Forteanana (so named after the father of the supernatural, Charles Fort). Most of Nick's updates can be found on the blog MysteriousUniverse.org.

Recently, Nick targeted what appears to be an avid fascination of Hitler and his hand-picked henchmen with religious and ancient artifacts which it was felt contained great power and whose force could be transferred over to the Nazi regime to bolster their self-deluded march to racial and military supremacy.

Begins Redfern: "Just like the maniacal Hitler himself, a significant body of high-ranking Nazis, such as Richard Walther Darré, Rudolf Hess, Otto Rahn, and Heinrich Himmler had major, unsettling obsessions with matters of a supernatural and mystical nature. Rahn, for example, who made his mark in a wing of Nazi-Germany's greatly feared SS, spent a significant period of time deeply engaged in a quest to find the so-called <u>Holy Grail</u>, which, according to Christian teachings, was the dish, plate, or cup used by Jesus at the legendary Last Supper. That the Grail was said to possess awesome and devastating powers spurred the Nazis on even more in their attempts to locate it, and then utilize those same powers as weapons of war against the Allies.

"Acknowledged by many historians with being the ultimate driving-force behind such research, Heinrich Himmler was, perhaps, the one high-ranking official in the Third Reich, more than any other, most obsessed with the occult. In 1935, Himmler became a key player in the establishment of the Ahnenerbe, which was basically the ancestral heritage division of the SS. With its work largely coordinated according to the visions of one Dr. Hermann Wirth, the chief motivation of the Ahnenerbe was to conduct research into the realm of religious-themed archaeology; however, its work also spilled over into areas such as the occult – the latter, primarily from the perspective of determining if it was a tool that, like the Holy Grail, could be useful to further strengthen the Nazi war-machine. Then there is Trevor Ravenscroft's book, The Spear of Destiny, which detailed a particularly odd fascination Adolf Hitler had with the fabled spear, or lance, that supposedly pierced the body of Jesus during the crucifixion. Ravenscroft's book maintained that Hitler deliberately started the Second World

OCCULT SECRETS OF THE THIRD REICH

War with the intention of trying to secure the spear – again as a weapon to be used against the Allies – and with which he was said to be overwhelmingly obsessed.

"So the account went. However, Hitler utterly failed. Ravenscroft suggested that, as the conflict of 1939-1945 came to its end, the spear came into the hands of U.S. General George Patton. According to legend, losing the spear would result in nothing less than death – a prophecy that that was said to have been definitively fulfilled when Hitler, fortunately for the Allies, committed suicide."

ABOUT TIMOTHY GREEN BECKLEY – UFO & Paranormal Pioneer

Tim Beckley has had so many careers that even his own girlfriend doesn't know what he does for a living...Timothy Green Beckley has been described as the Hunter Thompson of UFOlogy by the editor of "UFO Magazine," Nancy Birnes. Since an early age, his life has more or less revolved around the paranormal. At the age of three his life was saved by an invisible force. The house he was raised in was thought to be haunted. His grandfather saw a headless horseman. Beckley also underwent out of body experiences starting at age six. And saw his first of three UFOs when he was but ten, and has had two more sightings since – including an attempt to communicate with one of these objects. Tim grew up listening to the only all night talk show in the country that revolved around the strange and unexplained. Long John Nebel's guests included the early UFO contactees who claimed to have visited other planets and built time machines in the desert. Tim was fascinated by everything that went bump in the night – or even in the daylight for that matter. Years later, Tim was to appear on Long John's show numerous times and over the years has been a frequent guest on hundreds of programs which have come and gone just like ghosts in the night.

He is a popular guest on Coast to Coast AM. Has appeared on William Shatner's "Weird Or What?" And an episode of "UFO Hunters" regarding the dreaded Men In Black. He has his own podcast, "Exploring the Bizarre," and runs MR. UFO's Secret Files, a new YouTube channel.

Tim started his career as a writer early on. At age 14, he purchased a mimeograph machine and began to publish the "Interplanetary News Service Report." Over the years he has written books on everything from rock music to the secret MJ12 papers. He has been a stringer for national tabloids such as The Enquirer and editor of over 30 different magazines (most of which never lasted more than a couple of issues). His longest running effort was the newsstand publication UFO UNIVERSE, which went for 11 years. Today he is the president of Inner Light/Global Communications and editor of "The Conspiracy Journal" and "Bizarre Bazaar." He is one of the few Americans ever to be invited to speak before closed-door meetings on UFOs presided over by the late Earl of Clancarty at the House of Lords in England. He visited Loch Ness in Scotland while in the UK and went home with a belief that Nessie was somehow connected with the dragons of mythology as well as strange discs engraved on cathedrals and ghostly phenomena. The Inner Light Publications and Global Communications' catalog of books and video titles now numbers over 200, including the works of Tim Swartz, Sean Casteel, T. Lobsang Rampa, Commander X, Brad Steiger, John Keel, Tracy Twyman, Wendelle Stevens and a host of many other authors. Tim probably knows more about the history of the UFO movement since the early 1950s than anyone today. Because of his fair and balanced approach, he made friends with everyone regardless of whether or not he believed their stories. Tim has written over 60 books himself and contributed to many more.

Tim is also known among horror movie fans as "Mr. Creepo." When asked about his major cinema influences, he mentions Nancy Reagan as having gotten him involved as a horror host. During the heyday of double features and Time Square grind houses, he worked as a movie review critic as well as a publicist for several small film companies. His own recent cinematic efforts include "Skin Eating Jungle Vampires" and "Blood Sucking Vampire Freaks."

SUGGESTED READING BY TIMOTHY GREEN BECKLEY:

OUR ALIEN PLANET-THIS EERIE EARTH

STRANGE SAGA

JOHN LENNON – WE KNEW YOU

SECRET PROPHECY OF FATIMA REVEALED

SUBTERRANEAN WORLDS INSIDE EARTH

THE MATRIX CONTROL SYSTEM OF PHILIP K DICK AND THE PARANORMAL SYNCHRONICITIES OF TIMOTHY GREEN BECKLEY

MYSTERIES OF MOUNT SHASTA

UFO SILENCERS—MYSTERIES OF THE MEN IN BLACK

SECRETS OF DEATH VALLEY

KAHUNA POWER

CASE FOR UFO CRASHES

UFO REPEATERS — THE CAMERA DOESN'T LIE

YOUTUBE CHANNEL—Mr. UFO's Secret Files

Exploring the Bizarre (Thursdays at 10 PM Eastern/7 Pacific)

KCORradio.com

Blog: spectralvision.wordpress.com

SUGGESTED READING BY NICK REDFERN:

SECRET HISTORY: CONSPIRACIES FROM ANCIENT ALIENS TO THE NEW WORLD ORDER

A COVERT AGENDA: THE BRITISH GOVERNMENT'S UFO TOP SECRETS EXPOSED

SECRET SOCIETIES: THE COMPLETE GUIDE TO HISTORIES, RITES AND RITUALS

SUGGESTED READING, BOOKS BY T. LOBSANG RAMPA:

TIBETAN SAGE

OCCULT SECRETS OF THE THIRD REICH

SAFFRON ROBE

JOURNEY TO AGHARTA

TWILIGHT: HIDDEN CHAMBERS BENEATH EARTH

DOCTOR FROM LHASA

THE HERMIT

MORE SUGGESTED READING:

MAN, BEAST, GODS OF AGHARTA: Discovering The Mysterious Lost Kingdom Of The Inner Earth And The Home Of The King Of The World, Authored by Ferdinandi Ossendowski, Dr. Raymond Bernard, Dragonstar. Introduction by Timothy Green Beckley

OCCULT SECRETS OF THE THIRD REICH

BEWARE OF DIE GLOCKE—NAZI "WONDER WEAPON" IN THE SKY: DID NORDIC-LOOKING STAR PEOPLE PROVIDE THE GERMANS WITH PLANS FOR A REVOLUTIONARY TIME TRAVEL DEVICE?

By Sean Casteel

"We cannot take credit for our record advancements in certain scientific fields alone; we have been helped by the people of other worlds . . . We should think of the craft in the New Mexico desert as more of a time machine than a space craft."

—Professor Hermann Oberth, Father of Rocketry

* * * * *

"When WWII ended, the Germans had several radical types of aircraft and guided missiles under development. The majority were in the most preliminary stages, but they were the only known craft that could even approach the performance of objects reported to UFO observers."

—Captain Edward J. Ruppelt, USAF Project Blue Book

* * * * *

On a recent airing of "Ground Zero," a nationally-syndicated, conspiracy-focused program heard in the U.S. on the I Heart Radio Network, researchers Tim Beckley and Tim Swartz shocked bombastic host Clyde Lewis and his thousands of listeners by declaring that NOT ALL unidentified flying objects originate from the stars. Some may have been developed here on Earth by a group of Nazi earthling scientists who were working in collaboration with a group of Nordic-looking extra-terrestrials channeling information to the German nationalists as far back as 1919.

This, say Beckley and Swartz, is partially the reason why there is no "Disclosure" in our future, because of fear that the American military would have to admit they have known about these "wonder weapons" in our sky ever since thousands of Nazi scientists and engineers were "legally" ushered into the United States under the highly classified "Operation Paperclip" program, which exonerated them from their war crimes, while many hundreds of other Nazis were executed or fled from the Fatherland.

While admittedly a sensational hypothesis, Beckley and Swartz, in collaboration with several other investigators, lay out their complex concept in a just released book, "Nazi UFO Time Travelers: Do We Owe The Future To The Fuhrer?" published by the Conspiracy Journal, an imprint of Beckley's Global Communications paranormal publishing complex. For over half a century, Beckley and his writers have taken on just about every conceivable topic related to UFOs and Fortean phenomena. The iconoclastic Beckley and Swartz, who also co-host a weekly podcast, Exploring The Bizarre on KCORradio.com, produced "Nazi UFO Time Travelers" with the added assistance of "Phenomena Magazine" editor Brian Allan from the UK and, in the interest of full disclosure, myself.

At the outset we should explain that we in no way intended to glorify the Third Reich. In some instances, others have used the Nazi UFO theory as a springboard to promote pro-Nazi propaganda, which was the farthest thing from our minds. But, in all honesty, this complex theory needs to be bought to the attention of others who refuse to examine any of the evidence, evidence which indicates that we could be dealing with a number of explanations for the UFO phenomenon all rolled up into one. But the uppermost concern here is the acknowledgment that some of the craft we have been seeing in our skies could have been manufactured in underground bunkers somewhere in Germany during various phases of the Second World War. And if, indeed, some of these craft can travel through time, well, then some of the older sightings of "wonder weapons" could be attributed to highly advanced, Germanic technology.

As Beckley explains the matter in the book's opening chapter, "Beyond the mere ability to fly what may still seem like technologically 'miraculous' aircraft is the haunting, troublesome possibility that the ships also function as time machines, bringing the ability to travel in time within human reach for the first time in recorded history. Devices like Die Glocke (translated as 'The Bell') may have been used to bend both space and time and give the Nazis the unthinkable power to explore the past freely and even to CONTROL THE FUTURE. Are we plummeting headlong toward a world under fascist domination – a nightmare in which grinning, sadistic, jackbooted thugs are waiting for us to 'catch up' in time with our own predestined subjugation to open worldwide rule by the Nazis, who are possibly hiding out on the surface of the moon or in 'secret cities' at the Poles? Do they lie in wait for us as the clock on our freedom runs down?"

The concept is a little tricky, but it involves the idea that the Nazis were able to move into the future and exert total control once they got there. That concept does, of course, sound "fringe" on the surface. But, according to Beckley, we should not assume that the Nazis acted "alone" in achieving such a feat. They obviously had help from "Aryan Space Brothers" who seized an opportunity to use the fledgling Nazis to further their own otherworldly ends. In other words, the aliens made building a time machine simple enough that mere humans, once properly instructed and provided with the raw materials, could accomplish the task sufficiently well in real-world terms.

What their motives were is open to dispute and debate. Some see the Aryan "Space Brothers" as friendly visitors from the future, while others wonder why they would want to share their secrets with a very negative group of earthbound scientists. Perhaps they were deceived by the attractive mediums who they thought they may have been related to. Or they could have simply lacked the information required to see their channels' coming evil before sharing their technology.

The history of Adolph Hitler and the Nazis has always included elements of their occult beliefs, but the new book goes back further in time, to the early 20th century, and the mediums associated with the Vril Society. The female mediums, referred to as true "Nordic beauties," began to channel messages from extraterrestrials whose origin was many light years away. The messages included the technical designs of advanced aircraft unheard of in their day in addition to a kind of "blueprint" for a time machine. Some years later, Hitler himself, along with several of his SS henchmen, came under the influence of the Vril Society as he began his rise to power in a Germany that was sick enough and corrupt enough to be mesmerized by his unchecked anti-Semitism and militaristic obsessions.

When combined with the high caliber of scientists the Nazis "recruited" to design weapons for the war effort, which included now-legendary names like Wernher von Braun and Hermann Oberth, the fact that they had alien "help" along the way makes some of their more exotic advances a little more plausible.

In fact, the scientists themselves talked openly about this alien help.

"We cannot take credit for our record advancements in certain scientific fields alone; we have been helped by the people of other worlds . . . We should think of the craft in the New Mexico desert as more of a time machine than a spacecraft."

So said Professor Hermann Oberth, one of the early fathers of rocketry and the mentor to the young Wernher von Braun.

Meanwhile, von Braun himself stated in 1959 that: "We find ourselves faced by powers which are far stronger than we had hitherto assumed, and whose base of operations is at present unknown to us. More I cannot say at present. We are now engaged in entering into a closer contact with those powers, and in six or nine months' time it may be possible to speak with more precision on the matter."

While neither Oberth nor von Braun specify that they were aided in their efforts by Aryan Space Brothers, they are nevertheless surprisingly candid in what they DID say for public consumption. Their openness may have been part of some larger strategy to steer the belief in UFOs in the direction of the Extraterrestrial Hypothesis (or the "ETH" for short) and therefore away from a darker point of origin in the blueprints and designs of the Nazis. In the decades-long campaign of disinformation waged against the truth of the UFO phenomenon, Oberth and von Braun may have simply been firing another salvo of confusion and subterfuge. Or were they simply being sincere in reflecting on their own invention processes? Was there an undeniable alien presence working alongside them? Like most unanswered questions about the UFO phenomenon, the answers await their time.

Another fascinating thread of the story that Beckley holds fast to is this: In many alien abduction accounts, especially the early stories from the late 1950s and early

OCCULT SECRETS OF THE THIRD REICH

1960s, the UFO occupants are said to speak in German and to speak English with unmistakable German accents.

The new book quotes a well-known contactee named Reinhold Schmidt who encountered an alien ship in Kearney, Nebraska, in 1957. After accepting the flying saucer captain's invitation to come onboard, Schmidt heard the captain and crew speaking to one another in "High German," a dialect that Schmidt had been versed in by his parents from his youth. Apparently unaware that Schmidt could understand them, the beings spoke to him with their Deutsche accents intact and made no effort to disguise their voices.

The 1961 abduction of New Hampshire couple Betty and Barney Hill is much better known than Schmidt's, but, when studying their case, there is an often overlooked moment when Barney, as he undergoes regressive hypnosis with post-trauma specialist Dr. Benjamin Simon, begins to panic when one of his alien abductors takes on the appearance of a Nazi in full uniform. Was this a glimpse into the aliens' "true" agenda? As an African-American in the early 1960s, Barney was certainly familiar with the oppressive fears that come from being a victim of racism. Did his unconscious mind somehow conjure the Nazi image as an expression of those fears? Or was it intended as a grim warning of future totalitarian domination?

The Nazis also cast a shadow over even the beginnings of the contactee movement in the 1950s. Many people will be familiar with the 1952 meeting between George Adamski and the androgynous, blond-haired, blue-eyed Aryan Space Brother who called himself Orthon. But one may not know that that first contact in the California desert was facilitated by Adamski's associate, George Hunt Williamson, who worked out the time and location for the landing in the days before it took place by using an Ouija board to communicate with the Space Brothers. Williamson was himself associated with right wing extremist William Dudley Pelley, an American Nazi-sympathizer who had served time in jail for sedition and anti-government rabblerousing. While Williamson would later disavow that he held any racist beliefs at the time, he did serve in Pelley's employ writing and editing pro-fascist pamphlets and magazines.

Admittedly, no one wants to give up the utopian hopes that accompany belief in the Space Brothers. But the fact that their physical appearance embodied the ideal of Aryan or Nordic "good looks" is not an easy one to ignore. In the case of the desert encounter between Adamski and Orthon, we have this to consider as well: the new book "Nazi UFO Time Travelers" offers a line drawing based on a plaster-of-Paris cast – taken at the site of the meeting – of the boot print of Orthon. One can easily discern a pair of swastikas engraved into the sole of the alien's boot, leading one to consider the possibility that the visiting alien followed "on the heels," so to speak, of the Nazis defeated some short few years before.

I think at this point we now have a clearer idea of just what Beckley is aiming for in "Nazi UFO Time Travelers." When one combines these seemingly disparate events with one another, they coalesce into a picture of the possible: Aryan aliens who matched their advanced knowledge and technology with willing scientists bent on controlling the world, a kind of fifty-fifty split between extraterrestrial and human efforts that resulted in the flying saucer phenomenon as we know it today.

But there is still more. One of the most generally agreed upon historical aspects of the Nazis/UFO theory concerns an aircraft called "Die Glocke," which is German for "The Bell." It was believed to be a product of both alien guidance and the work of topflight scientists like the aforementioned von Braun and Oberth.

A mockup of this purported airship is featured on the cover of "Nazi UFO Time Travelers," and it is indeed a bell-shaped aircraft, although what kind of propulsion system could enable such an ungainly monstrosity to fly at mind-bending speeds remains unknown. The Bell is also said to contain the time travel apparatus that is so essential to the story, but which remains an even deeper mystery than what kind of fuel propelled it through the skies. Some contend that the propulsion system is based either in the long sought after antigravity energy or some manipulation of electronic principles which can be tapped into throughout the universe.

In 1965, in Kecksburg, Pennsylvania, numerous witnesses saw an unknown object crash in the woods outside town. Locals reported that some kind of government/military cleanup crew was on the scene nearly immediately, which indicates that the federal interlopers had been following the craft's descent on radar. The witnesses say the object was put on the back of a flatbed truck under some kind of tarp covering and hurriedly hauled away. But it was still possible to discern that the clandestine cargo was a large, acorn-shaped object that could easily be said to have resembled the contours of the Nazis' Bell. In fact, the similarity is so remarkable that one hesitates to conclude that it's all a simple coincidence.

"Nazi UFO Time Travelers" also features a pair of chapters by Tim R. Swartz, who writes about a tangled trail of conspiracy and secrecy that involves pioneering inventor Nikola Tesla's research being commandeered by Nazi spies in their desperate quest to develop weapons for defeating the Allies. Swartz also contributes several anecdotal accounts of ordinary people who have experienced time distortion, missing time and other similar anomalies while within close proximity to a UFO. Time does more than stand still at such moments, and Swartz gives some needed insight into how ordinary, non-Nazi witnesses also encounter a kind of time that dances outside our normal understanding.

Brian Allan, a Scotsman of longstanding fame in the world of the paranormal, provides an introduction into the many elements of the Nazi/flying saucer theory that are essential to the reader's understanding, a kind of primer in the basics. Allan's writing is both caustic and amusing, which is treading a fine line when it comes to this kind of analysis of this heavy, some would say "grim," subject.

So, with "Nazi UFO Time Travelers: Do We Owe The Future To The Fuhrer?," a certain amount of license must be granted to the authors. While most UFO believers quite understandably like to ignore the links between flying saucers, alien abduction, Germanic origin stories and Nazi technology rumors, Beckley and his crew prefer to look these nightmarish ideas in the eye and report on them as objectively as possible.

Have we assembled a book of "inconvenient truths," to paraphrase environmental activist and former vice-president Al Gore? It might be more accurate to say "frightening possibilities," and then to commence praying for deliverance from a future world of high-tech Nazis leering at us from some beer garden around the next corner in time.

ABOUT SEAN CASTEEL

Sean Casteel is a freelance journalist who has been writing about UFOs, alien abduction and many other paranormal subjects since 1989. Sean's writing appeared in many UFO- and paranormal-related magazines, including "UFO Magazine," Tim Beckley's "UFO Universe," "FATE Magazine," "Mysteries Magazine," and "Open Minds Magazine," most of which are now defunct but were a major part of a thriving UFO press in their heyday. Magazines in the UK, Italy, Romania and Australia have also published Sean's work.

Sean has written or contributed to over 30 books for Global Communications and Inner Light Publications, all of which are available from Amazon.com. Sean's books include "The Heretic's UFO Guidebook," which analyzes a selection of Gnostic Christian writings and their relationship to the UFO phenomenon, and "Signs and Symbols of the Second Coming," in which he interviews several religious and paranormal experts about how prophecies of the Second Coming of Christ may be fulfilled.

To view and purchase books Sean has written or contributed to, visit his Amazon author page at: http://www.amazon.com/author/seancasteel

SUGGESTED READING (Available On Amazon)

NAZI UFO TIME TRAVELERS: DO WE OWE THE FUTURE TO THE FUHRER?

THE SECRET SPACE PROGRAM: WHO IS RESPONSIBLE? TESLA? THE NAZIS? NASA? OR A BREAKAWAY CIVILIZATION?

UFOs: NAZI SECRET WEAPONS?

THE OMEGA FILES: SECRET NAZI UFO BASES REVEALED

Also, visit Timothy Green Beckley's YouTube Channel – "Mr. UFO's Secret Files" https://www.youtube.com/user/MRUFO1100/videos

OCCULT SECRETS OF THE THIRD REICH

This piece will further expand your esoteric horizons and reveal many new and exciting avenues of investigation into Nazi Arcana. The Nazis left no stone unturned in their search for allies from the world of the gods, including searching through the lost secrets of the Norse mythology, the white-skinned Northerners from whom the Nazis claimed to have descended.

Here writer Hercules Invictus wishes to share with you a simple mental map of the larger cosmos as it is preserved in Norse Mythology (Note: The World Tree is mentioned in Greek Mythology as well, but surviving details are rather sketchy). It is his belief that the Vanir in the Northern Tales are the Hyperboreans – or northern peoples who dwell in a sunny paradise – of old.

THE TREE OF WORLDS
A Shamanic Map of Inner and Outer Space
By Hercules Invictus

In the cosmology of the North Lands, it is believed that a giant tree, Yggdrasil, joins the nine known worlds and holds them together. Yggdrasil has three principal roots from which it draws nourishment: one in the world of the gods, one in the boundary surrounding the river ocean and the last in Niflheim, the world of Elemental Water, Mist and Ice.

The World Tree itself is inhabited by a remarkable variety of beings, as are the worlds connected by it. And each of these has an integral role to play in the mythic drama that is destined to unfold.

In the realm of Elemental Air, high atop the World Tree, a great eagle is perched. It is said that the Light Elves rule the surrounding region, named Alfheim. The Alfar are sylvan beings with great power over nature, and are allied to the war-like Aesir. In Alfheim celestial deer feed on Yggdrasil's leaves.

A worm called Nidhogg and his squirming kin, forever hungry, gnaw at Yggdrasil's lowest root in Niflheim whenever their standard fare of decaying corpses runs low. It is said that the Tree of Worlds shudders in agony each time they bite.

The eagle and the worm are mortal enemies and almost always in conflict. A squirrel named Ratatosk conveys messages between them. Whether Ratatosk is a clever and mischievous being or simply a poor messenger is open to debate.

The Dwarves and Dark Elves live deep in the Elemental Earth realm fashioned from Ymir the Primal Giant's decaying corpse. They are the guardians of hidden treasures and startling secrets. They are also unsurpassed smiths and craftsmen of renown.

Muspellheim, the world of Elemental Fire ruled by Surt, is home to the Fire Giants, fierce beings who constantly hone their war crafts in preparation for the final battle.

The ocean's boundary was claimed by Belgemir's descendants, the Frost Giants and Ogres. It was named Jotunheim. Three weird sisters, all giant-kin, settled by the pool near YggDr.asil's root and slowly grew in wisdom. These were the first Norns.

Bordering Jotunheim is Midgard, the middle world formed by Ymir's brow. Here the Aesir created a man from an ash tree and a woman from an elm. These were the ancestors of mankind.

Vanaheim, a world whose existence eluded the Aesir in those early days, is home to the Vanir, god-like beings who are the objectifications and personifications of the forces of fertility.

The Realm of the Dead also came into being in the dawn of time and was most easily accessed through Niflheim. Though the shades that inhabited it lacked purpose and firm leadership until much later on in their history, the dead patiently waited, as they still patiently wait, for the end times, when they can fulfill their mission and finally end their anguish.

For the Aesir and their growing households: Asgard, the fairest of all worlds. Near Ygdrassil's root they built dwellings, temples and fortresses for themselves.

There are other peoples as well, such as the Trolls, whose origins are hard to trace. For as we have stated earlier, Yggdrasil joins the worlds together and allows for continued interaction between a diversity of beings from many distinctly different realms. Save for the primal regions, Muspellheim and Niflheim, there seems to be constant traffic between the other worlds.

One need not be a Norn to have foreseen that, inevitably, quarrels and misunderstandings would arise.

Would you know more?

© Hercules Invictus

ABOUT HERCULES INVICTUS

Hercules Invictus is a Lemnian Greek, a proud descendant of Argonauts and Amazons. He is openly Olympian in his spirituality and worldview, dedicated to living the Mythic Life, and has been exploring the fringes of our reality throughout his entire earthly sojourn. For over four decades he has been sharing his Olympian Odyssey with others.

OCCULT SECRETS OF THE THIRD REICH

Having relocated the heart of his Temenos to Northeastern New Jersey and the Greater New York Metropolitan Area, he is now establishing his unique niche locally and contributing to his community's overall quality of life. Hercules is also recruiting Argonauts to help him usher in a new Age of Heroes.

Hercules currently hosts The Elysium Project and Voice of Olympus e-radio shows on the Spiritual Unity Radio Network. He currently writes for The Magic Happens and Paranoia Magazine, has published two e-books on Kindle, Olympian Ice and The Antediluvial Scrolls, and has been contributing to Timothy Beckley's awesome anthologies.

Hercules founded or co-founded Mount Olympus LLP, Olympian Heroic Path, Olympian Shamanic Path, Cosmic Olympianism, the Regional Folklore Society of Northeastern PA and the Center for the Study of Living Myth in New Jersey. He also spearheaded many of the real-world Age of Heroes initiatives and the fictive Mythic Adventure tales.

For more information, please Friend him on Facebook or visit his website: http://www.herculesinvictus.net" http://www.herculesinvictus.net

OCCULT SECRETS OF THE THIRD REICH

MICHAEL X AND THE NAZI DARKNESS PREVAILS
By Sean Casteel

Timothy Green Beckley of Global Communications continues to do the UFO/ paranormal communities a great service by reprinting and updating long sought after books by the early pioneers of the various fields of endeavor, especially, but not limited to, UFOlogy. Beckley unearthed a triptych of wondrous works by Michael X that focused on the darker side of the flying saucer phenomenon. Beckley called the collection "Trilogy of the Unknown, A Conspiracy Reader," making it available on Amazon along with over 200 titles produced through his Inner Light – Global Communications – Conspiracy Journal brand.

In his introduction to "Trilogy of the Unknown," Beckley writes, "Michael X was one of the greatest avatars of the early UFO/New Age movement of the 1950s. He spoke with great articulation and sincerity at many of the well-attended outdoor conventions held annually at Giant Rock, a private landing strip just outside of Joshua Tree in the hot Mohave Desert of Southern California. He spoke calmly and collectedly about the arrival of the silvery spaceships, dubbed flying saucers, explaining how they were piloted by friendly space beings from this solar system and way beyond."

Michael X perceived the Space Brotherhood to be on a mission to elevate our consciousness and invite us to join a cosmic "League of Nations," a federation of spiritually advanced worlds who exist around us and in other dimensions.

"I guess you could call Michael X a guru of sorts," Beckley continues, "though he didn't head a religious cult nor was he looking to attract a fanatical following in the manner of other more self-absorbed 'masters' of universal wisdom. No! Michael X was an avatar in the truest sense of the word – an advocate for all humanity."

Michael X even went so far as to refuse to reveal his last name so that he didn't become part of a cult of personality. He chose the letter "X" as a reference to the mysteries of our world and the space and time we inhabit. As a result of his secretiveness, there is little known about his background beyond the fact that he was a salesman of some kind before he discovered UFOlogy. Beckley once spoke to Michael X, but the pattern of secrecy continued and Beckley learned nothing more than he had known before.

OCCULT SECRETS OF THE THIRD REICH

The aliens with whom Michael X communed were said to be from Venus, typical of the time period in which he wrote. His contact with them mainly consisted of telepathic voices, and they spoke to him about the secrets of good health and offered a new understanding of science, philosophy and religion that could possibly propel us forward into a New Age of reason and enlightenment. He wrote about what the Venusians had taught him in a series of very concise study guides, perhaps around 25 or so, according to Beckley. Many of his discourses had to do with holistic health and the aging process, very "time travel-ish" as Beckley put it, as if they were referring to a "future earth."

"But as it turns out," Beckley writes, "Michael X's career was not only involved with the sweetness and light aspects of the New Age movement, but he had also stumbled upon the darker side of UFOlogy, which frightened him to the point that he eventually left behind the work he loved so much. This is a little known 'secret' about Michael X that I don't believe has ever been presented before."

Beckley says that he obtained this information from Dr. Frank E. Stranges, the late author of "Stranger At The Pentagon" and a good friend of Michael X's. Apparently Michael X had run across some UFO-related secret and was deemed to have "gone too far."

"It should be noted that Michael X was the first researcher I know of," Beckley writes, "to have mentioned the UFO Nazi connection. He wrote about it in a very sensationalistic work called WE WANT YOU – IS HITLER ALIVE? Published in 1969, this was a thin volume containing information that Michael X considered vital, though he knew that the German vs. the Extraterrestrial Hypothesis he presented would not be a popular one and would doubtlessly draw massive amounts of criticism from people who might think he had turned against his space brother friends, who were decidedly Aryan in appearance, if that makes a difference.

"During one of his meditations," Beckley continues, "a 'voice' came to Michael X and gave him a specific place and time to meet for a face-to-face encounter with his supposed alien friends. They promised to reveal some information that had not been disclosed before that would be helpful in the dissemination of his work."

Michael X was sent to a secluded place in the Mojave Desert where he and his contacts could be free of prying eyes. When he arrived, he saw nothing but remained in his car, waiting. After a while, he saw the glint of something in the sunlight and assumed it was the spacecraft arriving. He began to walk toward where he had seen the light when all of a sudden he sensed terrible danger. He heard an inner voice warning him to flee the scene, and when he looked back he saw one of the men he had intended to meet lowering his rifle, which had been the object that had glittered in the sun, not any ship full of Venusian Space Brothers.

Shortly after, Michael X completely withdrew from the UFO/New Age community and has not been heard from to this day. When Beckley spoke to Michael X in this same timeframe, Michael X confirmed the details of the desert escape story though he refused to elaborate further on anything, other than that he was rather unhappy with the fact that Beckley had gone ahead and published the WE WANT YOU tract. Beckley now says he doesn't know whether Michael X is still alive or not, but that Michael surely wouldn't mind seeing his works republished for a certain kind of truth seeker to learn from.

Which brings us around again to "Trilogy of the Unknown."

"We present what might be considered to be information on the seamier side of the subjects at hand," Beckley writes. "Here is information on Nazi UFOs, which Michael X spoke about years before anyone else dared touch on the theory that German scientists had stumbled upon a revolutionary form of propulsion and had constructed disc-shaped devices that they had hoped would help them win the war. There is also a warning from the space people to get our tail off the moon and never return – OR ELSE! And if you think David Icke was the first to write about reptilians roaming the earth, guess again, for Michael X told about the existence of a race of serpents running around inside Rainbow City, located in Antarctica, as part of an inner earth contingent."

Along with the idea of aliens on the moon jealously guarding their territory and the underground race of terrifying, hostile serpents, a great deal has also been written and talked about regarding the belief that Nazi German scientists may have developed working flying saucer technology close to the end of World War II that was later suppressed by the victorious Allies. However, one may never have heard the following story, taken from the middle section of "Trilogy Of The Unknown" by Michael X.

Michael X relates the rise and fall of a German named Karl Michalek, who in 1958, while living in Santiago, Chile, began to write some very unusual articles. He sent his articles to a publication called "Neues Europa," or in English, "New Europe," which was published by Louis Emrich. Emrich printed everything Michalek sent him, and within a short time, Michalek had garnered a large following of readers. The small newspaper had at first printed articles of general interest, but as time passed, Michalek's messages began to dominate the publication. [Michael X is quick to acknowledge the similarity of his own name to Karl Michalek's, which he feels is an unfortunate coincidence that hopefully won't confuse people reading this account.]

"The German readers were fascinated," Michael X writes, "intensely so."

Just what was stirring up so much excitement? Michalek was calmly announcing in the "New Europe" that he was in positive contact with the governmental heads of the planet Venus. The name of the particular intelligent being from Venus who was acting as Michalek's present contact was "Ase."

"Ase and Michalek are desirous," Michael X writes, "of bringing about everlasting peace and order to our planet Earth. In his series of regularly appearing articles, Karl Michalek presented himself as a sincere, God-fearing man who believes in the almighty power of the Creator. He is against those world groups that are promoting war, which Michalek knows will destroy the planet."

Michalek also authored a book laying out his beliefs called "Michalek: The

OCCULT SECRETS OF THE THIRD REICH

Prophet of the New Era. Unearthly Forces and the Human Race."

He was not only egocentric enough to call himself a "prophet," he also declared himself to be "the spiritual bearer of this great idealistic world idea" and "the President of the coming majestic government of the World Republic of this Earth." He sent stern warnings to leaders like Nikita Khrushchev and Dwight Eisenhower not to meddle in his Venusians' plans for world conquest or Moscow and Washington would be wiped out.

Michalek also told his followers reading the "New Europe" that the ships from Venus would land on "X-Day," in December of 1958, in Berlin itself, causing great excitement among his loyal throng. Predictably, the day came and went and not a single UFO was seen. Michalek covered his embarrassment by saying that the President of Venus had passed away unexpectedly at the age of 193. Ase, Michalek's contact among the Venusians, was forced to delay the landing maneuver for a short period of time.

"Two years later, Michalek again predicted 'Der Tag X,'" writes Michael X. "This time he stated that it was fixed and irrevocable. The date of the Venus Fleet landing was to be April 21, 1960! Note how X-Day was set for one day after Hitler's birth month and day, April 20.

"April 21st arrived – uneventfully," Michael X goes on. "Again, for some unknown reason, the Venusian UFO fleet had seen fit to stay away. This time, the failure of the spaceships to arrive as Michalek had promised brought forth a storm of protesting letters from readers of the 'New Europe.' Because the predicted Venus landing didn't take place, the curve of Michalek's success has sunk into the negative realm, and Michalek has sunk with it. INTERPOL in Austria takes a very dim view of his claims and is opposed to him. Even Michalek's former staunch supporters, including the disillusioned publisher, Louis Emrich,, have fallen away."

But there is more. In 1959, Michalek claimed, "For some time now, I have been the one designated to be President of the highest governmental authority of the coming World Republic. I have been so designated by the power of the Chief Leader of the planet Venus."

Michael X then backtracks to 1945, a mere fifteen years previous to the time in which he was writing. Michael X says that when Hitler was drawing up his last will and testament, he did not name a second Fuhrer to succeed him. He chose Admiral Karl Doenitz as the next President of the Reich, Joseph Goebbels as Reich Chancellor, and Martin Bormann as the Party Minister.

From there, Michael X reasons that Hitler had secretly survived his supposed suicide in Berlin in 1945 and was in fact living in South America. This was easier to believe in 1960, when Hitler would have been in his early 70s. In any case, it was a surviving Hitler who was the true authority that Michalek served, not the disappointing Venusians.

"It is possible," Michael X writes, "that Karl Michalek is in actuality the illegitimate son of Adolph Hitler. Mind you, I say it is 'possible.' I do not claim it is the gospel truth or a proven certainty. No. It's a simple hypothesis and nothing more. So far, Michalek has not 'delivered the goods' in regard to his predictions of UFO landings, and his own broken promises have dubbed him a charlatan, a hoaxer on the grand scale. Those who formerly believed in him now DO NOT."

The point is that Michalek, as a Nazi conspirator and a member of a surviving Hitler's inner circle, did have knowledge of genuine UFOs, but of Nazi design as opposed to true extraterrestrial spacecraft.

"The Michalek story may be part of the Nazis' plans, a preliminary test phase that for some reason, perhaps a good reason, had to be discontinued. If our hypothesis is right, Hitler has the UFO secret. And if we could manage to look in on his Argentine Hideout, we'd no doubt see quite an armada of earth-built UFOs. Not only that. It is also likely we'd find the craft well-armed."

As an interesting side note, just as this article/review was being written, a news story appeared on the Yahoo! website with the headline "Did Hitler Have A Secret Son?" According to the article, until his death in 1985, a man named Jean-Marie Loret believed he was the only son of Adolph Hitler. The article says there is currently a renewed attention to his claim because of evidence from France and Germany that adds credibility to Loret's story.

"Loret claimed that his mother, Lobojoie Charlotte, met Hitler in 1914, when he was a corporal in the German army and she was sixteen. She described Hitler as 'attentive and friendly.' She and Hitler would take walks in the countryside, although conversation often was complicated by their language barrier. Yet, despite their differences, after an inebriated night in June 1917, little Jean-Marie was born in March 1918, according to Loret."

In evidence, Loret offered the results of two studies, one that proved his blood type is similar and another that proved his handwriting is similar to Hitler's. The evidence is inconclusive, but Loret's story continues to be investigated by a leading French newspaper called "Le Pointe." Meanwhile, the official story is still that Hitler died childless in 1945 at age 56.

So the work of Michael X manages to resonate even in the present time some 50-plus years later, and NOT ONLY in regard to the concept that at least some aspects of the UFO phenomenon might have had their roots in a Nazi space program developed at the end of World War II. Remarkably, Michael X, as we have seen, is the author/researcher who actually laid the groundwork for a theory that has become increasing popular.

In this book published by Beckley, there is much more to inhale and mull over. There is also Michael X's brave discussion of reptilian humanoids that may coexist along with mankind on planet Earth without our knowledge, and a bizarre group of serpent-like creatures living within the earth, both in caverns beneath our feet and possibly inside a grand paradise to be found at the North and South Poles. Then there is the very relevant warning given our astronauts and leaders that we should NEVER return to the Moon. And, amazingly enough, we might have heeded their demands since decades have passed and we have not ventured back to the lunar surface.

Perhaps when you can achieve that kind of universal meaning along with what might prove to be a nearly prescient eye into the future, you have truly been in contact with some kind of genuine alien presence – whether you claim they came from Venus, which today might be called laughable, or from some dimension where spirit and alien forms commingle and occasionally reach out to one of our fellow mortals for the sake of all of us.

SUGGESTED READING

"Trilogy of the Unknown – A Conspiracy Reader" is available on Amazon.com

Other works that can be found by Michael X on Amazon.com include:

"Venusian Health Magic – Venusian Secret Science"

"Vivenus Starchild and Flying Saucer Revelations: Two Flying Saucer Classics" by Vivenus and Michael X.

OCCULT SECRETS OF THE THIRD REICH

IMPLOSION: THE SECRET OF VIKTOR SCHAUBERGER
By Tim Cridland

Viktor Schauberger was an Austrian forest ranger who became fascinated with the motions of fish in mountain streams in the moonlight. His observations led him to the discovery of the power of imploding vortices and the hidden properties of moving liquids.

From this he was able to produce free energy and anti-gravity, among other inventions. Schauberger's research came to the attention of Adolf Hitler, who may have utilized some of this research in the Nazi flying saucer project. After the war, a U.S. mega-corporation tricked Schauberger into selling all the rights to his research – past, present and future – and then promptly suppressed it. Schauberger, who hoped his discoveries would lead to a better world, realized his mistake too late. He died in obscurity, within days of being cheated out of his life's work.

With information about him hard to obtain, Schauberger often seems more urban legend than real man, a mysterious Dr. X who can turn water into gasoline (in this case, energy) until the oil companies chase him away. This amazing booklet leaves no doubt that Schauberger was real, and his discoveries demand attention.

Schauberger advocated working with nature. While others were trying to "conquer" nature, he was watching the movement of fish, birds, streams and lakes. From this he discovered "implosion technology," the exact opposite of the explosive technology that powers the world today.

There are tales of floating rocks and streams flowing uphill, diagrams of structures that purify air and water, do-it-yourself experiments that make water levitate, insights into the Nazi flying saucer project and translations of his Austrian patents.

Will the environmental movement rediscover Viktor Schauberger? His implosion technology is just the right remedy for a world on the brink of ecological disaster.

OCCULT SECRETS OF THE THIRD REICH

ABOUT TIM CRIDLAND

Tim Cridland – popular by his stage name "Zamora the Torture King" – is a world famous American sideshow performer. He has mastered some unique techniques by using his knowledge of science, anatomy, hypnosis, martial arts and teachings of the Middle East, allowing him to overcome dangerous situations without any pain.

He possesses the ability to overcome all sorts of dangerous situations like electrification, fire eating, sharp swords and many more. He's been featured on multiple television shows where he performs his death-defying stunts as an entertainer.

He currently resides in Las Vegas, where he performs nationally and internationally, and appears annually on Knott's Berry Farm's Halloween Haunt in Buena Park, California.

SUGGESTED READING BY TIM CRIDLAND (AVAILABLE ON AMAZON.COM)

SECRET EXPLOITS OF ADMIRAL RICHARD E. BYRD: THE HOLLOW EARTH, NAZI OCCULTISM, SECRET SOCIETIES AND THE JFK ASSASSINATION

The next section of the present work is a more detailed and high-tech oriented examination of Viktor Schauberger's work.

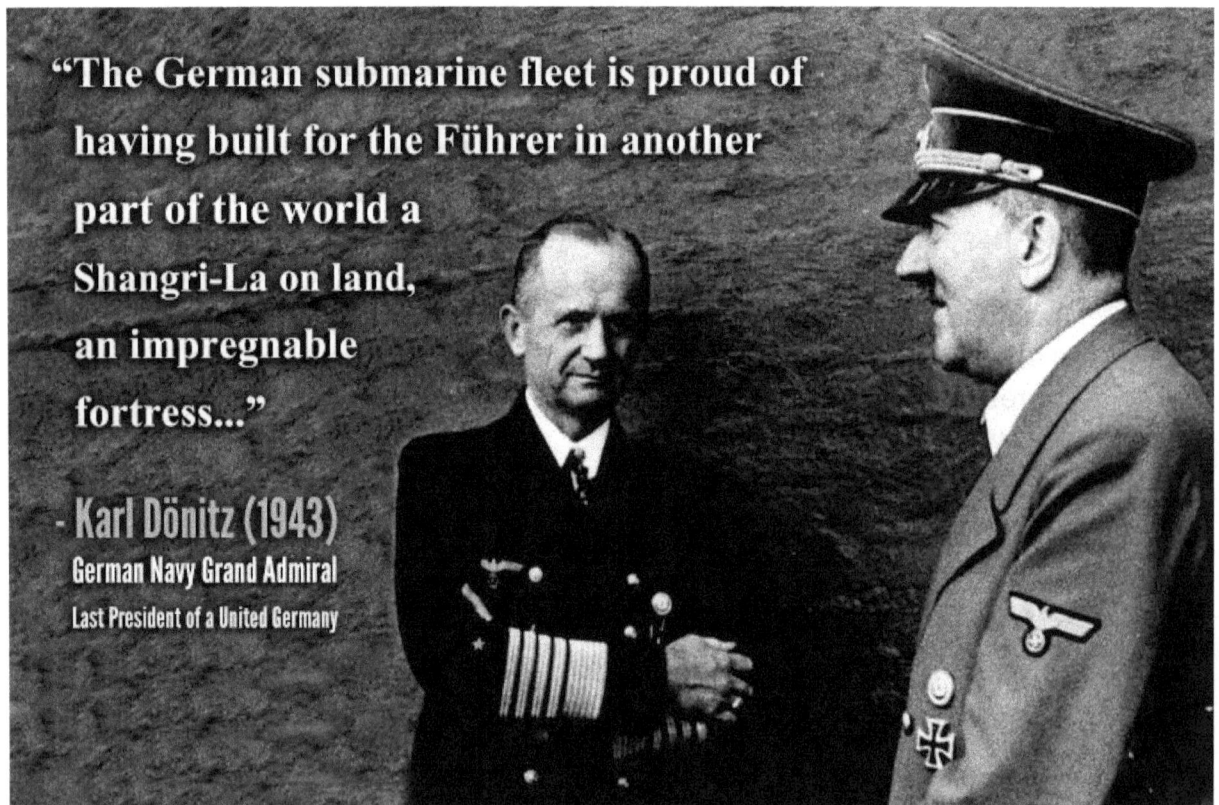

"The German submarine fleet is proud of having built for the Führer in another part of the world a Shangri-La on land, an impregnable fortress..."

- Karl Dönitz (1943)
German Navy Grand Admiral
Last President of a United Germany

IMPLOSION
VIKTOR SCHAUBERGER AND HIS AMAZING DISCOVERIES
Albrecht Giddings

It has been clearly and conclusively established already that technology in its various experimental and practical attempts to produce useful energy resorts only to pressure forces (water, steam, air or gas pressure) or that it makes either direct, or indirect use of the heat of combustion to produce expansion and explosion — again pressure forces — which it then converts to useful energy.

Thus we have established the fact that so far technology has only partly recognized the significance of Nature's polarity. Only after having explored the above mentioned deeper psychological factors do we begin to understand why it has seemed preferable to utilize the pressure component. This totally one-sided attitude in regard to the production of energy is responsible for the fact that the essential balance of the bipolar structure of the basic natural elements has been severely upset and all life on earth put in gravest danger of extinction.

All life has its secret in dipolarity. Without opposite poles there can be no attraction, and no repulsion. Without attraction and repulsion there can be no movement, and without the latter, no life. Light calls for darkness, because without darkness it would have no meaning. The alternation of warmth and cold, of day and night is also of greatest importance to our planet. While one side of the earth is cooling, its other side is getting warmer. These temperature differences produce a constant flux which results in a spiral rotation just as it happens with hot and cold air fronts whose meeting results in cyclones and hurricanes. There are even differences in the earth's weight, because on its warm side the weight increase is absolute and on the cold side specific. This, together with the magnetic forces, produces a declining rotational movement. The temperature differences exert a constant pressure which sets the masses in motion as it seeks compensation.

The counterpart of heat is cold; of the negative—positive; of the masculine—feminine, etc.

ALL OPPOSITE POLES ARE ESSENTIAL TO NATURE

Opposites represent an integral part of nature's course which, in reality, does not a describe a complete circle but a spiral. This observation, though of the greatest importance,has failed to attract the attention it deserves. All that lives (at this level of consciousness or being) moves between two opposites, between two poles — hence dipolarity — spiraling up- wards toward enlightenment and purification, or downwards through deterioration and degeneration toward ruin. This depends on whether the driving force is centripetal (that is, concentric — toward the center) or centrifugal (that is, excentric — toward the outside). The excentric or cenrifugal force leads to destruction, the concentric or centripetal force leads to growth and enrichment. This is equally true of material and of spiritual matters.

BALANCING NEGATIVE WITH POSITIVE

In the Tabula Smaragdina, the oldest of Arian Writs, we find the following significant words cut in the emerald: "Combine the heavenly with the earthly in accordance with the Laws of Nature, and health and happiness shall be yours as long as you live." Only the finest elements should be mated and blended if one wishes to obtain each time a finer and higher product. To mate, means to unite and to stimulate two opposites, the positive and the negative. The negative attracts the positive and the latter is drawn to the negative. Sunlight, which is positive, fertilizes the negative grain seed in the womb of the earth. A constant exchange of emissions between the positive atmosphere and the negative geosphere brings the seed to life. In this case it can be truly said: "She partly drew him down, he partly let himself sink." (Goethe: The Ballad of the Fisherman)

Union between the offspring of the earth and the descendants of the sun gives rise to life in the physical realm which is directed by the Etheric forces. The latter, on the other hand,have their own higher counterpart. The negative offspring of the earth capture the positive descendants of the sun and this produces a constant automatic movement. In the spring of the year,when the temperature and light conditions are relatively favorable, the positive rays of the sun (light) induce germination in the negative grains or seed. Therefore, to combine, means to stimulate and produce various gradients of potential. This in turn produces movement which is the very basis of life, so that everything is in constant flux (panta rhei).

Although the world is animated by a single universal force,this force can be divided into two contrasting elements — the pressure component, and the suction component. In this case,Nature's dipolarity expresses itself in the form of two differ exit types of motion. Each of these types manifests itself through certain specific phenomena and represents one of the two components of the force which animates and activates the whole universe. The secret of the normal and good life consists of achieving the proper balance or blend of these two components. (see "Tabula Smaragdina". This is pure Cabala. All occult science, East and West, bases itself on this principle, Chokmah and Bina, Osiris and Isis, Orpheus and Eurydice. The whirling Hooked Cross, the Swastika, is the symbol. Revolving counter-clockwise, centrifugal, it is negative. Revolving clockwise, centripetal, it is positive.)

OCCULT SECRETS OF THE THIRD REICH

USE CENTRIPETENCE TO OVERCOME GRAVITY

The pressure component leads to Centrifugence, friction, increased heat and gravitation; while the suction compoment leads to Centripetence, cooling, absence of friction and levitation — which makes it possible to overcome gravity. While friction may produce even white heat, fire. Centripetence produces a temperature drop which may reach what is known as the State of Anomaly which, in the case of water, +4° Centigrade. However, this is possible only if one uses Schauberger's suction spiral, a device which, on the whole, is still unknown.

Each living entity has its specific and characteristic point of Anomaly. This should be understood as the temperature or feverless condition, that is, the optimum degree of warmth required by its species to develop and proliferate.

Until now technology has recognized only one type of motion, the type which raises the temperature through friction and pressure. Even ancient tribes knew that fire could be produced by rubbing together wood or stones; but it took Viktor Schauberger to discover a new type of motion producing not heat, but a temperature drop, reaching at times the point of Anomaly. This can be accomplished by tightly winding or coiling either air or water through a spiral curved channel of special design.

In this process the medium — air or water — is drawn almost without friction toward a central point, condensed in a special manner and at the same time cooled. A biological vacuum (negative pressure) is created which, on its part, augments the suction acting on air or water. Until now this possibility has been overlooked in technology, and yet it offers totally new perspectives in regard to energy production. Friction creates in a machine conditions comparable to fever, conditions which cannot be normal, since they tax materials excessively and burn them out.

People and animals do not develop fever because of work. They may get hot but their blood temperature remains relatively constant. Normal conditions in machinery can be achieved by or through implosion and impansion with the best possible results in regard to the preservation of materials. It would seem obvious that man's duty is not to waste and squander as quickly as he can the resources of the earth, but to preserve and conserve them. Machinery design, therefore, should avoid all material waste and should ensure at the same time durability. Our unscrupulous modern technology and economy, unfortunately, have been moving in the opposite direction.

THERE ARE TWO WAYS TO GO

The two types of motion which nature employs give rise to the following phenomena:

(a) "Centrifugence"—resistance to friction—pressure—temperature rise—biological deterioration

(b) "Centripetence"—absence of friction—suction—temperature drop—biological improvement

"Centrifugence", which is a scattering of force, is slowed down by natural causes, because the resistance it encounters . grows as the square of its velocity, following the well known formula $W=MV^2$. Were it not for this fact, matter would risk being destroyed, or would be in danger of being broken up into atoms. The opposite is true of "Centripetence". Its effective force undergoes no deceleration, since there is virtually no friction, and grows, instead, as the square of its velocity. Centripetence contracts, conserves, condenses and therefore benefits life. It attracts and absorbs without producing pressure.

It is obvious therefore that as a result of the natural laws the effective power of centrifugal motion is never as great as that of centripetal motion, the first being destructive, the second constructive. Were the destructive force more powerful than the constructive force the universe would not exist. (The Christ is Centripetence. The Anti-Christ is Centrifugence.) Unfortunately our whole technology has committed the error of choosing the destructive force as a means to its own ends, and this tragic choice of the mode of propulsion and motivation, having completely disrupted the ratios and balance of nature, has brought it to a blind alley. Instead of applying by preference, as nature does, centripetence which permits producing energy almost at no cost, it has done the opposite. This has resulted in an over consumption of raw materials, in an explosion and exploitation of natural resources, until now the very destruction of atoms has been reached.

Centrifugence increases pressure and heat. Centripetence has a cooling effect and generates condensing reactive forces. It never cools beyond the point of anomaly. We know that while moderate chilling and moderate cold conserves, refreshes and preserves, rising temperatures lead to heat, putrefaction and combustion.

THE CABALISTIC PRINCIPLE OF BALANCE

In order to subsist, life must have both heat and cold. Exposure to excessive heat and light produces cancer in organic tissues (but living organic tissues); in dead organic tissues it produces rapid putrefaction and decay. Cold, on the other hand, preserves, consolidates and arrests disintegration. For this reason, food can be preserved only by applying cold. With the temperature at $+4°$ C. Thus cold is as important to life as warmth. Man must strike the golden mean between the two in order to realize the best conditions for his development and propagation.

All mechanical movement is the outcome of attraction and repulsion. However, the dominant factor regulating motion is not the pressure component, as assumed by our whole fire technology of steam pressure, hydraulics, electrical power, gas pressure, atomic fission, etc., but the suction component. So far, however, this component has been completely neglected by our technology and overlooked in mechanics. The tragic end of our civilization and culture is therefore inevitable, unless the new type of energy which can be produced by means of suction can be utilized in the form of implosion and impansion for industrial purposes.

In its second and higher phases, Centripetence generates magnetic forces, namely what is known as diamagnetism — a special type of vital energy lacking which no creature can survive.

As we see, there is one type of motion which determines a temperature rise, another which determines temperature drop. Now then, these systems of motion should be organized and adjusted in such a way as to have the constructive forces representing always over 50% of the total. When this ratio is exceeded, which of course should never be allowed to happen, synthesis becomes too rapid and there is maximum activation of the so-called etheric form of carbons, a maximum which equals approximately 94%, plus 4 to 6% condensed oxygen. Conversely, by destroying these products of synthesis one obtains a product containing only 4 to 5% high-grade substances and an excess of accumulated solar energy wastes, that is, complete peroxidation. (See also effects of radioactivity). A peroxidation of energy concentrates leads to a hyperacidity of the blood and lymph due to a deficiency of high-grade substances, then to cell damage, cell destruction and cancer.

Therefore, for the sake of his well-being, man should be careful not to resort to fire technology alone; that is, to that type of motion which produces friction and Centrifugence. In order to create for himself healthy, normal conditions, to get the best out of life — or make his life better, he should apply rather the planetary type of motion which is not Centrifugal, excentric, but primarily Centripetal, that is, concentric.

In nature there is definitely no such thing as homogeneous motion. The predominantly Centripetal type of motion which produces diamagnetic levitation is based exclusively on the spiral. Only this motion permits the planets to orbit freely around the sun following their predetermined paths. This could not be the result of gravitation alone, but also of their own powers of levitation. Only the proper balance between gravitation and levitation, between the attractive and the pressure forces makes it possible for the individual planets and the various solar systems to move along their courses, as parts of Spiral Nebulae.

THE SIGNIFICANCE OF THE SPIRAL

Without the Spiral there can be no levitation. This represents the opposite of gravitation — an observation which has yet to be made by orthodox science. All we know about levitation — that is, the art of overcoming gravity — has come down to us only through the Secret Teachings (for instance the Whirling Dervishes of the Middle East). The geometrical spiral is the basis of all planetary movement. It represents the motion which is employed by nature as a means of ascent and purification. In 1919 it was found by Viktor Schauberger that the spiral can be adapted to technical uses in the form of a suction impeller. Today only its opposite, the pressure impeller, is being used; while the suction impeller is still unknown.

Centripetal motion, in contrast to Centrifugal motion, is not circular but spiral. All that moves in a circle remains in one place both spatially and biologically and becomes arrested in its development. That which is arrested in its development is forced to regress. There is no standstill in nature; in the universe there is only advance and retreat.

Technologists are still quite unaware that the only path to growth and rise is the spiral. The consequences of this seemingly harmless oversight are nevertheless catastrophic. Centrifugence produces friction and friction produces fire. It eliminates water and robs the soil of its fertility. The soil, only temporarily stimulated by artificial fertilizers, is hastened in its truly cancerous process and becomes gradually barren. One of the economic consequences of this oversight is the looting of natural resources and their total depletion, which brings about political unrest, wars, increasing spiritual and sexual impotence, degeneracy and finally the end of culture and civilization.

"The spiral represents an upward path" (Infinity 1/10). Nature requires a type of motion which is primarily planetary,spiral, because this type heats neither the water, or as the case may be, the air serving as the medium of motion, nor the implosion motor — the design of which must embody the system of spiral curves presented by the original model — but which cools them instead to their natural point of anomaly.

This anomaly is the natural boundary line between the positive atmosphere and the negative geosphere with their different potentials. This explains nature s constant unrest. Optimum conditions for life are found within this boundary zone which,in humans and animals, is the normal blood temperature. Motors,too, have a certain atmospheric state of anomaly in which they function best or, as in the case of our current engines, in which their pressure and performance reach the highest peak.

THE LIFE BLOOD OF THE EARTH

When water, the life blood of the earth, is centrifuged or exposed to excessive, unfiltered solar radiation, its temperature rises. It develops a "fever", due to the decentralizing reactive forces which are generated in the process. This brings life to the harmful microorganisms which may be present in the water, since their growth is stimulated by higher temperatures. They begin to proliferate rapidly and deprive the physical primogeniture (water) of its vital energy, so that as soon as it has exceeded a certain temperature — this limit begins already at +9° Centigrade — it becomes lifeless and dies for lack of high- grade elements, becoming more and more shallow and unpalatable.

However, if we restore in this congenitally diseased, "cancerous" water its original, that is, primarily planetary, radio-axial movement by means of special vessels and devices, its temperature falls and the pathogenic bacteria die in the absence of temperature which allows them to proliferate. This does not mean, however, that cooling with ice or by other artificial means will restore the original properties of water which has been heated. This can be achieved only by using spiral geometric curves capable of restoring the water's diamagnetism and of re- generating its etheric forces.

Water deteriorates when its temperature exceeds a certain limit, whether due to overheating and overexposure to light, or to the action of compressor turbines, water wheels, pressure pumps, etc., whereupon such valuable fish as trout, salmon, etc.,can no longer breed. During the spawning season these species, as we know, have to migrate upstream toward the head of the river, where the water temperature is +4° C, since their young,lacking the necessary adaptability, can develop only at this temperature.

This is also the reason why the spiral should be used for technical purposes, releasing and making available unsuspected supplies of power. This however, can be accomplished not through explosion — the spiral cannot be used in internal combustion engines — but through impansion and implosion; not through destruction but through consolidation, synthesis and purification.

Today, preference is given in general to a type of motion which is centrifugal, thus excentric, resulting in high energy losses and being responsible for the criminally wasteful exploitation of natural raw materials, seeing that it wastes far more than it produces. This is a type of motion which represents in nature a cancerogenic factor.

Unfortunately, it has not occurred to science so far that Centripetence permits achieving the very opposite of what is produced by Centrifugence. Nature knows how to protect herself from all danger. It is quite helpless only when it faces such totally destructive devices as atomic bombs. Even Centrifugence is destructive because of heat and the decentralizing reflected radiations it produces. The opposite is true of Centripetence or the spiral movement.

ELIMINATION OF COSTLY FUELS AND NUCLEAR FISSION

This fact proves not only that truly unbelievable supplies of energy can be mobilized, but also that this can be done almost without expenditure, since the method requires neither costly fuels nor nuclear fission; and only a small amount of water or air, which is refined in the process. The pull of the suction spiral can yield any required amount of energy. Remembering that during hurricanes and cyclones the same suction forces are at work and that they lift easily tons of sea water, whole buildings, or even railroad trains which fall into their paths, one can imagine what could be achieved were it possible to produce them by mechanical means. A great visionary and inventor has been able to find the answer to this splendid riddle by submitting nature to a careful and close scrutiny.

In this case however, the difficulty was not how to discover the mysterious and resistance-less suction forces, but how to design the proper tubes, since ordinary round tubes cannot be used. It meant finding a tube design which would make it possible to control these forces. Viktor Schauberger was fortunate enough to wrest also this secret from nature, but for the time being it cannot be discussed due to the status of the patent rights. Truly careful observation can help solve even the most difficult problems.

Those still hampered by obsolete physical and technical concepts find it hard to understand such natural laws, because they are still firmly convinced that a motor must be supplied at one end with 100% energy in the form of coal, oil, water or the like, in order to deliver at the other 10 to 30% effective power. With Implosion this ratio is reversed! The temperature gradient can be utilized almost 100% since there are virtually no friction losses. In the case of the Implosion, an impulse starts the suction spiral, whereupon the whole turbine begins to breathe like a living organism; or, when water is used, to act like an arterial or venous circulatory system. It produces at the same time a biological vacuum and continues to function until the supply of energy which is stored in the material, that is, in the moving medium, has been used up.

FRICTION-LESS AND HEAT-LESS POWER

This amazing and hitherto unknown phenomenon can be explained by a friction-less movement of medium structures. This is exactly how nature solves the problem of friction-less and heat-less speed increases. The answer to this problem is a basic requirement in the production of power. Its cost is negligible, but it can produce the desired results only when the artificially accelerated flowing medium enters an advancing vortex whose suction force increases as the flowing medium gradually undergoes mechanical and specific condensation while being tightly coiled. A molecular suction point is formed on its own axis. This point draws the rapidly flowing medium from the walls toward the center, twisting it into a spiral which can be imagined as a screw within a screw. This prevents friction and reduces the temperature. Exactly the reverse is being done at present. As a result of Centrifugence, friction and resistance are increased; increased pressures lead to power losses and increased heat, all of which expresses itself in the form of excentric reactive forces which inhibit the synthesis of high grade elements. As we can see, an inevitable inhibiting atomic force is generated. This force which grows as the square of the velocity, represents nature's emergency brake. This would have been learned long ago, if nature had been observed with care.

A continuous movement produced by rotation is not the same as rotation produced by means of pressure. It does make a difference whether concentrates of basic materials contained in a moving medium are drawn, or compressed. Through intentional or unintentional pull and suction one can generate water spontaneously, while through pressure one can produce only fire. This is why in its processes of synthesis nature employs only the spiral motion, inasmuch as only the latter leads to healthy growth and development.

IMPANSION AND IMPLOSION ARE UNKNOWN

Impansion and Implosion are two terms which can be found in no dictionary, since they are still practically unknown. According to Viktor Schauberger, they are the opposite of expansion and explosion. While a gradual or sudden dilation leads to expansion and explosion, a gradual or sudden contraction or concentration of liquid or gaseous bodies, air, produces a negative pressure, and through the latter, impansion and implosion.

As a matter of fact, the production of energy requires a temperature gradient, either an upward gradient resulting from heat and pressure, or a downward gradient, resulting from cooling and suction — negative pressure. However, in natural processes itdoes make a difference whether the temperature is raised or lowered. A rise in temperature leads to expansion and explosion. Furthermore, the quicker this temperature rise, the greater the attending energy losses, inasmuch as they grow in proportion to the speed at which the energy rise takes place. The highest natural resistance forces are encountered in the case of the H-bomb explosions,when the heat released reaches up to a 100 million degrees Centigrade. After explosion, nature reduces this monstrous heat by applying suction forces. Suction always produces a natural temperature drop and acts like a brake on the pressure wave generated by the explosion, which would otherwise destroy the earth.

Therefore, an energy production method based on an upward temperature gradient, is the worst possible energy waste and a destructive process. The quicker the medium — air, or water — is cooled (this takes but a few seconds when the spiral rotates very rapidly), the greater the energy effect, since the friction-less contraction instead of meeting with increasing resistance, meets with lessening resistance. Not only water but also air are instantly cooled to their respective points of anomaly. And so we are forced to conclude that the stronger the pressure, the higher the energy losses; while on the other hand, the stronger the suction pull, the higher the energy output.

THE COLLAPSING EFFECT OF SUCTION

The impansion and implosion-producing temperature gradient shows various and hitherto unrealized aspects:

Suction is more powerful than pressure. Whereas pressure elicits resistance, suction results in general collapse attended by no resistance. Introversion is likewise more effective than extroversion, and represents the only possible means of physical and of spiritual ascent.

Suction, even when its graduation is not controlled, is more effective than explosive pressure. Therefore, when mechanically produced, it must be carefully adjusted and regulated according to certain definite rules. Its intensification, quite obviously, must be allowed to take place within a predetermined period of time and must be fully controlled.

Suction can cool even to the point of anomaly; when properly controlled it preserves and saves materials; it permits the effective energy output to attain its natural optimum level and its maximum development within the allotted cosmic time-span.

However, the mechanically produced temperature drop can reach anomaly (the geospherical and atmospherical zone of neutrality) only if the suction spiral is employed. The spiral concentrates and contracts. This contraction cools, and the cooling process creates a vacuum. The vacuum, again, has a sucking effect and as the spiral revolves faster and faster, the whole process generates a diamagnetic force which is merely a manifestation of the Etheric life-force without which there can be no life on earth.

OCCULT SECRETS OF THE THIRD REICH

VORTEX POWER EQUAL TO NUCLEAR POWER

Only a spiral contraction of the moving medium can produce a diamagnetic vacuum which leaves in its wake resistanceless suction. The higher the rate of flow the stronger the suction pull; which, as the flowing medium strikes certain nozzles produces an implosion. Those forces, which can be produced by rotation in a system of spiral geometric curves, are as powerful as nuclear forces.

The significant role of spiral motion in natural processes is demonstrated b whirlwinds, cyclones, typhoons, waterspouts, and finally by the whirlpools which occur in water. When cold and warm air masses meet over an ocean at a tangent, the resulting temperature drop and liberation of heat, plus the rotation of the earth, produce cyclones and hurricanes. Due to the rotation of the earth, winds flowing toward a low pressure area do not move in a straight line, but along a spiral. The strong effect of the earth's rotation on cyclones is demonstrated by the fact that south of the Equator they turn clockwise, while north of the Equator they turn counter-clockwise. Windspouts are a natural proof that a temperature drop is capable of releasing enormous energies.

In rivers, whirlpools are formed when the flowing masses of water encounter, and are deflected by, tear-drop shaped or egg-shaped stones of special composition, lying at the bottom of the river bed. The larger these stones and the greater the volume of water they deflect, the greater the temperature drop that is produced, and the larger the whirlpool that is formed.

Near Grein, Austria many boats and rafts used to perish in the waters of the Danube on account of such whirlpools. Many navigators tried to guide their rowboats through the eddies, but their offerings and prayers did not help and innumerable boats were lost because they did not have the power to pull out of the vortices. Finally, a simple man had the idea to break up the rocks lying on the floor of the river, rocks which had the shape of tear-Drops, and which were responsible for the dangerous eddies. As soon as this had been done, the whirlpools disappeared almost completely.

It was proved conclusively already twenty years ago by Viktor Schauberger to the famous hydrologist Prof. Forcheimer that when a stream of water is deflected tangentially by a stone of a certain shape and composition, and no larger than a child's head, the temperature of the water drops by 0.1 to 0.5° C. Such a temperature drop can reduce the temperature of one cubic liter of water 0.1° C. and is equivalent of 42.7 mkg effective power. The same is true of a temperature increase. In summer, to raise the temperature of a river such as the Danube (delivery about 800 cubic meters/second), for example, to 20° C. bathing temperature, it takes about 60 million PS or 45 million KW. This energy is freely supplied by the sun. We know that as it is being heated the water loses much of its natural properties, becoming first undrinkable, then dead, and finally putrid. In contrast, cooling to the point of anomaly +4° Centigrade, by imparting to it a spiral motion, restores its original properties, so it becomes once more like fine spring water. It is true that cyclones and hurricanes cause great damage due to the fact that they cannot be controlled. However, they are rare phenomena and their effects weigh less in the balance than those of fire, which in the form of lightning, storms and concomitant phenomena, is known in all parts of the earth, even where cyclones are never seen.

LIGHTNING, THE NATURAL PURIFYING AGENT

Of course, there is some value even to lightning which is a natural purifying agent cleansing the atmosphere by fire, freeing it of elements not yet ready for a higher developmental form which may have reached it due to excessive light and heat. The explosion of a storm precipitates these substances and produces an atmospheric discharge. Unfortunately it cannot eliminate radioactivity (from atomic fallout).

The return of the positively charged substances from the atmosphere to the earth leads, due to the planetary motion of the earth, to a polarity change, so that these substances are able to begin once more their physical ascent. The same happens in the spiritual realms. All that has not been sufficiently purified must return and go through the process of purification once more.

In nature this process of regression takes place normally, without disturbances, through expansion. (The symbol for this is the Swastika, or hooked cross, revolving counter-clockwise.) The latter should be understood as a slow dilation, produced by light and warmth, which gives rise to mild electrolytic processes which separate or dissociate the higher from the lower elements.

THE SIGNIFICANCE OF DIAMAGNETISM

The same diamagnetic vacuum which can be artificially created by impansion and implosion, can be found in the human chest, as accidentally discovered in 1908 by Prof. Sauerbruch who, nevertheless, could not know at that time that this diamagnetic phenomenon occurs not only in the human thorax, but in all living beings and even in the earth itself. (The symbol for this is the hooked cross revolving clockwise.)

Diamagnetism is generated when such a medium as air, water, or earth (necessarily containing dipolar trace elements) is forced to move primarily in a radioaxial, that is, spiral and centripetal manner, thus exactly like the earth.

Due to this totally unknown, yet primary method of synthesis, our planet is able to overcome gravitation, thus to levitate, to float in space and to move independently, condensing and refining its masses. Conversely, when the same medium is forced to move in the opposite manner, i.e., axioradially (being centirifuged), its movement generates an atomic hyperpressure, a dilating and rarifying heat which inhibits the absorption and resorption of superfluous elements, and so prevents the natural respiratory processes.

The rotation of the earth generates a diamagnetic force also in water. It enables, for example, the rainbow trout to remain almost stationary and motionless in the midst of a rushing stream, or to flee in case of danger with lightning speed, or —

during the spawning season —to move upstream by rising through the center of the cycloidal swirling magnetic axis of the water falls.

Let it be added that diamagnetism, although discovered by Faraday already in 1845, so far has found no practical application, because it represents a type of magnetism which cannot be adapted to fire technology, inasmuch as it checks excessive temperature increases and consequently prevents ignition in motors.

DIAMAGNETIC OR PARAMAGNETIC, THERE IS A DIFFERENCE

On the basis of certain personal significant observations, Faraday classified metals as paramagnetic and diamagnetic. The so-called magnetic — or better — paramagnetic metals are attracted by the magnet and show an axial arrangement; while the diamagnetic metals are repelled by the magnet and present an equatorial arrangement. It was found that the paramagnetic group contains not only iron, nickel and cobalt (whose magnetic properties have long been familiar), but also manganese, chromium, cerium, titanium, palladium, platinum, osmium, and almost all ferrous alloys. The diamagnetic group contains in the first place bismuth, then antimony, zinc, lead, copper, silver and gold.

For example, if a small bismuth rod suspended from a thread of raw silk is placed between the two poles of a very powerful electromagnet and made to swing horizontally, it is repelled by both poles. Therefore it positions itself at right angles (equatorially) to a line connecting the two poles; whereas an iron rod assumes an axial (normal) position to this line (NS).

On the strength of this behavior, all bodies can be classified either as paramagnetic or diamagnetic. It was discovered, furthermore, that glass, carbon disulphide, and other non-conductors are also highly diamagnetic. Each diamagnetic body, moreover, has a negative magnetic number, i.e., a number which gives the measure of its magnetic response.

Another interesting phenomenon is observed when liquids are magnetically tested. The liquids to be tested are put into thin-walled glass test tubes (or watch glasses) and placed near a powerful electromagnet whose poles are set very close together. In the case of magnetic liquids the contents of the test tube rise over the edges of the latter and gather together forming a little mound on the sides next to the poles. In the case of diamagnetic liquids, the samples in the test tubes expand axially, and contract equatorially, forming in the middle not a ridge, but a valley running equatorially to the two poles.

HOW TO GENERATE DIAMAGNETIC FORCES

In Viktor Schauberger's discoveries diamagnetism is a crucial factor, or rather a factor which changes the whole picture and brings it into relief. Schauberger found that when air, earth, or water is agitated and coiled (with light, heat and air excluded) radio-axially, i.e., from outside inwards, diamagnetic forces are generated.

Our present technology, which fails to recognize this type of motion, has been unable to produce diamagnetism, or to adapt it to practical purposes. It has applied, hitherto, only paramagnetic forces and Centrifugence, disturbing thereby the vital processes of synthesis.

As already stated, centripetal contraction produces a temperature drop which creates a vacuum. Not only the temperature drop but also the resulting vacuum can be measured, with a manometer. The temperature drop in question proceeds more rapidly or less, depending on the rate of speed of the swirling medium, and may reach anomaly. This process produces a specific condensation and volume decrease manifesting itself in the first stage in the form of an indrawing suction. In the second stage this suction produces in a hermetically enclosed space a biological vacuum which generates in the third stage the above mentioned type of magnetism which, in its turn, produces at the terminal end an implosion force which is the primary, all-animating, original atomic energy.

The present model of the atom, which is so familiar by now, is far from being the ultimate representation of matter. Even the lightest atoms are composed of a number of pulsating primary atoms. These are either positive or negative, either masculine or feminine, due to which they pulsate like spiraling microcosmic levro-or dextro-rotary hearts. Without diamagnetism —this extremely subtle type of etheric force — there can be no procreation and no progress, whether in the plant, the animal or the human kingdom. There can be no growth, no proliferation and no perfecting of the naturally multiplying generations.

Diamagnetism actually is a vital force, an atomic energy which is already etheric. which builds and sustains physical life in all its aspects. It has been stated by Profs. Warburg and Domagk that this cell building type of synthesis or vital force is possible only when the cells are supplied by the blood with sufficient oxygen, or Prana as it is more accurately called by the Hindoos, oxygen being only the coarser carrier of this far more subtle etheric force. This etheric energy is absorbed primarily by the various species of conifers and ever-greens, which store it in the tips of their needles. This explains why there is always an excess, not a deficiency, of oxygen in forests; these natural water reservoirs and air filtering plants store vital energy and dispense it to mankind. Oxygen deficiency, let us add, lends to the development of cancer cells and its effects can be eliminated only by supplying purified oxygen.

TOO MUCH OXYGEN IS DANGEROUS

There is a vast difference however, whether this oxygen is freely inhaled (as air) or forced into the lungs (as pure oxygen). Due to the vacuum in his chest, man is forced to inhale;but for example, a child given too much chemically pure oxygen from a cylinder may have blindness as a result, while an adult develops almost fatal pneumonia. It is generally known that even ordinary atmospheric oxygen produces blood decomposition when it is introduced by a hypodermic needle into the veins, because once in the blood it becomes aggressive, binds the blood albumen which has an opposite charge and has been weakened by disease, changing the metabolism in such a manner that instead of life-giving forces, atomic destructive energies are set into motion. These destructive energies which have predominantly an expanding and explosive effect, attack the structure of the cells, drastically extend their nuclei, and finally rupture them. A similar process takes place in the atomic reactor when pure carbon (graphite) is bombarded with unscreened cathode rays which produce a radiation rate so high it is almost imperceptible, and therefore potentially very dangerous.

Now then, when an organism that has been attacked by cancer is supplied with diamagnetically charged, high grade water containing up to 90% energized hydrocarbons (and correspondingly less used up oxygen) the negatively charged diamagnetic reduction elements bind and emulsify the excess oxygen and inactivate it by cooling it. As a result, the fever recedes and that, which Prof. Warburg calls the Vital Force, is restored. It concentrates in new cells, forcing them to proliferate steadily, arrests the development of the adjoining cancerous cells, and finally destroys them. Cancer, which is the result of fire (i.e., over heating and combustion) can be cured only by diamagnetic negatively charged high grade water, as established already in 1935. But although the production of such water would have benefitted millions of people, opposition supported by the medical authorities prevented the construction of water purification plants. Moreover, the first models of the equipment were destroyed during the war, so it has become possible to start collecting necessary data on the production of diamagnetic power by means of mechanical devices only recently, all such work having been stopped by the war and the ten years of Austria's military occupation.

Today we know at least that we are dealing with basic processes employed by Nature herself, that catalysts play in them an important role; and, naturally, that only those substances and materials can be used which are diamagnetic carriers.

Contrary to the concepts which hitherto have been considered in physics as valid, magnetism is not a quiescent field of force, but energy in flux. This was demonstrated long ago by the Vienese scientist, Felix Ehrenhaft. Ions can have a magnetic as well as an electric charge. The whole earth is permeated by spiraling centripetal magnetic currents. Spiral motion is especially typical of magnetism and constitutes the very basis of planetary motion and of all movement in the universe.

DIAMAGNETISM AND BREATH

Respiration binds elements belonging to the atmosphere with those belonging to the geosphere. In other words, it blends and emulsifies substances which have been purified by the diffusion apparatus (filter) with substances which have been filtered through the hermetically sealed blood and lymph systems. The emulsified product of this reductive blending process is represented in the crust of the earth by its physical primogeniture (tellurian waters), while in such higher life forms as plants, animals and humans, by sap or blood. Since neither blood nor sap can circulate without diamagnetism, and since there can be no diagmagnetism without the spiral motion, it is obvious why blood and sap do not move in a circle, but in cycloidal curves, coiling again the diffuse excess elements and combining them intimately in the presence of suitable catalysts (catalysts which Goethe used to call "connecting energy fields").

We are dealing in this case with extremely subtle rays which are released and activated when differently charged precious metals in infinitely fine dispersion are undergoing concentration due to the centripetal movement of the blood or sap, and which in their turn bring together oxygen and the excess products of digestion which have reached the blood, or sap, stream through the. intestinal filter.

This, however, is possible only when the median structures enclosing bipolarity charged sediments, which are just waiting for a natural triggering factor, are set in radioaxial motion and begin to unfold producing a diamagnetic vacuum. This diamagnetic vacuum is an atomic suction force which absorbs and draws in the oxygen from the ambient air. This oxygen, on the other hand, has to pass through certain filters, the skin, the rind, or bark, to absorb only the finest elements. Were it not so, the concentric pressure of the air would force in also less valuable elements.

Diamagnetic respiration is the opposite of atmospheric pressure, inasmuch as it draws in only excess diffuse oxygen, prana. This diamagnetic force is also behind the power of levitation which maintains the earth in a state of labile equilibrium and forces it to revolve around its own axis (called, in general, the magnetic axis). This diamagnetic force which acts axially in all directions, allows the earth to levitate spontaneously.

THE ALL-PERVADING FIFTH ELEMENT, AETHER

Diamagnetism is an emanation, or stream, of the universal ether (the fifth of the known basic elements, the other four being Fire, Earth, Air and Water, and their symbol, again, is the Swastika or Hooked Cross. The fifth element is the point or center on which the other four pivot). It produces constant suction whose surplus energy spirals upwards in a steady flow resulting in an endless inhalatory and exhalatory process, a process which can be mechanically reproduced.

Modern motors generate waves, and these waves impart a centrifugal or radioaxial movement to the surrounding masses of matter. The friction attending this process generates first heat, then fire. This is the end result of a reverse process of elementary compensation, be cause fire is an agent of combustion and therefore acts exactly like the pathogenic bacteria which are nature's purifying agents whose task it is to carry out the degenerative and destructive processes that protect life as a whole. When they are unable to perform this function, they must be aided by fire and burning This is Nature's way. However, it is catastrophic when man makes use of these destructive powers in building culture and civilization while at the same time furthering the proliferation of pathogenic bacteria in the waters by poisoning, overheating and sterilizing the latter, either by such mechanical means as compressor turbines, or by destroying the growth that protects the banks and shores.

The various types of machinery being used at present —centrifugal motors, propellers, agricultural machinery, etc. — are dangerous reactors. They release destructive atomic forces whose effects grow in proportion to the speed of rotation. It is obvious that they destroy the diagmagnetic axial force which absorbs and absorbs oxygen. They centrifuge the water and supply it with a constant stream of warm oxygen so that it asphyxiates and decomposes, all of which leads to the death of tellurian waters, of rivers and of seas.

TREES, SPRING WATER AND DIAMAGNETISM

It seems that until now few people have posed themselves the question why most springs are located high in the mountains and, furthermore, why only in wooded areas. (The latter is true even of springs situated in the lowlands.) It is an established fact that when a natural mountain spring is deprived of its tree covering and exposed to direct sunlight, it dries up and does not begin to flow again until after the protective shade has been restored. When permanently deprived of its natural shade, it either appears at another place, where adequate shade is avail- able, or vanishes forever.

Some mountain springs disappear never to return after having been exposed even to slightly stronger light for a longer period of time. It is also a fact that our supply of mountain water is shrinking as the protecting forests are being thinned and cut down. When the mountains are bare, rivers turn into thin trickles or dry up altogether, and when it rains they become raging torrents. With no trees to retain the waters, they rush into the valleys carrying destruction and silting up their estuaries with rocks and stones.

Thus, we are forced to reach the conclusion that when the forest dies, water dies too, and all life comes to an end, because without water there is no life.

The water of true mountain springs has a temperature of 4°C. just before coming to the surface. Under the influence of light this temperature rises very rapidly, because the positive charge of the atmosphere makes itself felt with lightning speed. When the effects of this positive charge are reinforced by those of direct light, rapid changes take place in the specific gravity of the flowing spring water. In other words, it becomes lifeless as it loses more and more of its diamagnetic powers of levitation.

THE LEVITATION OF CHARGED WATER

Diamagnetically charged water, blood, or sap can levitate. Water which is diamagnetically charged and enriched with carbonic acid refreshes and animates. Those who drink it feel better, healthier, despite its higher gravity.

Schauberger was moved by these observations to alter the polarity of water (or air) after it had been exposed to the action of the atmosphere and to make it negative once more by using a system of suction curves. The results he obtained were amazing. The water which had suddenly recovered its negative charge (in the presence of certain catalysts, with light and other factors excluded) rose high in a carefully insulated stand pipe of special design and made of special alloys — although the pressure was atmospheric — while the volume of water in the tank remained unchanged.

OCCULT SECRETS OF THE THIRD REICH

QUANTITATIVE AND QUALITATIVE ANIMATED WATER

This is how Viktor Schauberger discovered an artificial method of increasing water, as well as an answer to the question: What makes water, which has been negatively diamagnetically charged by the rotation of the earth, rise to the top of mountains, provided light has been excluded and there are trees giving it the necessary protective shade?

This discovery taught him how to create an artificial mountain spring and supplied him with proof that water influenced by the geosphere — that is, animated water — undergoes a quantitative increase and a qualitative improvement. In other words it grows and develops exactly like plants, animals or people when a soul is breathed into it.

Thus diamagnetism and levitation explain the mystery and origin of mountain springs. The planetary, spiral movement of the earth imparts to the tellurian waters under the surface of the earth a predominantly negative magnetic charge. The earth (geosphere) itself is also negatively diamagnetic, while the atmosphere is positively diamagnetic. Since opposite poles are attracted to each other, and like poles are repelled by each other, negatively charged water is repelled by the earth, i.e. it is lifted, while at the same time it is attracted by the atmosphere. Thus, pure water levitates and rises to the top of mountains, while predominantly positive water is repelled by the positive atmosphere and comes down to earth in the form of rain, to undergo its process of purification once more. When the earth happens to be also positively charged due to excessive sunlight, it can no longer attract rain, as in deserts.

Therefore an excess of light or fire is the enemy of water, and vice versa. It is left to man's reason to protect the mantle of vegetation covering the earth so as to preserve life. Under the present circumstances, however, this is not possible today because forests are being cut down all over the world. Steppes, sands and waste lands are advancing; even without atom bombing whole continents are heading toward destruction due to the exhaustion of their natural resources. They must sink to be reborn and emerge from the waters millions of years later. The eradication of the protecting and life-giving vegetation which mantles the earth is additionally hastened by radioactive peroxidation of the atmosphere.

Water loses its ability to ascend mountains when the soil is deprived of woods shading it from direct sunlight. Without this natural screen of trees, ground waters which are found at the deepest levels in deserts and closest to the surface in forests, are forced to recede. Thus the death of forests means the death of water and of all life. This is something which could not be overemphasized, since many are still unaware of this fact.

THE REGENERATION OF DISEASED WATER

Schauberger's discoveries prove among others that water can be multiplied and improved by applying planetary motion and simply imitating nature's methods, and conversely that when water is ruined by centrifugation and such devices as compressor turbines, water wheels, etc., it becomes devitalized, loses its power of levitation, ceases to breathe, asphyxiates and — with continued exposure to sunlight — recedes and vanishes altogether. Of course, in the bosom of Mother Earth this diseased water is gathered up again and its polarity reversed, whereupon it is re-generated and ready to reappear as a fresh and bubbling mountain spring at a new place, where it still finds the protective shade of trees it requires.

Be that as it may, our supplies of fresh water are steadily shrinking. In various branches of industry water experts worry and desperately search for a solution to the water problem. This search is bound to be fruitless unless they turn to Schauberger's discoveries and replace the present fire technology with a biotechnology that will protect and benefit life.

The water and the energy problems can be solved simultaneously if magnetism is produced by mechanical means, and all attempts to produce atomic energy are abandoned.

People can learn only by trial and error. Perhaps the error we made in applying fire methods indiscriminately was necessary to make us realize how dangerous it is to reverse and alter the natural basic motion (the one indicated by Nature as our only means of development) and how wrong it is to employ combustion and other destructive processes to build a civilization. This explains the decadence of our culture. When people use only excentric or centrifugal forces for technical purposes they deteriorate both morally and spiritually.

To use nuclear energy produced by the explosion and fission of atoms is a fatal blunder and a crime against humanity and against the earth itself. Hence it is only natural that the branch of science which has conjured up these horrors has found itself in a blind alley from which there would be no escape were it not for the discovery of diamagnetism, this universal life force without which there can be no respiration and no life. Fortunately, it can be mechanically produced and used to give earth, air and water the chance to breathe again.

The most convincing and obvious proof that life is gradually perishing can be found in the streams and rivers of our industrial areas were water is already so polluted by industrial waste waters and sewers that it resembles drainage from a manure pit. As a result our underground water and supplies of drinking water are gradually becoming unfit for human consumption. They are killing people, just as they have killed the fish which only a few years ago used to splash in them. Water chlorination is also harmful to the human organism. Today the Rhine and the Weser are Europe's most polluted rivers. Actually they are no longer rivers but streaming sewers, as stated by the German Minister of State, Dr. Seebolm.

WATER IS THE "BLOOD" OF THE EARTH

Healthy blood is the life carrier of the human organism. Pure water plays the same role in the economy of the earth. Thus the preservation of life requires that water be kept pure. But water can be pure and wholesome only when it is charged by a magnetic flux which not only stimulates the proliferation of apathogenic bacteria but also animates and regenerates it.

OCCULT SECRETS OF THE THIRD REICH

The general public is still oblivious to the seriousness of the water problem, although it is from this that disaster will come(even without atom bombs) in particular to our most developed areas. The water table is sinking, water is vanishing because its greatest enemy, but also its most important consumer — our fire technology — is poisoning it and burning it out. Our water economy, unaware of the true reasons, attributes its disappearance to a consumption exceeding the natural water supply. As a matter of fact, water consumption in industry and in homes is higher today than it was in the past.

But what causes these losses of underground waters? In the first place, deforestation and the exposure to strong light of regions which would be natural reservoirs had they not been ruined by the destruction of the geospherical diamagnetism. In the second place, the wrong and harmful methods by which rivers are being regulated. We have learned that it is a great mistake to grade river beds and to encase their banks in rigid stone walls. Viktor Schauberger fought for years both these methods and the destruction of forests with equal passion. Now, that many of his predictions have come true, and when it is mostly too late to undo the harm done, these mistakes are being recognized; but nothing is being done to remedy their con-sequences. In all truth, the only effective measure would be to apply Schauberger's discoveries.

THE SINUSOIDAL CURVE FOR CHARGED WATER

There is good reason why rivers wind and twist through valleys and plains. They are trying to preserve the primary form of the sinusoidal curve produced by the slightly declining planetary movement of the earth. The function of this curve is to create and maintain in rivers a diamagnetic axis which keeps their waters alive and pure and endows them with their carrying and towing capacity. When the meander is eliminated by regulation and, furthermore, when the vegetation protecting the banks(willows, alders, etc.) is destroyed, the resulting damage is threefold. First, the magnetic axis is destroyed and the river's carrying, towing and cleansing properties are impaired. Secondly,with the shading vegetation gone and the resulting overexposure to sunlight, the oxygen content of the water is overheated, becomes aggressive and it escapes; the water evaporates, dries out and decomposes. Thirdly, the graded river bed carries off water very rapidly instead of keeping it in the soil. The floor of the river sinks deeper and deeper, causing the underground water to escape and the table to drop; it "bleeds the land to death".

THE DECREASE IN FERTILITY OBVIOUS

The bed of the Rhine has already dropped one meter (and more in certain places) because it is graded and regulated — something which Viktor Schauberger tried to prevent in his days by installing suction spirals. The floor of the Danube between Ulm and Passau has been sinking at the rate of 1½ cm. a year since its regulation. In the Bavarian part of Swabia the River Wertach has cut so deep into the subsoil since it was regulated that its floor is now lies as much as ten meters below the level of its banks. This shows that its water has lost its magnetic axis and its powers of

55

magnetic levitation, its polarity having been changed to positive due to excessive insulation. As a further consequence it has cut through the adjoining horizons of underground water causing the latter to escape. This has reduced the fertility of the surrounding fields which are now threatening to change to a barren steppe.

The experts did not even guess until recently at the enormous importance of the diamagnetic properties of the earth and failed to realize that these properties were destroyed by the direct action of light or fire. The only thing that can keep the earth from becoming a desert, in order to protect the primary source of life, water, from death, is the art of multiplying and improving water.

Today the main question is: What is more important for the immediate development of the earth, water or fire? We know only too well that, indirectly, fire makes it possible to activate machinery; but it is a completely new discovery that by artificially producing and increasing water we can obtain better and cheaper energy and that we can restore, besides, the vegetation whose growth has been affected by an excess of fire.

Thus, by changes in technology to Implosion, not only would it be possible to solve the energy problem, but also to achieve complete freedom from nutritional problems.

An Implosion Motor is in every respect the opposite of an Explosion Motor. While the latter makes use of pressure forces produced by explosion, the implosion motor utilizes the suction forces of implosion. When pressure forces are applied, the particles they set in motion move away from the biological zero point, or zone of anomaly, being often heated until they are white-hot. A so-called heat barrier is produced by the resulting enormous friction resistance forces. One of the greatest problems in aircraft construction, for example, is how to overcome this barrier.

In the case of the implosion motor there is no—heat barrier and no sound barrier, because with friction almost entirely lacking, no heat is generated. On the contrary, due to the spiral contraction of the flowing medium there is cooling to anomaly, and this creates a vacuum which increases the suction pull. In this case the reactive power factor grows, because the medium which has been set in motion is radio-axially swirled almost without resistance while at the same time being mechanically and physically concentrated and correspondingly cooled. When nozzles 1 mm in "diameter are used, the flowing medium detaches itself — when its rotation reaches 1200 rpm — from the walls of the spiral channel and its flow rate rises to approximately 1290 m/sec. This corresponds to nearly four times the speed of sound. The larger the diameter of the spiral rotor, the slower can be the rotation of the impulsion motor which starts the suction motor.

An impulsion motor can coil and tighten water in a system of suction tubes spirally arranged around a conical shell into a homogeneous suction head and shoot it out through a special nozzle built into the bottom. When this stream of water, which is like a steel wire tapering to a suction point, is intermittently interrupted by a shutoff valve of special construction and made of a special alloy, a reactive back-pressure force is generated which acts in the same direction as the implosion motor. The speed of this back pressure force corresponds to the previously mentioned outflow rate. It supplies the rotor shaft with some

17.9 HP/lit/sec. through each 1 mm nozzle (i.e., an out outlet cross-section of 0.79 sq. mm, as selected on the basis of mathematical calculations) which can be utilized as a reactive projecting or lifting force.

In the case of an implosion engine having a diameter of 1 meter, the lower surface of the suction rotor measuring slightly over 5 meters in circumference could easily accommodate 100 or more nozzles, each with 3-6 outlets. Assuming 600 outlets had been installed, and with the rotor turning at the rate of 1200 rpm, the lower rotor shaft could be supplied with some 10,740 HP in the form of a cyclone-like projecting or lifting force.

Such an energy output exceeds even the present possibilities of a nuclear engine. A group of engineers and scientists from the University of Utah have designed a 7,000 HP nuclear railroad locomotive.

THE MASSIVE PROBLEMS OF NUCLEAR POWER

The estimated cost of this locomotive $1,200,000. The reactor will be 0.9 meters long, 0.6 m wide, and 0.9 m high. While it will be somewhat smaller than the above-mentioned implosion motor its capacity will be almost 4,000 HP lower. Furthermore, the nuclear reactor will have to be surrounded by a 200 ton screen to eliminate at least part of its deadly radioactive emissions. To install this giant nuclear locomotive on a single undercarriage would be impossible. It will require 12 supporting wheel axles and 24 wheels. Therefore it will be constructed as a dual unit having a total length of 48 meters.

The front part of the locomotive will house the reactor and motor. The trailer will carry ribbed, air-cooled heat exchanger tubes which will have to cool huge volumes of water of condensation. The basic cost of this locomotive will further be increased by the current costs of its nuclear fuel. It is estimated that these will reach $200,000 a year with the locomotive in full operation.

The implosion motor presents none of these disadvantages, namely, the heavy; 1.2 m thick lead screen, the trailer with its water cooling installations, and, last but not least, the fuel costs, inasmuch as the implosion motor runs on a small quantity of water uninterruptedly, like a living organism, until the water has been used up and the temperature gradient is exhausted.

Therefore the installation of implosion engines opens the path to dazzling possibilities. Implosion motors can be employed not only in stationary machinery, but also in all types of vehicles, cars, aircraft, ships, etc. They can replace all and sundry known types of motors and power engines.

THE NON-POLLUTING IMPLOSION MOTOR

Implosion motors are less expensive to construct, require no costly propellants and, moreover, permit biological exploitation so they have a positive effect.

OCCULT SECRETS OF THE THIRD REICH

While the present types of power machinery bring into play their centrifugal motion decentralizing reactive forces which lead to cancer, implosion motors produce by their centripetal motion condensing reaction forces and diamagnetism. In the first case we have, from the biological point of view, de-animating and regressive energies activated by back-pressure; in the second case, reactivated projecting and stimulating energies which result in biological improvement and growth.

Of course the mechanical production of diamagnetism requires exact measuring and control methods, because even the best medicine can be harmful when administered in excessive doses. The necessary data on the application of the constructive diamagnetic forces will have to be collected on the basis of practical findings.

OUR UNBEARABLE EXPLOSIVE POWER PLANTS

Still another and very important advantage of the implosion motor is that in operation it is both soundless and odorless;whereas, all combustion engines produce noise, smell, exhaust fumes and smoke, creating unbearable conditions when used in large numbers. Implosion motors on the other hand, run noiselessly, without smoke, exhaust fumes or smell. In nature planetary motion is soundless, crashing noises being the concomitant only of such destructive processes as storms.

It must be admitted that the design and construction of implosion motors presents great difficulties due to the fact that they imitate the prototype of life (not to mention a totally new technology which at the present time does not exist!). Their suction tubes must be arranged in a perfect spiral and therefore compasses cannot be used when working on their design. Also, they have no transmission shaft, while in all conventional power engines, which can produce energy only by means of circular, mostly centrifugal motion, the transmission shaft is an essential part. The type motion of a conventional engines represents, biologically speaking, a stationary spin, thus a backward motion, since in nature standstill is the equivalent of regression.

SUCTION TURBINES AND HOME POWER PLANTS

To begin with, implosion motors will have to be used as suction turbines and home power plants. During the transition period suction turbines will have to replace above all the compressor turbines now being used in our conventional power plants.

Schauberger's suction turbine will completely revolutionize the current power plant construction methods and will soon replace the present exclusive compressor turbine. The installation of suction turbines would result in substantial monetary and material savings. The fixed hydroelectric power plant and construction costs would be reduced at least by 70—80%, since no longer would it be necessary to build such costly installations as — to mention but a few — high dams and compression tunnels. Suction turbines, once they have been started, draw in water without further assistance, and therefore require only a fairly shallow basin for their inflow and outflow waters. Thus, substantial savings would be realized, particularly in such construction materials as cement, reinforced concrete, structural steel, etc., which could then be utilized for road construction (in most countries the latter is lagging), or other vital construction projects.

Water consumption being equal, the power output of suction turbines is 700 to 800% higher than the power output of compressor turbines. This means that countries which already have hydroelectric power plants could meet their power requirements over a longer period of years making use of their present facilities. It has been calculated, for example, that in Austria the maximum total power output of the present hydroelectric power plants (at least those which can be expanded) in full operation and with existing overhauled compressor turbine systems, is 40 billion kilowatts a year.

NEGATIVELY POLARIZED WATER

Besides, the present compressor turbines have seriously impaired the vital magnetic axis of flowing waters. This has drastically affected their buoyancy and towing capacity and, consequently, it has increased dredging costs. The polarity of the oxygen in the water is being changed by the compressor turbine systems. As a result it is becoming aggressive and it stimulates the proliferation of pathogenic microorganisms in the water. An additional consequence is that in the adjoining areas the water table is sinking. Due to the breakdown of the magnetic axis, the useful bacteria which, under normal conditions, are the natural purifying agents, are dying. This could be remedied by two different means: one, by installing suction turbines which restore the magnetic axis, and two, by placing suction spirals along the river beds.

It is an experimentally demonstrable fact that when healthy water has been centrifuged by compressor turbines or compressor blades for an hour, its pathogenic bacterial flora shows overnight a visible increase and, conversely, that such infected water can again be made into excellent spring water overnight by coiling it or swirling it for an hour by means of a suction spiral in a centripetal manner (in a manner restoring its negative polarity). Schauberger succeeded not only in changing sea water into fresh water by cold distillation with the aid of the suction spiral, but also generated power in the process.

The question of low-cost power production can be positively solved not only by equipping the existing large-scale hydroelectric works with suction turbines, but also by producing for home use small power generating units designed to operate on a few liters of water — or, at a later stage of development, on air.

This type of decentralized power supply system is much cheaper and far more practical. Many states would be spared the heavy expenditures entailed by the construction of large-scale power installations, inasmuch as such investments are covered by government funds, while home power plants would be purchased by private parties. These inexpensive units produce electricity at nominal cost and require no special attention. They would pay for themselves within a very short time and soon a number of industrial establishments, workshops and, above all, farms would have power plants supplying each of them with electricity according to the capacity of their units and their needs.

OCCULT SECRETS OF THE THIRD REICH

These home units present obvious advantages. In the first place they make the owner independent of other power networks. At the same time they appreciably reduce the consumption of high- voltage power and the number of the usual feed lines, in particular in regions still inadequately or unprovided with electricity. Secondly, they can be readily exported to economically undeveloped countries making it possible for the latter to avoid heavy power plant construction investments.

The home power unit based on the Implosion principle is in a developmental stage for the present (1954) since it is still necessary to determine which type of connection would be most suitable for this model.

IMPLOSION MOTOR IS A LIVING ORGANISM

The unit is like a living organism, because once the water on which it operates has been let in, it starts to circulate like blood in the human body. The upper part of the unit houses a small suction turbine which is started with all valves open. After the turbine has reached a certain number of revolutions per minute, a vertical circulation is started which resembles the circulation of the blood through the venous and arterial systems of the human or animal body, inasmuch as it follows a series of cycloidal spiral geometric curves.

Due to the circulatory movement produced by the suction and spiral channels, the water in the turbine is coiled, that is, swirled and drawn to the center almost without friction. The water, while being mechanically and physically coiled, cools rapidly and its temperature drops to anomaly. As it undergoes specific condensation a vacuum is created which, in its turn, produces a constant suction pull. We find exactly the same in the human chest which is forced to inhale air by a diamagnetically produced vacuum. This mechanism underlies all circulatory motion.

An excess hydraulic pressure is produced in a water tank which is located in the lower part of the unit. This excess pressure constantly forces the operating water upwards, through a lateral stand-pipe, At the same time the water is strongly pulled and en-trained in the same direction by the vacuum which is created by the pulling forces of the spiral suction tube, and it flows, carrying an overcharge of terrestrial (negative) magnetism. When the turbine reaches a certain number of revolutions per minute, the circulatory process within attains a speed several times higher than that of sound, and the molecularly condensed operating water leaves the suction spiral through special nozzles , forming an almost homogeneous suction head which revolves spontaneously around its own axis like a cyclone or hurricane.

This type of cyclone, however, can no longer be measured in the engine, because its intermittent swirls and sweeps take place within such brief time-spans and over such short distances that they can be registered by mechanical measuring instruments only if intercepted by special filter devices.

THE GENERATION OF COLD LIGHT, AND VACUUM LIFT

When this diamagnetically charged vertically emanating flow of energy is caught on pointed collectors (these must be carefully insulated on the outside) and conducted over further wire point spans (Brucken) into grounded vacuum tubes or bulbs, the inner surfaces of the evacuated bulb light up with a so-called cold or natural light. The intensity of this light increases as the reactor rotates faster and faster. This reactor is designed according to the laws of Nature, constructed of the right alloys, and properly insulated. Thus the construction of cold-current generators for use as home power plants will permit us to produce cheaper light and better light, because the present electron-electrical hot light production method arrests developmental processes and, with the existing type light bulbs, is harmful to the eyes.

The nearly homogeneous suction head is coiled in the Schauberger turbine around and into itself. Parenthetically speaking, the same has been observed just recently in cyclones. It has been established that the center of the vortex, which moves at the rate of 100 to 200 km/h, is surrounded by a second spiral which has been clocked at 800 km/h. The homogeneous suction head is deflected in the rotational direction of the suction turbine by check-valves (Bremsdusen — perhaps; intercepting nozzles?) of very special design. The heretofore almost unrecognized specific physical nature of suction and of the diamagnetism it generates increases the force of rotation — which is the actual motive power of the engine —a feature which represents the greatest advantage of the implosion engine in general, and of the home power plant in particular.

The energy thus derived from water or air must be checked and captured, otherwise the suction turbine would "run away", meaning that it would levitate! This can be prevented by connecting it to a dynamo, which makes it possible to produce also thermoelectric power.

The basic difference between the compressor and the suction turbine is that while the first rotates due to a great pressure gradient and converts only a fraction of this energy to electricity the other once having been started, draws in spontaneously its motor medium and takes advantage — against all hitherto known physical laws — of the descending temperature gradient.

It can be safely said that even today the Schauberger implosion technique can bring the entire energy problem, and in particular the whole electronics industry, into new paths where it could not be rivaled by even atomic energy. Implosion motors offer us for the first time the possibility of making practical use of diamagnetism, this foundation of the Life Force, and besides, to obtain cold light in various colors without the help of gases.

THE DIAMAGNETISM OF FLYING SAUCERS

Those who have attentively followed the ideas presented in the above must have been struck by the thought that the principles of modern aviation stand in direct contradiction to the natural processes of motion. The same propeller which is used by nature as a brake, serves in modern flight technology as a means of propulsion, but with enormous energy losses. It first whips or rams air back and then it produces a secondary effect the suction of which pulls the air vehicle forward. Similar processes of motion occur also with rocket aircraft and with nuclear aircraft now under construction. Pressure forces are used in every field of technology, instead of suction forces, although the latter are more effective, more economical, simpler, and above all more in keeping with the laws of nature, due to the fact that they create a vacuum and diamagnetism and require no propellant in the accepted sense of the word.

Although by now the great world powers must be acquainted with the principle of Flying Saucers. The USA has just recently requested permission to put into production rocket-base flying saucers. Even interplanetary bases are to be constructed using exclusively pressure forces. This proves that even these attempts to reach the outer spaces are biotechnically misdirected and that they will result in an enormous waste of money and materials. In the first place, interplanetary flight is possible only by suction force based on diamagnetism, thus on etheric force which pervades the entire universe. This force allows the heavenly bodies to float freely through space and to move along their proper orbits.

The universe can never be conquered by pressure forces or pressure radiation (druckstrahlen). Billions have been poured of late into this, as well as into atomic research; but it would be far better to spend this money on useful projects, because aviation of the future will resort primarily to levitation made possible by the suction spiral.

In the case of diamagnetic levitation, the force has to con- tend neither with a sound barrier nor with a heat barrier. The sound barrier does not enter the picture because the future air vehicles — whether disc or cigar-shaped — will be effortlessly moved forward by the steadily preceding suction pull. The opposite is true of our present aircraft (including the jet-propulsion rockets) with produce, like explosion, first compression and resistance, and only thereupon suction, giving rise at the same time to increasing friction and a high-invincible heat barrier. It releases as it breaks through the sound barrier a tremendous pressure wave which below, at ground level, splinters windowpanes, breaks doors and gates, and flattens roofs.

None of this occurs with flying discs which are propelled by diamagnetism, i.e., etheric forces. It goes without saying that Flying Saucers encounter no heat barrier since they generate a negative pressure and diamagnetism, Their metal or glass airframes are no more heated than the shell of an implosion engine. On the contrary, they cool to their specific zone of anomaly. It would be impossible to imagine more perfect air vehicles. They have no sound barrier, no beat barrier, and they require no costly propellant because they generate their own motive power, that is diamagnetism.

THE UNIVERSAL SOURCE OF ENERGY

An abundance of this energy, Diamagnetism, is available throughout the universe. Therefore, such a diamagnetic aircraft could travel around the earth not once, but two or three times at any given altitude without having to refuel. Actually, it could travel in outer space for years, or as long as the crew did not have to replenish its food supplies.

The following observations may serve as proof that the Flying Saucers are diamagnetically propelled. As already mentioned in our chapter on diagmagnetism, copper is a diamagnetic metal. When the UFO's fly at a relatively low rate of speed, they are surrounded by a light greenish hue. The spectral line, of burning copper has been observed to fall within this specific green. Furthermore, air samples taken from the atmosphere in the regions where, beginning in 1947, the UFOs have been frequently observed, have shown high concentrations of copper particles in very fine dispersion. On the other hand, air samples taken before the appearance of the Flying Saucers, show a complete absence of copper. Of course, none of the observations made so far regarding the UFO's speed, performance, take-off characteristics, and various light effects can be brought in line with the familiar laws of physics. This, however, is no proof that unknown types of air vehicles can not exist. After all, the mechanism of implosion and the nature of diamagnetism are ignored in modern physics and remain to be investigated and formally clarified.

The objection that man would not be able to tolerate the speeds at which, as determined by radar, the UFOs move is by no means valid. This assumption would be valid only if we considered existing with the conventional flying methods which bring pressure forces into play. How can we tell whether higher speeds would have any adverse effect on the human organism if only suction forces were to be used?

Undoubtedly, they key to the mystery of propulsion used by Flying Saucers can be found in the application of cycloidal spiral geometric curves. Only the latter would permit the UFOs to achieve the fantastic speeds of up to 60,000 km/h at which they have been seen to fly. Some of the maneuvers of these Saucers which we consider extraordinary are probably commonplace on other planets. It must be remembered that Flying Saucers have been observed for centuries, long before men representing our own civilization had mastered air travel.

ATOMIC EXPLOSIONS FORCED THEIR APPEARANCE

The mass appearance of the UFOs which, though still often disputed in official quarters so as to calm the general public, can no longer be denied in the face of factual evidence, appears to be connected with the effects of the atom bombs being exploded on our planet.

According to science, in our planetary system only the earth is inhabitable, wherefore it alone can be populated. This hypotheses is bound to be refuted some day by scientists, just as it was the case with the old geocentric concept of the world which placed the earth in the center of the universe and grandly permitted the sun to revolve around one one of its smallest satellites. We can rest assured that the countless solar systems of the universe must include a number of other habitable planets. We still ignore the number of fixed stars in our galaxy. Perhaps they number a hundred million, perhaps more, who can tell? But we do know that our whole galaxy is but a small island in a sea of innumerable galactic systems. Hence, what could be more illogical than to assume that the entire universe consists of a mass of meteoric iron or of a certain quantity of elements spinning in space with rhyme or reason; and, what could be more presumptuous than to believe that only the earth, this tiny grain of sand in comparison with the size of the universe, can be inhabited?

Other planets, no doubt, present different atmospheric and living conditions. It would not be surprising, therefore, if various and varying forms of life had evolved on separate planets. Indeed, even the principal human races of the earth show marked physical differences. Why then, should other planets not be in- habited by supermen who have reached a much higher level of development than the inhabitants of the earth, supermen who for thou- sands of years have been familiar with interstellar navigation made possible by the application of etheric forces. Unfortunately,when men dream of venturing forth into outer space, their only aim is conquest.

EVIDENCE OF ARRESTED SPIRITUAL DEVELOPMENT

War and destruction cannot be the only goals in this world. Those who see nothing else give proof of arrested spiritual development. Consequently it is highly dangerous to put into their hands this type of aircraft (though better this than nuclear types). Hence, it is of paramount importance to match technical advances with spiritual and religious progress, to broaden our world out- look and to develop our character. Man would do better to bring peace and order to his own native planet before planning to conquer strange worlds.

THE VIOLENT LORDS OF THE EARTH

What would happen, for example, if here on earth each man were to look upon his neighbors as robbers and aggressors, instead of treating them as peaceful and friendly guests? But the lords of this earth think only of violence and some of them even speculate in Martian real estate, selling the hide, one might say, before they have killed the bear. To men from other planets the inhabitants of the earth must appear as savages, not only because of their behavior, but also because of their nuclear technology which threatens not only the neighboring planets but our whole solar system, which might be said to represent a single higher organism — or perhaps an atom of the macrocosm. In view of this,people of other planets cannot remain indifferent to the fact that men of this earth have actually reached the possibility of disintegrating the earth.

It would be hopeless for people to dream of conquering other worlds, or for some of them to think that in the case of an atomic war they could migrate to another planet. It is obvious that conditions for life differ from planet to planet, being adapted to the existing spirituals level and biological development of their own inhabitants. Some day, when people will have matured spiritually, given up senseless struggle and their attempts to destroy the earth by means of atomic forces, they will discover hitherto unanticipated means of space travel. Individuals will not use large flying saucers but small, toy-like models. Many will own such aircraft because these will be, in all probability, much cheaper than our present day automobiles.

The aviation of tomorrow will be based on suction forces and levitation, which may sound like a dream of Utopia.

There will be, likewise, fantastic possibilities of transportation. During the coming centuries street traffic will take to the air. The serious road problems now plaguing our large cities will, where every fourth or fifth inhabitant has an automobile, will be solved. There is ample room in the air for vehicles to get out of each others way by going left, right, up or down. Take-offs, instead of being horizontal, will be almost vertical, making it possible for the owners of "implos" to use their yards and roofs as landing strips.

There will be no accidents due to mechanical failure or ignition trouble. Since implosion motors have no ignition system, they are not affected even by the impact of concentrated terrestrial rays (Erdstrahlen), which are erroneously believed to be a type of mysterious "death rays". It is unfortunate that science has done little in the way of investigating these terrestrial rays, which have in some cases been known to cause motors to choke.

The Flying Saucers, as far as is known, move soundlessly. Implosion motors are, likewise, noiseless in operation and this feature is one of their greatest advantages of attraction. Let us hope that some day they will eliminate the roar of our present of our present motors which shake the earth by their explosions.

MAN-MADE BARRIERS MUST GO

Speeds will be limited neither by the motor nor, presumably by the human organism. However, for the present their limits remain a matter of conjecture, inasmuch as the effects of suction flight on the human body are still unknown and will have to be studied.

Automobile and motorcycle races will become meaningless, for the reason that speed will have lost its magic attraction.

It can be taken for granted that the new methods of flight will affect politics. Instead of traveling, as today, by car or plane, people will find it cheaper to go by Implo; thus the time is bound to come when borders will no longer be capable of stopping the thousands of vacation-bound travelers hurrying by implosion aircraft to sea shores and mounts in search of rest and relaxation. The birds in the air can cross any state line at will, yet homo sapiens, this proud master of land, air and sea, is still stopped by the artificial barriers which he him- self has created in defiance of all natural laws.

Thus, only by eradicating national and political strife and the struggle for bread between nations and races, will it ever be possible to establish a universal world-wide Kingdom of Peace; and this can only be done if man's technical sciences and progress are based on the laws of Nature.

May the Implosion method help people to mature into peaceful and rational citizens of the world.

CONCERNING THE DEATH OF ELEMENTS, ESPECIALLY OF WATER

Elements die, as men die, on account of the corruption in them. As water at its death, as it were, consumes and devours its own fruit, so does the earth its own fruits. Whatever is born from it returns to it again, is swallowed up and lost, just as the time past is swallowed up by yesterday's days and nights, the light or darkness of which we shall never see again. It is no weightier today than yesterday, not even by a single grain, and will after a thousand years be of the same weight still. As it gives forth, so, in the same degree, it consumes. The death of the water, however, is in its own proper element, in that great terminus and centre of water, the sea, wherein the rivers, and what- ever else flows into it, die and are consumed as wood in the fire. Rivers, indeed, are not the element of water, but the fruit of that element, which is the sea; from this they derive their origin, and in this they receive both their life and their death.

CLIPS, QUOTES & COMMENTS: THE IMPLOSION AT FIRST HAND!

While inventor Viktor Schauberger was perfecting his Implosion- Vacuum-Suction engines in Vienna in the 1950s, Flying Saucer contactees were experiencing it at first hand! For George Adamski it was when he approached a landed Scout saucer on the California desert, Nov. 20, 1952. Well, not actually landed but producing just enough lift to float off the ground.

"The ship was hovering above the ground, about a foot or two at the far side from me, and very near to the bank of the hill. But the slope of the hill was such," writes Adamski in "Flying Saucers Have Landed", "that the front, or that part of it closest to me, was a good six feet above the earth. The three-ball landing gear was half lowered below the edge of the flange that covered them, and I had a feeling this was a precautionary act just in case they had definitely to land. Some of the gusts of wind were pretty strong and caused the ship to wobble at times. When this took place the sun reflecting on the surface of the ship caused beautiful prismatic rays of light to reflect out from it, as from a smoky diamond. This was observed, too, by the six others who maintained a steady watch from a distance.

"Nearing the ship I noticed a round ball at the very top that looked like a heavy lens of some kind. And it glowed. I wondered if it could be used as one end of a magnetic pole to draw their power from space as they were moving through it. . . And once, fora fleeting second, I saw a beautiful face appear and look but. I felt that whoever was inside was looking for the one who was still out with me, but no word was spoken. The face disappeared quickly (From the porthole on the side) but I noticed that this person, too, had long hair like the man I had been talking with.

"The lower outside portion of the Saucer was made like a flange, very shiny yet not smooth as a single piece of metal would appear. It seemed to have layers of a fashion, but they wouldn't be used as steps because they were in reverse of what steps would be. . .

"My space-man companion warned me not to get too close to it and he himself stopped a good foot away from it. But I must have stepped just a little closer than he, for as I turned to speak to him, my right shoulder came slightly under the outer edge of the flange and instantly my arm was jerked up and almost at the same instant was thrown back down against my body. The force was so strong that, although I could still move the arm, I had no feeling in it as I stepped clear of the ship. My companion was quite distressed about this accident, but he warned me and I alone was to blame. However, he did assure me that in time it would be all right. Three months later, his words have been proved true for feeling has returned and only an occasional shooting pain as of a deeply-bruised bone returns to remind me of the incident. . . "

It was a very real, physical reminder, too! Before leaving the Venusian asked for and received one of the exposed negatives Adamski had in a plate holder in his coat pocket, indicating that it would be returned to him later.

EVIDENCE FOR AN IMPLODING VORTEX

"... Where the entrance was, or how he went into the ship I do not know for sure, but as it silently rose and moved away, it turned a little and I saw a small opening about the centre of the flange being closed by what looked like a sliding door. Also I heard the two occupants talking together, and their voices were as music, but their words I could not understand.

"As the ship started moving, I noticed two rings under the flange and a third around the centre disk. This inner ring and the outer one appeared to be revolving clockwise, while the ring between these two moved in a counter-clockwise motion."

MHD, Magneto-Hydro-Dynamics is the fancy name for the science of the generation and controlled flow of a field of charged particles such as illustrated in the Flying Saucer drawing below. This accompanied a confidential report published in Hollywood in the 1960s by the Facts Uncensored Publishing Company. But for Adamski's arm to be jerked violently upward against the rim of the hovering Saucer the vacuum-creating flow of energy would have to come all the way out to the edge of that rim and around it and upward as we have shown in our adaptation of the Saucer drawing below. This also brings into play the full area of the parabolic curved upper surface of the craft for lift — as described by the Ganymede Saucer captain to Dino Kraspedon in Brazil in 1952, the same month of Adamski's experience!

"CREATE A VACUUM IN THE DIRECTION OF TRAVEL"

"We use the natural atmospheric pressure in the flying saucer," said Ganymede. "It is this which gives us the necessary propulsive force."

"If we maintain this pressure underneath the saucer and bring about a decompression on top, the craft will be given a terrific upward thrust which no known force can match. It is quite simple, my friend, we create a vacuum in the direction of travel. (This explains why UFOs have been seen to rise up straight and then tilt before moving horizontally in that tilted direction. RHC.)

"If we have low pressure on one side the other side is subject to the full atmospheric pressure. Any object, whatever its nature, can only be moved if some difference of energy potential is created. For example, with a saucer of 20 meters diameter, we get Pi times the radius squared = 3,141,600 square centimeters as the surface of the saucer. With an atmospheric pressure of 1.033 kilograms per square centimeter, we can calculate that the force operating on a saucer of 20 meters diameter is equal to 3,278,272.8 kilograms. This gives you some idea of what is involved, even the smallest type of saucer develops a thrust of approximately 3 million kg., whereas even your most powerful aeroplanes cannot develop more than a few thousand kilograms of thrust."

OCCULT SECRETS OF THE THIRD REICH

ATMOSPHERIC DRIVE

Though the title of Chapter Three of Kraspedon's book, "My Contact with Flying Saucers", is titled "Overcoming Gravity", this is not true Space Drive nor Contra-Gravity Drive because it depends on a vacuum created in the earth's atmosphere. Nor is there any hint in Ganymede's dialog with Kraspedon that an Imploding Vortex is central to the creation of the vacuum on the upper surface of the space craft. He frankly told Dino that they weren't ready then to reveal all of their secrets. However, Adamski got a little more detail from the Venusian when his photographic plate holder and film were returned to him at Alice Wells' home at Palomar Gardens, California a month later. The Venusian Scout Saucer few low over the place in the day time — so several good pictures could be taken of it— and the plate holder was tossed out into the yard.

Below is a reproduction of the image on the film in the plate holder when it was developed. Perhaps the Venusian hieroglyphics contain a practical explanation for Einstein's Unified Field Theory. Another, more striking example, which illustrates the awesome power of the inward-turning vortex claimed by Viktor Schaubarger, is the tornado. We are in the tornado season now and imploding vortexes are moving inexorably across the land, destroying everything in their path where the funnel touches down to the earth. Those who have been taken up in such imploding vortexes, and survived, report time changes which indicate this is a true Space Warp affecting the very structure of matter. The tornado is a crude Time Machine; so is the Flying Saucer, but more sophisticated, with its Space Warping power plant under constructive control!

Dr. Andrija Puharich, in his book "Beyond Telepathy", proves pretty conclusively, that Time is one of the essential factors in the Gravity equation. Change Time and you change Gravity, thus affecting the "glue which holds matter together. We review that highly important material in our lecture "Flying Saucers Uncensored"

Perceptive Associates will see a contradiction in the Flying Saucer propulsion idea illustrated on page 25 and that described by the French scientist, Dr. Petit, on page 34 of the May-June Journal. Dr. Petit says the imploding vortex works upwards "causing gases to rush out through the top of the UFO. But remarkably, a magnetic field pushes the gases downward along the craft's outer hull — providing lift".

At this point in time we cannot resolve the contradiction. The fact of George Adamski's arm being jerked upward at the Saucer rim would seem to indicate that the flow of charged particles is upward along the curved surface and inward at the top, as illustrated, rather than the reverse. Perhaps it works either way as long as a vacuum is created on the upper surface. Perhaps there is a third explanation not clear at this time. We welcome comment and observations by the Associates.

VICTOR SCHAUBERGER AND HIS WORK

"Implosion Instead of Explosion"

I was very impressed after reading this and attempted to find out more about it, such as subsequent developments or new research.

68

OCCULT SECRETS OF THE THIRD REICH

The Austrian Patent Office was contacted but gave no information. Mr. Schauberger's son ignores requests from this continent. Mr. Brandstatter's widow offered assistance, however, and I wrote to the people she referred me to. Both Mr. Brandstatter and Mr. Schauberger are now dead.

Victor Schauberger was a Forest Ranger before and after the First World War under Prince Schaumber-Lippe of Bavaria. This area was still a beautiful and unspoiled corner of the world then. One day, as often before, he was watching some trout standing motionless in the strong current of a mountain stream. For him, they had always been the symbol of the Man of Tomorrow who, he felt, would no longer need hard labor to sur- vive. When he disturbed them with his cane they didn't dash to the side, but always went forward into the current. Schauberger assumed that a force unknown to the science of the day was influencing their behavior.

The period that followed was difficult for him, that is until he discovered the Implosion Force. As happens to anyone harboring a new thought, no one understood him. He couldn't find a tradesman who would manufacture a spiral pipe with a dent in it. His criticism of fellow scientists caused him still more difficulties. He supported his theory with experiments but no one would listen as he was by then considered a dangerous outsider.

He was eventually found troublesome enough to warrant committing to an institution. He was, however, fortunate enough to have friends with influence and soon left, with a document in hand stating that he was in possession of all his faculties. He was henceforth the only one who could prove his sanity with- out the shadow of a doubt. Early publication of Schauberger's invention resulted in an invitation to work in America.

THE OIL COMPANY KISS OF DEATH

He came to Texas with his plans and models hoping to build a power plant for the home, which would make cheap electric power available. Unfortunately, the promises that had been made to him came to naught, and Schauberger, a very disillusioned man, became ill. He had consented under agreement to remain in Texas for three months. At the end of this period he was persuaded to sign the following contract before going home. Five days after landing in Europe, he died (1958).

(No wonder Schauberger's son wants nothing to do with America or Americans! This shabby treatment of the Austrian inventor proves that his Implosion motor was a threat to the established oil and nuclear power interests. So they murdered him with false promises, just as the Sick Industry broke the heart of Georges Lakhovsky in New York City in the early 1940s, with a research program on his Multi-Wave Oscillator which deliberately went nowhere. RHC.)

The Schauberger contract stated:

-that all of his patents would become the property of a consortium managed by a Mr. Donner.

-that any future inventions or developments would also be owned by this con-

OCCULT SECRETS OF THE THIRD REICH

sortium.

-that he would refrain from discussing any of it with other parties.

-that he would refrain from publishing.

-that all plans and models would remain with the consortium.

Like many inventors before him, Schauberger died poor, but his work and ideas are still alive. His son, Walter Schauberger, for one, is teaching about Schauberger's achievements in his Pythagoras-Kepler School.

Schauberger was a multi-faceted inventor. At the beginning of his career as a forest ranger he worked for a landowner whose young wife often went to the Riviera to play the casino at Monte Carlo. Always in need of money, her husband wanted to increase logging productivity. Oxen were then used to transport logs. This was slow and expensive. Schauberger suggested floating them down the creeks instead. He estimated the cost reduction at 90%. Engineers declared this was impossible since oak and beech are heavier than water and cannot float.

Schauberger knew his idea would work on cold winter nights if a spiral could be created in the flowing water, but that would have to be in a trough or flume with laths of larchwood nailed diagonally to implode the flowing water. The heavy logs went forward like bullets shooting out of a rifle. They twisted about their own axis without ever bumping against the walls of the trough, even at full capacity.

THE SPIRAL MUST BE HARMONIOUS

The spiral is subject to bipolarity. There are harmonious and inharmonious spirals, the same as with melodies. A spiral is harmonious when its radii are divisible by a whole number, i.e., 1 for the first coil, 1/2 in the second coil, 1/3 in the third coil, etc.

Nature uses egg shapes — one of its secrets. But it works slowly. Applying this principle would be inefficient in view of today's pollution and destruction. For this reason Schauberger wanted to speed up the natural processes. He observed that the planets orbit around the sun while at the same time spinning on their own axis. There is a double pattern as in waltzing. The spiral pipe incorporates this characteristic. It is conical and generally egg-shaped except for an inner bend along one quarter of its circumference. The shape causes the water to roll inwards under the action of the rotor on which the pipes are mounted.

The manufacture of such a pipe was at first difficult; but a solution was eventually found: a sheet of copper was cut to the harmonious measure, bent in the shape of a pipe, welded along its length (embodying, of course, the irregular ovoid mentioned above). The impossible was made possible. We know that Nature uses the spiral in many ways: hurricanes, twisters, tornadoes, streams and ocean currents. The Tesla coil, for instance, seems to work through this principle, or perhaps works better because of it. When the last three inches of the secondary winding are tapered and conical, the coil gives a better performance (e.g., the end where you attach the MWO antenna).

70

OCCULT SECRETS OF THE THIRD REICH

ISKUSIN AND ISKAD0R

Dr. Rudolf Steiner, M.D., the founder of Anthroposophie, found that the sap of both summer and winter mistletoe made a good remedy against cancer when injected. He called it Iskador. He described cancer as a disorder of the cell structure for which summer and winter mistletoe, when used together, could work wonders because of their regulating ability. Furthermore,during the process there is a build-up of a sort of electrical energy as the drops fall; this electrical energy, although aside effect,' seems to be the main healing force. This energy initially got lost during the mixing of the mistletoe as it was done by centrifuge. Dr. Med. Karl Roller, who was oriented to spiral force, reversed the process and used centripetal force which conserved the electrical property of the medicine. He called the drug Iskusin. (Electricity created by falling drops will be discussed later.)

THE WATER WHIRL IN PRACTICE

The pollution affecting the river Elbe in West Germany made it impossible for the city of Hamburg to use it as a source of drinking water. Deep wells had to be drilled and it was found that the water contains carbonic acid which is corrosive and endangered the City's water system. Carbonic acid can be neutralized with lime, at a ratio of 100 grams of lime to one cubic meter of water, or 6.6 tons of lime to 66,000 cm. of water, to be mixed during a 24-hour period. Lime and water were mixed spirally by a mixer, the upper portion of which had a saucer-like shape with a diameter of 83" and was 23 1/2" deep. A whirling arm of 3 1/4" diameter was driven by a motor. Not only did the centripetal motion do all the mixing, but also reduced the need for lime by 50% in each well. The city uses six such mixers.

THE GOLDEN PLOUGH

Because of his experience with all kinds of water problems, Schauberger was nicknamed "water magician". He was once invited to Bulgaria in connection with the problem of farmland drying out. The Bulgarians were then using steam plows, the plough- shares being made of steel. Strangely enough, there was no Drying out in the old Turkish settlements where wooden ploughs were still being used. Could the material used for the plough- shares be the reason for the difference? Back home in Austria, Schauberger made experiments. His ploughshares were covered with copper plates. The result was surprising, up to 60% more harvest. New experiments show an increase of up to 100%.

The use of steel has disadvantages; it has no magnetic permeability. The earth magnetism gets cut and diverged. This creates turbulent energy fields, a chaos; but more important is the grinding off of tiny steel particles because of the fast working methods of today. The fine steel dust combines with the oxygen. The result is oxidation and rust, which not only deprive the soil of some of its oxygen — at the same time killing some of the micro-organisms in the soil — but also causes the groundwater to sink. In time the soil dries out. You can prove this by putting a small quantity of rust dust into water. This is sufficient to prevent falling drops from generating electricity.

Another experiment was used to put galvanic elements into the ground. A copper plate was attached to one side of a container of water and a zinc plate to the other. This created an electric field, its radiation saturated the surrounding soil and the growth rate doubled.

BACK TO MESMER

It looks like we are back to Mesmer's experiment! If putting copper and zinc plates in water creates electricity that improves the growth rate of plants in that area, what would this do to men and women? It would be interesting to experiment in a bathtub. Leave the plates in some water for a day or two to create a build-up, then just add some hot water to fill the tub at the desired temperature. Perhaps some of the Associates would like to participate in this experiment and share their impressions with us?

A large technical company in Germany produces garden tools made from copper and byrillium, made after Schauberger's discovery. So far they are being used only in private homes and nurseries. Copper-byrillium tools are not as hard as steel; there is more deterioration; but this is helpful as it puts trace minerals back into the soil and creates bioelectricity without which there is little growth.

THE WATER TORNADO IN ACTION

A motor turns the conical rotor in the middle of the tower. The pipes are mounted with the larger opening on the rotor. The smaller end, with the jet in it, reaches almost to the wall on which a wavy steel ring is positioned. When the rotor with the pipes turns, the centrifugal force presses the water out through the jets against the wavy or rippled steel ring, which causes a recoil and relieves the motor. The centrifugal force in the winding pipes creates a suction on the bottom part and so make an almost perpetual movement. The Air Model works the same way, only upside down.

The Schauberger Biotechnic Ltd. in Switzerland manufactures an air purifier. A ventilator blows the polluted air into the egg-shaped housing. The Air rolls itself in and compressed at the bottom. Beneath the egg shape is a container with water, connected to the housing with a pipe. When the whirl is created, the water rises from the bottom through the pipe and mixes with the air,cleaning it. The clean air leaves through the top and the water flows back down depositing the dirt on the bottom.

FIRE IN THE WATER

"It is true that science has not yet solved the riddle of the water-jet, but Schauberger;should not tell such fairy tales as that rolling pebbles in water disperse sparks which make the Rhine river glow at night. That makes it hard to take such a man seriously." Such remarks were often made when someone discussed Schauberger's theories. Prof. Dr. Zimmerman heard it often and, when visiting Schauberger, talked about it.

Schauberger laughed, took two pebbles out of a drawer, filled a pail with common tap water and moved to a darker corner of the room. As he rolled the stones against one another in the water, Dr. Zimmerman could observe the flying sparks which had the same force as if it had been done in the air. Cold light: it was almost as in a fairy tale. "Once in Yugoslavia it failed," said Schauberger. "I had in mind to demonstrate this to a group of unbelievers, got the pebbles out of the river, but got no sparks. Then it dawned on me the stones had been on a long journey along the river bed and had lost their power. Take only pebbles from a mountain or the upper part of the river; better still, break the stones and use both halves."

Friction creates heat in the water as in the air. To create sparks, oxygen is needed and we find oxygen in water as well as in air. The legend about the glowing Rhine river may not be a fairy tale after all. When the strong river cur- rent pushed the rocks downstream, and the stones bumped against each other, then in the darkness of the night the dispersing of the sparks could be clearly seen (the water in those days was still clear and unspoiled;. Today, after grading the riverbed and its shores, the polluted water has lost its magic.

IS THE HOME POWER PLANT NEAR?

In different places in Austria and Germany, tests are being done with great enthusiasm on home power plant models. The greatest obstruction has been finding ways to construct the shape of the spiral pipes. This problem has now been solved with an accuracy and ease that were not possible in Schauberger's time. First, a wooden model was made. The profile of the outside will be the profile of the inside of the pipe. To achieve this, the wooden model has a two-piece form adjusted around it in some flexible material. After the material has hardened, the model will be taken out and wax poured in its place. The wax core will then have the shape of the wooden model and requires special handling.

First, it will be covered with a kind of epoxy or some-thing similar in which powdered copper has been mixed. The second coat is made of layers of fiberglass tapes to reinforce it since it will be the wall of the pipe. Another coat of epoxy or other strong material finishes the product. After all coats have hardened a little heat makes the wax flow out and the spiral pipe is completed. And what is the status of power plants in America?

ONE MILLION WATTS WITH A TORNADO MACHINE

Victor Schauberger's friends have not forgotten the bad experience he had in the U.S. Since his plans and models remained here, they keep a watchful eye across the Big Pond for any news about related inventions. Special attention was given to a newspaper report about an American engineer who suggested using wind energy by creating a man-made whirlwind in a silo- like tower. Ing James Yen, working for the Grumman Aerospace corporation, estimates that a turbine of only six feet in diameter could deliver two million watts. It would take a conventional turbine measuring 200 feet in diameter to produce the same results The silo-like tower is steady, has an open top and is open on one side. The wind enters the tower through the wing-like opening, starts a whirl and this, in turn, reduces the atmospheric pressure in the center. A vacuum is created, forcing air through the turbine. The sucked air makes it spin. Mr. Yen expects much from the comparably small turbine. Experiments in wind channels confirm his theory. He is confident that it would be possible to build whirl-wind generators with a capacity of 100 and even 1000 megawatts. Let us hope the atomic age is over soon!

NEUTRALIZING GRAVITY WITH LENTICULAR FLOW

"It was spawning time. I took my post, on a clear moonlight night, close to a waterfall hoping to catch a fish poacher. I could see every move of the fish in the crystal-clear water. Suddenly,the fish moved toward the sides. A very large trout had come up-stream. It swam along the fall as if in search of something, its motion like a winding dance, then finally disappeared beneath what looked like a sheet of glimmering metal under the moonlight. I noticed there was a whirlpool at the foot of the narrowing water-fall. The trout floated out of this vortex and up the waterfall as if drawn by an invisible force.

"Once at the crest, it was pushed out of the water and landed a few yards up-stream. I was so excited by what I had seen I forgot all about the poacher and went home to think about it. I saw this phenomenon many times after that, but no scientist could give mean explanation.

"Later in the same winter I shot an alpine goat across a deep ravine. It slipped and fell down into the ravine. I could hear it bouncing over the ice on the frozen river below. I was unhappy about this as I expected the horns to be broken. Slowly I made my way down the icy slope. To my pleasurable surprise the goat was intact and dry. After cleaning it out, I threw the guts into the water which was calm at that spot, as well as crystal-clear and six to eight feet deep. I watched them sink and noticed some movement between the stones on the bottom. Although some were size of a man's head, they moved to and fro as if they were electrically charged. Defying the laws of gravity they went from side to side as if alternatively attracted and repulsed by one another. I began to doubt my own eyes as a stone the size of a man's head spun then floated upward. It was egg-shaped.

"The next moment it was floating on the surface surrounded by a ring of open water and tossing gently. There followed another and another, until most of the egg-shaped stones were floating. Only the smooth, ovoid stones had this property, the angular ones remained motionless at the bottom. My first thought was that they must be electrically charged as this phenomenon reminded me of the light which appears under water when milky hued pebbles rub against each other.

"I didn't know at that time that a number of forces were at work to create a light effect as well as overcome the laws of gravity to bring these stones to the surface. I crossed the newly formed bridge and went home. Years later I learned that the Ankara river which originates in Lake Baikal in Central Russia is the site of a similar phenomenon, which makes it possible for the local farmers to cross the river in winter.

A LAKE RECREATES ITSELF

"Remarkable phenomena can be observed on the Lakes of Desolation in the Hartzau valley of Austria, after a long hot spell. I was sitting on the shore of such a lake on a hot day wondering whether to go for a swim when I noticed that the water started to move in a circle. Trees which had been imbedded in the sand after a landslide were pulled loose and carried away by the merry-go-round. As the speed of the circling water increased, the floating debris moved closer and faster toward the middle of the lake. Once they reached the center, the trunks tilted upward and were sucked in with great force so the shores were cleaned like a peeled banana — or like people whom a cyclone sets back down on earth almost naked. None of the trees resurfaced.

"Shortly afterward the lake calmed down. This, however, was only the calm before the storm. The bottom of the lake started rumbling and suddenly a spout as high as a house shot up out of its center with a thundering noise, spinning upon itself and overflowing from the top like a fountain. A short while later the spout collapsed sending waves to splash against the shore. I had witnessed the renewal of a lake devoid of fresh water tributaries.

Here ends Viktor Schauberger's personal report. His discoveries represent only a fraction of the many ways Mother Nature uses a spiral combined with an egg shape. The expression "the egg of Columbus" should be "the egg of Viktor Schauberger. After all, Columbus made the egg stand, but Schauberger made the egg outstanding!

UPSETTING MEDICAL ORTHODOXY

"The uterus, for instance, is egg-shaped. To many scientists it is now obvious that the uterus, because of its shape, is sucking the egg through the Fallopian tube and not, as believed by orthodoxy the Fallopian tube conveying it downward. Similarly, William Harvey's theory of 1618 that the heart is pumping the blood through the body no longer holds water. Some medical scientists recognized long ago that the blood is making the heart contract and not vice versa. This was corroborated as far back as 1892 by Dr. Karl Schmidt and 1927 by Dr. Martin Mendelson, by cardiologists Harlicek in 1937 and Genta in 1958, as well as Dr. W. Simonis in 1970. Everyone knowledgeable about the function of the heart realizes how little it can be compared with a pump.

Embryologie teaches that there is at first a primary fluid circulation within the tissue of the embryo and, much later, the heart starts to form. The tender cardiac valves have only a thickness of .15 mm Hg (about 4 inches of mercury); they are completely passive; there is no sign of an active pump. Suction, because of the eggshape, does most of the work, or better, implosion. It is a kind of ram pump and no more.

The Japanese, K. Nishi, points out that the red blood cells could never be pushed through the fine capillaries since some of them have a much smaller diameter than the red blood cells themselves. Amending the theory concerning the functioning of the heart would lead to better diagnosis and therapy.

A HEART-LIKE CONTAINER

Dr. Karl Roller had a problem mixing Drugs. He did not want to apply centrifugal force. Schauberger, whom he consulted, suggested that the liquid be shaken instead of the container.

"You have to build a heart-like container with a small, two-armed propeller on the bottom. Then you have the reversed movement." Replied Roller, "But then you'll have a centrifugal force again."

"Yes," said Schauberger, "but that will bring into play a suction in themiddle of the container." It shouldn't be necessary to have the propeller built into the bowl; one driven by an electric drill, like that used to stir paint should do. Dr. Roller remembered an experiment made by Dr. Rudolph Steiner on conserving plant juice without alcohol by using rhythm on rose petals and distilled water in a heart-shaped bowl, and having his wife swirl the contents to create a whirlpool,each morning and evening.

Dr. Roller remember an experiment an experiment made by Dr. Rudolph Steiner on conserving plant juice without alcohol by using rhythm. He made a bowl in a heart shape and put in some rose petals and distilled water. The water became red from the petals and scented. Each morning and evening his wife would swirl the contents of the bowl to create a whirlpool at the center. Seven? years later the liquid was still fresh; it looked like an old Greek wine, and that without any preservatives, although the scent was lost.

Now we can understand how a lake without fresh water ingress can rejuvenate itself by creating its own implosion. Ordinary tapwater will show improvement as well as distilled water. Laboratory examination does not show the energization of the water, but only a few changes.

UNTREATED TAP WATER

After Swirling 6-7 part water, put on a glass slide so that it can be projected and magnified on a screen. Let dry at 64-68° (18-20°C), then observe the crystallization. Spring and spiral-treated water look identical but tap water is cloudy. Fig. 1 shows a 20% copper chloride solution; beside chaos there isn't much to see. Fig. 2 is a 5% solution and not very promising either. But if we add, as in Fig. 3, only a few Drops of fruit juice to it, there is a change in the crystal formation. There is beauty. Fig. 4 contains distilled water and Fig. 5 shows the same distilled water treated in the egg-shaped bowl; substantiation has taken place. There is life in the water instead of chaos. You see an eccentrical point from which rays are emitted. You can get the same result by using a few Drops of healthy blood, as in Fig. 6% The District or Kiel in West Germany uses this method to determine the quality of milk. The test can show whether the animal was fed with organically grown fodder or not. This method may be the answer to the borderlander's attempt to show visible proof of the influence of generators, radionics, pyramids, cones,ELF wave devices, etc.

THE CONDENSING PRINCIPLE FOR LIFT

Even for the readers familiar with borderland research, the thought of a stone floating on water is hard to accept. We have been taught that what goes up must come down and that there is no escape from gravity. But is it so? Gravity can only be efficacious where the envelope around the object, air or water, is lighter or thinner than the matter itself. Any object will start to hover as you compress, that is, condense, it s envelope. This is where Archimedes' law comes in. If we put an egg in a glass of water it will sink to the bottom. Now add salt to the water and when the salt is dissolved, the egg rises and surfaces. Where is the gravity effect? The water surrounding the egg has become more dense. The envelope can be saturated in more than one way to achieve uplifting. For example, on a cold winter night the water in mountain streams is cold and that makes it dense.

When Dr. Jarl, M.D. studied at Oxford he had the friendship of a Tibetan student. Years later, during a journey to Egypt, he met his old friend again and was invited to spend some time in Tibet, which he did. One day his friend took him to a place near a cloister where construction was in progress. In a steep cliff, 250 meters above ground there was a cave.

Monks were busy building a wall on a small plateau in front of the cave. The spot could only be reached from the top of the cliff with the help of a rope. On the ground below lay a smooth, flat stone with a depression in its center, one meter across by 15 centimeters deep. A stone block about 1x1 1/2 meters was put in the bowl. At a distance of 63 meters from the bowl 19 musical instruments (ragdongs) were placed side by side in a 90° arc The radius of 63 meters had been carefully measured. The instruments consisted of 13 drums and 6 trumpets. Eight of the drums were 1 meter wide and 1.5 meters long. Four were medium-sized, 0.7x1m. The only small one was 0.2x0.3m. They were made from thick sheet metal, 3mm thick, weighed 150 Kg each and one end was open. Behind the instruments stood a row of monks, as shown in the drawing on the next page.

The priest who stood behind the small drum gave the signal to start the "concert". The instruments made a loud noise and the monks sang a mantra. For the first four minutes nothing happened. The tempo increased and suddenly the stone started to sway. Then the block shot upward with increasing speed toward the opening. Three minutes later it landed on the platform. Whenever a projected stone split, it was thrown back by the monks above. Within an hour it was possible to lift 5 or more tons.

CENSORSHIP FROM THE BRITISH MIRO

Dr. Jarl had heard about the Tibetan stone raising. Others, like Linauer, Spalding and Father Huc spoke about it. At first Jarl thought it was a sort of hypnotic trick; then he made movies of the anti-gravity phenomenon; but the British company Dr. Jarl worked for declared the movies their property and they were not to be disclosed until 1990 when, after 50 years, they shall be released. This could be the way the Great Pyramid at Cairo, Egypt was built.

In the book "The Egyptian Heritage", by Mark Lehner, based on the Readings of Edgar Cayce, published by the Cayce Foundation, we find this question, page 88, Q.14: "How was this particular pyramid at Gizeh (a suburb of Cairo) built?"

Answer: "By those forces in nature as make for iron to swim. Stone floats in the air in the same manner. This will be discovered in 1958."

(Could be! Flying Saucers landed at Edwards Air Force Base, California in 1954. In 1955 the U.S. Air Force engaged Martin Aircraft company to set up an Advanced

Design project at Baltimore to crack the secret of antigravity. In three years they could have done it. RHC)

Here is an experiment easier to duplicate! At the turn of the century an assistant at the University of Vienna made a discovery that could have changed physical theory, had it not been forgotten!

A pressure of 5 atmospheres (73 psi)forced tap water down a pipe. The jet at the bottom of the pipe had a diameter of about 0.2-0.3mm. The higher the pressure the better the result. About 30-40cm beneath the jet a metal container insulated on the outside with paraffin (overlap- ping the top edge) was placed; it is important to have the container isolated against ground. A wire led from the container to an electroscope.

When a paraffin plate was held in an angle a short distance from the thin water thread, the electrometer registered a charge of 10,000 volts! Connecting the wire to a neon tube would make it glow. A question arose: Why must the paraffin plate be at a certain angle? Later a Swedish research group extended this experiment by using a second jet at a distance of 60 cm from the first. The result was a double charge. This was accomplished by crossing isolated conductors from one water thread to the container of the other and vice versa. The loop through which the water thread goes must be horizontal and at a certain height, to be found by experimentation. Then came a big surprise: as soon as the static electricity field had reached a certain density, the water thread beneath the loop split and each single thread of water reversed its course and rose upward. Even with 73 psi pressure behind it, the water had lost its heaviness and danced around in the air.

DIFFUSION a la VIKTOR SCHAUBERGER

Viktor Schauberger, inventor of the implosion—generator had no doubt the Atlanteans knew the catalistic secret and therefore had silent airplanes.

He was fascinated by flying and even more by the gliding of birds high in the sky with no obvious physical effort. He also observed a similar phenomenon in mountain streams where trouts could stand motionless in a strong current, and, if disturbed, would shoot, like an arrow, not to one side, but strait ahead into the stream. Did he ever find an explanation?

There are other phenomena as well. Rivers in some places in Europe literally flow up hill. One such river is in the Tatra Mountains located in the Balkans. On a stretch of 15 Kilometers the river climbs 64 meters. Reports in the media about such striking occurrences are ignored by science, because no explanation can be given, and deeper investigation might result in a collapse of the well established "Law of Gravity".

In the opinion of Viktor Schauberger such phenomena as climbing rivers is related to the motions of birds and trouts and its explanation could revolutionize our science and if properly handled, could cut energy cost to almost nothing.

OCCULT SECRETS OF THE THIRD REICH

THE TRANSFORMING MEDIUM OF WATER

In his view, science made a big mistake by describing water as H2O. If water could be put into a formula, it should read: Water is an ideal medium for transformation into an accumulator or transformer, and only the way it is moved determines whether it will be magnetic or electric. Such currents are of organic origin and decompose water into its basic substance (Hydrogen—Carbon—Oxygen) H-C-O.

Under certain conditions, its carbon (C) unites with the oxygen (O) to form organic electricity. The freed hydrogen (H) shoots upward, spinning, attracting and absorbing the missing C & O from its environment and forms water again. If we break this tornado with a propeller or turbine, mounted within a pipe of proper dimension, the result will be that 4000 liters of air per second rushing with a speed of 200 kilometers per hour, will yield a force of 1000 horse-power, but only 4 horse-power are needed to break up 4000 liters of air. The remaining 996 hp. are free energy. This phenomenon is based on thermoelectric forces such as in cyclones or tornadoes which can be observed. Such implosion processes can be duplicated in small machines that give enormous power.

Similar reactions take place in the lungs of birds and in the gills of fish. The absorbed air or water touches organic catalysts which diffuse it; the split-off hydrogen acts like a magnet on the carbon and oxygen surrounding it, diffusing it in such a manner that in front of the opening of a machine, or the mouth of a bird or fish, the pressure sinks below 100 mm, leaving a vacuum which will push an airplane, bird or fish, forward.

The disaster in the thirties of the American airship,"Acron," and the German airship, "Hindenburg," have probably been caused by diffusion of their gases. The Acron was filled with helium and its diffusion causes rain, where as hydrogen turns into fire(Hindenburg). An analogue to the helium synthesis can be found in the natural process of rain.

At that time people did not pay much attention to this, since 50 years ago these analytic kinds of synthesis was almost unknown.

INTEGRATION OF THE LIFEBLOOD OF THE EARTH

Readers of the "Pendulum" who are also readers of "Country Living Books," "Trees," "Rural Economy," the "Soil Magazine" or "Organic Husbandry," may remember my writings on the discovery of an ancient system of Land Water Control, the introduction of which has invariably been followed by an amazing improvement in health and fertility (both animal and vegetable) in the areas concerned.

"What gave you the idea in the first place?", I am constantly asked, in conversation. I can only reply in the words of a famous scientist, "Ideas come out of space!"

The idea, upon which my work has been based, is as follows:"That it is possible to induce rainfall, as it touches the earth,to commence to move towards specially prepared focal points, where it will commence to spiral downwards, to replenish underground streams and centers of moving water, beneath the earth's surface;

instead of streaming off, on. or near, the surface of the land; filling the surface water channels far too rapidly and causing mud and floods to make their appearance."

ANCIENT KNOWLEDGE

This idea was quickly followed by the amazing discovery that the idea had evidently been in the minds of the ancient agriculturists, who first brought these islands (British Isles) to fertility, out of swamp and forest!

Not only here, in this Gloucestershire valley, but all over England, and in parts of Wales too, there are to be found the necessary earthworks and the chequer-board pattern of field and pasture,which are parts of the System; although, now, completely prevented from functioning by the application of modern ideas of Land drainage.

Modern drainage increases the rate of surface run-off, and pre- vents the far more rapid inward rotational movement. No puddles form where inward rotation of water is functioning; and in such areas there is no mud! Earth and water become permanently dissociated and air takes the place of stagnant water in the soil, wher- ever rainwater is allowed ot percolate the earth with a natural inward spiral move- ment. This action can be induced by man, and adapted in accordance with his needs.

The radiesthetist will be, it seems certain, most interested in that part of the discovery which is connected with the incidence of disease; and of the effects on disease which follow the introduction of this method of Land Water Control in any given area.

NEW LIFE IN THE VALLEY

In Farts of this valley, where I have not yet been permitted to set the System working, many dead and dying trees are to be seen. In areas where the ancient focal spots have been once more set to work, the diseased limbs, and the cankered bark of the trees, have all been shed, or smothered in new, healthy growth.

The corky excrescences which covered the twigs and branches of the elm trees, immediately began to shrivel up, and then to drop off, once the water of an area had started to move spirally inwards. Where, before, there were diseased growths, now there may be seen shining, healthy tissue, full of lenticels and growing at a rapid pace. The elm leaves may have been not much bigger than one's thumbnail, but now there will come, on the younger elm branches, large,tender, bright green leaves, which might be mistaken for nut leaves.

Willow trees—old and pollarded—may have been falling apart, riddled with the tiny holes of parasites. Now "new trees" will take their place. The splits are actu- ally mended by new tissue which grows rapidly up the edges of the split portions, reuniting them and enabling the tree to take on the appearance of a new one, as new bark covers the whole area in succeeding years.

In our valley, the waterside rushes, which, formerly, grew for awhile and then turned yellow and died away, now grow right up to flower and fruit!

As for the rushes in the boggy valley pastures—where are they?

The little acre known as "Poor Land" or the "Parish Field," which I rent from the Parish Council, was, when I took it over, in January 1939, a mass of rushes and water weeds. Some, then called it "Rushy Meadow." Now, there is not a rush to be seen! The rushes have been grazed to extinction by my farm animals, which, previously would eat but little of the sour herbage of this low lying pasture; which, nearly every winter, disappears for a while under many feet of Severn floods, which sweep across the three-mile-wide Valley; which is believed to have been, in previous days "less subject to waters." (vide the 16th century historian Leland).

THE HUMAN LINK

What place have human beings in this long-forgotten System, which I have rediscovered?

We have no "roots" like plants. We, and the animals, move from place to place. We, and they, may gain great benefit from eating produce which is obviously more healthy; from the new-textured, sweet-smelling, and richly colored soil which is now to be seen wherever the System is working.

Is there more than this? I think there is.

In this System, allowance is made for tidal movements in the waters of the earth -the rythmic "back-and-forth" of free water, which may be observed on the surface of the sea, but which, manifestly, cannot end at the sea shore. This movement must extend throughout the earth's surface, and outwards into space, also.

Much is written regarding the "stress" of modern times. I am convinced that much of this stress is connected with that unremitting onward "forward-traction" of the waters of the country-side—as though the "arteries" of the earth had been severed, while the "veins" had long since ceased to function!

COSMIC INTERCONNECTIONS

I look upon the Moon as having a similar function with regard to the Earth, as the Heart of man has with regard to his Body.

In this connection, it is interesting to note that the Ancient Chaldeans of Ur, (who, it seems probable, understood the principles which I have rediscovered) accounted the "Goddess of Fertility" to be none other than "Nin-Gal" the Goddess of the Moon!

There should be, I am convinced, (by practical experiment) a possibility for the earth's waters to draw back and forth, as well as on and on!

It also seems probable to me, that cosmic rays, coming out of space, need a healthy, and balanced environment in which to work naturally,—and therefore beneficiently in the service of mankind.

May it not be during sleep (when we are, as it were, "rooted to an area), that the influences which spell the difference between health and disease are at their strongest—for we, as we rebuild our defenses during rest, are then surely, most subject to external influences?

SECRETS OF THE SYSTEM

What are the secrets of this new (or very old) System? What are we to do,that we may start the System at once? Can we start in our own gardens? Yes, we can!

We cannot, however, get full results until the "Powers that Be" in Land drainage, see the light also.

"We are under Whitehall," I have been told by Land drainage engineers. "We are paid for our work and we must do as we are told. We can see that you have changed the texture of the soil. We know you are right, but—the Ministry of Agriculture says that all rivers and streams must flow straight to the sea; and dams of earth and stone are not permissible, according to modern drainage ideas!"

In our gardens, we may begin, however. That circular flower bed is the focal point. Make it, first, a "saucer,"—a depression—made firm with a few stones in the centre. Then, on the "saucer," place a mound of earth. In the surface of this mound you will set your plants and seeds. Mound it as high as possible by adding humus to lighten the soil. Mound your flower borders also. Never let them be flat. Air pressure will then drive the rainfall towards the "cores" of the flower beds and flower borders. Thence it will spiral downwards.

You will have started inward rotation. In time, no doubt, others will follow!

"For as the rain cometh down, and the snow from heaven, and returneth not thither, but watereth the earth, and maketh it bring forth and bud, that it may give seed to the sower and bread to the eater.

"So shall My Word be that goeth forth out of My Mouth; it shall not return unto Me void, but it shall accomplish that which I please, and it shall prosper in the thing whereto I sent it.

"For ye shall go out with joy, and be led forth with peace: the mountains and the hills shall break forth before you into a singing, and all the trees of the field shall clap their hands.

"Instead of the thorn shall come up the fir tree, and instead of the brier shall come up the myrtle tree: and it shall be to the Lord for a Name, for an everlasting sign, that shall not be cut off."

The ideas of the author have some resemblance to those of Dr. Schauberger but were evolved separately over a period of years. The principle enunciated should be capable of being followed with ease overseas where Ministerial interference with agriculture is less evident.

APPENDIX

Viktor Schauberger's Flying Saucer Research

What Happened to the Production drawings?

It only became known after the war, that aircraft resembling Schauberger's prototype had been further developed in several other production workshops. The most informative data about this is without doubt the report by Hermann Klaas, an engineer from Muhlheim in the Ruhr, who had collaborated on the plans and who at the time had published a detailed report, complete with photocopies of sketches and original documents, in the Wuppertal paper, Bergische Wochenpost (ceased publication): "I still have drawings of a model "flying disc" which I built in 1941; perfected by the Germans, in all truth this invention flew with almost unbelievable success. It had a diameter of 2.4 metres with a small, very fast running special electric motor (there were no petrol-engined models at that time), which had been "obtained" by courtesy of the Luftwaffe. It climbed straight up into the air so suddenly that unfortunately it hit the workshop ceiling and crashed to the ground in pieces.

The model which actually flew can be seen in the accompanying pictures and also those versions begun firstly in Bohemia and later in Breslau (where the Miethe group worked), which embodied a stronger ramjet-pipe (like the VI rockets). The three models approximate the Ballenzo-Schriever-Habermohl prototype, even as far as the incorporation of the jet nozzles. The jets must be able to swivel in order to achieve the "colloidal effect", which enables the "flying disc" to climb vertically (Miethe built better models later on). On the first model, and also on the other models, the outer rim, made of high-grade metal alloys, was solid (without vents).

When this disc had gained height or had attained the desired altitude so that the thrust from the rear exhaust nozzles began to take effect, the disc transferred from vertical to horizontal flight Naturally this control system was not simple. It was only on later designs that the "slotted rim" was incorporated, so that the jets could be swiveled in all directions. These flying discs are today being built not only in the West, but also in the U.S.S.R.

There was, of course, a whole range of further designs, though unfortunately no entirely completed prototypes. In the beginning neither Miethe nor Habermohl could get hold of a simple jet pipe. It could only be "supplied" via the agency of a Luftwaffe sergeant"

THE "FLYING SAUCERS" OF THE THIRD REICH

Years later, on the 27 th July 1956, the Munich periodical Das Neue Zeitalter published an article headed "Hitler built Flying Saucers" ... "The Austrian forester Viktor Schauberger was the inventor and discoverer of this new motive power—implosion, which, with the use of only air and water, generated light, heat and motion. In the implosion-motor a diamagnetism was developed which made the lifting power possible By means of a suction screw-impeller, which revolved from the outside towards the inside along a cycloid spiral space-curve, the same force is generated which creates waterspouts, typhoons, cyclones or hurricanes through the effect of suction. Qn the 19th February 1945 near Prague, the first test of an unmanned "flying disc" took place. In three minutes it climbed to a height of 15,000 metres and attained a horizontal speed of 2,200 km/h; it could hover motionless in the air and could fly as fast backwards as forwards. This "flying disc" had a diameter of 50 metres."

On the 14th of August 1956, volume 31, the Munchener Illustrierte printed an article in which engineer Rene Couzinet's wooden model was displayed, whose external appearance was similar to Schauberger's design. Apparently, however, Couzinet was still far from achieving a working model, for Schauberger commented on the article in a letter dated 11/8/56 as follows: "One look (at the model) told me that the man is still miles away from the achievement of diamagnetic levitation power, for Couzinet has probably employed the effect of direct suction, whereas Nature uses indirect, i.e. reactionary suction force ... what various papers have published is also incorrect, namely that I might have copied typhoons, cyclones, etc, which occur in warm zones."

It should be noted in passing, that judicial circles in West Germany and abroad have posed the question as to whether Hitler was able to flee to safety in such an aircraft at the end of the war. In any case, it is a proposal put forward in Mattern's book, UFO—The Ultimate Secret Weapon of the Third Reich.

A book by Rudolf Lusar entitled German Weapons and Secret Weapons of the 2nd World War and their Further Development, now in its fourth edition, was published in 1962 by J.F. Lehmann in Munich. In it the author dedicated awhole chapter to the "flying saucers" of the Third Reich, wherein it was stated: "The development, which had cost millions, was almost complete by the end of the war. No doubt the existing models were destroyed, although the plant in Breslau, where Miethe worked, fell into the hands of the Russians, who removed all the material and technical personnel to Siberia,where further work on these " flying saucers" has been carried on with much success. Schriever just managed to get out of Prague in time, Habermohl, on the other hand, must be in the Soviet Union. The former German designer Miethe is in the USA and, as far as can be determined, is designing "flying saucers" for A. V. Roe & Co. The machines, which have been observed to date, have diameters in the order of 16, 42, 45 and 75 metres and they are supposed to develop a speed of up to 7,000 km/h. Already in 1952 "flying saucers" had been indisputably recognized over Korea and according to press reports, were also observed and reported during NATO maneuvers in Alsace in the spring of 1954."

The magazine Hobby took up the theme again in its 26th issue and quipped with the headline "When saucers learned to fly," whereas a company newspaper made reference to "Secret Service Cases". In addition, we have been presented with many other publications on this theme, some of which are highly interesting, in which there is no lack of amazing references to design drawings and models supposed to have fallen into Allied hands at the end of the war.

It would indeed require a hard-working and conscientious chronicler to sift through such a profusion of data. But, as the old saying goes, "There is no smoke without fire'. Through the information supplied us by Walter Schauberger, which has provided us with much documentary evidence, much of the above will be made clear. We would, however, like to keep a certain distance from comments which reflect only isolated opinions. Everyone can draw his own conclusions from such views as have here been quoted.

In connection with many such reflections, a letter written by Viktor Schauberger to a friend on the 2nd August 1958 is very informative. The following are extracts: "The 'flying saucer' which was flight-tested on the 19th February 1945 near Prague and which attained a height of 15,000 metres in 3 minutes and a horizontal speed of

2,200 km/h, was constructed according to a model I built at Mauthausen concentration camp in collaboration with the first-class engineers and stress-analysts assigned to me from the prisoners there. It was only after the end of the war that I came to hear, through one of the workers under my direction, a Czech, that further intensive development was in progress: however, there was no answer to my enquiry. From what I understand, just before the end of the war, the machine is supposed to have been destroyed on Keitel's orders. That's the last I heard of it. In this affair, several armament specialists were also involved who appeared at the works near Prague, shortly before my return to Vienna, and asked that I demonstrate the fundamental basis of it: The creation of an atomic low-pressure zone, which (develops in seconds when either air or water is caused to move radially and axially under conditions of a falling temperature gradient."

THE USA INTERVENES

Particularly instructive is another letter by Schauberger to the same friend dated 23rd January 1958. "An American aircraft consortium offered me $3,500,000 to divulge the secret of the UFO. to three of their experts. A similar offer was made by Canadian interests. Both groups wanted to come here to see everything ... I answered ... until the signing of an internationally valid provisional agreement, nothing would be demonstrated. (These gentlemen, however) wanted to see first and sign later, which I categorically rejected. From the Germans it was suggested that I should secretly act as consultant on two major government projects for which I was to receive a commensurate fee. I declined, because I did not want the secrets to be drawn out of me and then, as always happened before, to receive a kick in the pants... I am no businessman, but a simple observer of Nature who has absolutely no contractual experience... Whenever I was overly trustful, always had to pay for it miserably... The professors believe they are able to correct wise Nature and they do everything back to front (in relation to what Nature actually does)... And now we're all in a fine mess. I will have nothing whatsoever to do with such bankrupts."

Despite these misgivings, discussions with Bonn did, in the end, take place. Essential to these discussions, inter alia, was the conditions that investigations into the hydraulic processes resulting from Schauberger's research and development, including the evaluation of earlier experiments, were to be verified on a strictly scientific basis by expert opinion from the Stuttgart Institute of Technology (Technische Hochschule Stuttgarts).

This report by experts was published verbatim in the quarterly magazine Komische Evolution, which regularly publishes the results of the latest scientific research in the sphere of Schauberger's theories and findings.

While discussions with Bonn were still under way, two representatives from the "Washington Iron Works" suddenly appeared at Schauberger's home: Messrs Karl Gerchsheimer from Texas and Norman Dodd from New York. During the American Occupation, Gerchsheimer was the US plenipotentiary for Wurzburg. He spoke fluent German with a Bavarian accent "We are here on behalf of a large American corporation whose spokesman is Robert Donner from Colorado. It is desired that Schauberger's ideas and findings be translated into fact as soon as possible in the USA. Money is available in unlimited quantity."

650 MILLION DOLLARS FOR "PROJECT IMPLOSION"

Later on it became known that the 650 million dollars was supposed to have been the first installment of the committed capital, notably at a time when the value of the dollar on the international market was twice that of today. Viktor's son, Walter Schauberger, also became involved in "Project Implosion". He was supposed to contribute his knowledge and scientific co- operation to the common cause of the scheme and to be prepared for a longish sojourn in the USA accompanied by his family. From the Americans' point of view, this requirement seemed justified, for even before the beginning of the 2nd World War, Walter Schauberger had played an important role in a series of his father's fields of research. At the beginning of the War, Walter was severely wounded and having had his leg amputated, was discharged from the field hospital

Both were opposed to an extended stay in the USA, however. In principle, they were prepared to assist for a limited period only. To clear up these and various other questions, the two Americans then returned to the USA. When they reappeared in Austria again, things really began to get moving. Very much now in evidence were the words "Top Secret", whose outward expression, inter alia, manifested itself in the constant care of both Schaubergers, which they, however, nevertheless experienced as a rigorous surveillance. Even clothing coupons were issued. Entry visas for the USA, for which one could often wait months in those days, were arranged within minutes and with a validity for an immediate period of four years. Thus father and son received a foretaste of the powerful arm of Uncle Sam whenever the question of dollars was involved. This first taste, however, was not to remain with them for long.

Gerchsheimer arranged for all the various records, calculations, drawings, even technical literature, together with all models, designs and pertinent apparata, which had been collected from a variety of places, to be quickly packed into five giant, watertight containers, which were immediately dispatched overseas. These days were distinguished by hectic bustle and activity and cast their shadows over the approaching difficulties in the New World.

A few days later, Viktor and Walter Schauberger were already in New York, where the US Chamber of Commerce had prepared a splendid reception followed by a banquet attended by high-ranking military personnel.

The Situation Becomes More and More Acute

The workshops themselves were located in Texas. It later came to light that the nearest human habitation was about ten kilometres away. All mail was scrutinized by Gerchsheimer personally, and the isolation was thus complete. Eric A Boerner, formerly an engineer with the Junkers Company in Germany, but whom in the USA had been raised to the position of director of the"Cosmotron" accelerator project in Brookhaven, took pan in one of the first conferences. Gerchsheimer had brought him in as an expert on questions regarding energy. At this conference Viktor Schauberger unexpectedly renewed his acquaintance with one of his former coworkers, a certain Renner from Salzburg. According to an entry in the documents related to this affair, which are in our possession, "Rennets transfer to the USA was very close to being a kidnap."

"Project Implosion can be started," Boerner declared. "Schauberger's basic considerations and ideas tally with recently ascertained facts, which,largely through the mathematical-physical endeavors and new interpretations of his son, Walter Schauberger, have been significantly extended. . . As energy is problem No. 1 for the USA, its solution requires a total commitment and that both Schaubergers remain in the USA for eight years. . . " Questions and objections were rigorously curtailed.

At a second conference, Viktor Schauberger flatly refused to stay on inthe USA even one day longer than the agreed period of three months. "Otherwise I refuse to talk" he declared categorically. A third and last conference took place at which Gerchsheimer announced that it had been decided to authorize Viktor Schauberger's return journey. At the same time he handed him a contract comprising several pages in English with the request that it be signed immediately, although he well knew that Schauberger was unable to read English. "We must leave for the airport in ten minutes", urged Gerchsheimer and glanced nervously at his watch. An extremely lively argument ensued which became considerably more heated when Walter Schauberger was informed that he would in no way be permitted to return to Europe with his father. On the contrary, it was desired that he be placed under contract Once again the tempting phrase: Money is no object.

WILD WEST METHODS DOMINATE

The Americans seemed to have entirely failed to grasp that it was precisely their Texan behavior that so disgusted their Austrian guests. With wild threats and honeyed promises, Gerchsheimer tried to induce Walter at least to remain. When he finally realized that all his efforts were to no avail, he was quite taken aback. Meanwhile Viktor Schauberger had reached the end of his nervous tether and had signed the contract after its essential features had been orally translated for him. At that point he would have signed anything required of him, for he was motivated by one single idea: To get away from the present company and to return to Austria.

This contract, of which we have a photocopy, is a typical example of unscrupulous American insatiability. In it Viktor Schauberger not only made over to those clever Yankees all rights to his patents, but also all his ideas, thoughts and discoveries, past as well as future. Moreover, he was not even allowed to talk about them with others. This contract degraded him to an empty shell, for his brain, his intellect, aye his whole being and all his thoughts had become the "property" of that US organization.

Apparently the enforcement of Schauberger's signature was a typical American show, for afterwards the room was suddenly filled with smiling faces. No one paid any attention to the time and all at once there was any amount of it. They only wanted to celebrate to the full the "conclusion of the agreement".

OCCULT SECRETS OF THE THIRD REICH

Towards midnight on the 20th September 1958, both Schaubergers finally arrived back in Linz. Then began the last 100 hours of Viktor Schauberger's life. However, no one had the slightest presentiment of it. His sudden death on the 25 th September 1958 precipitated a riot of rumor that Schauberger had already been in poor health for some time before the tribulations of a long journey for this 74 year old man. No doubt the final blow was his deep disillusionment over the humiliating outcome of his American trip and above all, that fateful contract with which he had totally delivered himself up to the Americans. "I don't even own myself any longer," he said utterly dejectedly to friends a few hours before he returned to his home.

WHAT DID THE AMERICANS REALLY WANT?

In the meantime, 20 years have elapsed. From the Americans nothing further has been heard, and just as little is know of "Project Implosion", which in those days is supposed to have been launched with such great elan. All the various design drawings, plans, calculations and models were left behind in the USA. The question arises; What did the Americans really want to achieve? In the final analysis, was it indeed only the "Flying Disc" project in which, long before the trip to America, the widest variety of groups on the other side of the Atlantic had already shown such surprising interest? Because Schauberger, in the face of demands for the facts, had displayed the greatest restraint, a reticence in no way diminished by offers of millions of dollars, the possibility cannot be ruled out that, by way of Schauberger's main interest-implosion, it was hoped to reach the real goal (flying discs).

IMPLOSION and LIVING WATER both carry references to the use of implosion technology for anti-gravity propulsion and we are shown pictures of Schauberger's model saucers. Again accepted this wholeheartedly. I still agree with the principle, but still would like to see some operational equipment before I pass judgement. The serious research of T. Townsend Brown presents hard evidence that the field around a capacitor inan electric oscillating circuit is electrogravitic in nature. Eric P. Dollard, Borderland's resident "Wireless Engineer," has shown through his researches with Tesla Technology that the capacitive field (which he terms the dielectric field) is implosive in nature and produces the same illumination effects as Reich's Orgone. So here we see a relationship between the implosive effects of water and the possibilities of anti-gravity; and the implosive effects of the dielectric field and the possibility of anti-gravity. Reich manipulated the Orgone streams around the earth to produce changes in the weather. Nikola Tesla was experimenting with weather engineering via his large Magnifying Transmitter at Colorado Spring. This manipulation was effected, not by ELF transmissions as is popular to believe (with no proof), but by the propagation of the dielectric field, which is the organic side of electricity and has been here shown to be in direct relationship with Orgone.

Herein reside the keys to a beneficial technology and the solution to the mechanics of anti-gravity. These matters have not really been suppressed — the teeming masses of humanity on this planet are not responsible enough, or spiritually aware enough to deal with the ramifications of universal energy and true freedom. Concerning this concept, Nikola Tesla had this to say, "I am unwilling to accord to some small-minded and jealous individuals the satisfaction of having thwarted my efforts. These men are to me nothing more than microbes of a nasty disease. My project was retarded by laws of nature. The world was not prepared for it. It was too far ahead of time. But the same laws will prevail in the end and make it a triumphal success."

This brings us to the stories of the suppression of Viktor Schauberger's technology. and the demise of his home power unit. These freshly translated articles show that the power unit never worked—in fact it exploded rather than imploded. The author of the German articles, Leobrand, can be non other than Leopold Brandstatter, author of IMPLOSION STATT EXPLOSION. As an astute student should, Leobrand carries on beyond the work of the teacher and shows the problems with Schauberger's view on flow design and such.

I now believe more firmly than ever in Schauberger's work. It can be put into the proper perspective — the balance of implosive and explosive forces, working in harmony and balance. This is the true path of natural energy — the Cosmic Pulse of Life. With this new perspective in English it is hoped that the small flame kindled here will help fan the fires of enlightened research and perhaps humanity can move in the direction of preservation of our fragile ecosphere.

VIKTOR SCHAUBERGER AND THE SECRETS OF NATURAL ENERGY

"When a man dies the bell tolls. When the forest dies and with it a whole people perishes, not a finger is lifted. It is known that for the death of a people the death of a forest has proceeded it."

A hundred years ago, a man called Viktor Schauberger was born into his role as a guardian of the earth. Among the magnificent Austrian forest he grew up wanting only to become a forest warden "like my father, grandfather, great-grandfather and his father before him." But life was to take him far from the peace and solitude of great mountains. Instead he was to lead the struggle to preserve the earth, the forests and rivers, attacking the exploitation of Nature as early as the 1920's.

He gave the world a vision of how technology could be transformed to give free, unpolluting energy. He warned of the consequences facing humankind if the present death—oriented technology continues. He died, betrayed by the same powers who promised to make his Dreams a reality, commercial gangsters who took all and gave nothing back to the world.

Olof Alexandersson's biography of Schauberger helps give back to us a hero, someone the authorities prefer forgotten like Reich, Tesla and others who looked to Nature to help solve the world's problems. This is the first book in English to describe Schauberger's prophetic work. But back to the story...

As a child Viktor was at home in the forest. One of his ancestors from an ancient Bavarian aristocracy moved to Austria and started a branch of the family devoted to the husbandry of the forests and their wildlife. Their motto was "Fidus in Silvis Silentibus"—Faithful to the Quiet Forests—their crest showed a tree trunk garlanded with wild roses.

OCCULT SECRETS OF THE THIRD REICH

From an early age Viktor was an astute observer of nature. He learned directly from nature, closely studying-the relationship between the earth, the trees and water. But water "the life blood of the earth" became his consuming passion and he set out to discover its laws and characteristics—the secrets of its power.

Far from being an inorganic substance, Schauberger perceived water to be alive, and with its own cycle of birth and transformation into higher forms of energy. He spent hours studying the flow of natural waterways, how water currents become stronger in the early hours of the morning when it is coolest, and particularly during full moon.

He remembered the stories of his ancestors who utilized their knowledge of water to transport logs down from the high forested mountains. They built constructions down the mountainsides which forced the water to flow in serpent-like spirals.

"I knew that my father transported hundreds of thousands of cubic metres of beechwood over long distances, never, however, during the day, but at at nights and generally when the moon shone. The reason for doing it this way, as my father often explained, was because water exposed to the sun's rays is tired and lazy and therefore curls up and sleeps. At night, however, and especially in moon light, the water becomes fresh and lively and is able to support the logs of beech and silver fir which are in fact heavier than water."

By the end of World War 1, Schauberger was given responsibility for a large wilderness area of almost untouched forest, employed by an Austrian prince. But the prince had problems. He needed money;he needed a way to transport his timber down from the remote forest. Schauberger built water flumes based on his own observations and the knowledge of his ancestors. A water snake undulating through a dam gave Schauberger the final key to success with his flumes. By imitating its movements, a combination of vertical and horizontal curves, the water chutes carried heavy logs effortlessly. Experts came from all over Europe to study the construction, and Schauberger was offered a position with the government. He travelled all over Austria for several years supervising other constructions which were equally successful — but here Schauberger first encountered the professional jealousy and interference that was to mark his life.

He had observed how the streams reacted when the trees were cut down. No longer protected from the sun, the waterways became blocked and the springs that fed them dried up. He began to warn the authorities of the dangerous changes that occur when man disrupts the natural harmony of the forests.

But the large timber companies that sprang up everywhere, with encouragement from the state, had only one goal; to transform trees into money as quickly as possible. Schauberger's log flumes had allowed the commercial exploitation of virgin forests which had been inaccessible to the foresters and he had to witness the brutal damage done to natural forests destroyed by short-sighted greed. Angry and disillusioned, he resigned from the government and continued exploring the mysteries of water under private employment.

OCCULT SECRETS OF THE THIRD REICH

IMPLOSION OR EXPLOSION

"There exist two forms of motion within Nature—one that breaks down, the other that builds up and refines; both always work in cooperation with one another. The form of motion which creates, develops, purifies and grows is the hyperbolic spiral... the spiraling of nebulae in space, in the movement of our planetary system, in the natural flow of water, blood and sap.

"The destructive and dissolving form of movement is centrifugal, in Nature."

The whole of modern technology is based on the idea of breaking down through heat, combustion, explosion. It exemplifies man's single-minded pursuit of destruction and decomposition. To Schauberger, the splitting of the atom and the development of nuclear energy is an offense against Nature. "One can make use of atomic power through the biotechnology of implosion."

He developed his Trout Turbine, named after his observations of trout moving upstream. Later renamed the Implosion Machine, it could generate power without fuel. "The implosion motor is centripetally operated. It produces its own driving source through the diamagnetic use of water and air. It does not require any other fuel such as coal, oil, uranium or energy derived from atom splitting, since it can produce its own energy (atomic power) by biological means in unlimited amounts—almost without cost."

VIKTOR SCHAUBERGER'S BIOLOGICAL SUBMARINE

The biological submarine once had the attention of the German War Lords, but Viktor Schauberger made it look as though it were not very useful, as in his opinion, biotechnology is for supporting progress and not for destruction. This submarine idea was taken from the observation of fish, especially of trout, which can stand motionless in a flowing stream, just by taking water in and out This process has two functions, first it creates a vacuum in front of the mouth into which the fish gets sucked, and at the same time provides food, as the water contains all that the fish needs. While the food goes into the digestive system, the water is forced through the fan-like structure of the gills, which not only absorb the oxygen needed, but also push the water backwards. This specially compressed water does not mingle right away with the rest, it glides along the conical body like a wedge and shoves it forward. In addition, on the scales it forms little whirls which enhance the push further.

However, Viktor Schauberger was not the sole observer of this phenomenon. Before him others not only formed the same idea but even constructed prototypes with some results. One inventor, A. Borner, came to the conclusion that the speedy motion of a fish is relative to the size of its gills. He constructed a boat with a precise opening in its bow, where a turbine sucked in water like a fish, and pushed it out through slit-like exit ports in such a way that it glided along the hull like a sheet, not only separating it from the friction of the outside water, but also giving it an additional push forward. Further, he applied such skin depressions like sharks have on his ship's hull, presuming that they cause small swirls, and so increased the forward motion. Borner even incorporated the slippery skin layer that fishes have by apply-

91

ing oil to the hull to reduce friction. He hoped all this would bring a 60-80% reduction in fuel. Indeed, experiments with his boat FORELLE, meaning trout', achieved twice the speed, while still using the same amount of fuel.

Apparently, Borner did not know the spiral vortex, which is an invention of Viktor Schauberger. If properly applied, it will not only increase speed, but also reduce fuel consumption to a minimum!

Water Schauberger, Viktor's son, shows such a submarine. His biotechnical submarine has a movable bow, which gives the boat the flexibility fish have. The conical and rifled water-intake permits a variable step-up, creating a strong torque on the water, which, after entering the implosion turbine, will be intensified to such a pitch, that now its recoil (resonance) is driving it instead of the motor, as biotechnical applications always have a pull and push action. Such a turbine consist of tapered-down pipes with inside rifling which are bent into spirals. Such FREE ENERGY is not a question of time, rather the will to use it, as it already exists, giving us a chance to move on water, under it and in the air using only a fraction of the energy we use today!

VIKTOR SCHAUBERGER; THE REPULSINE,
UFO'S AND FLYING SAUCERS OF NAZI GERMANY

It was nearly the end of WWII. At that same time, scientist Viktor Schauberger worked on a secret project. Johannes Kepler, whose ideas Schauberger followed, had knowledge of the secret teachings of Pythagoras that had been adopted and kept secret. It was the knowledge of Implosion (in this case the utilization of the potential of the inner worlds in the outer world). Hitler knew—as did the Thule and Vril people—that the divine principle was always constructive. A technology however that is based on explosion and therefore is destructive runs against the divine principle. Thus they wanted to create a technology based on Implosion. Schauberger's theory of oscillation (principle of the overtone sequence, monochord) takes up the knowledge of Implosion. To put it simply: Implosion instead of Explosion! Following the energy paths of the monochord and the implosion technology one reaches the realm of antimatter and thus the cancellation of gravity.

Whatever might have been thought of Viktor Schauberger in Austria, word of his abilities and the statements contained in his new book, "Our Senseless Toil—the Source of the World Crisis", evidently reached others ears, including those of Adolf Hitler. At a time when the relations between Austria and Germany were at an all-time low, Viktor Schauberger was summoned to an audience with the Reich Chancellor Hitler, in Berlin. Special papers were arranged and all the documentation carried out within one day. Suddenly Viktor Schauberger left for Berlin and a meeting with Hitler, who greeted him warmly as a fellow countryman, telling him that he had studied all the reports about his work thoroughly and was very impressed with what he had learned.

Thirty minutes had been allocated for the discussions, which Prof. Max Planck had been requested to attend as scientific adviser shortly before he was rudely deposed from his position as Privy Counselor. This exchange of views eventually lasted 11 hours, during which Schauberger explained the destructive action of contemporary technology and its inevitable consequences. He contrasted this with all the processes of natural motion and temperature, of the vital relation between trees, water and soil productivity, indeed all the things he considered had to be thoroughly understood and practiced in order to create a sustainable and viable society.

When Viktor had finished his explanations, Max Planck, who had remained silent, was asked his opinion about Viktor's natural theories. His response was the remarkable and revealing statement that "Science has nothing to do with Nature". Pausing for a moment to take in this astonishing admission, Viktor then referred to the proposed four-year plan, the so-called Goering Plan, stating that, "not only was the time frame far too short, but, if instituted, it would gradually undermine and ultimately destroy Germany's biological foundations. As a result, the Third Reich would last only ten instead of the boasted 1,000 years. " (Viktor was not far out in his estimate!)

During the earlier part of the discussion, Hitler had been enthusiastic, but he became greatly perturbed at what he had just heard and ordered his technical and economic advisers, Keppler and Wiluhn, to discuss with Schauberger what could be done. Once outside the door, these two men demanded to know how Viktor had got in there in the first place. Angered at their truculently condescending air, he replied " Through the same door I've just come out of! " Seeing that his ideas had no hope of acceptance, and leaving them gaping, he returned to his hotel and left for Austria the following morning. Keppler and Wiluhn, however, were to get their revenge later, after the Anschluss on March 13th, 1938.

Once again he was the victim of deceit and his ideas were usurped, for, in a later letter to his son Walter, he wrote that copies of the preliminary application had been fraudulently obtained by Prof. Ernst Heinkel, the famous aircraft designer, through a firm of patent attorneys, Lehmann-Harlens in Berlin. By mining the information contained in this document, Heinkel obtained insights into how a jet-engine could be produced, even though he misinterpreted its findings; his first prototype exploded due to his lack of proper understanding. With a certain absence of principle, he then sought Viktor's collaboration in the project. Although some initial discussion eventually took place, Viktor did not cooperate, having become aware of what Heinkel had done, and further contact between the two men ceased. Using his ill-gotten gains, however, Heinkel persevered with his research, which culminated in the construction of the first successful jet-plane, its first flight being on August 27th, 1939.

Although Heinkel never had the honesty to reveal the source of the ideas for his invention, keeping all the kudos for himself, this jet plane was nevertheless built as a direct result of Viktor's theories. Viktor Schauberger is therefore the real father of the present jet age. He even went as far as to state that in order to develop and build fast-flying, supersonic aircraft successfully, the bodily forms of deep-sea fish should be copied. Today's 'stealth bombers' very much emulate these forms. In 1939 Viktor's personal research virtually came to an end, all the materials he needed being appropriated for war production. In 1941, however, he was summoned by Air Marshal Ernst Udet to discuss the growing crisis of energy production and means of solving it. Premises were subsequently set up near Augsburg for research and development, all of which came to nothing partly due to the death of Udet and partly because it was bombed by the Allies in 1942.

In 1943, despite his incapacitating war wounds and 58 years of age, Viktor was declared fit for active duty and was inducted into the Waffen-SS, very much under duress. He came under the control of Heinrich Himmler, who forced him into research to develop a new secret weapon. Provided with suitable accommodation at Schloss Schonbrunn, the nearby Mauthausen Concentration Camp to supply the workforce of prisoner engineers, Viktor was threatened with his life if he did not comply with orders and carry out this research. In spite of these threats, however, Viktor put his foot down and demanded from the SS Command the absolute right to select the various engineers he needed. He further demanded that any technicians he chose were to be removed entirely from the camp, fed properly, dressed in normal civilian clothes and billeted in civilian accommodation, otherwise they would be unproductive. As he explained, people who live in fear of their lives and under great emotional stress could work neither consistently nor creatively. Surprisingly the SS agreed and so Viktor selected somewhere between twenty and thirty engineers, craftsmen and tradesman from Mauthausen, to be accommodated in various houses near the plant.

When they were all assembled, Viktor exhorted them to work as hard as they could, but under no circumstances were they to attempt to escape, otherwise his own life would be forfeit. They set to work with a will, and, while not understanding what Viktor was trying to achieve, they nevertheless carried out his instructions faithfully. Two machines were eventually built, one called a 'Repulsator' and the other a 'Repulsine', reflecting their forces of recoil. Accurate information about them is difficult to obtain, because after the end of the War all top-secret information was confiscated by the Allies—the Russians, French, English and Americans—and is therefore no longer available to the general public. Let's run this by again, with particular emphasis on the Repulsine, both the A & B models.

Viktor Schauberger, an Austrian forester who observed the effects of nature—especially of water, privately met Adolf Hitler in 1934 to discuss the fundamental principals of agriculture, forestry, and water engineering. While Hitler was impressed by Schauberger's radical ideas for utilizing water power in new and dynamic ways, he was also displeased that Schauberger was not willing to participate in work for the Third Reich. Subsequently and unfortunately for Schauberger this meant that once Austria was annexed in 1938 and war broke out in 1939 the SS would come searching for him and his ideas based on his patents for an "air turbine" and "procedure for lifting liquids and gases" from 1935 and the "warm-cold" machine built for Siemens in 1937 but destroyed in an unauthorized test.

OCCULT SECRETS OF THE THIRD REICH

In 1940, Schauberger began construction of the Repulsin(e) discoid motor in Vienna with help of the Kertl company. He patented his idea on March 4, 1940 in Austria under patent 146,141. But very soon afterwards he was reported by the Viennese Association of Engineers to the SS who placed Schauberger in a mental hospital in Mauer-Ohling. Schauberger was then forced to work with Messerschmitt on liquid vortex cooling systems and Heinkel concerning applications of water towards aircraft engines. At this point Heinkel received reports on the early Repulsin A. At Mauthausen, under orders from Heinrich Himmler himself, Schauberger was to carry out research and development for the Third Reich war effort. He was given approximately 20-30 prisoner engineers to proceed with his research into what was termed "higher atomic energies". For this Schauberger was given special dispensations from the SS for both himself and fellow engineers.

The construction and perfection of the Repulsin A model discoid motor continued until one of the early test models was ready for a laboratory test that ended in disaster. The model was 2.4 meters in diameter with a small high-speed electric motor. Upon initial start-up the Repulsin A was set in motion violently and rose vertically, quickly hitting the ceiling of the laboratory, shattering to pieces. The SS were not pleased and even threatened Schauberger's life, suspecting deliberate sabotage. Replacement models were built, but by 1943 a more improved design, the Repulsin B model was constructed with the SS objective of developing this motor for an odd SS bio-submarine which Schauberger named the "Forelle" (Trout) due to its configuration of a fish with a gaping mouth!

The Repulsin models operated in the following way: When the main electric engine is started, the Coanda effect begins to create a differential aerodynamic pressure between the outer and inner surface of the primary hull . At a higher speed, the vortex chamber becomes a type of high electrostatic generator due to the air particles, in high speed motion, acting as an electrical charge transporter. The Repulsin A will begin to glow due to strong ionization effect of the air. Now we have all the ingredients for a continuous and strong Aether flow along the main axis from the top to the bottom of the craft. The radial air pressure required for lifting 1 kg with the Coanda Effect is roughly 1.4 kg/cm2.

In the Repulsin B the vortex turbine has been improved for increasing the "Implosion Effect" and thus the lifting force . In the Repulsin B the upper membrane is fixed and the lower rotates at high speed. On the edge rim there are special shaped blades of boomerang configuration. There are 120 blades that are 3 degrees spaced around the rim. The enhanced vortex turbine increases significantly the "implosion" effect in the vortex chamber. This contributes to it being able to generate a stronger thrust than the centrifugal turbine used in the Repulsin A. By means of suction screw-impeller (which revolved from the outside towards the inside along a cycloid, spiral space curve) the same type of force is generated which creates twisters, cyclones, and typhoons through the effect of either suction or implosion. Work on the Repulsin B continued in 1944 at the Technical College of Engineering at Rosenhugel in Vienna.

OCCULT SECRETS OF THE THIRD REICH

Schauberger was finally released back to Leonstein, Austria that same year. It appears that the SS had discarded the idea of applying the Schauberger motor to a submarine when the benefits would greatly improve their work on the secret Flugkreisel which was taken from Rudolf Schriever back in 1941. By 1943 the machine had flown but proved to be unstable. The leader of the SS replacement team was Dr. Richard Miethe who proposed several Flugkreisel replacements with varied power plants, most of which relied on jets or rocket power, until it was learned that Schauberger had engineered a type of turbine machine that would create an up-current of axially-spinning air so powerful that the up-current's drag force would speed the whole machine higher and higher into the air with a thrust equal to 10,000 hp simply by moving "air" . The turbine was considered a priority for flight development into a manned machine by the SS. It is speculated that Miethe's final design built in Breslau that flew in 1944 was an enlarged manned Repulsin-type craft.

Schauberger meanwhile had his remaining discoid motors confiscated by the Russians and Americans at the end of the war. While AVRO Canada approached Schauberger for disc development along with a team led by Dr. Richard Miethe, Schauberger refused and instead devoted his remaining life to peaceful uses of his vortex technology by working on various civilian projects which included generators, and both water and air purification systems. In the late 1950s Schauberger visited the US and was again pressured into working on military disc designs. The pressure was even greater due to the fact that Schauberger's original Repulsin motors had fallen into Russian hands and the US suspected Schauberger's technology would appear as a nuclear armed aircraft over US soil. Schauberger refused to participate again but had his designs forcibly signed over to a powerful US consortium. He returned to Austria and died there 5 months later having been robbed of everything. A tragic end of life for the man everyone named the "Water Wizard". Compliments: Rob Arndt.

So, just what the happened to these flying machines after the war???

That is indeed a tough question to answer. It cannot be excluded that a small number of these craft/disks might have been built. The several photographs of UFOs that emerged after 1945 with the typical features of these German constructions suggest as much. Some say that some of them had been sunk into the Austrian Mondsee, others maintain that they were flown to South America or brought there in parts. It is certain though that if the crafts didn't get to South America, the plans that did allowed for new ones to be built and flown there, for an important part had been used in 1983 in the "Phoenix Project", the follow-on project of the 1943 "Philadelphia Experiment". This was a teleportation, materialization and time travel experiment of the U.S. Navy that was more successful than you could imagine in your wildest Dreams. There is enough material for another book, but it does not fit too well into our subject here. It all makes sense.

As far back as 1938, a German expedition to the Antarctic was made with the aircraft carrier Schwabenland (Swabia). 600,000 km2 of an ice-free area with lakes and mountains were declared German territory, the "Neuschwabenland" (New Swabia). Whole fleets of submarines of the 21 and 23 series were later headed towards Neuschwabenland. Today about one hundred German submarines are still unaccounted for, some equipped with the Walter snorkel, a device that allowed them to stay submerged for several weeks, and it can be assumed that they fled to Neuschwabenland with the dismantled flying disks or at least the construction plans. Again it must be assumed that since the test flights had been very successful some so-called flying saucers have flown directly there at the end of the war.

There is the question raised as to why in 1947, Admiral E. Byrd led an invasion of the Antarctic, why he had 4,000 soldiers, a man-of-war, a fully equipped aircraft carrier and a functioning supply system at his command if it was a mere expedition? He had been given eight months for the exercise, but they had to stop after eight weeks and high losses of planes, the causes of which are undisclosed even today. What had happened? Later Admiral Byrd spoke to the press: "It is the bitter reality that in the case of a new war, one had to expect attacks by planes that could fly from Pole to Pole ." Further he added that there was an advanced civilization down there that used their excellent technologies together with the SS.

Is this report true? Who really can answer that question?!

Norbert-Jurgen Ratthofer writes about the whereabouts of the Haunebu developments in his book "Zeitmaschinen" . Time Machines: "The Haunebu I, II and III space gyros and the VRIL I space flying disk had disappeared after May 1945... It is very interesting to note in this context that after its nineteenth test flight, the German Haunebu III is said to have taken off on April 21, 1945, from Neuschwabenland, a vast, officially German territory in the Eastern Antarctic, for an expedition to Mars, about which there is nothing further known. One year later, in 1946, the many sightings that suddenly occurred in Scandinavia of shining objects of unknown and definitely artificial origin caused a great stir among the Allies in East and West. Again one year later, in 1947, and well into the Fifties, a rising number of shining unknown flying objects, doubtlessly steered by intelligent beings, mostly round, disk- or bell-shaped, sometimes cigar-shaped, so-called UFOs appeared over North America. Today, we simply refer to flying saucers as UFO's. It is also true today that making mention of seeing an actual UFO is almost an act of ridicule, and throws serious doubt as to the person's credibility.

Good photographic material proves that the flying saucers had been sighted often since 1945. In a significantly high percentage of the cases where personal contacts with the people from the so-called UFOs was made, were with especially beautiful Aryan types, blond and blue-eyed and that they either spoke fluent German or another language with a German accent (reference: the Adamski case of 1952, the Cedric Allingham case of 1954 and the Howard Menger case of 1956). It is further said that color photographs taken by a night guard in West Germany in the Seventies exist of a landed and restarted flying disk that had both a knight's cross and a swastika on its hull.

OCCULT SECRETS OF THE THIRD REICH

The flying machines are well documented in photographs and films. There is the 60 minutes documentary "UFO—Secrets of the Third Reich". The American, Vladimir Terziski gave a three-hour speech at the September 1991 UFO conference in Phoenix, Arizona, where he showed slides of German saucers, construction plans and subterranean German bases. Also of interest are the book by the Italian air force commander Renato Vesco and the book by Rudolf Lusar "Die deutschen Waffen und Geheimwaffen des Zweiten Weltkrieges und ihre Weiterentwicklung" (The German Arms and Secret Weapons of the Second World War and Their Development), J. F. Lehmanns Verlag, Munich 1971. Also, we have the preceding articles from Author Rob Arndt. Makes ya wonder, doesn't it?

For the reader: "Ultima Thule" apparently was the capital city of the first continent peopled by Aryans. The Scandinavians have a tale of "Ultima Thule", the wonderful land in the high North, where the sun never sets and the ancestors of the Aryan race dwell. Hyperborea was up in the North Sea and sank during an ice age. According to alleged Thule texts they were technically very advanced and flew "Vril-ya", flying machines that today we call UFOs. These flying disks were capable of levitation, extreme speeds and the maneuvers known from today's UFOs due to two counter-rotating magnetic fields and they used the so-called Vril power as energy potential or fuel (Vril = ether, Od, Prana, Chi, Ki, cosmic force, Orgon..., but also from the academic "vri-IL" = as the highest deity = god-like), i.e. they take the energy from the Earth's magnetic field (free energy) so the story goes...or does it?!

Why have only few people heard of these things, or of the developments of Nikola Tesla, and Viktor Schauberger among which were free energy machines, energy transfer without cables, antigravitation and the changing of the weather by the aimed use of "standing waves"? What consequences would the knowledge about free energy forms and about the use of flying saucers, which only use a magnetic field for an energy source, have? Especially if every citizen would have access to it, for their cars for example? No more "Fill'er up!" No pollutants, no pollution of the environment. No nuclear power stations any more, people could no longer be kept locked within the boundaries of a country, and we all would have more free time because we wouldn't have to work to pay for heating, petrol and electricity (in this time one could think a lot, perhaps, about the true meaning of life). And these energy forms exist! The have been existing for at least ninety years and have been kept secret all this time. Why were they kept secret?

I leave it to the reader to ascertain the truth, if any, from this document. I find the information on Viktor Schauberger during the WWII era simply fascinating. Of course, a picture is worth a thousand words, and boy oh boy, do those pictures resemble Schauberger's Repulsine! The rest, take it for what it's worth: interesting reading, although no documented scientific facts can be ascertained. Original??? You bet!

Some of this information leaves one wondering what the heck is really flying around out there...are the UFO's that we have reports of seeing, even to this day, the remnants of this super-secret technology?! If so, then why are they only seen on rare occasions? One would think that if any country had this amazing technology at their disposal, that it would be implemented for the benefit of mankind. Even from just the standpoint of big-business and/or greed, the entity holding this technology would revolutionize transportation as we know it.

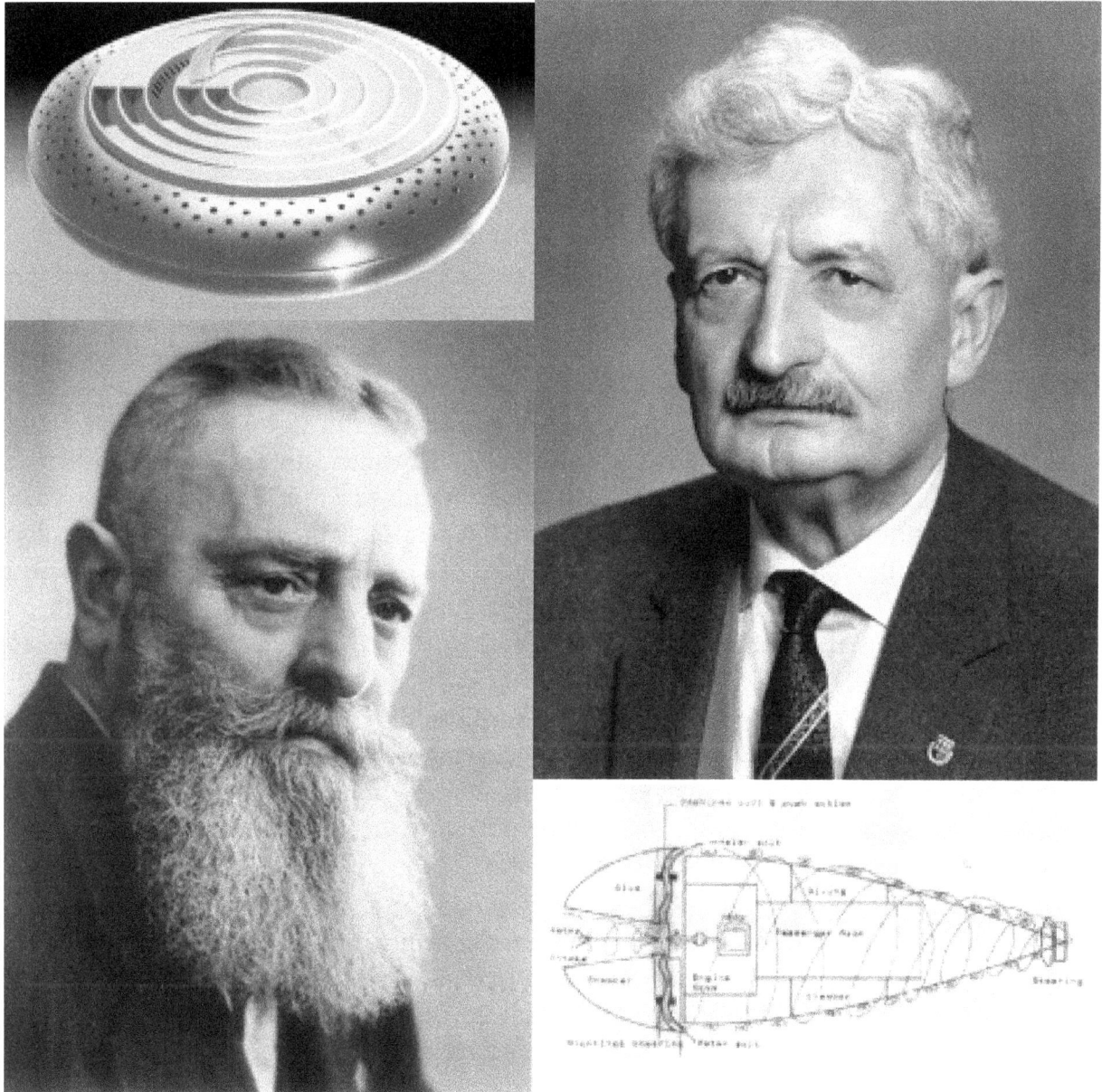

Schauberger's Repulsin disc. Professor Hermann Oberth in 1955, Dr. Viktor Schauberger, Schauberger's "Biological Submarine."

OCCULT SECRETS OF THE THIRD REICH

VIKTOR SCHAUBERGER COMES TO AMERICA
By Peter Moon

We here consider the fate of Dr. Schauberger, the scientist who carried the Vril Project with his "positive energy" technology and decried the Nazis as a false movement. In 1958, Viktor Schauberger and his son, Walter, were brought over to the United States under the strangest of circumstances.

Schauberger came to the United States because the Reich was in ruins and only America offered him any hope of fulfilling his Dreams. His personal motive was to integrate his implosion techniques and the Pythagorean model of the monochord into a holistic technology that would balance the planet. This was the same utopian ideal he had futilely shared with Hitler a quarter of a century earlier. Now, he hoped the conquering Americans, who had replaced the evil Nazis, would make good on history. Unfortunately, the Americans involved in this drama had an agenda all to themselves.

Viktor and Walter Schauberger should have noticed that something sinister was at work when they discovered that their visas were both stamped for a four year stay in America. Viktor had previously insisted on staying abroad for only three months, and his son was willing to stay for one year in total. This incident proved itself to be a premonition of much future frustration.

The primary operatives involved in bringing the Schaubergers to America were Karl Gerchsheimer and Robert Donner. Gerchsheimer was a natural scientist who understood the concept of implosion while Donner was financially connected and was the authority behind the maneuver. Upon the Schaubergers' arrival in America, the first objective was for Viktor to debrief his advanced knowledge to Gerchsheimer. This proved to be extremely frustrating to Gerchsheimer because Schauberger's training and terminology were entirely foreign to the textbook science that he was familiar with.

Gerchsheimer complained to Donner that he was getting nowhere. Donner was intent on getting the core knowledge of the man reputed to be Germany's most brilliant scientist. Upon hearing of Gerchsheimer's frustration, Donner flew immediately to the National Atomic Research Laboratory to verify the scientific validity of Schauberger's work. Some of you may recognize the National Atomic Research Laboratory. It is today known as Brookhaven Labs, the think tank where the Montauk Project was cooked up. After three days of discussions at Brookhaven, a written agreement was drawn up at the behest of Donner which arranged for a native German, Eric A. Boerner, to act as a go-between with Schauberger.

Boerner was a very curious creature and certainly a duplicitous one. He headed a design team at Brookhaven that worked on the Cosmotron Project. The Cosmotron was basically a particle accelerator. Technically, it was a proton (ionized hydrogen atom) accelerator or Synchrotron which made use of a large toroidal electromagnet to generate high electric and magnetic fields.

As a result of Donner's agreement, Schauberger was instructed to write down everything he knew about implosion, in the German language, without regard to whether it corresponded to textbook science. These reports were addressed to Mr. Eric A. Boerner, National Atomic Research Laboratory, Brookhaven, Upton, New York State. It was specifically stated in the reports that they were written at the behest of Mr. Robert Donner, or his representative, Mr. Karl Gercheimer, as per the agreement drawn up on the 15th, 16th and 17th of August 1958 at Brookhaven. Gersheimer then forwarded these reports on a daily basis to Boerner, who would translate them and disseminate the information to the Brookhaven scientists.

Boerner was not a physicist but an engineer, and through his association with the Cosmotron Project, the Schaubergers were conveniently led to misconstrue his true title. They thought he was the head of the Cosmostron Project when he was really just a German with sympathies to the Fatherland. Boerner did not have top secret clearance as a physicist but merely headed an engineering design team. The Schaubergers had been tricked. They thought they were providing information to the United States Government and the military. They knew implosion could create a bomb much more powerful than the hydrogen bomb. They would have been shocked to know the truth and consequences of their actions.

After the initial difficulties had been overcome in interpreting Schauberger's work, cartons and crates were sent for from Europe. The information therein would lay out the complete work of Schauberger and enable him to realize the fulfillment of technology in accordance with Mother Nature. Part of these papers were said to include an interpretation of the equation $E=mc^2$ that clarifies the way in which natural energies accumulate.*

It is obvious that Donner and his cronies at Brookhaven were striving after something much more grand than has ever been accomplished in the name of regular science. They were seeking to harness the morphogenetic grid itself and steer it to their own design. In the meantime, the Schaubergers were still being sold a bill of goods. They were told that this work was for the enhancement of all humanity and that the project would require a four-year period in which to be fully developed. The deceit was becoming more apparent but was still not being fully contemplated by the culturally displaced and overwhelmed Viktor Schauberger.

The Schaubergers eventually became uncooperative. Viktor went into the hospital for poor health while Walter blatantly forgot a key meeting on a trip to Colorado. There, he was to have met with executives of the Eastern Oil Company and the Trunk Line Company. The Schaubergers decided unto themselves that they were going home.

Donner was neither distressed nor intimidated. He ordered his lawyer to draw up a contract and told the Schaubergers they should sign the paper. He said it was all that was needed in order for them to leave the country. The Schaubergers were insufficiently skilled in English to understand the full meaning of the contract. After much argument, irritation and mistranslation, Viktor Schauberger relented. He was desperate to return to his country and was willing to do whatever it took. Without fully realizing what he was doing, he signed away all his patents, inventions and ideas. Additionally, he was committed to total silence.

It should not surprise anyone that Viktor Schauberger died only a few days after returning to his native home in Linz.

Schauberger's work was incorporated by the Brookhaven scientists and evolved into what we know today as HAARP, the High-frequency Active Auroral Research Program, which seeks to control the Earth's grid. It affects the weather as well as the minds of all living creatures. Fortunately, it is not a perfect system and has plenty of holes in it.

Although the history of the Schaubergers is involved and complex, it is just one tiny strand in a gigantic web of intrigue.

Excerpted from Peter Moon's book "The Black Sun" and used by permission
Peter Moon's books available at: www.SkyBooksUSA.com

ABOUT PETER MOON

Peter Moon was born in San Fernando, California, and grew up in both Southern and Northern California. Interested exclusively in athletics in his early years, he became interested in creative writing, science fiction and science during his high school years. His exploration of these fields, during the 1960s, led to an interest in Eastern Religion and Western Occultism which culminated in a unique career and association that focused on the private concerns of L. Ron Hubbard. Hubbard was a renowned science fiction writer who was an accomplished occultist but is also known as the controversial founder of Dianetics and Scientology, a movement which explored the brutal effects of mind control that have been inflicted on the human race and sought methods to free the human spirit from the confines of the human body.

Peter went out on his own in 1983 and moved to Long Island where his background in dealing with mind control phenomena and spiritual liberation enabled him to forge an association with scientist Preston Nichols, one of the world's foremost experts on electromagnetic phenomena. Nichols had been involved in strange experiments at the Montauk Air Force Station on Long Island which included the manipulation of time. Their collaboration in "The Montauk Project: Experiments in Time" and its sequels have now reached legendary proportions. Peter has continued his own investigation into the occult forces behind the Montauk Project and has also collaborated with Dr. David Anderson of the former Time Travel Research Center which has now been reincorporated as the Anderson Institute.

After Peter and Preston's books had been translated into the Romanian language, Dr. Anderson invited Peter to Romania, where he has pursued remarkable mysteries beneath the Romanian Sphinx in the Bucegi Mountains which have been published in "Transylvania Sunrise" by Radu Cinamar with Peter Moon. This book concerns the discovery of the most amazing archeological artifact in the history of Mankind, a chamber that contains a holographic record of the Earth's history as well as holographic readouts of human DNA and also of other species. This mysterious chamber also contains tunnels leading to secret locations beneath the Earth as well as other unimaginable technology. These pursuits are currently being followed in "Transylvania Moonrise" and additional sequels to this spectacular storyline. Peter currently lives on Long Island, New York.

SUGGESTED READING BY PETER MOON
THE MONTAUK SERIES, INCLUDING:
PYRAMIDS OF MONTAUK
THE MONTAUK PROJECT—EXPERIMENTS IN TIME
THE MUSIC OF TIME
THE HEALERS HANDBOOK
MYSTERY OF EGYPT

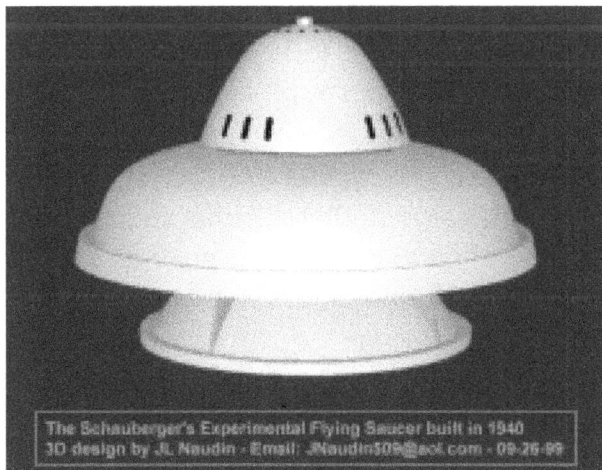

Models of Schauberger's Repulsin discs.

OCCULT SECRETS OF THE THIRD REICH

HOW THE VRIL GESELLSCHAFT
MAY HAVE DEFEATED THE THIRD REICH
By Tim R. Swartz

Long before Hitler and his brown-shirt thugs seized power in Germany, counter-culture, supernatural and mystical beliefs abounded in late 19th and early 20th century Austria and Germany. Rudolf Steiner's theories of anthroposophy and bio-dynamic blood, along with Helena Blavatsky's Great White Brotherhood of hidden Mahatmas in Tibet resonated with those who felt that world-rule was their ultimate destiny.

Occult practices were not a fringe spiritual activity to Nazism, they played a crucial role in the building of Hitler's Nazi Germany. The German Workers' Party, which became the Nazi Party in February 1920, was founded on January 5, 1919. The German Workers' Party was the creation of the Thule Society, an extreme-right, Aryan-theosophical organization that had been founded in 1918.

The Thule Society was named after "Ultima Thule," a fabled land that supposedly existed far beyond the Arctic Circle. The legend of Ultima Thule could be found in Greek and Roman mythology and the "German study group" believed the lost land was the original home of the "Aryan race."

Senior members of the Thule Society believed the master race were still living, hidden away in underground caverns and cities, located at various secret locations all across the planet. This subterranean society, called the Vril-ya, was said to have incredible technology, far beyond the reach of humans, including a universal energy source known as "Vril."

The idea of Vril came from a 19th century book called "The Coming Race," written by Edward Bulwer-Lytton. The book was very popular and the idea of Vril became well-known and filtered into everyday language as a word to refer to any revitalizing liquid. In fact, the brand name of the popular UK meat extract Bovril is a blend of "bovine" (cow) and "Vril" – as its makers wanted to suggest it was a powerful elixir.

The Vril Gesellschaft (Vril Society) was led by the Thule Gesellschaft medium Maria Orsitsch (Orsic) of Zagreb. Orsic was a young German nationalist who claimed to receive communications from an extraterrestrial race who had once lived in what is now Sumeria. These beings eventually departed Earth for planets circling the orange giant star Alpha Tauri, (Aldebaran) located about 65 light years from the Sun in the zodiac constellation of Taurus.

In 1919 Orsic had channeled information in a secret Templar script – a language unknown to her – with the technical data for the construction of a highly advanced spacecraft. According to author Jan van Helsing in his book "Secret Societies and Their Power in the 20th Century," the construction plans and the technical details that the Vril mediums received were so accurate that they led to the most fantastic idea men ever begot: the construction of a "Jenseitsflugmachine," a "flying machine for the other side" and the "Vril-Odin."

As well as receiving instructions on constructing space ships, the Vril mediums also were told that in order for Germany to gain its rightful place of world dominance, the Nazis' had to locate various objects of religious significance that had been hidden across the planet. The reasoning was that these objects channeled energies that originated beyond the known universe, and that whoever possessed these objects would also possess the powers of creation.

This began one of the strangest sagas of history, a period that researchers still dispute concerning its meaning and significance. During this time, the Nazis set up teams of well-financed researchers, archaeological and religious experts, hunting for supernatural treasures, religious relics and entrances to mystical underground cities.

THE AHNENERBE

The head of these secret Nazi expeditions was the Ahnenerbe ("Inheritance of the Forefathers"). This was a research group established by order of SS head Heinrich Himmler in 1935 (though it probably existed as early as 1928). It was expanded during the Second World War on direct orders from Adolf Hitler.

The Ahnenerbe had fifty different research branches named "Institutes," which carried out more than one hundred extensive research projects. Some of the institutes, particularly those responsible for Tibetan research and archaeological expeditions, were quite large. The public function of the Ahnenerbe was the publication of materials as part of the effort to investigate and "revive" Germanic traditions. Before the war, the Ahnenerbe set up its

own publishing house and went on to produce a monthly magazine (Germanien), two journals on genealogy (Zeitschrift für Namenforschung and Das Sippenzeichen), and countless monographs.

In private, the Ahnenerbe was part of Himmler's greater plan for the creation of a "Germanic" culture that would replace Christianity; a kind of SS-religion that would form the basis of the new world order after the end of the war. The directive for this new world order came from the channeled communications of the Vril mediums.

Heinrich Himmler, chief of the SS and architect of the death camps, was specifically named to be the one to herald the New Nazi Regime by gathering the "sacred objects of power" to present to Hitler. When these ancient artifacts were finally together in Berlin, the ancient Germanic gods, along with powerful alien overseers, would emerge once again into physical reality to bring planet Earth under their ultimate control.

THE OCCULT REICH

Modern scholars have dismissed the Third Reich's interest in occultism as pointless, wasteful, and even leading to their ultimate defeat. It has been pointed out that when he came to power, Hitler had a dowser scour the Reich Chancellery for cancerous "death rays." As well, before flying to Scotland Rudolf Hess had his horoscope drawn up by a personal astrologer, who obviously failed to see what the planets had in store for him after he was captured by the Allied forces.

None of this is really new information. The British realized the Nazis' weakness for the occult and parachuted faked copies of the astrological magazine "Zenit" into Germany which contained pessimistic horoscopes for the Nazis. However, Hitler was committed to the Vril mediums as they had proved to him the reality of their psychic abilities. Once firmly in charge, Hitler "turned against" astrology, tarot reading and all commercial uses of the supernatural. This was because he had been warned by Maria Orsic that others outside of the Vril Society could use paranormal methods to manipulate the public in ways outside of their control.

For Himmler and his followers, the declarations from the Vril mediums fit into their belief system perfectly. At the heart of the Nazi creed was the conviction that the Aryan race, from which true Germans were said to be descended, was superior to all others. Whether the Aryans came from Earth, or some other world, mattered little to Himmler. He saw this as the perfect way to gain and consolidate power, not only for the Nazi Regime, but also ultimately for himself.

Himmler saw that the concepts that true Germans were a "perfect race and that everyone else on the planet were of "impure blood" was a rallying cry to bring Germans together against a common enemy; Germany against the world. The real reason for the shadowy projects spanning the globe was to locate specific occult/religious objects; if proof of the reality of superhuman Aryans was also obtained during these expeditions, all the better.

These Vril Society directed expeditions were mostly left up to Himmler while Hitler ran the country. However, Hitler was obviously no stranger to the inner, occult,

1. Ghent Centerpiece: It was rumored that Jan van Eyck's "Adoration of the Mystic Lamb," held clues to the hidden location of the Holy Grail.

2. Holy Grail: Heinrich Himmler grew increasingly disillusioned with the Vril Gesellschaft when he was unable to locate the Holy Grail.

3. Holy Lance: The Vril mediums convinced Hitler that the Spear of Destiny was one of a number of sacred objects needed in order to rule the world.

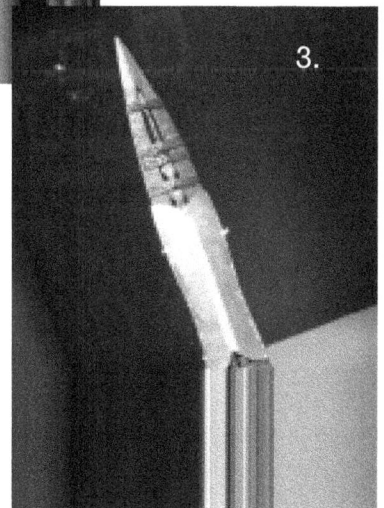

workings of his regime. Found within one of Hitler's prodigious libraries was the book "Magic: History, Theory and Practice" (1923), by Ernst Schertel. Hitler's copy has been thoroughly read, and its margins scored repeatedly. There is one particularly thick pencil line beside the passage: "He who does not carry demonic seeds within him will never give birth to a new world."

THE SEARCH FOR SACRED ARTIFACTS

What is known about the Ahnenerbe expeditions came about due to the discovery in 1945 of thousands of files hidden in a cave near Waischenfeld in Bavaria. Some of these documents show some details for Ahnenerbe's search for the needed sacred objects. One item in particular should be familiar to students of the esoteric, The Holy Grail.

The Grail figured prominently in European folklore as a powerful occult symbol, with the Order of the Knights Templar believed to have discovered either the "Grail" or the "Ark of the Covenant," or both, during their sojourn in Palestine at the site of Solomon's Temple.

Several studies have been made of the Templar cathedrals – Chartres in particular—to prove that the Templars left a coded message in stone revealing that they brought a sacred object of great value back with them from the East, an object whose tremendous, otherworldly power enabled them to finance, design, and build a series of magnificent churches all over France in an amazingly short period of time.

Selected scientists with the Ahnenerbe were certain that they had broken some of the secret codes left by the Templars concerning the hiding place of The Grail. On the night of April 10, 1934, two panels—the Just Judges and St. John the Baptist, from Jan van Eyck's famous painting, Adoration of the Mystic Lamb, were stolen from Saint Bavo Cathedral, in Ghent, Belgium. Often referred to as "The Ghent Altarpiece," it is a complex series of 24 scenes, with two doors and a central piece which is showing saints and apostles adoring the Mystic Lamb, or the symbol of Jesus Christ. From the panels to the left and to the right, pious hermits and pilgrims, Just Judges and Knights of Christ are approaching the ceremony in the middle. The upper register shows Christ as a King, between the Virgin Mary and John the Baptist, Adam and Eve. Inside, there are angels singing and making music.

Rumor had it that Himmler was convinced that the painting contained a coded map to the Holy Grail, among other of the desired sacred relics. The theory suggests that The Mystic Lamb should be read as a code with some of the panels incorporating documents or a map that led to the Holy Grail. The mystery remains as The Just Judges panel has never been recovered.

Another little known search for the Grail occurred in 1940 when Himmler visited the famous Montserrat Abbey near Barcelona, Spain. Andreu Ripol Noble, a monk who could speak German, was ordered by his superiors to greet Himmler during the visit. In an interview conducted years later, Noble related how Himmler came to Montserrat inspired by Richard Wagner's opera Parsifal, which mentions the Holy Grail could be in kept in"the marvelous castle of Montsalvat in the Pyrenees." Wagner is thought to have been inspired by the writings of the 13th troubadour Wolfram von Eschenbach and scores of other writers who claimed to know where the sacred chalice lay.

Himmler was also inspired by a folk song from Catalonia, the north-eastern region in which Montserrat lies, which has a cryptic reference to a "mystical font of life" that is situated in the area. According to Noble though, Himmler failed to find any trace of the Grail and left empty-handed.

Another scared artifact that Hitler did manage to get a hold of was the Spear of Destiny. According to the Gospel of John (19:31-37) as Jesus hung on the Cross a Roman centurion pierced his side with a spear. Christian tradition later named that soldier as Gaius Cassius Longinus. Over the centuries an object claimed to be this Holy Lance has passed through the hands of some of Europe's most influential leaders including Constantine, Justinian, Charlemagne, Otto the Great, the Habsburg Emperors. A legend has arisen that, "whosoever possesses this Holy Lance and understands the powers it serves, holds in his hand the destiny of the world for good or evil."

Eusebius of Caesarea, who became a spiritual advisor to Constantine, described the Holy Lance as it was at the height of Constantine's power in the Fourth Century: "It was a long spear, overlaid with gold. On the top was fixed a wreath of gold and precious stones, and within this the symbol of the Savior's name, two letters indicating the name of Christ by means of its initial characters – those letters the emperor was in the habit of wearing on his helmet at a later period. From the spear was also suspended a cloth, a royal piece, covered with a profuse embroidery of most brilliant precious stones and which, being also richly interlaced with gold, presented an indescribable degree of beauty to the beholder. The emperor constantly made use of this sign of salvation as a safeguard against every adverse and hostile power, and commanded that it should be carried at the head of all his armies."

In 1938, when Hitler arrived in Vienna to oversee the annexation of Austria, he also observed the transfer of the Hapsburg Crown Jewel collection, which included the Holy Lance, from Vienna to Nuremberg. The lance was kept in the hall of St. Katherine's Church, where it had once rested for nearly 400 years. However, during the war when Allied bombers damaged a portion of St. Katherine's, the many treasures looted by the Nazis and stored there were taken to another hiding place. In the confusion, the Holy Lance was inadvertently left behind.

The Holy Lance fell into the hands of U.S. soldiers on April 30, 1945. Later, the United States officially returned the Holy Lance to Austria, along with the other treasures that the Nazis had stolen. Today, the Spear of Destiny is kept in the Hapsburg Treasure House Museum in Vienna.

Trevor Ravenscroft was the first to reveal Hitler's obsession with the Holy Lance in his 1972 book "The Spear of Destiny, the Occult Power Behind the Spear Which Pierced the Side of Christ." Many historical scholars have dismissed Ravenscroft's book as being historically inaccurate. However, Dr. Howard A. Buechner, M.D., professor of medicine at Tulane and later L.S.U., told a strange tale in his two books "Hitler's Ashes—Seeds Of A New Reich" and "Adolf Hitler and the Secrets of the Holy Lance."

In his books, Dr. Bueschner writes that he was contacted by a former German U-boat submariner who claimed to have helped take the Spear of Destiny to Antarctica in 1945. Dr. Buechner was a retired Colonel with the U.S. Army who had served as a battalion surgeon in World War II. In the mid-1980s a "Capt. Wilhelm Bernhart" showed Buechner what was allegedly the log of the "Hartmann Expedition," including a hand-written letter of authenticity signed by "Hartmann," and photos of some of the objects recovered.

The former Nazi sailor claimed the Holy Lance, currently on display in the Hapsburg Treasure House, is a fake that had been deliberately left behind to be found later by U.S. troops. Dr. Bueschner says that in the final hours of the war, Hitler, disillusioned that the predictions of his success through the help of occult artifacts had failed, had them, including the Spear of Destiny, sent to a secret Antarctica base via submarine. Perhaps it was these sacred artifacts that Admiral Byrd's Operation Highjump was in search of.

DANCE WITH THE DEVIL

The failure of the Ahnenerbe and Himmler to obtain all of the sacred objects of power cast a spell of defeat against Hitler and his Third Reich. One is left to speculate whether or not the instructions giving by Maria Orsic were actually meant to be a subterfuge with no actual hope for success.

During the war, Orsic, along with other high-ranking members of the Vril Society, remained conveniently out of sight, obviously realizing that Hitler and the SS had the tendency to quickly turn on those they once trusted when things didn't go exactly as planned.

In March of 1945, an internal document of the Vril Gesellschaft was sent to all its members; a letter written by Orsic simply stated: "niemand bleibt hier" (no one is staying here). This was the last announcement from Vril, and since then no one has heard from Orsic or the rest of the Vril mediums.

It has been speculated that the Vril mediums took the now completed Vril 7 "Jäger" spaceship to Aldebaran to escape Hitler's fury. Perhaps they knew early on that the fate of Hitler and Germany was already set in place. In order to save themselves from almost certain death, they chose to give Hitler and Himmler just enough information to gain their trust, and then send them out on missions that would distract them long enough in order for the Vril Society to finish building their spaceship and escape.

The Third Reich provided the Vril Society with almost unlimited funds as well as scientists and engineers to build their spaceships in accordance to their channeled instructions; something they never could have accomplished by themselves. It would seem that Maria Orsic and the other members of the Vril Gesellschaft played the perfect shell game against the German Socialists. By providing clever lies that reinforced the Nazis' ideas that they were the Master Race, the Vril Society got what they needed, and perhaps prevented the Nazis from ultimately inflicting an even greater horror on the planet.

ABOUT TIM SWARTZ

Tim R. Swartz is an Indiana native and Emmy-Award winning television producer/videographer, and is the author of a number of popular books including The Lost Journals of Nikola Tesla, America's Strange and Supernatural History, Secret Black Projects, Evil Agenda of the Secret Government, Time Travel: A How-To-Guide, Richard Shaver-Reality of the Inner Earth, Admiral Byrd's Secret Journey Beyond the Poles, and is a contributing writer for the books, Sir Arthur Conan Doyle: The First Ghostbuster, Brad Steiger's Real Monsters, Gruesome Critters, and Beasts from the Darkside, and Real Ghosts, Restless Spirits and Haunted Places. As a photojournalist, Tim Swartz has traveled extensively and investigated paranormal phenomena and other unusual mysteries from such diverse locations as the Great Pyramid in Egypt to the Great Wall in China. He has worked with television networks such as PBS, ABC, NBC, CBS, CNN, ESPN, Thames-TV and the BBC. He has also appeared on the History Channels program "Ancient Aliens" and the History Channel Latin America series "Contacto Extraterrestre." His articles have been published in magazines such as Mysteries, FATE, Strange, Atlantis Rising, UFO Universe, Flying Saucer Review, Renaissance, and Unsolved UFO Reports. As well, Tim Swartz is the writer and editor of the online newsletter Conspiracy Journal; a free, weekly e-mail newsletter, considered essential reading by paranormal researchers worldwide. Tim is also the host of the webcast program "Exploring the Bizarre" heard Thursday nights at 10:00PM EST on kcorradio.com

SUGGESTED READING BY TIM SWARTZ:
ADMIRAL BYRD'S SECRET JOURNEY BEYOND THE POLES
LOST JOURNALS OF NIKOLA TESLA
TIME TRAVEL: FACT OR FICTION?
INVISIBILITY AND LEVITATION
MATRIX OF THE MIND
TELEPORTATION: A HOW TO GUIDE
PARANORMAL WORLD OF SHERLOCK HOLMES
NAZI UFO TIME TRAVELERS

OCCULT SECRETS OF THE THIRD REICH

< The Vril mediums all wore their hair extremely long, an uncommon hairstyle at the time. They believed that their long hair acted as a cosmic antennae to receive alien communication.

> Maria Orsitsch (Orsic) was the leader of the "Vrilerinnen," the beautiful young mediums of the Vril Gesellschaft.

< In September 1939, Germany made its third "New Swabia" expedition to Antarctica under instructions by the Vril mediums to search for a city of "Aryan Masters" hidden within subterranean caverns.

> The Ahnenerbe sponsored an expedition to Tibet from May 1938 to August 1939, led by German zoologist and SS officer Ernst Schäfer

OCCULT SECRETS OF THE THIRD REICH

NAZIS AND THE ALDEBERAN ALIENS
By Brad Steiger

The Coming Race (1871), a novel by the occultist Edward Bulwer-Lytton, was set in the Earth's interior, where an advanced civilization of giants thrived. In this story, the giants had built a paradise and discovered a form of energy so powerful that they outlawed its use as a potential weapon. This force, the Vril, was derived from the Black Sun, a large ball of "Prima Materia" that provided light and radiation to the inhabitants of the Inner Earth.

The symbol of the Black Sun is suggestive of the plight of the sun when, according to Norse myths, the great wolf Fenrir will swallow the solar orb at the beginning of the Wolf Age. Like many secret groups, there appears to have been more than one order—those who followed the Golden Sun and those who followed the Black Sun. The Black Sun, like the Swastika, is a very ancient symbol. While the Swastika represents the eternal fountain of creation, the Black Sun is even older, suggesting the very void of creation itself. The symbol on the Nazi flag is the Thule Sonnenrad (Sun Wheel), not a reversed good luck Swastika. The Black Sun can be seen in many ancient Babylonian and Assyrian places of worship.

THE OLD ONES, THE ELDER RACE THAT CAME TO EARTH LONG AGO

There are persistent legends in nearly every culture that tell of an Elder Race that populated the Earth millions of years ago. The Old Ones, who may originally have been of extraterrestrial origin, were an immensely intelligent and scientifically advanced species who eventually chose to structure their own environment under the surface of the planet's soil and seas. The Old Ones usually remain aloof from the surface dwellers, but from time to time throughout history, they have been known to visit certain of Earth's more intelligent members in the guise of an alchemist or a mysterious scientist in order to offer constructive criticism and, in some cases, to give valuable advice in the material sciences.

The Buddhists have incorporated Agharta, a subterranean empire, into their theology and fervently believe in its existence and in the reality of underworld supermen who periodically surface to oversee the progress of the human race. According to one source, the underground kingdom of Agharta was created when the ancestors of the present day cave dwellers drove the Serpent People from the cav-

OCCULT SECRETS OF THE THIRD REICH

erns during an ancient war between the reptilian humanoids and the ancient human society.

By the 1840s, the legend of Agharta had already been widely circulated among the mystically minded in Germany. According to this ancient tradition, the Master of the World already controlled many of the kings and rulers of the surface world by exercising his occult powers. Soon this Master and his super race would launch an invasion of Earth and subjugate all humans to his will.

SECRET SOCIETIES IN GERMANY WANTED TO BE
FOUND WORTHY OF THE ALIEN MASTERS OF THE WORLD

The secret societies formed in Germany in the late nineteenth and early twentieth centuries wanted desperately to prove themselves worthy of the super humans that lived beneath the surface of the planet and they wished to be able to control the incredibly powerful Vril force. This ancient force had been known among the alchemists and magicians as the Chi, the Odic force, the Orgone, the Astral Light.

In 1919, Karl Haushofer, a student of the Russian mystic George Gurdjieff, founded the Brothers of the Light Society in Berlin, and soon changed its name to the Vril Society. The Vril Lodge believed that those who learned control of the Vril would become master of himself, those around him, and the world itself, if he should so choose. The members of the Vril Society were well aware of the Astral Light's transformative powers to create supermen out of ordinary mortals. Such members of the Lodge as Adolf Hitler, Heinrich Himmler, Hermann Goring, Dr. Theodor Morell, Hitler's personal physician, and other top future Nazi leaders, became obsessed with preparing German youth to become a Master Race so the Lords of the Inner Earth would find them worthy above all others when they emerged to evaluate the people of Earth's nations.

As Haushofer's Vril grew in prominence, it united three major occult societies, the Lords of the Black Stone, the Black Knights of the Thule Society, and the Black Sun. The Vril chose the swastika, the hooked cross, as its symbol of the worship of the Black Sun. While these societies borrowed some concepts and rites from Theosophists, Rosicrucians, and various Hermetic groups, they placed special emphasis on the innate mystical powers of the Aryan race. Theosophist Mme. Helena Blavatsky listed Six Root Races—the Astral, Hyperborean, Lemurian, Atlantean, Aryan, and the coming Master Race. The Vril and its brother societies maintained that the Germanic/ Nordic/ Teutonic people were of Aryan origin, and that Christianity had destroyed the power of the Teutonic civilization.

MEDIUM MARIA ORSIC CONTACTS ARYAN ALIENS FROM ALDEBERAN

In 1921, Maria Orsic (Orsitch), a medium in the society, now renamed Vril Gesellschaft, began claiming spirit messages originating from Aryan aliens on Alpha Tauri in the Aldeberan star system.

It was while the Vril Gesellschaft was meeting at an old hunting lodge near Berchtesgarden, that the mediums received remarkable news. Maria Orsic, who led

114

the Vrilerinnen, a group of beautiful young women psychics in the society, began to receive messages from Aryan aliens on Alpha Tauri in the Aldeberan star system. Maria and a sister medium named Sigrun learned that a half billion years ago, the Aryans, also known as the Elohim or Elder Race, began to colonize our solar system. The aliens spoke of two classes of people on their world—the Aryan, or master race, and a subservient planetary race that had evolved through mutation and climate changes. On Earth, the Aryans were identified as the Sumerians until they elected to carve out an empire for themselves in the hollow of the planet.

Maria, Sigrun, and the other members of the Vrilerinnen, Traute, Gudrun, and Heike, began to receive transmissions that dictated diagrams and blueprints of advanced flying machines, complete with the mathematics and physics to go with them. The mediums, contrary to popular feminine custom of the day to wear bobbed or short hair, wore their hair long to serve as better receptive antennas for the alien messages.

ALIEN TRANSMISSIONS HELP TO BUILD A FLYING SAUCER

By 1921, some say that a working model of what would one day be called a "flying saucer" had been built. Working in underground bases with the Aryan alien intelligences who had chosen the German people as their earthly successors, the Vril Gesellschaft mastered antigravity space flight, established space stations, accomplished time travel, and developed their spacecraft to warp speeds.

In 1922, members of Thule and Vril Gesellschaft claim to have built the Jenseitsflugmaschine, the Other World Flight Machine, based on the psychic messages received from the Aldeberan aliens and channeled through Maria, Sigrun, and the other mediums. W. O. Schulmann of the Technical University of Munich was in charge of the project until it was halted in 1924, and the craft was stored in a hangar at Messerschmitt's Augsburg location.

GERMAN SCIENTISTS BECOME FASCINATED WITH ROCKETS

The fascination with rockets by conventional German scientists who were not associated (or perhaps even aware of) the Vril Gesellschaft began in 1923 with Dr. Hermann Oberth's book By Rocket to Interplanetary Space. There were many other books that advanced the cause of spacecraft development that appeared in Germany in the mid-1920s.

In 1927 the Verein Fuer Raumschi[fahrt (Society for Space Travel) was organized with Wernher von Braun and Willy Ley among its members. The VFR produced the world's first rocket-powered automobile, the Opel-Rak I, with Fritz von Opel in 1928. Further experiments were made with railway cars, rocket sleds, crude vertical takeoff and landing aircraft. Some successful rocket launches were made from the Rakentenjlugplatz (rocket airfield) near Berlin.

When Adolf Hitler seized power in Germany in 1933, the Nazi party took over all rocket and aircraft development, and all astronautical societies were nationalized. In 1937 the Peenemuende group was formed under the direction of Walter Dornberger and Wernher von Braun.

OCCULT SECRETS OF THE THIRD REICH

HITLER AUTHORIZES THE CONSTRUCTION OF FLYING DISCS

Hitler authorized the construction of the Rund flugzeug, the round, or disk-shaped vehicle, for military use and for space flight. A few years later, the Fuhrer officially abolished all secret societies, but sources indicate that the Vril Gesellschaft continued its work unabated in the strictest of secrecy.

THE THIRD REICH'S EXPEDITION TO DISCOVER INNER EARTH

In April, 1942, Nazi Germany sent out an expedition composed of a number of its most visionary scientists to seek a military vantage point in the hollow earth. Although the expedition of leading scientists left at a time when the Third Reich was putting maximum effort in their drive against the Allies, Goering, Himmler, and Hitler are said to have enthusiastically endorsed the project. Steeped in the more esoteric teachings of metaphysics, the Fuehrer had long been convinced that Earth was concave and that a master race lived on the inside of the planet.

The Nazi scientists who left for the island of Rugen had complete confidence in the validity of their quest. In their minds, such a coup as discovering the opening to the Inner World would not only provide them with a military advantage, but it would go a long way in convincing the Old Ones, the Masters who lived there that the German people truly deserved to mix their blood with them in the creation of a hybrid master race to occupy the surface world.

Some maintain that rather than receiving a late night visitor dressed as a quiet, mannerly, and respectable burgher as had the alchemist Helvetius, Hitler's encounter with a Vril master from the inner Earth was far more dramatic. According to Hermann Rauschning, governor of Danzig, Hitler was shaken by the visit and declared that the "new man" was already living among them and that he was "intrepid and cruel." The Fuhrer admitted that he was afraid of him.

ALIENS HELP NAZIS MASTER ANTIGRAVITY SPACE FLIGHT

UFO researcher Vladimir Terziski firmly believes that an "alien tutor race" secretly began cooperating with certain German scientists from the Thule, the Vril, and the Black Sun societies in the late 1920s. With help from extraterrestrial intelligences, Terziski postulates, the Nazis mastered antigravity space flight, established space stations, accomplished time travel, and developed their spacecraft to warp speeds. At the same time the aliens "spread their Mephistophelean ideas" into the wider German population through the Thule and Vril societies.

Terziski maintains that antigravity research began in Germany in the 1920s with the first hybrid antigravity circular craft, the RFZ-1, constructed by the secret Vril society. In 1942-43 a series of antigravity machines culminated in the giant 350-foot-long, cigar-shaped Andromeda space station, which was constructed in old zeppelin hangars near Berlin by the research and development arm of the SS.

Shortly before the Third Reich collapsed in 1945, Wernher von Braun, Hermann Oberth, and about eighty other top scientists were smuggled out of Nazi Germany by the Allies. The allies also captured various documents, files, plans, photographs, and designs. However, one specific file, containing discoid-shaped aircraft disappeared.

GIANT UNDERGROUND LAUNCH PADS ARE BUILT BY SLAVE-LABOR

In 1938 Hitler's aide, Martin Bormann, had ordered the careful mapping of all mountain passes, caves, bridges, and highways and began selecting sites for underground factories, munitions dumps, and food caches. Giant underground workshops and launching pads, known as "U-plants," were established in which top German scientists would be assigned the task of creating secret weapons. A slave-labor force of 250,000 was required to complete work on such fortresses. Networks of tunnels and assembly plants were fashioned in Austria, Bavaria, and northern Italy.

Allied intelligence had learned of work at the Luftwaffe experimental center near Oberammergau, Bavaria, to create Project Feuerball (Fireball), an aerial device designed to confuse Allied radar and interrupt electromagnetic currents. Efforts were accelerated to perfect the craft in 1944, but work seemed to have been shifted to the development of the Kugelblitz (Round Lightning), a round, symmetrical airplane, quite unlike any previous flying object known in terrestrial aviation history.

DE HAVILLAND AIRCRAFT MADE A NAZI SAUCER FLY – FOR AWHILE

A friend of ours who once worked as a design engineer at the De Havilland aircraft plant in Canada told us that Canadian intelligence had taken plans for an advanced circular aircraft that had been found at Peenemuende, site of the Nazi rocket experimental complex from 1937 to 1945, and presented them as a challenge to the scientists at De Havilland.

"We actually made the 'flying saucer' fly-for a while," our friend said. "We never mastered the complete techniques of the propulsion system to keep the bloody thing in the air for very long at a time."

NAZI SPACE SCIENTISTS ARE SCOOPED UP BY PROJECT PAPERCLIP

Before the smoke had barely cleared from the final resistance in Nazi Germany, Major General Hugh Knerr, Deputy Commanding General for Administration of US Strategic Forces in Europe, acknowledged that the U.S. was "alarmingly backward" in many areas of research, and he ordered the U.S. occupation force to seize both the "apparatus and the brains" that had created the advanced scientific accomplishments of the Nazi scientists or the United States would remain several years behind.

While it was agreed that the United States should scoop up as many German scientists as possible, the occupation force then had to circumvent its own law that no former member of the Nazi Party could immigrate to America. Of the 1600 scientists and their dependents who had been assembled for immediate relocation in the United States, even a superficial inquiry revealed that at least 1200 of them had been avowed Nazis. Informed of this intelligence, President Harry S. Truman decided that it was in the national interest of the United States to gain technological superiority and the scientists were allowed to waffle and declare that they had only been "nominal Nazis" and had not actively supported Nazi military efforts.

OCCULT SECRETS OF THE THIRD REICH

The relocation of the scientists still had to be conducted in utmost secrecy, for the war had been costly and bitter with many American lives lost. The U.S. public at large would not respond favorably if they found out that many of the scientists being given a free ride to the States had worked in laboratories that had been constructed by Nazi slave labor and death camps. The scientists and their family members who were selected by the Joint Intelligence Objectives Agency had paperclips binding their scientific papers to the standard immigration forms, hence the name "Operation Paperclip."

As we stated in our Conspiracies and Secret Societies: The Complete Dossier (Visible Ink Press, 2006), Operation Paperclip was not made public until after the first astronauts had set foot on the Moon in 1973. The eminent Dr. Hubertus Strughold, the "father of space medicine," was one of the prominent physicians who entered the United States under Operation Paperclip. In 1977, the Aeromedical Library at the USAF School of Aerospace medicine was named after Dr. Strughold.

Operation Paperclip also allowed entrance to the United States to Reinhard Gehlen, Nazi Intelligence mastermind, who helped Allen Dulles restructure the OSS (Office of Strategic Services) into the Central Intelligence Agency (CIA); Klaus Barbie, the "Butcher of Lyon"; Otto von Bolschwing, infamous for Holocaust abuses; and the SS Colonel Otto Skorzeny. In 1984, Arthur Rudolph, who had been awarded NASA's Distinguished Service Award in 1969, left the United States rather than face charges for Nazi war crimes.

VON BRAUN TELLS PRESS THAT "POWERS" KNOCKED THE JUNO II ROCKET OFF-COURSE

Long before Operation Paperclip was finally disclosed, the general public was well aware of the participation of such individuals as Dr. Wernher von Braun and Dr. Hermann Oberth, widely recognized as the "father of modern rocketry," as having been integral to the success of the United States space program.

Late in 1958, after the peculiar malfunction of the Juno II rocket, von Braun was quoted in West German newspapers as saying that the rocket had strangely gone off course, as if it had been "deflected."

On January 1, 1959, he told a reporter for Newes Europa that "we feel ourselves faced by powers which are far stronger than we had hitherto assumed....More I cannot say at present. We are now engaged in entering into closer contact with these powers and in six or nine months' time it may be possible to speak with more precision on the matter."

Who exactly were the far stronger "powers" on whom von Braun placed the blame for the malfunction of the Juno II? Had he been, after all, familiar with the interactions of the Vril and other German secret societies with the Aryans from Alderberan?

DR. OBERTH ADMITS THAT GERMANS WERE HELPED BY ALIENS FROM OTHER WORLDS

The rocket scientist's enigmatic reference recalled an earlier comment by his mentor, Dr. Oberth, who protested the accolades for the Germans' brilliant accomplishments in pioneering rocket designs by stating: "We alone cannot take the credit for our record advancement in rocket technology. We have been helped by people from other worlds."

Just who were these mysterious people "from other worlds" who had served as the tutors that enabled Nazi scientists to create a technology unparalleled on Earth?

CANADIAN AND U.S. FAILURES TO CREATE FLYING SAUCERS
FROM ROCKET BASE PLANS SEEM TO PROVE
THAT THE NAZIS HAD HELP FROM ALIENS

On February 16, 1953, the Canadian Minister for Defense Productions released information to the Canadian House of Commons that Avro-Canada, a Canadian aircraft manufacturing company, was engaged in developing plans for a "flying saucer" that would be able to fly at 1,500 miles an hour and lift up and descend vertically. Avro projected that their proposed vehicle would make all other forms of supersonic aircraft obsolete.

It was no secret that the Canadians had retrieved some of the research from the German rocket base at Peenemuende that had been directed by Walter Dornberger and Wernher von Braun in the production of the vergeltungswaffe, the V-2 rocket that had ravaged London, and this announcement seemed clear evidence that they had been successful in assembling one of the Nazi's secret craft.

As if not to be outdone by the Canadians, on February 15, 1955, the Air Technical Intelligence Center, together with the Wright Air Development Center at Wright-Patterson U.S. Air Force Base in Dayton, Ohio, revealed that the Air Force proposed building jet-propelled "flying saucers" under the code name of Project Silverbug.

Circular, saucer-shaped, like the classic UFOs that civilians had been sighting since at least 1947, the largest of the proposed saucers would weigh 26,000 pounds and would be powered by radically advanced jet engines that would be able to lift the craft to an altitude of 36,090 feet in about one minute and 45 seconds. The cruise speed of these remarkable vehicles would be Mach 3.48 and the operating ceiling would be able to soar to 80,600 feet. By way of comparison, today's F-15 fighter jet has a similar performance range, but it was developed more than 20 years after the proposed saucers of Project Silverbug.

For some UFO researchers, this rare disclosure from the Air Force seemed proof that the German occult Vril Society really had made contact with extraterrestrials who had given the Nazis their technological advantage at the onset of World War II. Others spoke of the Nazi discovery of a downed UFO and the intense work of the German scientists and engineers to reverse-engineer the alien spacecraft.

A large number of UFO researchers remain convinced that the U.S. Air Force continued to develop the saucer-shaped superships at Area 51 in Nevada and that many of the huge "motherships" sighted in the skies recently have been our very own flying saucers built on the alien-inspired craft first constructed by the Vril Society.

OCCULT SECRETS OF THE THIRD REICH

WHAT HAPPENED TO THE MEDIUMS
WHO CHANNELED THE ALDEBERANS, THE ARYAN MASTERS?

Research sources are vague as to the eventual fate of Maria Orsic. Some say that Maria, Sigrun, Traute, Gudrun, and Heike were transported by the Jenseitsflugmaschine, the Other World Flight Machine, to live eternally with their extraterrestrial guides on another planet. Another source has Maria escaping to Acapulco where Admiral Wilhelm Franz Canaris had established a submarine base in 1945. Rumors had circulated that the two had had a clandestine love affair. Others maintain that all five of the lovely mediums went with Vril members by submarine to establish a secret base in Antarctica in 1943.

Those who know of Admiral Richard Byrd's claim of finding a "new world" in Antarctica are also those who remind us that the Americans, Canadians, British, and Russians did not snatch up all the German scientists. Some point out that as many as 130 scientists who were working on the secret Vril projects disappeared immediately at the war's end. Simultaneously, a number of German Freight U-boats capable of transporting 850 metric tons each vanished from official inventory. And, at the same time, several airliners capable of flying very long distances seemingly disappeared from Tempelhof Air Base. Shortly after these aircraft and submarines had mysteriously vanished, officials noted that tens of millions of marks in gold bullion and precious stones were missing from the Reichsbank.

A STRANGE MEETING WITH GERMAN SCIENTISTS
AND THEIR ALIEN FRIENDS

A most intriguing question that may always remain unanswered is whether or not the Vril Society divided its membership after contact was established with the Aldeberans and sent some of its alien-inspired scientists to the United States.

In 1969, when I [Brad] was living in Chicago, I received a telephone call from Ray, an executive in a large advertising agency who asked me to appear as a consultant at a meeting of an executive from a major airline, some investment counselors, and a group of people who claimed to be a secret group of German scientists who had been working with extraterrestrials—or non-Terrans, as the aliens preferred. The scientists claimed that they were now willing to share a number of inventions that the larger Earth society could use: A powder that transformed common tap water into smokeless, non-pollutant, no-knock fuel, and a liquid that would totally fireproof any surface upon which it had been sprayed. The advertising executive wanted me to advise him and his friends just who the hell these "people" were.

For the first meeting I asked my friend Glenn, a former detective, to accompany me. We met in a private home not far from O'Hare Airfield. There were three principals:

*Ray, the advertising executive whom I had met before, was a former jet pilot who had chased UFO's in Korea and had been on their trail ever since.

*Bill, an executive with a major airline, who was dedicated to solving the UFO enigma and able to travel anywhere at a moment's notice to investigate any UFO report firsthand.

*The member of the secret society who had been chosen to negotiate for the fuel base and the fireproofing solution.

In addition to these individuals, I was never really introduced to any of the others who, apparently, were the investment counselors, and a number of stoic, silent men and women who were apparently members of the secret society of German scientists and their alien or non-Terran allies.

One of the alleged non-Terrans, a tall redheaded woman with very strange, staring eyes, was extremely hostile to me, complaining that in one of my books I had said that some UFO's may not have the most friendly of intentions. She retreated after a time to a corner of the room with the other members of the silent non-Terran/ German scientist group.

DID THE FUEL WORK?

Yes, Ray said. He had used it in his lawnmower all summer with good results. An attorney used it in his Lincoln Continental for several months, and he had been told by mechanics that the motor was in excellent condition.

A jarful was mixed and handed around the room. There seemed to be little odor. Glenn dipped in a finger and touched it to his tongue. Little taste—maybe a bit like kerosene. We poured a bit out and touched a match to it. Instantly it poofed into smokeless flame.

DID THE FIREPROOFER WORK?

We were informed that a demonstration had been arranged at a nearby airfield. A mixture of oil and gasoline consuming an old fuselage had been extinguished within seconds with but one squirt from a fire extinguisher filled with the substance.

Ray felt he could get backers to raise the money the group was asking for the formulas.

LEARNING THE MYSTERIOUS ALLIANCE
OF THE SECRET SOCIETY AND THE ALIENS

In subsequent late-night meetings with the negotiator for the group, we learned that he had been trained by the German scientists who worked closely with the non-Terrans from Aldeberan. He was a rarity among the group in that he was not of German descent, but was an Italian-American.

According to his account, at the end of World War I, Dr. Rhinelander (as we shall call him) was a member of a secret society in Germany that had been contacted by a group of non-Terrans, the Aryans from Alderberan, and told that he would be given the plans and assistance to build marvelous aerial craft that would run on a propulsion system totally unknown to the earth science of the day. If he wished to receive this information, he must form a group of scientific disciples and immigrate to a certain coal-mining community in the Midwest, U.S.A.

Dr. Rhinelander agreed, and as soon as possible, the Germans immigrated to the designated area. It was important to be near these nearly played-out mines, Dr. Rhinelander was told, because the fuel he would need for the crafts would be made from a by-product of coal.

Dr. Rhinelander and his fellow scientists established themselves in the community, beginning their day when the last whistle sounded in the mines. While the other miners trudged for the bars, home, supper, and bed, the scientists entered their laboratories and set about to fulfill the time schedule that had been set for them by their mysterious benefactors. Eventually, through the apparently unlimited funds provided by the non-Terrans, Dr. Rhinelander was able to buy up old mines to convert into spacious laboratories and to employ large numbers of the indigenous community.

Those who wished to work for Dr. Rhinelander had first to pass a rigorous physical examination and a tortuous, maddening psychological examination. If one were accepted, he was given a special diet and was required to submit to a regular testing of his blood, "to see if it stayed right."

When the first craft was completed about 1924, Dr. Rhinelander had such confidence in his brilliant daughter's abilities as a pilot that he permitted her to captain the maiden flight of the aerial craft that had been designed according to their tutors' specifications.

Although the takeoff was accomplished without incident, the craft was no sooner free of the Earth's atmosphere when a similar but larger vehicle appeared and literally "caught" the ship piloted by Ms. Rhinelander within its metallic structure.

The alarmed and confused German scientists were then informed that another group of non-Terrans had objected to the intervention of Dr. Rhinelander's benefactors. They were not eager for Homo sapiens to have the secrets of interstellar travel. In fact, they would seek to delay humankind's leap to other worlds as long as possible.

HOSTILE ALIENS HAD NOT APPROVED OF THE UNION
OF EARTHLINGS AND ALDEBERANS

In spite of this interference by a hostile extraterrestrial group, Dr. Rhinelander became determined to master space travel and to negotiate for the return of his daughter. Two more vehicles were lost to the opposing factor of non-Terrans before the Germans perfected a means of avoiding capture. Dr. Rhinelander's daughter and the other crew members were never returned, although the Terrans were assured that these people were being well cared for on another world.

Dr. Rhinelander had finally accomplished space travel in the 1930's, but it seemed to matter little. He grieved over the loss of his daughter and became diverted from his work. Concurrently, the unlimited financial funding that they had enjoyed seemed to be curtailed. Chaos began to permeate their once splendid structure of efficient order.

At the time of Dr. Rhinelander's death, the group was approaching poverty, and now the scientists wished to sell the formulas to the non-pollutant fuel and the fire-proofer. Even though they remained in close contact with the non-Terrans in their underwater bases, the scientists had little inclination to attempt more than an occasional foray into the night skies with their two surviving craft.

ENCOUNTERING MAIDS FROM THE GERMAN MOON BASE

I went along on a midnight meeting in some seedy bar where we were to rendezvous once again with the negotiator. It rained so hard that night that it must have kept even UFO's out of the sky, because the man did not show to deliver the formulas.

Although the negotiator failed to keep his appointments, it was not long before Ray found himself confronted by attractive young women who claimed that they had gone to school on a base on the Moon that had been established by German scientists in the 1930s. Ray telephoned me and appealed for help. He said that the women could answer any technological question that he, a former Air Force jet pilot, could throw at them without hesitation.

Excitedly, he told me that he had taken one of the Moon Maids for dinner a couple of nights before in an attempt to ply her with alcoholic beverages to loosen her tongue. She had put away enough drinks to topple a horse without slurring a syllable, without contradicting any previously disclosed aspect of her story, and without once excusing herself to go to the ladies' room.

I turned down the opportunity to come along for the next "for sure" transfer, and I was hardly surprised when Ray told me that our mysterious salesman had not shown on that occasion, either.

Were the strange group of German scientists and alleged aliens that we met that night in Chicago really a splinter group of the Vril Society who had made their spacecraft work in hidden bases in the United States? Or were they clever frauds who tried to exploit the romance of secret societies and extraterrestrial mentors into just another scam? If they were merely scammers, however, why did they never take the money that was offered to them several times and run? From my point of view at the time, it seemed that the group that had met with us had somehow violated the code of their larger society and had been ordered to break off contact with those outsiders who wished to buy their formulas.

Ray kept in touch for quite some time, and he proved to possess a rare degree of determination. He told me of a number of midnight meetings, which the other parties never kept. On occasion, he was "tailed" by three dark men in dark automobiles, who proved to be unshakable.

But he never managed to track down those magical formulas, and he never received another telephone call from the mysterious secret society.

As a footnote, although outlawed in Germany, the Vril society has recently resurfaced in Italy where it is known as Causa Nostra (Our Cause). Membership is restricted to women only, and the principles are said to be those established by Maria Orsic, the original Vril Chefin, and the Vril Gesellschaft of Sigrun, Traute, Gudrun, and Heike. Maybe this time, their extraterrestrial contacts will reveal themselves to the world at large. Or maybe the non-Terrans, the aliens, have been walking among us unnoticed for years now.

ABOUT BRAD STEIGER

Brad Steiger is a world renowned author of over 175 books with over 17 million copies in print. His titles include: "Mysteries of Time and Space," "Real Ghosts, Restless Spirits and Haunted Places," "Conspiracies and Secret Societies: The Complete Dossier," "Touched by Heaven's Light," "American Indian Medicine Power," "Strangers from the Skies," "Project Bluebook," "The Rainbow Conspiracy," "Real Encounters, Different Dimensions and Otherworldly Beings," and many more. Steiger first began publishing articles on the unexplained in 1956; since then he has written more than 2,000 paranormal-themed articles. From 1970-73, his weekly newspaper column, "The Strange World of Brad Steiger," was carried domestically in over 80 newspapers and overseas from Bombay to Tokyo. He was born in Fort Dodge, Iowa, on February 19, 1936. He is married to Sherry Hansen Steiger, author and co-author of over 22 books. They have two sons, three daughters, and ten grandchildren. Keep up with Brad at his Facebook, https://www.facebook.com/Brad.Steiger.Author or the Steiger website www.bradandsherry.com.

SUGGESTED READING, BOOKS BY BRAD STEIGER:
CONSPIRACIES AND SECRET SOCIETIES
REAL ENCOUNTERS, DIFFERENT DIMENSIONS AND OTHERWORLDLY BEINGS
REAL MONSTERS
REAL GHOSTS
SEX AND THE SUPERNATURAL

Hitler believed the Spear of Destiny would help him conquer the world!

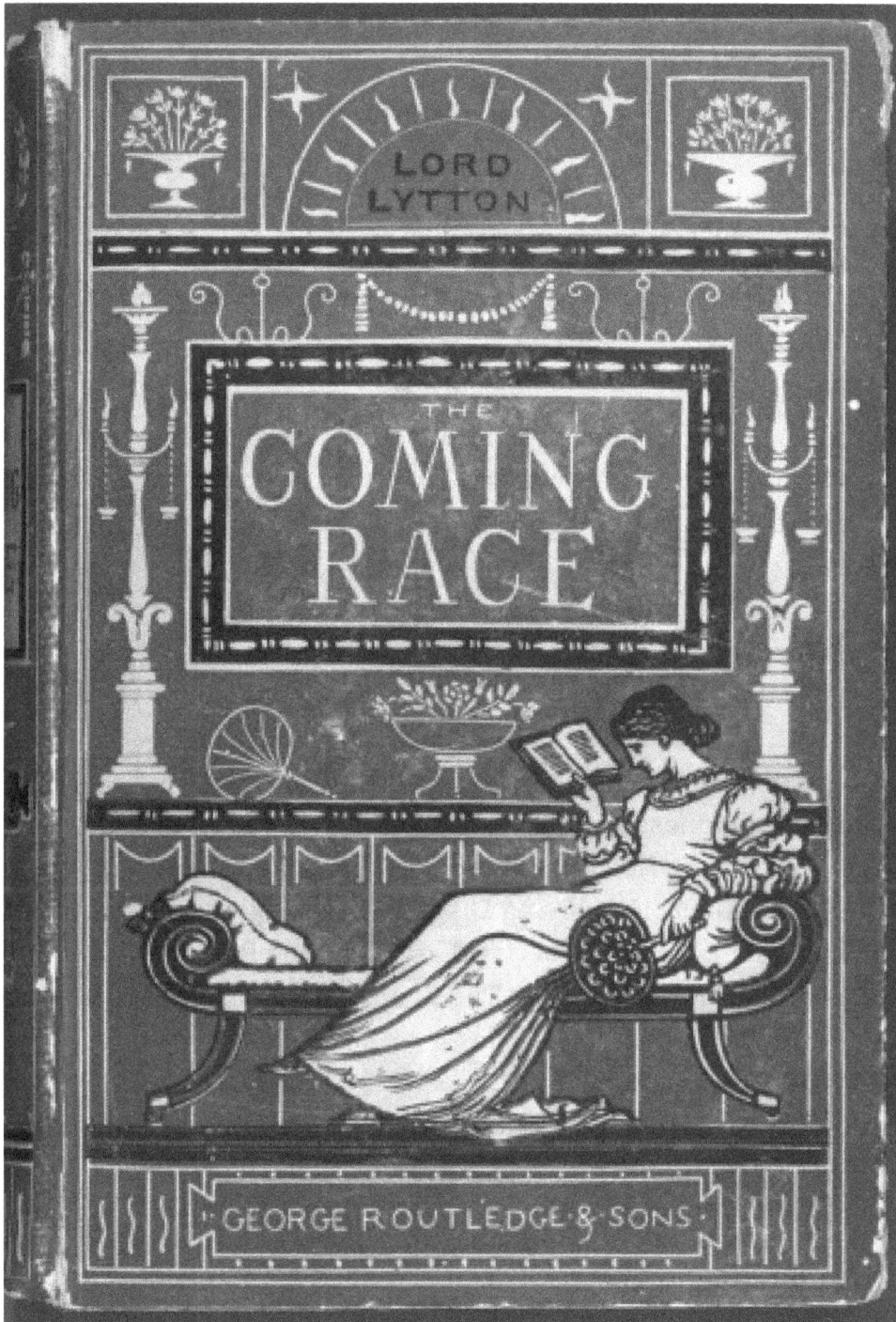

The Vril Gesellschaft was inspired by the 1871 novel "The Coming Race,"
written by Edward Bulwer-Lytton.

OCCULT SECRETS OF THE THIRD REICH
Téodoro Rampalé

Contents

INTRODUCTION: SEARCH FOR A MAP OF HELL

This book is concerned with one of the most controversial notions of the late twentieth century, one that is so bizarre and appalling in its implications that serious historians have consistently dismissed it as the worst kind of nonsense. Put simply, the notion is this: that the shocking nightmare of Nazism and the destruction it wrought throughout the world were the result of an attempt by Hitler and his cohorts to contact and enlist the aid of supernatural forces in their bid for domination of the planet. Upon reading this, older readers may be put in mind of the lurid but enjoyable occult thrillers of Dennis Wheatley, such as Strange Conflict, which deals with Nazi magical practices in a highly sensational way, and may dismiss the idea for that reason. Other readers may well pause to consider the hideous excesses practiced by the Nazis and be dismayed that the defining tragedy of the twentieth century should be trivialized

OCCULT SECRETS OF THE THIRD REICH

by such an idea.

There is no doubt that the subject of the Third Reich inspires a deep and abiding fascination to this day, with the origin of the awful cruelties perpetrated in its name still the subject of intense debate. Ever since Hitler's death in the Fuhrerbunker in 1945, historians, psychologists and theologians have attempted to understand and explain the frightful aberration that was Nazism. One of the foci around which discussion of Hitler moves is the question of where he stands in the spectrum of human nature. As the journalist Ron Rosenbaum notes, the very existence of this spectrum suggests an extremely uncomfortable question: 'is Hitler on a continuum with previous and successive mass murderers, explicable within the same framework, on the extreme end of the same spectrum of the human nature we supposedly share with Jeffrey Dahmer and Mahatma Gandhi?" Or is he something else entirely, existing outside the continuum of humanity, evil in some absolute, ultimate way? The theologian Emil Fackenheim believes that such was the magnitude of Hitler's crimes that we must consider him as representing a 'radical evil', an 'eruption of demonism into history'. (2) Hitler's evil is seen by thinkers like Fackenheim as existing beyond the bounds of ordinary human behavior (however appalling). Indeed, to them it is so extreme that it transcends the field of behavioral science and enters the realm of theology: in other words, Hitler's ultimate nature can only be completely understood by God.

The industrialized mass murder perpetrated by the Nazis resonated irresistibly through the latter half of the twentieth century, and is certainly the principal contributing factor to what the British historian Norman Davies calls 'a demonological fascination with Germany'. In summarizing the historiography of the Western Powers, Davies states: 'Germany stands condemned as the prime source both of the malignant imperialism which produced the First World War, and of the virulent brand of fascism which provoked the Second.' (3) In the post-war years, this contributed to the 'Allied scheme of history' in which the West presented (and still presents) itself as the pinnacle of civilization, morality and altruism. While the numerous reasons why this is far from the truth lie beyond the scope of this book, the attitudes that have accompanied the Allied scheme are of extreme importance with regard to our continuing fascination with the Nazis. Davies writes of 'The ideology of "anti-fascism", in which the Second World War of 1939-45 is perceived as "the War against Fascism" and as the defining event in the triumph of Good over Evil.' (4) It is easy to understand, therefore, how such defining events (particularly those separated from us by a mere 55 years) can tenaciously maintain themselves in the public consciousness.

While historians have tended to concentrate on the many important economic, social and historical factors that influenced Nazi ideology, somewhat less attention has been paid to the Nazis' fascination with arcane and esoteric belief systems, in spite of their undeniable influence upon Hitler and the architects of National Socialism in the years leading up to and including the Second World War. The purpose of this book, therefore, is to attempt to make some sense of the irrational and benighted realms of Nazi occultism and pseudoscience, and to attempt an explanation of the strange attraction they held for their proponents.

Given the human capacity for myth-making, it is perhaps unsurprising that the known history of the Third Reich should have given rise, in subsequent decades, to the assertion that the Nazis were, quite literally, in contact with an evil, transhuman intelligence that chose to exert its influence over humanity through the living conduits of Hitler and other high-ranking members of the Reich. In the course of this book, we shall see that the intellectual fathers of National Socialism, aggressively anti-Semitic Pan-German and volkisch nationalists like Guido von List, Jorg Lanz von Liebenfels and Rudolf von Sebottendorff, cultivated an undeniable and profound interest in occultism, theosophy, the idea of Atlantis as a lost Aryan civilization, and the magical powers inherent in the very blood of racially pure Germans. That Hitler's immediate subordinates themselves dabbled in occult sciences such as astrology is also beyond doubt. Occultism played a significant role in the formation and rituals of the SS; and it is also a matter of historical record that the Nazis embraced cock-eyed cosmological theories such as Horbiger's World Ice concept (which provided them with an opportunity to denounce the ideas of the Jewish Albert Einstein).

In the decades since the end of the war, some historians have seen Nazi occultism as evidence of the essential irrationality underlying the Third Reich, and as a salutary lesson regarding the power that myth can exercise over the human mind. This point of view is, of course, based on the fact that occultism (however important it may be in the history of the human quest for understanding) is not an accurate way of describing the nature of the Universe. The concepts, beliefs, attitudes and actions we shall encounter in this book, however, are based on the opposite notion, that occultism is a genuine and useful system with which to apprehend and influence the workings of Nature.

If we take Fackenheim's belief that Hitler represents an 'eruption of demonism into history', which can only truly be understood by God, and apply it to the subject of Nazi occultism, it becomes clear that the various claims for the reality of genuine Nazi occult power were inevitable. One can easily imagine the thought processes of the writers who have made these claims: the Third Reich was an atrocious aberration in the history of humanity, an utter catastrophe even by our usual bloody standards. How could it have come about? If Hitler was uniquely evil, why was he so? What was it in his mind, his nature, his essential attributes and the actions to which they gave rise that took him beyond the continuum of human behavior and placed him at the level of the absolute, comprehensible only to the creator of the Universe? If his evil extended beyond the human, is it possible that its origin lay beyond the human?

In view of the extreme nature of Nazi crimes, the idea that an evil external to humanity (a cosmic evil) exists and that leading Nazis actually attempted to make contact with transhuman entities in their pursuit of world domination and the creation of an Aryan super-race maybe seen by many as distasteful in the extreme, and demeaning to the memory of those who suffered and died under Hitler's tyranny. It is an uncomfortable notion, to be sure, and one that, as the British writer Joscelyn Godwin notes, occupies 'that twilight zone between fact and fiction: the most fertile territory for the nurturing of mythological images and their installation in the collective imagination'. (5) However, it is for this very reason that the idea of genuine Nazi occult power demands our attention: it has become an important (if unwelcome) aspect of the history of the Second World War and the second half of the twentieth century.

At this point, I should clarify my reasons for and intentions in writing this book. The prevalence of the Nazi-occultism idea is such that I considered it worthwhile to attempt an evaluation of it—especially in view of the fact that humanity stands on the threshold of a new millennium more or less intact. With the arrival of the year 2018, human culture finds itself in an intriguing position, the nature of which might best be captured by the British writer Thomas De Quincey's statement that the present is the confluence of two eternities, the past and the future. As we look with curiosity, hope and some trepidation to the new century and the new millennium before us, we will also, of necessity, look back at the thousand years we have just left behind, and in particular at the century that has just ended—without doubt the bloodiest and most violent, but also the century that saw more and greater scientific advances than any other in the history of our species. And yet, despite the myriad scientific and technological advances that have carried us to this point in our history, it cannot be said with any confidence that science itself has triumphed over mythology. In some ways, this is by no means a bad thing: human beings are not machines, and a worldwide culture based exclusively on hard scientific principles would be intolerable to human nature, which is fascinated by spirituality, mythology and mystery.

However, this inherent need in human beings to mythologize can seriously hinder the quest for truth, particularly historical truth. As the British historian Hugh Trevor-Roper put it, 'reason is powerless against the obstinate love of fiction'. When he wrote this, Trevor-Roper was referring to the so-called 'Hitler survival myth', the idea that the Fuhrer did not die in the Berlin bunker in 1945, but somehow managed to escape —according to various versions, to South America, to Antarctica, and even to a monastery in Tibet. As a historian and British intelligence officer, Trevor-Roper was given the task of establishing Hitler's fate by the then-head of Counter-intelligence in the British Zone of Germany, Sir Dick White. He made his report to the Four-Power Intelligence Committee in Berlin on 1 November 1945, and the report inspired one of the finest history books ever published, The Last Days of Hitler (1947). In this book, Trevor-Roper calmly establishes beyond all reasonable doubt that Hitler did not survive the end of the Second World War. Nevertheless, the Hitler survival myth continued to circulate, particularly in far-right and neo-Nazi circles, and can still be encountered occasionally to this day.

This mythopoeic capacity is brought to bear in the absence of verifiable data. In the case of the Hitler survival myth, in September 1945 no one knew for certain what had happened to the Fuhrer: he had simply disappeared. This gave rise to numerous speculations, particularly from journalists, that he had somehow managed to escape from the ruins of Berlin as his Thousand-Year Reich imploded to the dimensions of his bunker. When Trevor-Roper's final report was delivered, stating that Hitler had died by his own hand and that all other theories were 'contrary to the only positive evidence and supported by no evidence at all', it drew criticism from some quarters. 'The critics did not indeed deny the evidence that was produced, but they maintained that there was still a possibility of escaping so final a conclusion; they maintained that the body that had been burnt was that not of Hitler but of a "double" introduced at the last minute ...' (6)

Trevor-Roper's use of the phrase 'a possibility of escaping' is interesting and very significant with regard to the present book, since the idea of escaping from a final conclusion to the horror of Hitler resonates powerfully with the fact that Hitler himself managed to escape human justice through suicide. Indeed, as more than one commentator has suggested, Hitler managed a twofold escape: not only did he elude punishment for his crimes but he has also eluded explanation, as noted earlier. This inability on our part to arrive at a satisfactory explanation for Hitler has been called 'evidentiary despair' by Ron Rosenbaum, who illustrates the concept with comments from historians such as Trevor-Roper, Alan Bullock and the Jewish-studies scholar Alvin Rosenfeld. Trevor-Roper still considers Hitler a 'frightening mystery', while Bullock states that the more he learns about Hitler, the harder he finds him to explain. Rosenfeld sums up the problem best: 'No representation of Adolf Hitler has seemed able to present the man or satisfactorily explain him.' (7)

Of course, there have been many attempts to explain the mind of Hitler, to chart the process that took him from unprepossessing Viennese down-and-out to the assassin of European Jewry. Surprisingly (indeed, shockingly), the debate that has continued for more than half a century concentrates partly on the question of whether or not Hitler can accurately be described as 'evil'. Our first reaction to this might be that it is the easiest question to answer that has ever been posed, to echo Alan Bullock's 'If he isn't evil, who is?' Nevertheless, the ease with which we seem to be able to answer this question is illusory and, in addressing ourselves to it, we find ourselves grappling with one of the oldest problems of humanity: the problem of the nature of evil itself. As Rosenbaum reminds us, 'it doesn't matter what word we choose to apply to Hitler', it does not alter the number of people who suffered and died. 'How we think about Hitler and evil and the nature of Hitler's choice is a reflection of important cultural assumptions and divisive schisms about individual consciousness and historical causation, the never-ending conflict over free will, determinism, and personal responsibility.'8 It is important to emphasize that to question the use of the word 'evil' as applied to Hitler is not to minimize in any way the enormity of his crimes (which were inarguably horrific). However, our intuitive sense of the existence of evil and the certainty with which we perceive its presence in Hitler is little help in our search for a definition of it. Rosenbaum informs us that during the course of interviews with many historians, conducted as part of the research for his remarkable book Explaining Hitler: The Search For the Origins of His Evil, he discovered to his surprise that many were reluctant to call Adolf Hitler evil.

Rosenbaum is instructive on the problems of defining evil in terms sufficiently accurate to allow a serious and rigorous discussion of the primary motivating factors in Hitler's crimes:

[I]n the realm of scholarship, it's remarkable to discover how many sophisticated thinkers of all stripes find themselves unwilling to find a principled rationale for calling Hitler evil, at least in the strict sense of doing wrong knowingly. The philosophical literature that takes these questions seriously makes a distinction between obviously evil deeds such as mass murder and the not-always-obvious nature of the intent of the doer, preferring the stricter term 'wickedness' to describe wrongdoers who do evil deeds knowing they are doing wrong. I was drawn to the philosophical literature on the problem of wickedness ... by another defining moment in my encounters with Hitler explainers: my conversation in London with H. R. Trevor-Roper, former Regius Professor of Modern History at Oxford, one of the first and most widely respected postwar Hitler explainers. I'd asked him the deceptively simple question I'd begun asking a number of Hitler explainers: 'Do you consider Hitler consciously evil? Did he know what he was doing was wrong?' (9)[Original emphasis]

Trevor-Roper's answer was an emphatic No: Hitler was convinced of his own rectitude. Although his deeds reached an extreme of awfulness, he committed them in the deluded belief that they were right. Rosenbaum also points out that the assumption that Jewish people themselves might be expected to be the first to reject this 'rectitude argument' is also flawed, as evidenced by the statement of Efraim Zuroff, director of the Simon Wiesenthal Centre's Jerusalem headquarters, and the chief Nazi-hunter in Israel. When asked if he thought Hitler was conscious he was doing wrong, Zuroff almost shouted: 'Of course not! Hitler thought he was a doctor! Killing germs! That's all Jews were to him! He believed he was doing good, not evil!' (10) (Original emphasis.)

The acceptance by many historians of the rectitude argument leads Rosenbaum to a tentative and very interesting conclusion: 'that beneath the Socratic logic of the position might be an understandably human, even emotional, rejection—as simply unbearable—of the idea that someone could commit mass murder without a sense of rectitude, however delusional. That Hitler could have done it out of pure personal hatred, knowing exactly what he was doing and how wrong it was.' (11) (Original emphasis.) Allied to this is the so-called Great Abstraction Theory of history, which places emphasis on profound and inevitable trends at the expense of the activities of single personalities as formulated in the now-unfashionable Great Man Theory. According to the Great Abstraction Theory:

'Nothing could have prevented the Holocaust. No one's to blame for the failure to halt Hitler's rise. If it hadn't been Hitler, it would have been "someone like Hitler" serving as an instrument of those inexorable larger forces.' (12) The alternative, which is considered unthinkable by many historians and philosophers, is that a single human being wanted to bring about the Holocaust—a human being ... a member of our species. (The reader may detect a similarity between this notion and the reluctance by some to allow Hitler to be placed within the continuum of human behavior mentioned earlier.)

While the implications of the Great Abstraction Theory may serve as a form of consolation (nothing could have prevented the Holocaust from happening: it was the result of uncontrollable historical forces), it has been rightly criticized in some quarters for its implicit removal of Hitler from the position of sole creator of the Final Solution. In the last analysis, he remains the greatest enigma: any attempt to explain seriously the origin and nature of the evil of the Third Reich must centre on Adolf Hitler— not as a pawn of larger forces, but as the prime mover of Nazism.

All of which brings us back to the central question, phrased memorably by Rosenbaum: what made Hitler Hitler? What turned him from an apparently ordinary, undistinguished human being into the very embodiment of wickedness, the destroyer of more than six million innocent people? According to Yehuda Bauer, a founder of the discipline of Holocaust Studies, while it is possible in theory to explain Hitler, it may well be too late. The deaths of crucial witnesses and the loss of important documents may have resulted in our eternal separation from the means to answer the question, to draw an accurate map of the hell Hitler created on Earth.

Of course, there have been numerous theories put forward, including the suggestion that Hitler's anti-Semitism derived from the unproven seduction and impregnation of his paternal grandmother, Maria Schicklgruber, by a Jew, resulting in the birth of his father, Alois Hitler. According to this theory, Hitler exterminated the Jews in order to exterminate what he perceived as the poison in his own blood. Another conjecture has it that Hitler discovered an affair between his half-niece, Geli Raubal, and a Jewish music teacher, and that he either drove her to suicide or had her murdered. This resulted in a desire for murderous vengeance against the Jews. Yet another theory suggests that the death of Hitler's mother in 1907 was in some way made more painful by the malpractice of her Jewish doctor, Eduard Bloch, for which Hitler, once again, exacted terrible vengeance.

(13) As we have just seen, the desperate search for an adequate explanation of Hitler has resulted in a number of contradictory theories, many of which are built on flimsy evidence. Interestingly, this search has also generated a mythology of its own, revolving around what Rosenbaum calls 'the lost safe-deposit box. A place where allegedly revelatory documents—ones that might provide the missing link, the lost key to the Hitler psyche, the true source of his metamorphosis—seem to disappear beyond recovery." (4) This mythology was inspired by real events in Munich in 1933, when Fritz Gerlich, the last anti-Hitler journalist in that city, made a desperate attempt to alert the world to the true nature of Hitler by means of a report of an unspecified scandal. On 9 March, just as Gerlich's newspaper, Der Gerade Weg, was about to go to press, SA storm troopers entered the premises and ripped it from the presses.

Although no copy of the Gerlich report has ever been found, rumors have been circulating for many years about the ultimate fate of the information with which Gerlich hoped to warn the world of the danger of Hitler, one of which involves a secret copy of the report that was smuggled out of the premises (along with supporting documentary material) by one Count Waldburg-Zeil. Waldburg-Zeil allegedly took the report and its supporting documents to his estate north of Munich, where he buried them somewhere in the grounds. According to Gerlich's biographer Erwin von Aretin, however, Waldburg-Zeil destroyed them during the war, fearful of what might happen should they be discovered by the Nazi authorities.

Rosenbaum informs us of an alternative version of these events, involving documents proving that Geli Raubal was indeed killed on the orders of Adolf Hitler. According to von Aretin's son, the historian Professor Karl-Ottmar Freiherr von Aretin, his father gave the documents to his cousin, Karl Ludwig Freiherr von Guttenberg, co-owner of the Munchener Neueste Nachrichten, who put them in a safe-deposit box in Switzerland. Guttenberg was killed following his involvement in the attempted coup against Hitler on 20 July 1944. For the sake of security, he had not told anyone the number of the safe-deposit-box account.

The idea that somewhere in Switzerland there lies a set of documents containing information that might be of some help in explaining the transformation of Adolf Hitler from man to monster is a powerful one, and has generated more than one subsequent controversial claim. There is, for instance, the account given by a German novelist named Ernst Weiss, according to which the voice Hitler claimed to have heard while recovering from war injuries in a hospital at Pasewalk summoning him to a mission to avenge Germany following her surrender in 1918, was actually that of Dr. Edmund Forster, a staff psychiatrist at the hospital. Forster 'sought to cure Hitler's hysterical blindness by putting him in a hypnotic trance and implanting the post-hypnotic suggestion that Hitler had to recover his sight to fulfill a mission to redeem Germany's lost honor'. (15)

Weiss, who apparently befriended Forster, claimed that the psychiatrist discovered a dreadful secret during the course of Hitler's treatment, a secret with the potential to unlock the future Fuhrer's psyche and which Forster took with him when he fled Germany in 1933. Shortly before his suicide (to which he was driven by the Gestapo), Forster took his Pasewalk case notes to Switzerland and placed them in a safe-deposit box in a bank in Basel. As an added security measure, Forster rewrote the notes in a cipher of his own devising, the key to which he took to his grave.

As Rosenbaum notes, the unreadable cipher in the lost safe-deposit box is a powerful metaphor for the elusive explanation of Hitler:

These lost-safe-deposit-box stories clearly serve as expressions of anxiety about—and talismans against—an otherwise apparently inexplicable malignant evil. In fact, despite the despairing tone of the safe-deposit-box myths, they represent a kind of epistemological optimism, a faith in an explicable world. Yes, something is missing, but if we don't have the missing piece in hand, at least it exists somewhere. At least somewhere there's the lost key that could make sense of the apparently motiveless malignancy of Hitler's psyche ... A missing piece, however mundane or bizarre ... but something here on earth, something we can contain in our imagination, something safely containable within the reassuring confines of a box in a Swiss bank. Something not beyond our ken, just beyond our reach, something less unbearably frightening than inexplicable evil. [Original emphasis.] (16)

If I have relied rather heavily on Rosenbaum's work in the last few pages, it is because it is of considerable relevance to our concerns in the present book. When I began to think about writing Invisible Eagle, my intention was to attempt an evaluation of the evidence for Nazi involvement with occultism and black magic. In the course of my preliminary reading, however, it became clear to me that, while early racist organizations like the volkisch movement and the Pan-Germans were most certainly influenced by occultist notions, the evidence for Adolf Hitler and other leading Nazis as practicing black magicians was decidedly weak. Nevertheless, in the decades since the end of the Second World War, an elaborate mythology has developed around this very concept, the details of which (as lurid as they are unsubstantiated) have been presented in a number of popular books, mainly in the 1960s and early 1970s.

The reason for this, it seems to me, has a great deal to do with what we have been discussing in this Introduction: the need—desperate and perhaps doomed to failure—to arrive at an adequate explanation for the catastrophic wickedness of Hitler and the Nazis. Indeed, this notion first arose during the actual war years and was adhered to at first principally by members of the Spiritualist community, and later by many others (it is estimated that by 1941 as much as 25 per cent of the British population had some belief in the paranormal). An interest in occultism and Spiritualism became a great comfort to those who had lost loved ones either overseas or in the Blitz, since it held the potential to establish for them the reality of an afterlife, a world of the spirit where their sufferings would be at an end, replaced by ultimate peace and love. For many people with an interest in esotericism, it became evident that the war was very much a war between Good and Evil in the cosmic sense: a battle between the powers of Light and Darkness. The Nazis were using (or perhaps being used by) monstrous occult powers, and the only way to have even a chance of stopping them was to employ the opposing magical powers of goodness and love. This the Spiritualist community did, paying special attention to British pilots fighting in the Battle of Britain. It is a little-known fact that there was an additional battle being waged at the time, by Spiritualists giving psychic aid to the brave pilots defending the nation's skies. This came to be known as the Magical Battle of Britain.

The Spiritualists were in turn aided in their efforts by the white witches who feared that a Nazi invasion of Britain would see their extermination. By raising their own occult forces, they hoped to stave off the invasion in the summer of 1940. Traveling to the Kent coast, the witches threw a substance known as 'go-away powder' into the sea. Made according to an ancient recipe, this substance, combined with certain potent magical spells, had the effect (so the witches believed) of raising an impassable psychic barrier around the shores of Britain. Another coven travelled to the Hampshire coast with the intention of raising a magical cone of power that would turn back the advancing forces of Darkness. Indeed, magical operations were carried out by covens all over the country, concentrating on the idea of confusing the minds of Hitler's High Command and making them think that to invade Britain would be too difficult. (In the autumn of 1940, the invasion of Britain was postponed indefinitely.)

At this point, I should pause to note that at various points in this book I shall be using two phrases that at first sight might appear to be synonymous but which actually have very different meanings. The first is 'Nazi occultism', by which I mean the Nazi belief in the occult and supernatural; the second is 'Nazi occult power', by which I mean the belief of occultists and crypto-historians that the Nazis wielded genuine supernatural powers, achieved through their alleged contact with transhuman intelligences. It will become clear in the course of the book, I hope, that the latter concept, while far less verifiable in historical terms, is nevertheless of considerable importance in the mythology of the twentieth century and the manner in which we view reality today.

That said, let us now turn to a brief overview of the subjects that we shall be examining in the following pages. This survey can in many ways be categorized as conspiracy literature. As such, it presents certain problems both for the writer who explores it and the reader who agrees to accompany him or her. With regard to Invisible Eagle, it will become clear that the early sections refer to data that have been verified and are accepted by professional historians. However, as the reader proceeds through the book, it will also become clear that ideas about the involvement of leading Nazis with occultism and black magic grow more outlandish and less believable, particularly when presented by writers who have little or no official training in the history of fascism and the Second World War.

It might therefore appear to the reader that this book itself is only half legitimate, based as it is partly on verifiable historical data and partly on bizarre and spurious notions that have few claims to historical accuracy. Such a conclusion would, however, be a mistake: the various claims made regarding Nazi involvement with the occult have come to occupy a central place in the mythologizing of the Third Reich that has developed in the years since the end of the Second World War. Just as the Nazis mythologized the history of their so-called 'Aryan' ancestors in order to legitimize (in their own minds, at least) their claims to racial superiority, so they themselves have, to a great extent, been mythologized by writers in the fields of occultism and conspiracy theory.

The result is that a body of wild historical speculation now exists alongside what we know for certain about Nazi Germany, and it is an unpalatable but undeniable fact that this speculation forms a significant element in the public attitude to Hitler and the Nazis. However spurious the ideas that we shall examine in the later stages of this book, it is essential that we do discuss them in order to gain some understanding of the awful fascination the Third Reich still holds for us.

Thus, in Chapter One, we will examine the origins of occultist belief in Nazi Germany in movements such as volkisch nationalism and Pan-Germanism, the adoption of Theosophical concepts, the development of the occult-racist doctrine known as Ariosophy, and the occult societies that were used as conduits for the propagation of racist esotericism and the doctrine of Aryan supremacy. In Chapter Two, we will concentrate on the bizarre mythology adopted by the Nazis, which centered on the idea of a lost Aryan homeland in the far North, and will examine the occult origin of the swastika.

The first two chapters contain information that is historically verifiable and accepted by serious historians. With Chapter Three, we find ourselves departing from this path of respectability and entering what the French writers Louis Pauwels and Jacques Bergier call the Absolute Elsewhere: an intellectual realm of extreme notions that is the equivalent of Godwin's 'twilight zone between fact and fiction'. Much of the remainder of this book will deal with these notions, not through any misguided belief in their veracity but rather in an attempt to establish the reasons for their inclusion in the mythology that has been imposed upon the history of the Third Reich in the last five decades. Chapter Three, therefore, will introduce us to the mysterious Vril Society and its use of a vast and hidden power known as 'vril' and said to be wielded by a race of subterranean superhumans. In Chapter Four we will travel to Tibet to examine the curious notion that the Nazis were in contact with certain high lamas, through whom they intended to ally themselves with the powerful race living beneath the Himalayas. Chapter Five will be devoted to an examination of one of the most enduring myths regarding Nazi occult power: that of Hitler's quest for the so-called Spear of Destiny, the Holy Lance said to have pierced the side of Christ during the crucifixion and whose possession would enable those who understood its mysteries to control the world. In Chapter Six we will chart the origins and ritual practices of the SS and attempt to establish how much of what has been written regarding its use of black magic is true. Chapter Seven will see us plunging ever deeper into the Absolute Elsewhere, where we will encounter the fantastic principles of Nazi cosmology, including the theory that the Earth is hollow (a theory that has enjoyed more or less constant currency in certain UFO circles—the fringe of the fringe, one might say).

Although at first sight it might appear out of place in a book dealing with the subject of Nazi occultism, I have devoted Chapter Eight to an examination of the radical and highly advanced aircraft designs on which the Nazis were working towards the end of the war, and which were captured, along with many of the scientists and engineers who were attempting to put them into practice, by the Allies in 1945. I have included this subject because it provides a connection between the alleged occult philosophy of the Third Reich and the sinister but increasingly popular concept of Nazi survival to the present day. It has been suggested by a number of researchers and commentators that modern sightings of UFOs (unidentified flying objects) may be due to the development by America and Russia of captured Nazi secret weapon designs. It is certainly beyond dispute that both Allied and German air crews encountered highly unusual aerial phenomena over Europe in the form of small (three-to four-foot diameter) illuminated spheres, which appeared to follow their fighters and bombers and interfered with the electrical systems of the aircraft.

These glowing balls of light were known as 'foo fighters'. Others (including certain neo-Nazi groups) have suggested in all seriousness that some UFOs are actually operated by Nazis and are powered by vril energy, and that the Third Reich survives today in the icy fastnesses of the North and South polar regions, in particular the region of Antarctica known as Queen Maud Land (so named by Norwegian explorers) which the Nazis claimed for Germany in 1939 and renamed Neu Schwabenland.

Later we will examine the notion of Nazi survival in various secret locations, which has it that the Third Reich (or, perhaps more accurately, the Fourth Reich) is alive and well and continuing its quest for world domination. Finally, in the Conclusion we will attempt a summing up of the material we have covered.

By the end of the book, I hope to make it clear that the history of Nazi occultist beliefs, in combination with the attempt to enlist the Nazis' quest for genuine supernatural power to explain the motivations of Hitler and the Third Reich, has resulted in an elaborate mythological system that has had a definite influence upon our attitude to the practice of official secrecy and the putative abuses of political and economic power in the post-war world. The structure of belief we will be discussing is thus twofold: on the one hand, we can identify the pernicious esotericism of the Nazis themselves and the revolting cruelties it engendered; and on the other, the modern mythological system that has developed in the years since the end of the Second World War, and which has Nazi occultist beliefs as its starting point. Readers will find themselves embarking on a journey into realms both outre and unsettling; we will of necessity be exploring concepts from which most academics would turn away with the utmost disdain. We will look at claims and beliefs that most rational people would find it hard to accept anyone could seriously entertain—were it not for the atrocities committed in their name that have irreparably demeaned our species. And we will see how the frightful and irrational concepts of Nazi mysticism and pseudoscience have survived to the present day to cast a fearsome shadow over the future.

OCCULT SECRETS OF THE THIRD REICH

1—ANCESTRY, BLOOD AND NATURE
THE MYSTICAL ORIGINS OF NATIONAL SOCIALISM
AN HISTORICAL PERSPECTIVE

We must begin our journey in the convulsed but well-mapped territory of nineteenth-century Europe, in which arcane and esoteric concepts might be expected to be far removed from the complex political processes, intellectual rationalism and rapid industrialization occurring at the time. Nevertheless, the origins of the Nazi fascination with occult and esoteric belief systems can be traced to the political, cultural and economic conditions prevalent in Prussia and Austria in the second half of the century. As noted by the British authority on the history of the Third Reich, Nicholas Goodrick-Clarke, Austria in the late 1800s was the product of three major political changes: 'These changes consisted in the exclusion of Austria from the German Confederation, the administrative separation of Hungary from Austria, and the establishment of a constitutional monarchy in the "Austrian" or western half of the empire." The German Confederation had been created by the Congress of Vienna to replace the Holy Roman Empire, and lasted from 1815 to 1866; it consisted of a union of 39 German states, with 35 monarchies and four free cities. Its main organ was a central Diet under the presidency of Austria. However, the establishment of the confederation failed to meet the aspirations of German nationalists, who had hoped for a consolidation of these small monarchies into a politically unified Greater Germany.

As a step towards the ascendancy of Prussia over Austria and the unification of Germany under Prussian dominance, Otto von Bismarck provoked the Austro-Prussian War in June 1866, using the dispute over the administration of Schleswig-Holstein as a pretext. In this conflict, also known as the Seven Weeks' War, Prussia was allied with Italy, and Austria with a number of German states, including Bavaria, Wurttemberg, Saxony and Hanover. Prussia easily overcame Austria and her allies. Austria was excluded from German affairs in the Treaty of Prague (23 August 1866). The war notwithstanding, Bismarck considered Austria a potential future ally and so avoided unnecessarily weakening the state, settling for the annexation of Hanover, Hesse, Nassau, Frankfurt and Schleswig-Holstein. (These moderate peace terms were to facilitate the Austro-German alliance of 1879.) The war resulted in the destruction of the German Confederation, and its replacement with the North German Confederation under the sole leadership of Prussia. The defeat of Austria was an additional blow to German nationalism: Austrian Germans found themselves isolated within the Habsburg Empire, with its multitude of national and ethnic groups. A look at the political divisions within the empire will give some idea of the extent of its multiculturalism. They included:

Austria; the kingdoms of Bohemia, Dalmatia and Galicia-Lodomeria; the arch-duchies of Lower Austria and Upper Austria; the duchies of Bukovina, Carinthia, Carniola Salzburg and Styria; the margraviates of Istria and Moravia; the counties of Gorizia-Gradisca, Tyrol and Vorarlberg; the crownland of Austrian-Silesia; Bosnia-Hercegovina; Lombardy (transferred to Italy in 1859), Modena (transferred to Italy in 1860), Tuscany (transferred to Italy in 1860) and Venetia (transferred to Italy in 1866); and the town of Trieste. (2)

As Goodrick-Clarke states, fears that the supremacy of the German language and culture within the empire would be challenged by the non-German nationalities resulted in a conflict of loyalties between German nationality and Austrian citizenship. This in turn resulted in the emergence of two principal nationalist movements: volkisch nationalism and the Pan-German movement, which we will discuss anon.

The second major change was the Ausgleich ('Compromise') of 1867, whereby the Habsburgs set up the Dual Monarchy of Austria-Hungary. The intention was to curb the nationalist aspirations of Slavs in both states, inspired by Slavs in the Ottoman Empire (including Serbs, Montenegrins and Albanians) who had taken advantage of the Turkish decline to establish their own states. As noted by the American historian Steven W. Sowards, 'The former revolutionaries [of 1848]—German and Magyar—became de facto "peoples of state", each ruling half of a twin country united only at the top through the King-Emperor and the common Ministries of Foreign Affairs and of War'. (3)

However, according to Norman Davies, the Ausgleich only served to make matters worse:

There was no chance that the German-speaking elite could impose its culture throughout Austria, let alone extend it to the whole of the Dual Monarchy. After all, 'Austria was a Slav house with a German facade'. In practice the three 'master races'—the Germans, the Magyars, and the Galician Poles—were encouraged to lord it over the others. The administrative structures were so tailored that the German minority in Bohemia could hold down the Czechs, the Magyars in Hungary could hold down the Slovaks, Romanians, and Croats, and the Poles in Galicia could hold down the Ruthenians (Ukrainians). So pressures mounted as each of the excluded nationalities fell prey to the charms of nationalism. (4)

The Ausgleich resulted in aspirations towards autonomy among a number of groups within the Austro-Hungarian Empire; the empire as a whole was home to eleven major nationalities: Magyars, Germans, Czechs, Poles, Ruthenians, Slovaks, Serbs, Romanians, Croats, Slovenes and Italians. The largest and most restless minority consisted of about 6.5 million Czechs living in Bohemia, Moravia and Austrian Silesia. However, their desires for autonomy were constantly frustrated by the Hungarian determination to preserve the political structure established by the Ausgleich.

German nationalism had been frustrated on two main occasions in the first half of the nineteenth century: at the Congress of Vienna in 1815, and after the revolutions of 1848. According to Goodrick-Clarke:

As a result of this slow progress towards political unification, Germans increasingly came to conceive of national unity in cultural terms. This tendency had begun in the late eighteenth century, when writers of the pre-Romantic Sturm und drang movement had expressed the common identity of all Germans in folk-songs, customs, and literature. An idealized image of medieval Germany was invoked to prove her claim to spiritual unity, even if there had never been political unity. This emphasis on the past and traditions conferred a strongly mythological character upon the cause of unification. (5)

He goes on:

The exclusion of Austria from the new Prussian-dominated Reich had left disappointed nationalists in both countries. Hopes for a Greater Germany had been dashed in 1866, when Bismarck consolidated the ascendancy of Prussia through the military defeat of Austria, forcing her withdrawal from German affairs. The position of German nationalists in Austria-Hungary was henceforth problematic. In 1867 the Hungarians were granted political independence within a dual state. The growth of the Pan-German movement in Austria in the following decades reflected the dilemma of Austrian Germans within a state of mixed German and Slav nationalities. Their program proposed the secession of the German-settled provinces of Austria from the polyglot Habsburg empire and their incorporation in the new Second Reich across the border. Such an arrangement was ultimately realized by the Anschluss of Austria into the Third Reich in 1938. (6)

The idealized, romantic image of a rural, quasi-medieval Germany suffered under the program of rapid modernization and industrialization undertaken by the Second Reich. For many, who saw their traditional communities destroyed by the spread of towns and industries, the foundations of their mystical unity had become threatened. In addition, these anti-modernist sentiments resulted in the rejection of both liberalism and rationalism, while paradoxically hijacking the scientific concepts of anthropology, linguistics and Darwinist evolution to 'prove' the superiority of the German race.

A set of inner moral qualities was related to the external characteristics of racial types: while the Aryans (and thus the Germans) were blue-eyed, blond-haired, tall and well-proportioned, they were also noble, honest, and courageous. The Darwinist idea of evolution through struggle was also taken up in order to prove that the superior pure races would prevail over the mixed inferior ones. Racial thinking facilitated the rise of political anti-Semitism, itself so closely linked to the strains of modernization. Feelings of conservative anger at the disruptive consequences of economic change could find release in the vilification of the Jews, who were blamed for the collapse of traditional values and institutions. Racism indicated that the Jews were not just a religious community but biologically different from other races. (7)

The Volkisch Movement and Pan-Germanism

As mentioned earlier, the fears and aspirations of German nationalists led to the formation of two highly influential movements, volkisch nationalism and Pan-Germanism. The intention of the volkisch movement was to raise the cultural consciousness of Germans living in Austria, particularly by playing on their fears for their identity within the provinces of mixed nationality in the Austro-Hungarian Empire. The word volkisch is not easy to translate into English, containing as it does elements of both nationalism and a profound sense of the importance of folklore. The main principles of volkisch thought were the importance of living naturally (including a vegetarian diet); an awareness of the wisdom of one's ancestors, expressed through the appreciation of prehistoric monuments; and an understanding of astrology and cosmic cycles. (As more than one commentator has noted, there is a distinct and rather sinister similarity between these principles and those of the modern New Age movement.)

The ideas of the volkisch movement were propagated through educational and defense leagues called Vereine. In 1886, Anton Langgassner founded the Germanenbund, a federation of Vereine, at Salzburg under the banner of Germanic Volkstum (nationhood). The Vereine were particularly popular amongst young people and intellectuals; such was their popularity, in fact, that an unsettled Austrian government dissolved the Germanenbund in 1889, although it re-emerged in 1894 as the Bund der Germanen. Goodrick-Clarke estimates that by 1900, as many as 150,000 people were influenced by volkisch propaganda.

According to the historian of Nazism, Eugene Davidson, the followers of the volkisch movement: believed the troubles of the industrial order—the harshness, the impersonality, the sharp dealing, the ruthless speculators—would only be exorcised by a return to Ur-Germanism, to the German community, the ancient Teutonic gods, and a Germanic society unsullied by inferior, foreign intrusions. Nations might endure such foreign elements, but a Volk was an organic unity with a common biological inheritance. The culture-bearing Volk of the world, incomparably superior among the races, was the German; therefore, the only proper function of a German state was to administer on behalf of the Volk; everything international was inferior and to be rejected. A sound economy would be based on agriculture rather than on industry with its international, especially Jewish influences; and in religion, a German God would have to replace the Jewish God. (8) [Original emphasis.]

Volkisch ideology was propagated through a number of racist publications, one of the most virulent of which was the satirical illustrated monthly Der Scherer, published in Innsbruck by Georg von Schonerer (1842-1921), a leader in the movement, whom Davidson describes as 'anti-Catholic, anti-Semitic, and often ludicrous'. (9) The anti-Catholic and anti-Semitic articles in Der Scherer were accompanied by drawings of fat priests and big-nosed Jews, the latter a prototype of the Jewish stereotype that would be later used in National Socialist propaganda. In one picture, a

Jew and a priest are sitting on a mound of writhing people, who represent the Volk, while another shows the Devil in Hell, with a sign saying: 'Spa for Jews and Jesuits.' (10)

Jews were consistently attacked from two directions: volkisch anticlerical groups linked them with the reactionary Church, while clerical anti-Semites linked them with volkisch heathenism. Jews were therefore seen as 'either godless socialists or capitalist exploiters ... and the hidden, international rulers of financial and intellectual life'. (11) As we shall see later, these views would survive Nazism, and have extended their pernicious influence through various right-wing groups active today. One Catholic paper, Die Tiroler Post, wrote in 1906 that the goal of the Jew was world domination, while another, the Linzer Post, defended anti-Semitism as no more than healthy self-preservation. In the same year, the volkisch Deutsche Tiroler Stimmen called for the extermination of the Jewish race. (12)

If the volkisch movement attempted to raise German national and cultural consciousness, Pan-Germanism operated in a more political context, beginning with the refusal of Austrian Germans to accept their exclusion from German affairs after the Austro-Prussian War of 1866. The movement originated among student groups in Vienna, Graz and Prague, which were inspired by earlier German student clubs (Burschenschaftern) following the teachings of Friedrich Ludwig Jahn (1778-1850). Jahn, a purveyor of volkisch ideology, advocated German national unity, identity and romantic ritual. These groups advocated kleindeutsch (or 'little German') nationalism, which called for the incorporation of German Austria into the Bismarckian Reich. As Goodrick-Clarke notes, 'This cult of Prussophilia led to a worship of force and a contempt for humanitarian law and justice.'

(13) Georg von Schonerer's involvement with Pan-Germanism transformed it from a nebulous 'cult of Prussophilia' into a genuine revolutionary movement. Following his election to the Reichsrat in 1873, Schonerer followed a progressive Left agenda for about five years, before making demands for a German Austria without the Habsburgs and politically united with the German Reich. Schonerer's Pan-Germanism was not characterized merely by national unity, political democracy and social reform: its essential characteristic was racism, 'that is, the idea that blood was the sole criterion of all civil rights'. (14)

The Pan-German movement experienced something of a setback in 1888, when Schonerer was convicted of assault after barging into the offices of Das Neue Wiener Tageblatt and attacking the editor for prematurely reporting the death of the German emperor, Wilhelm I. He was sentenced to four months' imprisonment, lost his title of nobility (15) and was deprived of his political rights for five years.

When the Austrian government decided in 1895 that Slovene should be taught in the German school at Celje in Carniola, and two years later the Austrian premier, Count Casimir Badeni, ruled that all officials in Bohemia and Moravia should speak both Czech and German (thus placing Germans at a distinct disadvantage), the flames of nationalism were once again fanned throughout the empire. The result was that the

Pan-Germans, together with the democratic German parties, followed a strategy of blocking all parliamentary business, which in turn led to violent public disorder in the summer of 1897.

By this time, Schonerer had identified an additional enemy in the Catholic Church, which he regarded as inimical to the interests of Austrian Germans. 'The episcopate advised the emperor, the parish priests formed a network of effective propagandists in the country, and the Christian Social party had deprived him of his earlier strongholds among the rural and semi-urban populations of Lower Austria and Vienna.' (16) The association of Catholicism with Slavdom and the Austrian state could further be emphasized, Schonerer believed, by a movement for Protestant conversion; this was the origin of the slogan 'Los von Rom' ('Away from Rome'). The movement claimed approximately 30,000 Protestant conversions in Bohemia, Styria, Carinthia and Vienna between 1899 and 1910, (17) although it was not at all popular among either the volkisch leagues or the Pan-Germans, who saw it as 'a variation of old-time clericalism'. (18) For that matter, the Protestant Church itself was rather dissatisfied with Los von Rom, and felt that its profound connection of religion with politics would make religious people uneasy. By the same token, those who were politically motivated felt religion itself to be irrelevant.

By the turn of the century, Pan-Germanism could be divided into two groups: those who, like Schonerer, wanted political and economic union with the Reich, and those who merely wanted to defend German cultural and political interests within the Habsburg empire. These interests were perceived as being radically undermined, not only by the Badeni language decrees, but also by the introduction in 1907 of universal male suffrage. This could only exacerbate the growing German-Slav conflict within the empire, and was one of the main factors in the emergence of the racist doctrine of Ariosophy, which we will discuss later. In 1853-55, Arthur de Gobineau had written an essay on the inequality of races, in which he had made claims for the superiority of the Nordic-Aryan race, and warned of its eventual submergence by non-Aryans. This notion, along with the ideas about biological struggle of Social Darwinism, was taken up at the turn of the twentieth century by German propagandists who claimed that Germans could defend their race and culture only by remaining racially pure. (19)

The volkisch nationalists and Pan-Germans found further inspiration in the work of the zoologist Ernst Haeckel who, in 1906, founded the Monist League to spread his racist interpretation of Social Darwinism. Seven years earlier, Haeckel's colleague, Wilhelm Bolsche, had written a book entitled Vom Bazillus zum Affenmenschen (From the Bacillus to the Apeman), in which he had described the 'naked struggle for dominance between the zoological species "Man" ' and 'the lowest form of organic life [microscopic organisms]'.

(20) This 'struggle for dominance' was to have a profound effect upon the development of German anti-Semitism in the early years of the twentieth century. Hitler would later express his own anti-Semitism in these biological terms, in order to de-

prive Jews of all human attributes. On one occasion in 1942, for instance, Hitler said: The discovery of the Jewish virus is one of the greatest revolutions the world has seen. The struggle in which we are now engaged is similar to the one waged by Pasteur and Koch in the last century. How many diseases must owe their origin to the Jewish virus! Only when we have eliminated the Jews will we regain our health. (21)

GERMAN THEOSOPHY

The revival of Germanic mythology and folklore in Austria in the last two decades of the nineteenth century was of enormous importance to the development of Nazi esotericism and cosmology, yet it must he viewed in the context of a much wider occult revival that had been taking place in Europe for about one hundred years. The central concepts of what would become Western occultism, such as Gnosticism, Hermeticism and the Cabala, which originated in the eastern Mediterranean more than 1,500 years ago, had been largely banished from Western thought by the scientific revolution of the seventeenth century.

At this point, it is worth pausing to consider the meanings of these concepts. Gnosticism (gnosis simply means direct knowledge), as practiced by early Christian heretics, contains two basic tenets. The first is dualism, which can, according to Michael Baigent and Richard Leigh, be defined thus:

Dualism, as the word itself suggests, presupposes an opposition, often a conflict, between two antithetical principles, two antithetical hierarchies of value, two antithetical realities. In dualism, certain aspects or orders of reality are extolled over others. Certain aspects of reality are repudiated as unreal, or inferior, or evil. In its distinction between soul and body, between spirit and 'unregenerate nature', Christianity is, in effect, dualist. (22)

The second tenet concerns the evil of matter:

Matter was rejected as intrinsically evil. Material creation, the phenomenal world, was deemed to be the handiwork of a lesser and malevolent god. In consequence, matter and material creation had to be transcended in order to attain union with a greater and truer god, whose domain was pure spirit; and it was this ' union that the term 'gnosis' signified ... [Gnostic] thinking had probably originated in the similar dualism of Persian Zoroastrianism. It was subsequently to surface again in Persia, under a teacher known as Mani, and to be called Manicheism. (23)

Hermeticism derives from Hermes Trismegistus ('the thrice-greatest Hermes'), the name given by the Greeks to the Egyptian god Thoth, the god of wisdom and of literature. To the Greeks, this 'scribe of the gods' was author of all sacred books, which they called 'Hermetic'. The ancient wisdom of Hermes is said to reside in 42 books, the surviving fragments of which are known as the Hermetica. The books of Hermes were written on papyrus and kept in the great library of Alexandria. When the library was destroyed by fire, most of this wisdom was forever lost; however, some fragments were saved and, according to legend, buried in a secret desert location by initiates.

Hermetic works such as The Divine Pymander and The Vision describe the means by which divine wisdom was revealed to Hermes Trismegistus, and also contain discourses on the evolution of the human soul. The Tabula smaragdina or Emerald Tablet is said to contain the most comprehensive summation of Egyptian philosophy, and was of central importance to the alchemists, who believed that it was encoded with the mystical secrets of the Universe. Hermes Trismegistus is said to have been the greatest philosopher, king and priest, and was also a somewhat prolific writer, being credited with 36,525 books on the principles of nature. A composite of the Egyptian god Thoth and the Greek god Hermes, both of whom were associated with the spirits of the dead, Hermes Trismegistus was the personification of universal wisdom. However, it is likely that the writings attributed to him were actually the anonymous works of early Christians.

The third element in the threefold foundation of Western occultism was the Cabala, the mystical system of classical Judaism. Translated from the Hebrew as 'that which is received', the Cabala is founded on the Torah (Jewish scriptures) and is a kind of map, given to Adam by angels and handed down through the ages, by which our fallen species may find its way back to God. The primary document of Cabalism is the Sefer Yetzirah (Book of Creation), which was possibly written in the third century by Rabbi Akiba, who was martyred by the Romans. According to the Sefer Yetzirah, God created the world by means of 32 secret paths: the ten sephirot (or emanations by which reality is structured) and the 22 letters of the Hebrew alphabet.

Between 1280 and 1286, the Spanish Cabalist Moses de Leon wrote the Sefer ha-Zohar (Book of Splendor), the primary document of classical Cabalism. It is centered upon the Zohar, a body of teachings developed by the second-century sage Rabbi Simeon bar Yohai during his meditation in a cave near Lod, Israel. In the Zohar, God is referred to as Ein-Sof (without end), and as such cannot be represented or known by fallen humanity. The human goal is to realize a union with God and, since all of reality is connected, thereby to elevate all other souls in the Universe.

In the West, Cabalism came to form a principal foundation of occultism, with its magical amulets and incantations, seals and demonology, and its concentration on the power inherent in the letters of the Hebrew alphabet. Christian occultists focused on the Tetragrammaton YHVH, the unspeakable name of God, through which it was possible to gain power over the entire Universe. (24)

The occult revival in Europe came about primarily as a reaction to the rationalist Enlightenment and materialism of the eighteenth and early nineteenth centuries. This lamentably but necessarily brief look at its esoteric origins brings us to the emergence of Theosophy in the 1880s. The prime mover behind Theosophy was Helena Petrovna Blavatsky (1831-1891). Her parents, Baron von Hahn, a soldier and member of the lesser Russian-German nobility, and Madame von Hahn, a romantic novelist and descendant of the noble house of Dolgorouky, led a somewhat unsettled life: the baron's regiment was constantly on the move. Madame von Hahn died in 1842, when Helena was eleven, an event which seems to have contributed to her waywardness and powerful sense of individuality.

OCCULT SECRETS OF THE THIRD REICH

At seventeen she married Nikifor Blavatsky, Vice-Governor of Yerevan in the Caucasus, and 23 years her senior in July 1848. The marriage failed after only a few weeks and Helena left her husband with the initial intention of returning to her father. However, she suddenly decided instead to leave her family and country behind, boarded a steamer on the Black Sea and headed for Constantinople. (25) For the next 25 years, she wandered through Europe, Asia and the Americas. Although she may have had an allowance from her father, she also supported herself in a variety of ways, including as a bareback rider in a circus, a piano teacher in London and Paris, and also as an assistant to the famous medium Daniel Dunglas Home. This is pretty much all that is known with any certainty about this period in her life: the rest is a confusing jumble of rumor, contradiction and legend, much of which originated with Blavatsky herself.

During a trip to the United States in 1873, Blavatsky observed the enormous popularity of Spiritualism. She had arrived with no money and had to live in a hostel for working women, doing menial jobs such as sewing purses. At about this time, she met Henry Olcott (1832-1907), whose New Jersey family claimed descent from the pilgrims. Apparent financial difficulties forced Olcott to take up farming in Ohio, at which he seems to have excelled, gaining a position as Agricultural Editor of the New York Tribune, until the outbreak of the Civil War, in which he fought as a signals officer in the Union Army. When the war ended, Olcott headed to New York to study for the Bar, and established a law practice there in the late 1860s. (26) In spite of a fair degree of success in his profession, Olcott seems to have been rather dissatisfied with his lot: his marriage was not happy, and eventually he divorced his wife. In search of some form of intellectual diversion, he became interested in Spiritualism.

As his interest in the subject grew, Olcott began to investigate individual cases of alleged psychic manifestations, including those occurring on the Eddy farm at Chittenden, Vermont. His investigation of the events at Chittenden (which included spirit materializations) were written up as articles for a New York paper, the Daily Graphic. On 14 October 1874, Olcott met Blavatsky at the Eddy farmhouse during one of his many visits there. Blavatsky had been intrigued by the articles she had read in the Daily Graphic, and had decided to cultivate Olcott's friendship.

Greatly impressed with her apparent mediumistic skills, Olcott became Blavatsky's devotee and publicist. From then until 1875, when she founded the Theosophical Society, Blavatsky earned a comfortable living as a medium, only falling on hard times when the nationwide interest in Spiritualism began to wane. In 1877, Blavatsky published Isis Unveiled, an exposition of Egyptian occultism that, she claimed, had been dictated to her by spirits via a form of automatic writing, and which argues, essentially, for the acceptance of occultism (hidden laws of nature) to be accepted by orthodox science. Its effect—the book sold widely—was to soothe the minds of those whose religious faith had been undermined by scientific rationalism, in particular the theories on evolution and natural selection of Charles Darwin. Perhaps unsurprisingly, the book was fiercely attacked in scholarly circles both for intellectual incompetence and out-and-out plagiarism, with one critic identifying more than 2,000 unacknowledged quotations. (27)

Central to the mythos Blavatsky constructed for herself was her experience of living and traveling for seven years in Tibet. (The number seven is of considerable magical significance, and is the number of years required for initiates into occult mysteries to complete their apprenticeship.) (28) She made the rather astonishing claim that she had studied with a group of Hidden Masters in the Himalayas, under whose guidance she had reached the highest level of initiation into the mysteries of the Universe. It is, however, extremely unlikely that a single white woman with a considerable weight problem and no mountaineering experience could have made the arduous trip up the Himalayas, succeeded in finding these 'Hidden Masters', and done so without being spotted by the numerous Chinese, Russian and British patrols that were in the area at that time. (29)

One of the Tibetan adepts with whom Blavatsky studied was named Master Morya. She actually met him at the Great Exhibition in London in July 1851 (although she claimed to have met him in visions on numerous occasions previously). Master Morya was a member of the Great White Brotherhood of Masters, immortal, incorporeal beings who had achieved ultimate enlightenment, but had elected to remain on Earth to guide humanity towards the same goal. We shall have a good deal more to say on the Great White Brotherhood in Chapter Five, but for now let us return to Madame Blavatsky.

In 1879, with the Theosophical Society not doing particularly well at recruiting converts, Blavatsky decided to go to India, a logical choice in view of the emphasis placed on eastern philosophy in Isis Unveiled. She and Olcott enjoyed a warm reception from various members of Indian society, including the journalist A. P. Sinnett and the statesman Alien O. Hume. In 1882, they moved the society's headquarters to Adyar, near Madras. The new headquarters included a shrine room in which the Hidden Masters would manifest in physical form. However, while Blavatsky and Olcott were away touring Europe, Emma Coulomb and her husband, who had managed the household but been dismissed after repeatedly attempting to secure financial loans from the society's wealthy members, decided to take their revenge by publishing letters said by them to have been written by Blavatsky and which contained instructions on how to operate the secret panels in the shrine room, through which the 'Masters' appeared.

Unfortunately for Blavatsky, it was at this time that the Society for Psychical Research (SPR) decided to investigate the mediumistic claims of Theosophy. Needless to say, when the Coulombs' revelations of trickery came to light, the SPR issued a scathing report on Blavatsky and her claims.

Injured by the scandal and with her health failing (she would later die of Bright's Disease), Blavatsky left India and settled in London, where she began work on her second and (it is generally acknowledged) greater book, The Secret Doctrine (published in 1888). Comprising two main sections, 'Cosmogenesis' and 'Anthropogenesis', the book is nothing less than a history of the Universe and intelligent life. The Secret Doctrine is allegedly a vast commentary on a fantastically old (several million years) manuscript called The Stanzas of Dzyan, written in the Atlantean language Senzar, and seen by Blavatsky in a monastery hidden far beneath the Himalayas. The Stanzas tell how the Earth was colonized by spiritual beings from the Moon. Humanity as we know it is descended from these remote ancestors via a series of so-called 'root races'.

Lack of space prevents us from going too deeply into the contents of The Secret Doctrine. Suffice to say that at the beginning of the Universe, the divine being differentiated itself into the multitude of life forms that now inhabit the cosmos. The subsequent history of the Universe passed through seven 'rounds' or cycles of being. The Universe experienced a fall from divine grace through the first four rounds, and will rise again through the last three, until it is redeemed in ultimate, divine unity, before the process begins again. (We would perhaps be well advised to resist the temptation to compare this scheme with the similar-sounding Big Bang/Big Crunch theory of universal evolution proposed by modern physicists: there is little else in the Stanzas that orthodox science would find palatable.)

Each of these cosmic rounds saw the rise and fall of seven root races, whose destiny mirrored exactly that of cosmic evolution, with the first four descending from the spiritual into the material and the last three ascending once again. According to Blavatsky, humanity in its present form is the fifth root race of Earth, which is itself passing through the fourth cosmic round. (The reader may thus find it a considerable relief that we have a long period of spiritual improvement ahead of us.) The first root race were completely noncorporeal Astral beings who lived in an invisible land; the second race were the Hyperboreans, who lived on a lost polar continent (we will examine the important concept of Hyperborea in detail in the next chapter); the third root race were the Lemurians, fifteen-foot-tall brown-skinned hermaphrodites with four arms, who had the misfortune to occupy the lowest point in the seven-stage cycle of humanity. For this reason, the Lemurians, who lived on a now-sunken continent in the Indian Ocean, suffered a Fall from divine grace: after dividing into two distinct sexes, they began to breed with beautiful but inferior races, this miscegenation resulting in the birth of soulless monsters. The fourth root race were the Atlanteans, who possessed highly advanced psychic powers and mediumistic skills. Gigantic like the Lemurians and physically powerful, the Atlanteans built huge cities on their mid-Atlantic continent. Their technology was also highly advanced, and was based on the application of a universal electro-spiritual force known as Fohat—similar, it seems, to the vril force (see Chapter Four). Unfortunately for the Atlanteans, although they were intelligent and powerful, they were also possessed of a childlike innocence that made them vulnerable to the attentions of an evil entity that corrupted them and caused them to turn to the use of black magic. This was to result in a catastrophic war that led to the destruction of Atlantis. (30) The fifth root race, from which we today are descended, was the Aryan race.

OCCULT SECRETS OF THE THIRD REICH

Theosophy placed a heavy emphasis on the importance of reincarnation and the concept of hierarchy. Through reincarnation, the movement's followers could imagine themselves to have participated in the fabulous prehistory of humanity in a variety of magical, exotic and long-lost locations, while feeling assured that their souls were on a definite upward trajectory, heading for spiritual salvation and ultimate unity with God. Of equal importance to the cosmic scheme were hierarchy and elitism. As mentioned earlier, the Hidden Masters or Mahatmas of Tibet, such as Master Morya and Koot Hoomi, were enlightened beings who had decided to remain on Earth to guide the rest of humanity towards spiritual wisdom. This concept, along with Blavatsky's own claim to hidden occult knowledge, is clearly based on the value of authority and hierarchy. Indeed, this value is illustrated by the fate of the Lemurians, whose miscegenation caused their Fall from divine grace. The only section of that society to remain pure was the elite priesthood, which eventually retired to the wondrous city of Shambhala in what is now the Gobi Desert (more of which in Chapter Four) and which is linked with the Hidden Masters of Tibet. (31)

As we have already noted, the central tenets of Theosophy offered a way for people in the late nineteenth century to maintain their religious faith (or, at least, their faith in the existence of some form of spirituality in the cosmos) while simultaneously accepting the validity of new theories, such as evolution, that threatened to undermine their previously held world view. However, for many people in Europe and America, scientific rationalism, rapid industrialization and urbanization presented another threat to their long-established way of life. As an antidote to the fears and uncertainties of modern life, Theosophy was particularly readily accepted in Germany and Austria. As Goodrick-Clarke notes, it was well suited to the German protest movement known as Lebensreform (life reform). 'This movement represented a middle-class attempt to palliate the ills of modern life, deriving from the growth of the cities and industry. A variety of alternative life-styles—including herbal and natural medicine, vegetarianism, nudism and self-sufficient rural communes—were embraced by small groups of individuals who hoped to restore themselves to a natural existence ... Theosophy was appropriate to the mood of Lebensreform and provided a philosophical rationale for some of its groups.' (32)

Interest in Theosophy increased in Germany with the founding of the German Theosophical Society on 22 July 1884 at Elberfeld. Blavatsky and Olcott were staying there at the home of Marie Gebhard (1832-1892), a devotee of occultism who had corresponded frequently with the famous French occultist and magician Eliphas Levi (Alphonse Louis Constant) (c. 1810-1875). Its first president was Wilhelm Hubbe-Schleiden, then a senior civil servant at the Colonial Office in Hamburg. Hubbe-Schleiden, who had travelled extensively throughout the world and was a keen advocate of German colonial expansion abroad, was instrumental in gathering the isolated Theosophists scattered throughout Germany into a consolidated German branch of the society. Hubbe-Schleiden also did much to increase occult interest in Germany through the founding in 1886 of his periodical Die Sphinx, a scholarly blend of psychical research, the paranormal, archaeology and Christian mysticism from a scientific viewpoint. As such it was firmly Theosophical in tone, and included contributions from scientists, historians and philosophers. (33)

Another great popularizer of scientific occultism in Germany was Franz Hartmann (18381912), who had also led a highly eventful life in Europe and the Americas, following a number of careers such as soldier, doctor, coroner and mining speculator. Already interested in Spiritualism, Hartmann was converted to Theosophy after reading Isis Unveiled and decided to travel to Adyar to meet Blavatsky and Olcott in 1883. So impressed was Blavatsky with him that she appointed him acting president of the Theosophical Society while she and Olcott travelled to Germany to start the branch there. Hartmann remained there until 1885, when the Theosophists left India following the Coulomb scandal.

Hartmann went on to found the occult periodical Lotusbluthen (Lotus Blossoms), which ran from 1892 to 1900 and was the first German publication to feature the swastika on its cover. (34) (In eastern mysticism, the swastika is a symbol with many positive connotations; we will examine it in detail in the next chapter.) The increased public interest generated by this periodical prompted a number of German publishers to issue long book series dealing with a wide range of occult and esoteric subjects, including the work of Annie Besant and Charles Leadbeater who took over the Theosophical Society on Blavatsky's death in 1891.

The German branch of the society had been dissolved in 1885 when the Theosophists left India, but was replaced by a new society founded in Berlin in August 1896 as a branch of the International Theosophical Brotherhood in America, with Hartmann as president. Also on the executive committee was one Paul Zillmann, who founded the monthly Metaphysische Rundschau (Metaphysical Review) and who would later publish the works of the Ariosophists (whom we shall meet shortly). By 1902, German Theosophy, which had hitherto suffered from internecine rivalry, became far better coordinated under the two main centers at Berlin and Leipzig.

In 1906, a Theosophical Publishing House was founded at Leipzig by Hugo Vollrath, a disciple of Hartmann's, possibly to counter the new influence in occult circles of Theosophist Rudolf Steiner, whose mystical Christian stance did not endear him to Annie Besant whose own outlook was firmly Hindu. (Steiner would later leave and form his own Anthroposophical Society in 1912.) The Theosophical Publishing House produced a large number of occult magazines and book series, in competition with other publishers such as Karl Rohm, Johannes Baum and Max Altmann who had turned their attention to this potentially lucrative field.

The public interest in occultism quickly grew in Vienna, which already had its own tradition of esotericism and interest in paranormal phenomena. New occult groups were founded, including the Association for Occultism, which had its own lending library, the Sphinx Reading Club and the First Viennese Astrological Society. (35) In fact, it was in Vienna that the seeds of Germanic occult racism were most liberally sown. The public disquiet at economic change, scientific rationalism and rapid industrialization and the threat they appeared to pose to traditional 'natural' ways of life was palliated not only by occultist notions of the centrality and importance of humanity within the wider cosmos (of the essential meaningfulness of existence), but also by the volkisch ideology that assured Germans of the value and importance of their cultural identity. This combination of culture and spirituality was expressed most forcefully through the doctrine of Ariosophy, which originated in Vienna.

ARIOSOPHY

The bizarre theories of Ariosophy constituted a mixture of racist volkisch ideology and the Theosophical concepts of Madame Blavatsky. (As with the philosophy of Nietszche, Blavatsky's ideas were hijacked and warped by German occultists and it should be remembered that neither of these two would have advocated the violence and suffering that would later be perpetrated by the Nazis: indeed, Nietszche disavowed anti-Semitism and called German nationalism an 'abyss of stupidity'.)

The two principal personalities behind Ariosophy were Guido von List (1848-1919) and Jorg Lanz von Liebenfels (1874-1954), both of whom added the undeserved particle 'von' (denoting nobility) to their names. Born in Vienna to a prosperous middle-class family, List Dreamed of the reunification of Austria with Germany, and hated both Jews and Christians for the attacks he perceived them to have made upon German culture, spirituality and territorial rights. A journalist by trade, List also wrote novels about the ancient Teutons and the cult of Wotan, whose hierarchy he came to call the Armanenschaft, a name derived from his spurious interpretation of a Teutonic myth. According to the Roman author Tacitus in his Germania, the Teutons believed that their people were descended from the god Tuisco and his son, Mannus. Mannus had three sons, after whom the ancient German tribes were named: Ingaevones, Hermiones and Istaevones. With no scholarly evidence to back him up, List decided that these names referred to the agricultural, intellectual and military estates within the Germanic nation. The word Armanenschaft derived from List's Germanization of Hermiones, the intellectual or priestly estate, to 'Armanen'. List claimed that the profoundly wise Armanenschaft was the governing body of the ancient society.

(36) List's codification of his beliefs regarding the ancient and racially pure Teutons led to a profound interest in the symbolism of heraldry and the secrets allegedly contained in the runic alphabet, an interest that included the mystical significance of the swastika which he identified (at least in terms of its power and significance) with the Christian Cross and the Jewish Star of David. (As indicated earlier, we shall examine the origin and meaning of the swastika in the next chapter.) By 1902, as a result of a period of enforced inactivity following a cataract operation that left him blind for eleven months, List had devoted much thought to the nature of the proto-Aryan language he believed was encoded in the ancient runes.

His occult-racist-mystical theories, including an exposition on the Aryan proto-language, did not find particular favor with the Imperial Academy of Sciences in

OCCULT SECRETS OF THE THIRD REICH

Vienna, which returned without comment a thesis he had sent. Nevertheless, the anti-Semitic elements in German and Austrian society began to take note, and in 1907 a List Society was formed to provide financial aid in his researches. List's spurious historiography and archaeology provided a pseudo-scientific basis for both racism and extreme nationalism, and enabled the German Volk to trace their ancestry back to the splendor and racial purity of the ancient Teutons and their cult of Wotanism.

The cult of Wotan arose primarily from List's beliefs regarding the religious practices of the ancient Teutons, whom he considered to have been persecuted by Christians in early medieval Germany. In List's view, the Old Norse poems of Iceland, Norway, Denmark and Sweden, the Eddas, were actually chronicles of the myths of the ancient Germans. The Eddas were composed of songs, manuals of poetry and works of history telling the story of the ancient Teutonic pantheon of gods and the numerous secondary divinities who were their cohorts. In fact, we have almost no record of the myths and beliefs of the ancestors of the Germans and Anglo-Saxons. According to conventional studies of mythology:

For the Germanic tribes of the West, the ancestors of the Germans and Anglo-Saxons, documentary sources of information are sparse. Latin historians like Caesar and Tacitus had at their disposal only second-hand information and they attempted to explain Teutonic religion in terms of Roman religion. For instance, Donar, the thunder-god, became for them Jupiter tonans. Woden received the name Mercury and Tiw [the sky-god] was called Mars. The missionaries, monks and clerks who, from the eighth century, pursued their work of conversion and were at the same time the first to write the German language could, had they wished to, have given us a complete picture of German mythology in the early centuries. But their chief concern was to save souls. Hence they scarcely alluded to pagan myths except to condemn them. We should know practically nothing of the old German beliefs if 'popular' tales and epics had not preserved much that pertains to secondary divinities, demons, giants and spirits of all sorts. (37) [Original emphasis.]

In the Eddas, Wotan (whose name derives from the word in all Germanic languages meaning fury, and which in modern German is wuten, to rage) was the god of war, whom dead heroes met in Valhalla. It was Wotan who gained an understanding of the runes after being wounded by a spear and hanging from a tree for nine nights, and who related the eighteen runic spells that held the secrets of immortality, invincibility in battle, healing abilities and control of the elements. In Norse legend, the runes are not only a system of writing but also possess an inherent magical power. Goodrick-Clarke describes List as 'the pioneer of volkisch rune occultism', (38) since he was the first to link the runes of a certain written series with Wotan's runic spells. 'List attributed a specific individual rune to each of Wotan's verses, adding occult meanings and a summary motto of the spell. These occult meanings and mottoes were supposed to represent the doctrine and maxims of the rediscovered religion of Wotanism. Typical mottoes were: "Know yourself, then you know everything!" ... and "Man is one with God!" ' (39)

OCCULT SECRETS OF THE THIRD REICH

The central tenet of Wotanism was the cyclical nature of the Universe, which proceeded through a series of transformations: 'birth', 'being', 'death' and 'rebirth'. This cyclical cosmology was a primal law and represented the presence of God in Nature. Since Man was part of the cosmos, he was bound by its laws and thus required to live in harmony with the natural world. 'A close identity with one's folk and race was reckoned a logical consequence of this closeness to Nature.' (40)

List also utilized Theosophical concepts in his development of Wotanism, in particular those of Max Ferdinand Sebaldt von Werth who wrote extensively on Aryan sexuality and racial purity. Sebaldt believed that the Universe was whisked into being by the god Mundelfori, and that its fundamental nature was one of the interaction of opposites, such as matter and spirit, and male and female. Aryan superiority could therefore only be achieved through a union of racially 'pure opposites'. In September 1903, List published an article in the Viennese occult periodical Die Gnosis that Drew heavily on this idea, referring to ancient Aryan cosmology and sexuality. The phases of this cosmology were illustrated with variations on the swastika, the Hindu symbol of the Sun, that List appropriated and corrupted to denote the unconquerable and racially pure Germanic hero.

(41) List was also heavily influenced by legends of lost civilizations and sunken continents, such as the fabled lands of Atlantis and Lemuria, and by the theosophical writings of Madame Blavatsky. He went so far as to compare the Wotanist priesthood with the hierophants of Blavatsky's The Secret Doctrine. Theosophical concepts also formed the basis of his Die Religion der Ario-Germanen (1910), in which he devoted considerable space to the Hindu cosmic cycles which had inspired Blavatsky's concept of 'rounds' or cosmological cycles. List identified the four rounds of fire, air, water and earth with 'the mythological Teutonic realms of Muspilheim, Asgard, Wanenheim and Midgard, which were tenanted respectively by fire-dragons, air-gods, water-giants and mankind'. (42) These realms lie at the centre of the Nordic creation myth. At the dawn of time, there was nothing but a vast, yawning abyss. Niflheim, a realm of clouds and shadows, formed to the north of the abyss, while to the south formed the land of fire called Muspilheim. When Ymir, the first living being and the father of all the giants, was slain in battle, his body was raised from the sea and formed the earth, Midgard. (43) According to List, the Ario-Germans were the fifth race in the present round, the preceding four corresponding to the mythical Teutonic giants.

Wotanist doctrine held that the natural evolutionary cycle of the Universe was from unity to multiplicity and back to unity. The first stage of this evolution (unity to multiplicity) was represented symbolically by anticlockwise triskelions and swastikas and inverted triangles. The second stage (multiplicity back to the unity of the godhead) was represented by clockwise and upright symbols. In this scheme, the Ario-German was seen as the highest possible form of life, since he occupied the 'zenith of multiplicity at the outermost limit of the cycle'. (44)

List was a fervent believer in the lost civilizations of Atlantis and Lemuria, and claimed that the prehistoric megaliths of Lower Austria were actually Atlantean artifacts.

In his Die Ursprache der Ario-Germanen (The Proto-Language of the Ario-Germans) (1914), he included a chart comparing the geological periods of Earth with a Hindu kalpa (4,320,000,000 years), which also corresponded to a single theosophical round. We will have much more to say on the Ariosophist belief in lost civilizations later in this chapter, and in the next.

For now, let us turn our attention to the other principal personality in Ariosophy, List's young follower Jorg Lanz von Liebenfels, who founded the notorious anti-Semitic hate sheet Ostara and created the Order of the New Templars in 1907. Like his mentor List, Liebenfels had a middle-class Viennese upbringing, which he would later deny in favor of an imagined aristocratic background.

Liebenfels chose as a headquarters for the Order of the New Templars a ruined castle, Burg Werfenstein, perched on a cliff on the shores of the River Danube between Linz and Vienna. He was obsessed with the idea of a Manichaean struggle between the 'blond' race (characterized by creativity and heroism) and the dark 'beast-men', who were consumed with lust for 'blonde' women and who were bent on the corruption of human culture. Two years earlier, Liebenfels had established the racist periodical Ostara (named after the pagan goddess of spring) that called repeatedly for the restoration of the 'blond race' as the dominant force in the world. This could only be achieved through racial purity, the forced sterilization or extermination of inferior races, and the destruction of socialism, democracy and feminism. (45)

These racist concerns led Liebenfels to conceive the bizarre notion of founding a chivalrous order based on the monastic and military orders of the Crusades. As Goodrick-Clarke notes, Liebenfels had been drawn since childhood to 'the Middle Ages and its pageant of knights, noblemen, and monks. His decision to enter the Cistercian noviciate owed much to these sentiments, and it is likely that his adult desire to identify with the aristocracy derived from similar fantasies.' (46) Liebenfels's fantasies also included holy orders, which perhaps naturally resulted in an intense interest in the Order of the Knights Templar. This interest was fueled by the medieval Grail Romances, which were at the time enjoying a widespread popularity due to their treatment by Richard Wagner in his operas. To Liebenfels and many of his contemporaries, such romances were significant in their painting of the Grail Knights as searchers after sublime and eternal values: this view provided a powerful antidote to the hated modern world with its rampant industrialization and materialism.

The most renowned and applauded Order in Christendom at the time of the Crusades was undoubtedly the Knights Templar, and Liebenfels developed a fantasy in which these knights became champions of a racist struggle for a Germanic order that would enjoy a hegemony over the Mediterranean and the Middle East. According to Goodrick-Clarke:

In 1913 he published a short study, in which the grail was interpreted as an electrical symbol pertaining to the 'panpsychic' powers of the pure-blooded Aryan race. The quest of the 'Templeisen' for the Grail was a metaphor for the strict eugenic practices of the Templar knights designed to breed god-men. The Templars had become the key historical agent of [Liebenfels's] sexo-racist gnosis before 1914. (47)

At this point, it is worth looking very briefly at the history of the Knights Templar and how their rise and fall influenced Liebenfels's Weltanschauung (world view). The Order of the Knights Templar became one of the most powerful monastic societies in twelfth-century Europe, and came to symbolize the Christian struggle against the infidel. In AD 1118, a knight from Champagne named Hugh of Payens persuaded King Baldwin I of Boulogne (whose elder brother, Godfrey, had captured Jerusalem nineteen years before) to install Payens and eight other French noblemen in a wing of the royal palace, the former mosque al-Aqsa, near the site where King Solomon's Temple had allegedly once stood in the Holy Land. The Order later comprised three classes: the knights, all of noble birth; the sergeants, drawn from the bourgeoisie, who were grooms and stewards; and the clerics, who were chaplains and performed non-military tasks. (48) Choosing the name Militia Templi (Soldiers of the Temple), (49) they vowed to defend the mysteries of the Christian faith and Christians traveling to the holy places. The Order initially derived its power from St Bernard of Clairvaux, head of the Cistercian Order, and from Pope Honorius II, who officially recognized the Templars as a separate Order in 1128. (50) It is believed that the Templars took their inspiration from the Hospitallers, who protected Catholic pilgrims in Palestine and pledged themselves to a life of chastity and poverty.

The Seal of the Templars showed two knights riding on a single horse—a sign of their poverty (at least in their early days); the design was retained for decades after the Order had become one of the richest of the time. (51) The vast wealth that the Templars were to acquire was partly the result of the Order's exemption from local taxes, coupled with their ability to levy their own taxes on the community. The Templars honored their vow of poverty for the first nine years of their existence, relying on donations from the pious even for their clothes. Their battle standard was a red eight-pointed cross on a black-and-white background; their battle cry was 'Vive Dieu, Saint Amour' ('God Lives, Saint Love'), and their motto was 'Non nobis, Domine, non nobis, sed Nomini Tuo da gloriam' ('Not for us, Lord, not for us, but to Thy Name give glory'). (52)

Over the next century and a half, the Templars amassed a truly staggering amount of wealth, property (with over seven thousand estates in Europe) and power, and had branches throughout Europe and the Middle East, all run from their headquarters in Paris. This led to jealous rivalries, and during the Crusades rumors began to circulate that the Templars were not the pious Christian knights many believed them to be. Attention was focused on their secret rituals, which their enemies claimed were centered upon their worship of Allah; others suspected them of actually worshipping the demon Baphomet, practicing horrendous black magic rites involving sodomy, bestiality and human sacrifice, of despising the Pope and the Catholic Church, and various other crimes.

In 1307, King Philip IV of France, heavily in debt to the Templars, decided to use these rumors in an attempt to engineer their downfall. On 13 October, he seized their Temple in Paris and arrested the Grand Master, Jacques de Molay, and 140 Templars, whom he subjected to horrible tortures in order to secure confessions. Philip persuaded Pope Clement V to authorize the seizure of all Templar properties. Pope Clement abolished the Order in 1312 at the Council of Vienne, and transferred its properties to the Hospitallers, in return for the money Philip claimed was owed by the Templars. (53)

Jacques de Molay was promised life in prison if he made a public confession of the Order's crimes. Instead, he made a public proclamation of the Order's innocence of all crimes with which it had been charged, and for this he was burned at the stake. However, this was apparently not the end of the Knights Templar: there have been persistent rumors that those Templars who managed to evade capture fled to Scotland disguised as stonemasons and created the society of Freemasons. It has also been suggested that a Templar named Geoffroy de Gonneville received a message from de Molay shortly before his death and took it to a group of Templars meeting in Dalmatia. The message stated that the Order would be revived in 600 years' time. Before disbanding, the Templars at this meeting allegedly created the Order of the Rose-Croix, or Rosicrucians.

(54) To Lanz von Liebenfels, the brutal suppression of the Knights Templar and the appropriation of their wealth and property represented the victory of racial inferiors over a society of heroic men. The result was racial chaos, the corruption of 'ario-Christian' civilization and the disorder of the modern world. (55) For this reason, Liebenfels decided to resurrect the Order in the form of his Ordo Novi Templi (ONT). He described the Order as an 'Aryan mutual-aid association founded to foster racial consciousness through genealogical and heraldic research, beauty-contests, and the foundation of racist Utopias in the underdeveloped parts of the world'. (56)

The early activities of the ONT revolved around festivals and concerts, with hundreds of guests being shipped in by steamer from Vienna. They were routinely reported in the press, thus ensuring a wider audience for Liebenfels and the racist ideas presented in Ostara. Membership of the ONT was naturally restricted to those who could prove that they were of pure Aryan blood and who would vow to protect the interests of their (racial) brothers.

Two years before he founded the ONT, Liebenfels had published a book with the incredibly odd title Theozoologie oder die Kunder von den Sodoms-Afflingen und dem Gotter-Elektron (Theo-zoology or the Lore of the Sodom-Apelings and the Electron of the Gods). The word 'theo-zoology' was arrived at through the amalgamation of Judaeo-Christian doctrine and the principles of the then-burgeoning field of life-sciences. Using the Old and New Testaments as departure points, Liebenfels divided his book into two sections, the first dealing with the origin of humanity in a race of beast-men (Anthropozoa) spawned by Adam. In his warped and bizarre view of antiquity, Liebenfels utilized new scientific discoveries such as radiation and radio communication, which at that time had a powerful hold on the public imagination.

Liebenfels applied these discoveries in his description of the gods, which held that they were not really gods at all, but higher forms of life (Theozoa) who possessed fantastic mental faculties including telepathy (which was actually the transmission of electrical signals between the brains of the Theozoa). Through the millennia, these god-men gradually lost these faculties through miscegenation with the beast-men of Adam, until their telepathic sense organs became atrophied as the pineal and pituitary glands of modern humanity. As Goodrick-Clarke notes, (57) Liebenfels based this declaration in part on the work of the zoologist Wilhelm Bolsche (1861-1939), who in turn seems to have been inspired by Theosophy. At any rate, Liebenfels believed that the only way for Germans to reclaim their ancient godhood was through the enforced sterilization and castration of 'inferior races', to prevent the pollution of pure Aryan blood. (58)

The second section of Liebenfels's book concerned the life of Christ (whose powers were once again electrical in nature) and the redemption of the Aryan people, who had been corrupted by the promiscuous activities of the other races of Earth. This idea of the Aryan struggle against the pernicious vices of other races in effect replaced the traditional Judaeo-Christian concept of the struggle between good and evil. Liebenfels argued for the most extreme measures in the pursuit of Aryan re-deification: since the poor and underprivileged in society were identified with the progeny of the inferior races, they would have to be either exterminated (by incineration as a sacrifice to God), deported or used as slave labour. This constituted the inversion of traditional Judaeo-Christian compassion for the poor, weak and handicapped in the new form of Social Darwinism, with its central tenet of survival of the fittest at the expense of the weakest. These horrific methods of ensuring the survival of pure-blooded Aryans proposed by Liebenfels would, of course, become hideous reality in the Third Reich.

Although List's and Liebenfels's ideas were inherently hateful and violent, they remained just that: ideas. Many of their followers became more and more restless and dissatisfied with their lack of action against the perceived threat to the Aryan race from the various inferior beings with whom they were forced to share their nation, in particular the Jews, who were blamed for the perceived evils of urbanization, industrialization and the threat to the traditional rural way of life of the Aryan peasant-hero. Many came to believe that the time for scholarly theorizing was past, that the time for direct action had come.

THE GERMANENORDEN

In May 1912, a meeting was held at the Leipzig home of Theodor Fritsch. At this meeting were approximately twenty prominent Pan-Germans and anti-Semites. Their purpose was to found two groups to alert Germans to the dangers to small businesses they perceived as arising from the influence of Jewish business and finance. These groups were known as the Reichshammerbund and the Germanenorden (Order of

Germans). Born on 28 October 1852, Fritsch, the son of Saxon peasants, had trained as a milling engineer, and had edited the Kleine Muhlen-Journal (Small-Mills Journal). In common with other activists of the time, his anti-Semitism arose principally from a fear of rapid industrialization, technology and mass production, driven by international Jewish influence, and the threat it posed to small tradesmen and craftsmen.

In spite of his political leanings, Fritsch decided against becoming a candidate for either of the two German anti-Semitic parties, the Deutsch-Soziale Partei and the Antisemitische Volkspartei, which had been established at Bochum in 1889, since he did not believe that anti-Semitism would prove successful in parliament. As Goodrick-Clarke notes, Fritsch's 'conviction in the ineffectiveness of parliamentary anti-Semitism proved to be correct. When more than one party existed after the Bochum conference, their competition led to a reduction in the number of successful anti-Semitic candidates at the Reichstag elections.'

(59) In addition, the merging of the two parties in 1894 as the Deutsch-Soziale Reformpartei resulted in a significant reduction in anti-Semitism in favor of 'an appeal to more conservative and middle-class economic interests'. (60) At this time, in the mid-1860s, racist writers such as the French aristocrat Comte Vacher de Lapouge and the Germanized Englishman Houston Stewart Chamberlain were influenced by biology and zoology, and were concentrating more on 'scientific' studies of race (although they were, of course, nothing of the kind). It was these writers who identified the Jews as the greatest threat to the supremacy of the Aryan race, and attempted to back up their ideas with reference to physical characteristics such as hair and eye coloring, and the shape of the skull. (61) For de Lapouge, Jews were more pernicious than any other race because they had insinuated themselves so completely into European society, (62) while Chamberlain in particular did much to popularize mystical racism in Germany. According to Stanley G. Payne:

Beyond the Aryan racial stereotype (tall, blond, blue-eyed) [Chamberlain] affirmed the existence of a special 'race soul' that created a more imaginative and profound spirit in Aryans and produced a 'German religion', though the latter was still (in part) vaguely related to Christianity. The ultimate anti-Aryan and most bitter racial foe was the Jew. Chamberlain combined Social Darwinism with racism and thus emphasized an endless racial struggle on behalf of the purity of Aryanism and against Jews and lesser peoples [including Slavs and Latins], virtually creating a scenario for race war. (63)

In order to fulfill his ambition to create a powerful anti-Semitic movement outside the ineffectual parliament, Fritsch founded a periodical called the Hammer in January 1902. By 1905, its readership had reached 3,000. These readers formed themselves into Hammer-Gemeinden (Hammer-Groups), changing their name in 1908 to Deutsche Erneuerungs-Gemeinde (German Renewal Groups). '[T]heir membership was interested in anti-capitalist forms of land reform designed to invigorate the peasantry, the garden city movement, and Lebensreform.' (64)

OCCULT SECRETS OF THE THIRD REICH

The Reichstag elections of January 1912 saw a humiliating defeat for Conservatives and anti-Semites, who lost 41 of their 109 seats, while the Social Democratic Party increased their seats from 43 to 110. (65) In the Hammer, Fritsch favorably reviewed a violently anti-Semitic book entitled Wenn ich der Kaiser war! (If I were Kaiser!) by the chairman of the Pan-German League, Heinrich Class, and decided that the time was right to act in the formation of an anti-Semitic organization that would not be subject to the control or influence of any party.

As already stated, at the meeting in Fritsch's Leipzig home on 24 May 1912 two groups were established: the Reichshammerbund, which combined all existing Hammer-Groups, and the Germanenorden, whose secret nature reflected the conviction of anti-Semites that Jewish influence in public life could only be the result of a secret international conspiracy and as such could only be combated by a quasi-Masonic lodge whose members' names would be withheld to prevent enemy infiltration. (66)

Germanenorden lodges were established throughout Northern and Eastern Germany that year, and called for the rebirth of a racially pure Germany from which the 'parasitic' Jews would be deported. By July, lodges had been established at Breslau, dresden, Konigsberg, Berlin and Hamburg. By the end of 1912, the Germanenorden claimed 316 brothers. (67) The main purpose of these lodges was to monitor Jewish activities; in addition, lodge members aided each other in business dealings and other matters.

The Germanenorden was heavily influenced by the doctrines of Ariosophy. Any German wishing to join the order was required to supply details of hair, eye and skin color, and also had to prove beyond any doubt that they were of pure Aryan descent. Anyone suffering from a physical handicap—and for that matter, anyone who looked 'unpleasant'—was barred from membership. Ariosophy also inspired the emblems used by the Order. According to Goodrick-Clarke: 'From the middle of 1916 the official Order newsletter, the Allgemeine Ordens-Nachrichten, began to display on its front cover a curved-armed swastika superimposed upon a cross ... Although the swastika was current among several contemporary volkisch associations in Germany, it was through the Germanenorden and the Thule Society, its successor organization in post-war Munich, that this device came to be adopted by the National Socialists.' (68)

The initiation rituals of the Germanenorden were somewhat bizarre, to say the least. Initiation would take place in the ceremonial room of the lodge, where the blindfolded novice would encounter the Master, two Knights in white robes and horned helmets, the Treasurer and Secretary with white Masonic sashes, and the Herald, who stood at the centre of the room. 'At the back of the room in the grove of the Grail stood the Bard in a white gown, before him the Master of Ceremonies in a blue gown, while the other lodge brothers stood in a semicircle around him as far as the tables of the Treasurer and Secretary. Behind the grove of the Grail was a music room where a harmonium and piano were accompanied by a small choir of "forest elves".' (69)

Upon commencement of the ceremony, the brothers sang the Pilgrims' Chorus from Wagner's Tannhauser, while the brothers made the sign of the swastika. The novice was then informed of the Order's world-view, and the Bard lit the sacred flame in the grove of the Grail. 'At this point the Master seized Wotan's spear and held it before him, while the two Knights crossed their swords upon it. A series of calls and responses, accompanied by music from Lohengrin, completed the oath of the novices.' (70)

With the outbreak of the First World War in 1914, the Germanenorden began to suffer problems, both with membership and finance. Many members of the Order were killed in action, and the Order's chief, Hermann Pohl, feared that the war would ultimately result in its destruction. At that time, Pohl's leadership abilities were coming under attack from several high-ranking members who were becoming tired of the emphasis he placed on ritual and ceremony of the type indicated above. On 8 October 1916, representatives of the Berlin lodge suggested that Pohl should be relieved of his position, to which Pohl responded by declaring the formation of a breakaway order, the Germanenorden Walvater of the Holy Grail. The original Order was then headed by General-major Erwin von Heimerdinger. (71)

Following the schism of 1916, the Germanenorden became seriously weakened, with many members confused as to its status (many assumed that it had been disbanded).

However, the end of the war in November 1918 saw attempts to revive its fortunes and influence. Grand Master Eberhard von Brockhusen believed that the Order would benefit from a constitution, which he succeeded in establishing in 1921, 'which provided for an extraordinarily complex organization of grades, rings, and provincial "citadels" (Burgen) supposed to generate secrecy for a nationwide system of local groups having many links with militant volkisch associations ..,' (72)

In the post-war period, the Germanenorden's verbal violence was transformed into murderous activities against public figures. The new Republic was, of course, despised as a symbol of defeat, and it was the Germanenorden that ordered the assassination of Matthias Erzberger, the former Reich Finance Minister and head of the German delegation to Compiegne (one of the so-called 'November criminals') (73) who had signed the armistice. His killers, Heinrich Schulz and Heinrich Tillessen, had settled in Regensburg in 1920, where they met Lorenz Mesch, the local leader of the Germanenorden. Since they had become interested in volkisch ideology after the end of the war, and were heavily influenced by its propaganda, the Order chose them to assassinate Erzberger, which they did in August 1921.

From 1921, the Germanenorden became the focus for right-wing and anti-Semitic sentiments in the hated Weimar Republic. When Rudolf von Sebottendorff joined Hermann Pohl's breakaway Germanenorden Walvater in 1917, the seed of the legendary Thule Society was sown.

THE THULE SOCIETY

The mythology surrounding the Arctic realm of Thule has its origins in another myth, that of Atlantis. Although the 'lost continent' of Atlantis was held for centuries to have existed in the Atlantic Ocean 'beyond the Pillars of Hercules' (according to Plato in two of his dialogues, the Timaeus and Critias), this view was challenged in the late seventeenth century by the Swedish writer Olaus Rudbeck (1630-1702) who claimed that the lost civilization, which had conquered North Africa and much of Europe 9,000 years before, had actually been centered in Sweden.

This curious notion was taken up in the mid-eighteenth century by a French astronomer and mystic named Jean-Sylvain Bailly (1736-1793) who came to the conclusion that the great achievements of civilizations such as Egypt and China were the result of knowledge inherited from a vastly superior antediluvian culture that had resided in the far North. According to Bailly, when the Earth was younger, its interior heat was much greater, and consequently the North Polar regions must have enjoyed a temperate climate in remote antiquity. Combining this idea with his belief that such climates are the most conducive to science and civilization, Bailly identified Rudbeck's Atlanteans with the Hyperboreans of classical legend. The placing of this high civilization in the far north resulted in the Nordic physique (tall, blond-haired and blue-eyed) being seen as the ultimate human ideal.

The origin of the Nazi concept of Thule and the Thule Society can be traced to Guido von List, Jorg Lanz von Liebenfels and Rudolf von Sebottendorff (1875-1945). As we have already noted, all three added the particle 'von', suggesting noble descent, to their otherwise undistinguished names. As Joscelyn Godwin observes in his study of Polar mythology, Arktos (1993), 'One of the hallmarks of master-race philosophy is that no one is known to have embraced it who does not consider himself a member of that race. And what is more tempting, having once adopted the belief that one's own race is chosen by Nature or God for pre-eminence, than to put oneself at its aristocratic summit?' (74)

As we have seen, in 1907, Liebenfels founded the ritualistic and virulently racist Order of the New Templars, which had the dubious distinction of serving as the prototype for Heinrich Himmler's SS (Schutzstaffel). Liebenfels was an avid student of Madame Blavatsky, who developed the notion that humanity was descended from a series of 'Root Races' that had degenerated throughout the millennia from a pure spiritual nature to the crude and barbarous beings of the present. According to Blavatsky, the origin of the anthropoid apes could be explained as the result of bestiality committed by the Third Root Race of humanity with monsters. Liebenfels in effect hijacked this concept and twisted it in the most appalling way, claiming that the non-Aryan races were the result of bestiality committed by the original Aryans after their departure from the paradise of their northern homeland, a lost continent he called Arktogaa (from the Greek, meaning 'northern earth').

These ideas found favor with Guido von List, like Liebenfels a native of Vienna, who was instrumental in the development of the volkisch movement. As we saw earlier, this movement was characterized by a love of unspoiled Nature, vegetarianism, ancient wisdom, astrology and earth energies. List had already played a crucial role in the founding of the secret, quasi-Masonic Germanenorden, whose aim was to counter what its members saw as the corruption by Jewry of German public life that was clearly the result of a secret international conspiracy. The Germanenorden was still active during the First World War, publishing a newsletter and placing advertisements in newspapers inviting men and women 'of pure Aryan descent' to join its ranks. It was in response to one of these advertisements that Rudolph von Sebottendorff met the leader of the Germanenorden, Hermann Pohl.

Sebottendorff had originally intended to be an engineer; however, having failed to complete his studies at the Berlin-Charlottenburg Polytechnic, and thus having little chance of qualified employment in Germany, he decided to go to sea. In 1900, after service on a number of steamships, and an abortive career as a gold prospector in Western Australia, Sebottendorff made his way first to Egypt and then to Turkey, where he immersed himself in a study of the Turkish people and cultivated an intense interest in occult science and ancient theocracies.

By 1916, Sebottendorff, now married, had settled in Bad Aibling, a fashionable Bavarian spa. At their meeting in Berlin in September of that year, Sebottendorff learned of Pohl's conviction that contamination by other races (particularly Jews) had robbed the Aryan race of its knowledge of magical power, and that this knowledge could only be regained through racial purity. On his return to Bad Aibling, Sebottendorff immediately set about organizing a recruitment campaign for the Germanenorden in Bavaria.

In 1918, Sebottendorff met an art student named Walter Nauhaus who had been badly wounded on the Western Front in 1914 and had been invalided out of the war. Nauhaus shared Sebottendorff's intense interest in the occult, and soon became an invaluable colleague in the Bavarian recruitment campaign for the Germanenorden. It was Nauhaus who suggested that the name of the order be changed from Germanenorden to Thule Gesellschaft (Thule Society), in order, according to Goodrick-Clarke, to 'spare it the unwelcome attentions of socialist and pro-Republican elements'. (75) The ceremonial foundation of the Thule Society took place on 17 August 1918. The society met at the fashionable Hotel Vierjahreszeiten in Munich, in rooms decorated with the Thule emblem: a long dagger, its blade surrounded by oak leaves, superimposed on a shining, curved-armed swastika.

On the eve of the Armistice that signaled German defeat in the First World War, the Thule Society, appalled at the prospect of the Kaiser abdicating, not to mention the revolution in Bavaria which had seen the seizure of authority by the Soviet Workers' and Soldiers' Councils, held a meeting on 9 November 1918, at which Sebottendorff made an impassioned exhortation to his fellow Thuleans:

Yesterday we experienced the collapse of everything which was familiar, dear and valuable to us. In the place of our princes of Germanic blood rules our deadly enemy: Judah. What will come of this chaos, we do not know yet. But we can guess. A time will come of struggle, the most bitter need, a time of danger [...] I am determined to pledge the Thule Society to this struggle. Our Order is a Germanic Order, loyalty is also Germanic. [...] And the eagle is the symbol of the Aryans. In order to depict the eagle's capacity for self-immolation by fire, it is colored red. From today on our symbol is the red eagle, which warns us that we must die in order to live. (76)

The Thule Society continued to meet at the Hotel Vierjahreszeiten, while Sebottendorff extended its influence from the upper and middle classes to the working classes via the use of popular journalism. He achieved this by purchasing for 5,000 marks a minor weekly newspaper, published in Munich and called the Beobachter, in 1918. Renaming the paper the Munchener Beobachter und Sportblatt, Sebottendorff added sports features to attract a more youthful, working-class readership for the anti-Semitic editorials that had been carried over from the paper's previous proprietor, Franz Eher. (In 1920, the Munchener Beobachter und Sportblatt became the Volkischer Beobachter, which would later be the official newspaper of the Nazi Party.)

On 26 April 1919, seven members of the Thule Society were captured by Communists and taken to the Luitpold Gymnasium, which had served as a Red Army post for the previous two weeks. The hostages included Walter Nauhaus, Countess Hella von Westarp (secretary of the society) and Prince Gustav von Thurn und Taxis (who had many relatives in the royal families of Europe). Four days later, on 30 April, the hostages were shot in the cellar of the Gymnasium as a reprisal for the killing of Red prisoners at Starnberg. The killing of the Thule Society members had the effect of catalyzing a violent popular uprising in Munich that, with the aid of White troops entering the city on 1 May, ensured the demise of the Communist Republic.

In 1918, Sebottendorff had succeeded in extending the journalistic influence of the Thule Society to the working classes by asking a sports reporter on a Munich evening paper, Karl Harrer, who had an intense interest in volkisch ideology, to form a workers' ring. This small group met every week throughout the winter of 1918, and discussed such topics as the defeat of Germany and the Jewish enemy. At the instigation of Anton drexler, the workers' ring became the Deutsche Arbeiterpartei (German Workers' Party) (DAP) on 5 January 1919. In February 1920, the DAP was transformed into the National Socialist German Workers' Party (NSDAP). By that time, the party had already been infiltrated by an army spy whose orders had been to monitor its activities. Instead, he supported it, drafted new regulations for the committee, and soon became its President. His name was Adolf Hitler.

THE EDDA SOCIETY

As we saw earlier in this chapter, Guido von List and his followers believed that the Icelandic Eddas were chronicles of the ancient Aryans. List's occult-historical system was elaborated upon by Rudolf John Gorsleben (1883-1930), a playwright-turned-journalist who was born in Metz and grew up in Alsace-Lorraine (annexed by the German Reich in 1871). In this environment, in which people's loyalties were divided between France and Germany, Gorsleben was exposed to Pan-German nationalism and succeeded in tracing his ancestry back to a fourteenth-century noble family in Thuringia. (77)

At the outbreak of the First World War, Gorsleben fought first in a Bavarian regiment and then in a unit attached to the Turkish army in Arabia When the war ended he went to Munich, where he became involved with the Thule Society and right-wing politics. During an eventful three years, Gorsleben became Gauleiter of the South Bavarian section of the Deutschvolkischer Schutz- und Trutzbund, an anti-Semitic group that was competing with the early Nazi Party. He formed associations with right-wing figures such as Julius Streicher, who would later edit the Nazi organ Der Stunner, and Lorenz Mesch, the Germanenorden chief who had been instrumental in the assassination of Erzberger.

Through his periodical Deutsche Freiheit (German Freedom) -later renamed Arische Freiheit (Aryan Freedom)—Gorsleben disseminated his occult racist ideas, which centered upon the concept of racial purity and the reactivation of the occult powers that every Aryan possessed but which had become atrophied. With these magical powers once more at their fullest, the Aryan would hold complete sway over the processes of nature, and would thus be in a position to dominate and rule the world. He reiterated the volkisch notion that racial mixing was not only detrimental to the superior partner but also that a female could be tainted merely by intercourse with a racial inferior, and that all subsequent offspring, even if conceived with a racial equal, would likewise be tainted. (78)

With regard to the Eddas, Gorsleben believed that the Scandinavian runes contained an inherent magical power that provided those who understood their significance with a spiritual conduit through which could flow the force that drives the Universe itself. By far the most powerful was the asterisk-like hagall rune, since within it could be found hidden all the other runes. In addition, Gorsleben was perhaps the first occultist to promote the magical significance of crystals, which he considered to be three-dimensional projections of the runes. According to this theory, the spirit of every human individual can be correlated to a specific type of crystal that can be apprehended through the faculty of mediumship.

In November 1925, Gorsleben founded the Edda Society in the medieval town of Dinkelsbuhl in Franconia. The treasurer of the society was Friedrich Schaefer, an associate of Karl Maria Wiligut, who would come to exert a great influence upon Heinrich Himmler. When Gorsleben died from heart disease in August 1930, the Edda Society was taken over by Werner von Bulow (1870-1947), who had designed a 'world-rune-clock' which illustrated the correspondences between the runes, the zodiac, numbers and gods.

(79) Bulow also took over the running of Gorsleben's periodical, and changed its name from Arische Freiheit to Hag All All Hag, and then Hagal. Although the primary intention of the Edda Society was to conduct research into the ancient Aryan religion through the interpretation, via the runes, of Norse mythology, the history of the lost Atlantean civilization and the numerous prehistoric monuments of Europe, it nevertheless declared its allegiance to National Socialism in 1933, stating in an article in Hagal that the rise of Nazism was occurring in accordance with universal laws. Hagal also included material on the ancestral clairvoyant memories of Wiligut, which

were felt to be of extreme significance to an understanding of the ancient occult heritage of the Germanic people.

Interestingly, not all rune scholars subscribed wholeheartedly to the racist, anti-Semitic interpretation of the Eddas. For example, one rune occultist, Friedrich Bernhard Marby (1882-1966), synthesized rune scholarship with astrology after encountering the writings of Guido von List. In his paper Der eigene Weg (established 1924) and his book series Marhy-Runen-Bucherei (begun in 1931), Marby emphasized the health benefits gained from meditation on the runes. He was denounced as an anti-Nazi by the Third Reich in 1936, and sent first to Welzheim concentration camp, and then to Flossenburg and Dachau, and was only freed when the camps were liberated by the Allies in April 1945.

(80) Although he lacked the virulently racist outlook of the other volkisch occultists of the period, Marby subscribed to a similar theory to that espoused by Liebenfels: namely, the essentially electrical nature of the cosmos, inspired (as noted earlier) by the recent discovery of radiation and the new uses to which electricity was being put. In Marby's opinion, the Universe was awash with cosmic rays, which could be both received and transmitted by human beings. In addition, the beneficial influences of these rays could be increased by adopting certain physical postures in imitation of rune-forms (a practice with an obvious similarity to yoga).

In 1927, Siegfried Adolf Kummer (b. 1899) founded a rune school called 'Runa' at dresden. Runa concentrated on the practice of ritual magic, including the drawing of magic circles containing the names of the Germanic gods and the use of traditional magical tools such as candelabra and censers. During these rituals, the names of runes were called out and rune shapes were traced in the air as an aid to the magical process. Like Marby, Kummer was denounced by Wiligut, who considered their methods disreputable. (81)

Other occultists were more concerned with astrology and more overtly paranormal (in today's parlance) subjects than rune occultism. Georg Lomer (1877-1957) trained as a physician, but after encountering Theosophy turned his attention to alternative methods of medicine, particularly the use of Dream symbolism and palmistry in the diagnosis of illness. By 1925, Lomer had added astrology to his occult interests, resulting in a synthesis of pagan Germanic mysticism with astrology. As Goodrick-Clarke observes: 'In common with the other post-war Aryan occultists, Lomer essentially used occult materials to illuminate the forgotten Aryan heritage.' (82)

The defining element in the occultism practiced in Germany and Austria in the late nineteenth and early twentieth centuries was the perceived evil and corruption of the modern world, particularly that of the despised Weimar Republic with its stench of defeat, weakness and decadence. For people like List, Liebenfels, Sebottendorff and their followers, the future of humanity lay not in industrialization, urbanization and international finance (which they saw as causing the destruction of traditional, rural ways of life and the brutalization of their ancestral homelands) but in the resurgence of ancient Aryan culture and the maintenance of racial purity. For the Aryans were heirs to a fabulous mystical legacy stretching far into prehistory, all the way back to the lost realms of Atlantis, Lemuria, Hyperborea and Ultima Thule. From out of the mists of time shone this lost Golden Age of giants and god-men endowed with fantastic, superhuman abilities but who had been subsumed through miscegenation with inferior races—and were now gone. The volkisch occultists hoped, through their activities, to forge a magical and cultural link with these lost times, and through racial segregation and later genocide re-establish the global hegemony of the Aryan Superman.

Having completed our survey of Germanic occultism as developed and practiced around the turn of the twentieth century, we must now leap back several thousand years into the past and turn our attention to that lost Golden Age itself. We are about to enter the strange realm of crypto-history, which will require us to travel far from Germany in the inter-war years—indeed, far from the orthodox view of humanity's entire history. In this way, we shall be able to identify the mythological origins of volkisch occultism in the legends of the lost Aryan homeland. In the following chapter, we will find ourselves traversing the icy fastness of the far North, as well as an ancient sea in what is now the Gobi Desert. We shall also reacquaint ourselves with Madame Blavatsky and her theories of the Root Races of humanity; and, by the end of the chapter, we will have examined the origins, mystical significance and ultimate corruption of the swastika, at which point we will have prepared ourselves for the harrowing journey into the nightmarish world of Nazi occultism itself.

2—FANTASTIC PREHISTORY
THE LOST ARYAN HOMELAND

As we have seen, the idea of a fabulous and mysterious homeland of the Aryan people, lying hidden somewhere in the far northern latitudes, was not an invention of the Nazis but had a rich provenance not only in the tradition of Western occultism but also in the burgeoning science of anthropology. (Indeed, the very concept of an 'Aryan Race' owed its existence as much to philology as any other branch of enquiry.) (1)

Until the Enlightenment, of course, biblical tradition had been assumed to be the ultimate authority on the origin and history of humanity, that origin being Mount Ararat on which Noah's Ark made landfall after the Deluge. This idea made sense even to those scientists of the Enlightenment who rejected biblical authority, since mountainous regions would have provided the only possible protection against natural disasters such as the putative prehistoric flood.

The German Romantics were greatly attracted to Oriental philosophy and mysticism, in particular the Zend-Avesta, the sacred text of the ancient Persians. Thinkers of the calibre of Goethe, Nietzsche, Arthur Schopenhauer and Richard Wagner found in the Orient a system of philosophy and historiography that allowed them to abandon the unsatisfactory world view of Judeo-Christianity. (2) As Joscelyn Godwin notes, allied with this admiration for the Orient was a rediscovery of the German Volk, the pre-Christian Teutonic tribes whose descendants, the Goths, had brought about the final destruction of the decadent Roman Empire. The problem faced by the German Romantics was how to forge a historical connection between themselves and the Orient, which they considered to be the cradle of humanity and the origin of the highest human ideals.

Godwin asks, concerning the early Teutons:

But where had those noble and gifted tribes come from? Were they, too, sons of Noah, or dared one sunder them from the biblical genealogy? The time was ripe to do so. The French Encyclopedists had set the precedent of contempt for the Hebrew scriptures as a source of accurate information. The British School of Calcutta, with their Asiatic Researches, had revealed another world, surely more learned, and to many minds philosophically and morally superior to that of Moses. If the Germans could link their origins to India, then they would be forever free from their Semitic and Mediterranean bondage. (3)

Of course, in order to establish and strengthen the link between the Germans and the Orient, Hebrew had to be abandoned as the original language of humanity, to be replaced by Sanskrit, the language of classical Hinduism. Instrumental in the forging of this link was the classical scholar Friedrich von Schlegel (1772-1829), who attempted to establish a historical and cultural contact between the Indians and the Scandinavians through which the Scandinavian languages could have been influenced by the Indian. Schlegel solved this problem by supposing that the ancient Indians had travelled to the far north as a result of their veneration for the sacred mountain, Meru, which they believed to constitute the spiritual centre of the world.

It was actually Schlegel who coined the term 'Aryan' in 1819 to denote a racial group (as opposed to a group of people speaking the Proto-Indo-European language, which is the proper definition of the term). Schlegel took the word 'Aryan', which had already been borrowed from Herodotus (who had used the word Arioi to describe the people of Media, an ancient western Asian country in what is now northern Iran) and applied to the ancient Persians, and connected it spuriously with the German word Ehre, meaning honor. At that point, the word 'Aryan' came to denote the highest, purest and most honorable racial group." (4) This historical scheme was added to by other thinkers such as the anti-Semitic Christian Lassen, who claimed that the Indo-Germans were inherently biologically superior to the Semites.

The philologist Max Muller would later urge the adoption of the term 'Aryan' instead of 'Indo-Germanic', since the latter term did not include other European peoples who could, like the Indians and Germans, trace the origin of their languages to Sanskrit. According to the historian Leon Poliakov, by 1860 cultivated Europeans had come to accept that there was a fundamental division between Aryans and Semites. Godwin expresses this dogma in straightforward terms: ' (1) Europeans were of the Aryan Race; (2) This race had come from the high plateaus of Asia. There had dwelt together the ancestors of the Indians, Persians, Greeks, Italians, Slavonians, Germans, and Celts, before setting off to populate Europe and Asia.' (5)

As we noted in Chapter One, the ideas of Charles Darwin were hijacked at this time by the proponents of Aryan racial superiority, and the concept of the survival of the fittest was readily applied to the interaction between racial groups (however spurious and misguided this system of grouping might have been). Darwin's assumption that evolution through natural selection would necessarily result in gradual improvements to each species was inverted by Aryan racism, which maintained that the White Race had long ago reached perfection and was being corrupted and undermined through miscegenation with inferior races.

As Godwin informs us, plans were being laid in some quarters for the biological 'improvement' of the human race back in the late nineteenth century. The French writer Ernest Renan believed that selective breeding in the future would result in the production of 'gods' and 'devas':

A factory of Ases [Scandinavian heroes], an Asgaard, might be reconstituted in the center of Asia. If one dislikes such myths, one should consider how bees and ants breed individuals for certain functions, or how botanists make hybrids. One could concentrate all the nervous energy in the brain ... It seems that if such a solution should be at all realizable on the planet Earth, it is through Germany that it will come. (6)

THE POLAR PARADISE

In their desire to rediscover the ultimate mythical and cultural roots of their self-designated master race, the proponents of Aryanism turned away from the heat of the biblical Mesopotamian Eden and looked instead to the cool and pristine fastness of the Far North. The eighteenth-century polymath Jean-Sylvain Bailly (1736-1793) had already done much of the groundwork for a radical re-interpretation of humanity's origin with his highly original combination of Eastern mysticism and astronomy. According to Bailly, the ancient cultures of Egypt, Chaldea, China and India were actually the heirs of a far older body of knowledge, possessed in the distant past by a long-lost superior culture living in the antediluvian North. (7)

Bailly believed that it was this ancient culture that invented the zodiac in around 4600 BC. After the Flood, members of this civilization moved from northern Asia to India. For Bailly, this assertion was supported by the similarity of certain legends in later cultures living far from each other: for example, the legend of the Phoenix, which is found both in Egypt and in the Scandinavian Eddas (discussed in Chapter One). Bailly equated the details of the Phoenix's death and rebirth with the annual disappearance of the Sun for 65 days at 71° North latitude. He went on to compare the Phoenix with the Roman god Janus, the god of time, who is represented with the number 300 in his right hand, and the number 65 in his left (corresponding, of course, with the 300 days of daylight and 65 days of darkness each year in the far northern latitudes). Bailly thus concluded that Janus was actually a northern god who had moved south with his original worshippers in the distant past. In support of his theory, Bailly also cited the legend of Adonis, who was required by Jupiter to spend one third of each year on Mount Olympus, one third with Venus and one third in Hades with Persephone. Bailly connected this legend with conditions in the geographical area at 79° North latitude, where the Sun disappears for four months (one third) of the year. (8)

To Bailly, this strongly suggested the preservation of the ancient knowledge of a hitherto unknown Nordic civilization, which had been encoded in numerous legends passed down to subsequent cultures. These ideas corresponded somewhat with the work of one Comte de Buffon, who had concluded in 1749 that the Earth had formed much earlier than the Christian date of 4004 BC (although Buffon's date of 73,083 BC is still quite far from the Earth's actual age of approximately 4,000 million years). Buffon made the logical suggestion (within his scheme of creation) that the polar regions would have been the first to cool sufficiently to allow the development of life, and therefore placed the first human civilization in the far northern latitudes. For Bailly, this was ample justification for his own ideas concerning the Arctic region as the cradle of humanity. The reason for the southerly migration of this first civilization became obvious: since temperate climates are the most conducive to social, intellectual and scientific advancement, it clearly became necessary to move away gradually from the polar regions as they became too cold and the temperatures in the southern latitudes cooled from arid to temperate. The migration was finally complete when Chaldea, India and China were reached. (9)

The idea of a polar homeland for humanity was also elaborately developed by the Indian Bal Gangadhar Tilak (1856-1920) who wrote an epic work, The Arctic Home in the Vedas, while in prison in 1897 for publishing anti-British material in his newspaper, The Kesan. Published in 1903, Tilak's book concentrates on the age and original location of the Indian Vedic civilization, from its origin in the Arctic around 10,000 BC, through its destruction in the last Ice Age; the migration to northern Europe and Asia in 8000-5000 BC and the composition of the Vedic hymns; the loss of the Arctic traditions around 3000-1400 BC; to the Pre-Buddhistic period in 1400-500 BC. (10)

Tilak's reading of the ancient Vedic texts supported his assertion of a prehistoric homeland in the far north, describing as they did a realm inhabited by the gods where the sun rose and fell once a year. Godwin has this to say regarding Tilak's interpretation of the Vedic hymns:

The hymns are full of images that make nonsense in the context of a daily sunrise, such as the Thirty Dawn-Sisters circling like a wheel,' and the 'Dawn of Many Days' preceding the rising of the sun. If, however, they are applied to the Pole, they fall perfectly into place. The light of the sun circling beneath the horizon would be visible for at least thirty days before its annual rising. One can imagine the sense of anticipation felt by the inhabitants, as the wheeling light became ever brighter and the long winter's night came to an end."

Tilak's ideas on the origin of humanity were further developed by the Zoroastrian scholar H. S. Spencer in his book The Aryan Ecliptic Cycle (1965), in which he examines the Zoroastrian scriptures in much the same way that Tilak examined the Vedic texts. Spencer compared events in the scriptures with the various positions of the sun during the precession of the equinoxes. (At this point, we should pause briefly to examine this phenomenon. The rotational axis of the Earth is not perpendicular to the plane occupied by the Solar System: instead, it is tilted at an angle of 23 1/2 0. Due to gravitational forces from the Sun and the Moon, the axis of the Earth's rotation 'wobbles' very slightly; or, to be more precise, it describes a circle. As the planet rotates, its axis also rotates, describing a complete circle once every 26,000 years.) In this way, Spencer was able to date with considerable accuracy the events described in the Zoroastrian scriptures. Spencer set the date for the first appearance of the Aryans in the polar regions at 25,628 BC, during the Interglacial Age. The Aryans were forced to leave their homeland as the environment grew steadily colder and more hostile, and enormous reptiles began to appear. (How the reptiles themselves could have withstood the cold is another matter.) According to Spencer, the advent of the Ice Age that scattered the Aryans from their pleasant homeland was just one of a number of global catastrophes that proved the downfall of at least three other ancient civilizations: Atlantis, Lemuria and the culture occupying what is now the Gobi Desert. (12) According to Spencer, the Aryan tradition influenced the great civilizations of Egypt, Sumer and Babylon. From Hyperborea to Atlantis

The great Russian occultist Helena Blavatsky, whom we met in Chapter One, had considerable information to divulge on the nature of the lost civilizations whose philosophy and knowledge were passed down, in frequently garbled form, to the great civilizations of the Middle and Far East. According to Blavatsky, who claimed to have consulted a fantastically old document entitled the Stanzas of Dzyan while in Tibet, our remote ancestors occupied a number of lost continents, the first of which she describes as 'The Imperishable Sacred Land', an eternal place unencumbered by the sometimes violent fates reserved for other continents, that was the home of the first human and also of 'the last divine mortal'.

The Second Continent was Hyperborea, 'the land which stretched out its promontories southward and westward from the North Pole to receive the Second Race, and comprised the whole of what is now known as Northern Asia'. The 'Second Race' refers to one of the Root Races. Blavatsky continues:

The land of the Hyperboreans, the country that extended beyond Boreas, the frozen-hearted god of snows and hurricanes, who loved to slumber heavily on the chain of Mount Riphaeus, was neither an ideal country, as surmised by the mythologists, nor yet a land in the neighborhood of Scythia and the Danube. It was a real continent, a bond-fide land which knew no winter in those early days, nor have its sorry remains more than one night and day during the year, even now. The nocturnal shadows never fall upon it, said the Greeks; for it is the land of the Gods, the favorite abode of Apollo, the god of light, and its inhabitants are his beloved priests and servants. This may be regarded as poetized fiction now; but it was poetized truth then. (13) [Original emphasis.]

The Third Continent was Lemuria (so called by the zoologist P. L. Sclater in reference to a hypothetical sunken continent extending from Madagascar to Sri Lanka and Sumatra). Blavatsky claimed that the gigantic continent of Lemuria actually existed, its highest points now forming islands in the Pacific Ocean.

The Fourth Continent was Atlantis. 'It would be the first historical land, were the traditions of the ancients to receive more attention than they have hitherto. The famous island of Plato of that name was but a fragment of this great Continent.' (14)

In her description of the Fifth Continent, Blavatsky evokes images of cataclysmic seismic shifts in the land mass of the Earth:

The Fifth Continent was America; but, as it is situated at the Antipodes, it is Europe and Asia Minor, almost coeval with it, which are generally referred to by the Indo-Aryan Occultists as the fifth. If their teaching followed the appearance of the Continents in their geological and geographical order, then this classification would have to be altered. But as the sequence of the Continents is made to follow the order of evolution of the Races, from the first to the fifth, our Aryan Root-race, Europe must be called the fifth great Continent. The Secret Doctrine takes no account of islands and peninsulas, nor does it follow the modern geographical distribution of land and sea. Since the day of its earliest teachings and the destruction of the great Atlantis, the face of the earth has changed more than once. There was a time when the delta of Egypt and Northern Africa belonged to Europe, before the formation of the Straits of Gibraltar, and a further upheaval of the continent, changed entirely the face of the map of Europe. The last serious change occurred some 12,000 years ago, and was followed by the submersion of Plato's little Atlantic island, which he calls Atlantis after its parent continent. (15)

Blavatsky claimed to have read in the Stanzas of Dzyan that the Earth contained seven great continents, 'four of which have already lived their day, the fifth still exists, and two are to appear in the future' In The Secret Doctrine, she calls them Jambu, Plaksha, Salmali, Kusa, Krauncha, Saka and Pushkara. She continues:

We believe that each of these is not strictly a continent in the modern sense of the word, but that each name, from Jambu down to Pushkara, refers to the geographical names given (i) to the dry lands covering the face of the whole earth during the period of a Root-Race, in general; and (ii) to what remained of these after a geological [cataclysm]: and (iii) to those localities which will enter, after the future cataclysms, into the formation of new universal 'continents,' [or] peninsulas ... each continent being, in one sense, a greater or smaller region of dry land surrounded with water. [Original emphasis.] (16)

Aside from the Stanzas of Dzyan, Blavatsky drew on a huge number of religious texts, including the Hindu Puranas, which speak of a land called Svita-Dvipa (Hyperborea), or the White Island, at the centre of which is Mount Meru, the spiritual centre of the world. (We will have more to say of Mount Meru in Chapter Four.) If we accept the attributes given to Mount Meru in the sacred texts of the Hindus—including its height of 672,000 miles—then it must be conceded that the mountain does not exist anywhere on the physical Earth. This has led Orientalists to speculate that the White Island and Mount Meru are situated in what might best be described as another dimension occupying that same space as Earth and which is visible (and reachable) to beings possessing a sufficiently advanced spirituality. (17)

The legendary realm of Hyperborea also formed a centerpiece in the writings of the French occultist Rene Guenon (1886-1951) who, like Blavatsky (whom he nevertheless considered a charlatan), claimed to have received his information from hidden Oriental sources. Guenon's Hyperborea is very similar to Blavatsky's, although its origin is placed much more recently. According to Guenon, the present cycle of humanity began a mere 64,800 years ago in the Hyperborean land of Tula (Thule). Along with the later Atlantean civilization, which lasted for 12,960 years (or half of one precessional cycle), Hyperborea was the origin of all religious and spiritual tradition in our own modern world. Guenon also wrote of Mount Meru, although in symbolic terms: 'It seems from his essays on symbology that Guenon did not regard Meru as an actual mountain situated at the North Pole, but rather as a symbol of the earth's axis that passes through the pole and points to the Arktoi, the constellations of the Great and Little Bears. (Guenon also claimed that the inclination of the Earth's axis at 23 1/2° was a result of the Fall of humanity.)' (18)

At this point, we should pause to consider a question that may have occurred to the reader: assuming the existence of the prehistoric Root Races of humanity, why have none of their remains ever been discovered and excavated by archaeologists and palaeontologists? Apart from the obvious but not particularly satisfactory answer that the vast majority of the Earth's fossil record has yet to be discovered, it should be remembered that, according to Guenon, Blavatsky and the other Theosophists, the early Earth and its fabulous primordial inhabitants were not solid, corporeal entities, but were composed of a rarefied spiritual substance that only later descended into the material state. It is for this reason that their remains have never been discovered. (19)

For a basic chronology of the Earth according to this system, we can look to Godwin, who summarizes the development of Guenon's work by Jean Phaure. Between 62,000 and 36,880 BC was the Golden Age (Krita Yuga), which lasted for one full precessional cycle (25,920 years) beginning with the Age of Leo. This was the period before the descent into matter, when Paradise existed. Then came the period from 36,880 to 17,440 BC, the Silver Age (Treta Yuga), lasting 19,440 years. This age lasted from Leo to Sagittarius, and included the descent into matter. It also saw the rise of Hyperborea and the other continents of Lemuria and Mu. This was followed by the period from 17,440 to 4,480 BC, the Bronze Age (Dvapara Yuga), which lasted for half of one precessional cycle, and from Scorpio to Gemini. This age saw the fall of Atlantis around 10,800 BC, the colonization of other parts of the world by Atlantean refugees, the biblical Flood and the invention of writing. The period between 4,480 BC and AD 2000 is the Iron Age (Kali Yuga), which lasts for 6,480 years, from Taurus, through Aries to Pisces. This period includes our own history. The cycle ends with the Millennium and the beginning of the Age of Aquarius. Phaure has no problem with an incarnated humanity living in the Arctic, and suggests that they were able to do so with the aid of a spiritual energy source unknown to our own narrow, materialistic science. In support of this, he cites the case of certain Tibetan adepts who are able to live quite happily in the frigid Himalayan regions with little clothing. (20)

It is easy to see how the central tenets of Theosophy—the ancient and fantastic civilizations, the origins of the Aryan race and that race's position of high nobility—were attractive to the German occultists and nationalists who so hated the modern world of the late nineteenth and early twentieth centuries. As the researcher Peter Levenda observes:

'Modernism in general was seen as being largely an urban, sophisticated, intellectual (hence "Jewish") phenomenon, and this included science, technology, the Industrial Revolution, and capitalism.' (21) The doctrines of the Theosophists successfully fused science and mysticism, taking Darwin's theories regarding natural selection and the survival of the fittest and applying them to the concept of a spiritual struggle between the races of Earth (resulting in the Aryan race), which was a necessary component in the evolution of the spirit. (22)

Levenda continues:

It should be remembered that Blavatsky's works ... appear to be the result of prodigious scholarship and were extremely convincing in their day. The rationale behind many later Nazi projects can be traced back -through the writings of von List, von Sebottendorff, and von Liebenfels—to ideas first popularized by Blavatsky. A caste system of races, the importance of ancient alphabets (notably the runes), the superiority of the Aryans (a white race with its origins in the Himalayas), an 'initiated' version of astrology and astronomy, the cosmic truths coded within pagan myths ... all of these and more can be found both in Blavatsky and in the Nazi Party itself, specifically in the ideology of its Dark Creature, the SS. It was, after all, Blavatsky who pointed out the supreme occult significance of the swastika. And it was a follower of Blavatsky who was instrumental in introducing the Protocols of the Elders of Zion to a Western European community eager for a scapegoat.

(23) It will be remembered that the notorious document known as the Protocols of the Elders of Zion was an anti-Semitic forgery created by the Okhrana (the Czarist secret police) and occultists in St Petersburg and Paris to discredit the enemies of Rachkhovsky, the head of the Okhrana in Paris. (24) Produced in St Petersburg in 1902 and translated into German in 1919, the document purported to be the minutes of a meeting of the putative secret Jewish world conspiracy, (25) a conspiracy that, it appeared, was approaching the fulfillment of its goals. The Protocols indicated that Democracy, Communism and international commerce had been successfully infiltrated and taken over by the Jews, who 'had "infected" all governments, all commerce, all of the arts and media'. (26) Information regarding the Protocols was initially provided to the press by a Madame Yuliana Glinka, a believer in Spiritualism who would do much to promote the anti-Semitic falsehoods contained within the document.

As is well known, Hitler himself came to believe wholeheartedly in the veracity of the Protocols, which formed a principal basis for his own anti-Semitism:

To what an extent the whole existence of this people is based on a continuous lie is shown incomparably by the Protocols of the Wise Men [Elders] of Zion, so infinitely hated by the Jews. They are based on a forgery, the Frankfurter Zeitung moans and screams once every week: the best proof that they are authentic. What many Jews may do unconsciously is here consciously exposed. And that is what matters. It is completely indifferent from what Jewish brain these disclosures originate; the important thing is that with positively terrifying certainty they reveal the nature and activity of the Jewish people and expose their inner contexts as well as their ultimate final aims. The best criticism applied to them, however, is reality. Anyone who examines the historical development of the last hundred years from the standpoint of this book will at once understand the screaming of the Jewish press. For once this book has become the common property of a people, the Jewish menace may be considered as broken. (27)

Hitler's reference to the Frankfurter Zeitung is especially interesting and ironic, in view of the startling and intriguing suggestion made by that paper's Munich correspondent, the anti-Nazi Konrad Heiden. Heiden began reporting on Hitler's activities in 1921; when Hitler took power in 1933, Heiden was forced to flee to France. In his biography of Hitler, Der Fuehrer, written in exile and published in 1944, Heiden suggests a profound connection between Hitler and the Protocols, a connection which is summarized by Rosenbaum:

Heiden's stunning conjecture, which deserves attention because of his intimate acquaintance with the Hitler Party from the very beginning of the Fuhrer's rise, was that the secret of that rise lay in Hitler's adapting the modernized Machiavellian tactics attributed to his archenemy, the Elders of Zion, and putting them to his own use in manipulating the media, subverting the institutions of the state, and Grafting his own successful conspiracy to rule the world. Heiden argues that Hitler did not merely adopt the counterfeit Jewish conspiracy as his vision of the world, he adopted the tactics falsely attributed to Jews by Czarist forgers as his own—and used them with remarkable success. A success that made Hitler himself a kind of creation of a counterfeit. [Original emphasis.]

(28) I hope the reader will forgive this seeming digression from the subject we were discussing: while the apparent influence of the Protocols on Hitler may seem a long way from the lost Aryan homeland of the prehistoric north, it is worth introducing the idea at this point, not only because it was a supporter of Blavatsky who promoted the Protocols in western Europe but also because it is of profound importance to the rest of our study. If Heiden was correct in his conjecture, and Adolf Hitler, and hence Nazi Germany, were the creation of a counterfeit, this demonstrates quite convincingly the power and influence that bizarre falsehoods can have over the collective psyche of a people. This will have special significance in the last three chapters of this book, which will deal with Nazi cosmology and the belief in a hollow Earth, the theory that German scientists were responsible for the wave of UFO sightings in the late 1940s (and perhaps still are responsible for such sightings today), and the persistent rumors regarding the survival of key Nazis in a hidden Antarctic colony.

Before moving on, however, we must return briefly to Blavatsky and Theosophy in order to address the implication that the movement possessed fascist elements. In spite of its proclamation of the supremacy of the Aryan race (not to mention Madame Glinka's unfortunate promotion of the Protocols), Theosophy was not inherently fascist, and Blavatsky herself did not become overtly involved in politics (29) (Indeed, although it had inspired a large number of German occultists and nationalists at the turn of the century, Theosophy would later be attacked and suppressed by the Nazis, along with all other organizations showing any resistance whatsoever to Hitler.) (30) Nevertheless, some of Blavatsky's followers, most notably Annie Besant (1847-1933), became active in politics. In Besant's case, it was Indian politics, and it was under her presidency after Henry Olcott's death in 1907 that the Theosophical

Society became an important element in the Indian Nationalist Movement. As Levenda notes, the Nazis would later attempt to exploit Indian nationalism and the desire for home rule by claiming a similarity of ideals and objectives between Indian nationalism and National Socialism. (31)

ICELAND AND ANTARCTICA

It is a matter of historical record that the Nazis mounted expeditions to Iceland, Antarctica and Tibet (the Tibetan expeditions will be examined more closely in the next chapter). The true reasons for these expeditions, however, have been the subject of considerable debate throughout the decades since the end of the war. As we have already noted, the Nazi concept of Thule can be traced to Guido von List, Jorg Lanz von Liebenfels and Rudolf von Sebottendorff, who conceived of it as the ancient homeland of the Aryan race. (At some time between the third and fourth centuries BC, Pytheas of Massilia undertook a voyage to the north. He reached Scotland, and sailed on for six more days, probably reaching the North Shetland Islands. He then claimed to have reached the land of Thule, which may have been Iceland, or perhaps Norway, before encountering a frozen sea.)

(32) The volkisch fascination with the Scandinavian Eddas led von Sebottendorff to conclude that the supposedly long-vanished land of Thule was actually Iceland. This link with the lost Aryan homeland prompted an intense interest in the possibility of discovering further clues to their remote history, indeed, to their very origin, among the caves and prehistoric monuments of the island. (33)

According to Peter Levenda, an organization called the Nordic Society was established at Lubeck by Alfred Rosenberg (1893-1945), the Nazi mystic, philosopher, editor of the Volkischer Beobachter and later Reich Minister for the occupied eastern territories. The society counted among its members representatives from Norway, Sweden, Finland, Denmark and Iceland, who were drawn together in order to defend the Nordic nations against the Soviet, Jewish and Masonic threat. On 22 August 1938, the Volkischer Beobachter carried an article on one of the Nordic Society's meetings, at which Rosenberg was quoted thus:

'We all stand under the same European destiny, and must feel obliged to this common destiny, because finally the existence of the white man depends altogether upon the unity of the European continent! Unanimous must we oppose that terrible attempt by Moscow to destroy the world, the sea of blood into which already many people have dived!' (34)

Rosenberg explained his Thulean mythology in his book Der Mythus des 20. Jahrhunderts (The Myth of the Twentieth Century), published in 1930, which was a massive best-seller in Germany, despite the fact that it was widely considered to be appallingly-written nonsense. (Hitler himself, who, once in power, had little time for paganism, Thulean or otherwise, described it as 'stuff nobody can understand'.) (35) In the first chapter of the book, Rosenberg explains the basis of his belief in an ancient Aryan homeland in the north:

The geologists show us a continent between North America and Europe, whose remains we can see today in Greenland and Iceland. They tell us that islands on the other side of the Far North (Novaia Zemlya) display former tide marks over 100 metres higher than today's; they make it probable that the North Pole has wandered, and that a much milder climate once reigned in the present Arctic. All this allows the ancient legend of Atlantis to appear in a new light. It seems not impossible that where the waves of the Atlantic Ocean now crash and pull off giant icebergs, once a blooming continent rose out of the water, on which a creative race raised a mighty, wide-ranging culture, and sent its children out into the world as seafarers and warriors. But even if this Atlantean hypothesis is not thought tenable, one has to assume that there was a prehistoric northern center of culture. (36)

Despite these assertions concerning the great secrets of a long-vanished Aryan civilization that might be found in Iceland, Rosenberg, who was looked upon with a mixture of amusement and contempt by most of the leading Nazis, was not involved with the actual expeditions sent there. They were authorized by Heinrich Himmler under the auspices of the Ahnenerbe—the SS Association for Research and Teaching on Heredity. Levenda has retrieved numerous documents regarding these missions, some of which he includes in his fascinating study Unholy Alliance (1995). One of these documents, addressed to the Ahnenerbe from a Dr. Bruno Schweizer, contains a proposal for a research journey to Iceland, and is dated 10 March 1938:

From year to year it becomes more difficult to meet living witnesses of Germanic cultural feelings and Germanic soul attitudes on the classical Icelandic soil uninfluenced by the overpowerful grasp of western civilization. In only a few years has the natural look of the country, which since the Ur-time has remained mostly untouched in stone and meadow, in desert and untamed mountain torrents, revealed its open countenance to man and has fundamentally changed from mountainsides and rock slabs to manicured lawns, nurseries and pasture grounds, almost as far from Reykjavik as the barren coast section, a feat accomplished by the hand of man; the city itself expands with almost American speed as roadways and bridges, power stations and factories emerge and the density of the traffic in Reykjavik corresponds with that of a European city.

Dr. Schweizer goes on to bemoan the loss of ancient agricultural techniques such as forging, wood-carving, spinning, weaving and dyeing; along with the forgetting of myths and legends and the lack of belief in a 'transcendent nature'. After describing the lamentable rise of materialism that Drew people from rural areas to the city (and gave an unfavorable impression to good German visitors!), the doctor continues:

Every year that we wait quietly means damage to a number of objects, and other objects become ruined for camera and film due to newfangled public buildings in the modern style. For the work in question only the summer is appropriate, that is, the months of June through August. Furthermore, one must reckon that occasionally several rainy days can occur, delaying thereby certain photographic work. The ship connections are such that it is perhaps only possible to go to and from the

OCCULT SECRETS OF THE THIRD REICH

Continent once a week.

All this means a minimum period of from 5-6 weeks for the framework of the trip. The possible tasks of an Iceland research trip with a cultural knowledge mission are greatly variegated. Therefore it remains for us to select only the most immediate and most realizable. A variety of other tasks ... should be considered as additional assignments.

Thus the recording of human images (race-measurements) and the investigation of museum treasures are considered to be additional assignments. (37)

As Levenda wryly observes, it is not clear how the people of Iceland would have reacted to the taking of 'race measurements' or, for that matter, the 'investigation of museum treasures', which almost certainly would not have remained in the museums for very long!

German interest in Antarctic exploration goes back to 1873, when Eduard Dallman mounted an expedition in his steamship Gronland on behalf of the newly founded German Society of Polar Research. Less than 60 years later, the Swiss explorer Wilhelm Filchner, who had already led an expedition to Tibet in 1903-05, planned to lead two expeditions to Antarctica with the intention of determining if the continent was a single piece of land. Filchner's plans called for two ships, one to enter the Weddell Sea and one to enter the Ross Sea. Two groups would then embark on a land journey and attempt to meet at the centre of the continent. This plan, however, proved too expensive, and so a single ship, the Deutschland, was used. The Deutschland was a Norwegian ship specifically designed for work in polar regions, and was acquired with the help of Ernest Shackleton, Otto Nordenskjold and Fridtjof Nansen. The expedition reached the Weddell Sea in December 1911. Another expedition was mounted in 1925 with the polar expedition ship Meteor under the command of Dr. Albert Merz.

In the years running up to the Second World War, Germany wanted a foothold in Antarctica, both for the propaganda value of demonstrating the power of the Third Reich and also because of the territory's strategic significance in the South Atlantic. On 17 December 1938, an expedition was despatched under the command of Captain Alfred Ritscher to the South Atlantic coast of Antarctica and arrived there on 19 January 1939. The expedition's ship was the Schwabenland, an aircraft carrier that had been used since 1934 for transatlantic mail delivery. The Schwabenland, which had been prepared for the expedition in the Hamburg shipyards at a cost of one million Reichsmarks, was equipped with two Dornier seaplanes, the Passat and the Boreas, which were launched from its flight deck by steam catapults and which made fifteen flights over the territory which Norwegian explorers had named Queen Maud Land. The aircraft covered approximately 600,000 square kilometres, took more than 11,000 photographs of the Princess Astrid and Princess Martha coasts of western Queen Maud Land, and dropped several thousand drop-flags (metal poles with swastikas). The area was claimed for the Third Reich, and was renamed Neu Schwabenland.

Perhaps the most surprising discovery made by this expedition was a number of large, ice-free areas, containing lakes and sparse vegetation. The expedition geologists suggested that this might have been due to underground heat sources.

In mid-February 1939, the Schwabenland left Antarctica and returned to Hamburg. Ritscher was surprised at the findings of the expedition, particularly the ice-free areas, and immediately began to plan another journey upon his arrival home. These plans, however, were apparently abandoned with the outbreak of war.

At this point, orthodox history gives way to strange rumors and speculations regarding the true reason for the Third Reich's interest in Antarctica. It has been suggested, for instance, that the 1938-39 expedition had been to look for a suitable ice-free region on the continent that could be used for a secret Nazi base after the war. According to the novelist and UFO researcher W. A. Harbinson: Throughout the war, the Germans sent ships and aircraft to Neu Schwabenland with enough equipment and manpower (much of it slave labour from the concentration camps) to build massive complexes under the ice or in well-hidden ice-free areas. At the close of the war selected Nazi scientists and SS troops fled to Antarctica ...' (38)

Such speculations properly belong to the field known as 'Nazi survival', which we will discuss in depth in the final chapter of this book. Therefore, let us place them aside and turn our attention to another important element in the concept of a lost Aryan homeland: a symbol that once signified good fortune but was irreparably corrupted by the Nazis, and which now signifies nothing but terror and death.

THE SWASTIKA

In antiquity, the swastika was a universal symbol, being used from the Bronze Age onwards on objects of every kind. The word 'swastika' comes from the Sanskrit: su (Greek eu, meaning 'good'), asti (Greek esto, meaning 'to be') and the suffix ka. (39) The symbol means 'good luck' (the Sanskrit-Tibetan word Swasti means 'may it be auspicious'). According to Joscelyn Godwin, the shape of the swastika derives from the constellation Arktos, also known as the Great Bear, the Plough and the Big Dipper. To the observer in the Northern Hemisphere, this constellation appears to rotate around Polaris, the Pole Star (an effect caused by the rotation of the Earth). If the positions of Arktos in relation to Polaris are represented in pictorial form (corresponding to the four seasons), the result is highly suggestive of a swastika; in 4000 BC, they were identical to the symbol. It is for this reason that the swastika (aside from denoting good fortune) has been used to represent the Pole.

OCCULT SECRETS OF THE THIRD REICH

(40)

The swastika gained in importance in European culture in the nineteenth century, primarily in the fields of comparative ethnology and Oriental studies. The absence of the symbol from Egypt, Chaldea, Assyria and Phoenicia led the ethnologists to believe that the swastika was an Aryan sun-symbol. (41) Madame Blavatsky saw the significance of the symbol, and incorporated it into the seal of the Theosophical Society to signify the harmony of universal movement. According to Godwin: 'So innocent were the "good luck" associations of the swastika that during World War I, it was used as the emblem of the British War Savings Scheme, appearing on coupons and stamps.' (42)

The swastika appears in two forms: left-handed and right-handed. However, confusion quickly arises when one is faced with the question of how to define 'left' and 'right' with regard to this symbol. Some occultists and historians favor a definition based on the direction taken by the arms as they extend outward from the centre; while others prefer to define left' and 'right' in terms of the apparent direction of rotation. The confusion arises from the fact that a swastika whose arms proceed to the left appears to be rotating to the right, and vice versa.

Each swastika variant has been taken to mean different things by writers on the occult, such as the Frenchman Andre Brissaud who says that the counter-clockwise-spinning swastika represents the rotation of the Earth on its axis and is the 'Wheel of the Golden Sun', symbolizing creation, evolution and fertility. The clockwise-spinning swastika is, according to Brissaud, the 'Wheel of the Black Sun', representing man's quest for power in opposition to Heaven. (43) The Chilean diplomat, esotericist and Hitler apologist Miguel Serrano (b. 1917), whom we shall meet again in the final chapter, has another explanation of the left- and right-handed swastikas: the left-handed (clockwise-turning) symbol represents the migration of the ancient Aryan Race from its homeland at the North Pole, while the right-handed (counter-clockwise-turning) symbol—the one used by the Nazis—represents the destiny of the Aryans to return to their spiritual centre at the South Pole.

(44) Swastika with arms extending to left, apparent rotation to right / Swastika with arms extending to right, apparent rotation to left.

After informing us of the complexities attached to the interpretation of left- and right-handed swastikas, Godwin continues:

Whatever the validity of these theories, the ancient decorative swastikas show no preference whatsoever for one type over the other. The place where the left-right distinction is supposed to be most significant is Tibet, where both Nicholas Roerich and Anagarika Govinda observed that the swastika of the ancient Bon-Po religion points to the left, the Buddhist one to the right. Now it is true that the Bon-Pos perform ritual circumabulations counter-clockwise, the Buddhists clockwise, but almost all the Buddhist iconography collected by Thomas Wilson shows left-handed swastikas, just like the ones on the Bon-Pos' ritual scepter, their equivalent of the Buddhist vajra. One can only say that the swastika should perhaps be left-handed if (as in Bon-Po) it denotes polar revolution, and right-handed if (as in Buddhism) it symbolizes the course of the sun. But the root of the problem is probably the inherent ambiguity of the symbol itself, which makes the left-handed swastika appear to be rotating to the right, and vice versa. (45)

As we saw in the first chapter, the swastika gained popularity among German anti-Semitic groups through the writings of Guido von List and Lanz von Liebenfels, who took the symbol of good fortune and universal harmony and used it to denote the unconquerable Germanic hero. As might be expected, the counter-clockwise orientation of the swastika used as a banner by the National Socialist German Workers' Party (NSDAP) has also aroused considerable controversy in occult and esoteric circles.

According to the occult historian Francis King, when Hitler called for suggestions for a banner, all of the submissions included a swastika. The one Hitler finally chose had been designed by Dr. Friedrich Krohn, a dentist from Sternberg. However, the design incorporated a clockwise-turning swastika, symbolizing good fortune, harmony and spirituality.

Hitler decided to reverse the design, making the swastika counter-clockwise, symbolizing evil and black magic. (46) Here again, we encounter the problem of defining what is a right-and left-handed swastika. Was the Nazi symbol right-handed (traditionally denoting good) or left-handed (denoting evil)? In one sense, the Nazi swastika could be said to be right-handed because the hooked arms extend to the right; conversely, it could be said to be left-handed, since the apparent rotation is counter-clockwise. As the journalist Ken Anderson notes: 'What we are dealing with is subjective definition ... We can speculate that Hitler had chosen to reverse the cross because of the connotations of black magic and evil in Krohn's cross and for the purpose of evoking the positive images of good luck, spiritual evolution, etc., for his fledgling party!' (47) (Original emphasis.) Anderson gives the impression of having his tongue slightly in his cheek, but his interpretation is almost certainly correct, for two reasons.

Firstly, we must remember that Hitler himself had very little time for occult mumbo-jumbo, and was certainly not the practicing black magician many occultists claim him to have been (more on this in Chapter Five); and secondly, the idea that Hitler considered himself 'evil' (as he would have had to have done in order to take the step of reversing a positive symbol to a negative one), or that evil was an attractive concept for him is ridiculous. As we noted in the Introduction, one of the most terrifying and baffling aspects of Adolf Hitler is that he did not consider himself 'evil': as Trevor-Roper states, Hitler was convinced of his own rectitude, that he was acting correctly in exterminating the Jews and the other groups targeted for destruction by the Nazis.

In addition, Hitler himself makes no mention of such an alteration in his repulsive Mein Kampf. In view of the fact that he took most of the credit for the design himself, neglecting even to mention Krohn's name, he would surely have explained the reasons for his making such a fundamental alteration to the design of the NSDAP banner:

... I was obliged to reject without exception the numerous designs which poured in from the circles of the young movement ... I myself - as Leader - did not want to come out publicly at once with my own design, since after all it was possible that another should produce one just as good or perhaps even better. Actually, a dentist from Starnberg [sic] did deliver a design that was not bad at all, and, incidentally, was quite close to my own, having only the one fault that a swastika with curved legs was composed into a white disk

I myself, meanwhile, after innumerable attempts, had laid down a final form; a flag with a red background, a white disk, and a black swastika in the middle. After long trials I also found a definite proportion between the size of the flag and the size of the white disk, as well as the shape and thickness of the swastika. (48)

The reader will notice that Hitler says the submission he received that was quite close to his own had only one fault: the swastika had curved legs. Anderson is undoubtedly correct when he states that 'the major importance of the decision [was] - for a man who prided himself on being a thwarted artist of great merit - not some unidentified occultic myth, but rather balance and aesthetic value'. (49)

Hitler: by Carol Ann Rodriguez

OCCULT SECRETS OF THE THIRD REICH

3—A HIDEOUS STRENGTH
THE VRIL SOCIETY

We have now reached the point in our survey of Nazi involvement with the occult where we must depart from what is historically verifiable and enter an altogether more obscure and murky realm, a place that Pauwels and Bergier call the 'Absolute Elsewhere'. (1) Serious historians (at least, those who deign to comment on the subject at all) regard the material we shall be examining for the rest of this book with contempt—and, it must be said, not without good reason. Much of what follows may well strike the reader as bizarre and absurd in equal measure; and yet, as we shall see, amongst the notions we are about to address (products, apparently, of fevered imaginations) will be found unsettling hints of a thread running through the collective mind of humanity in the late twentieth century—ominous, dangerous and, by the majority, unseen.

As we shall see, the 'twilight zone between fact and fiction' can produce significant shifts in our collective awareness of the world, our place in it and the unstated intentions of those who rule us. The world view of those who subscribe to the idea of genuine Nazi occult power includes a number of outrageous conspiracy theories that revolve around the claim that many leading Nazis (including, according to some, Hitler himself) escaped from the ruins of Berlin and continue with their plans for world domination from some hidden headquarters. At first sight, these theories can surely have little to do with known reality. And yet, the idea that the American Central Intelligence Agency (CIA) could have smuggled many personnel from Nazi intelligence and the German secret weapons program into the United States in the post-war years might likewise seem outlandish—until we remember that this, too, is a documented historical fact. Project PAPERCLIP proves that some senior elements of the Third Reich did indeed survive in this way, their lives bought with scientific and military knowledge that the American government desperately wanted.

So, for the rest of this book, we shall concentrate on the elements of Nazi occultism that find no home in orthodox history but that nevertheless stretch their pernicious tentacles through modern popular and fringe culture and refuse to vanish in the glare of the light of reason. The Vril Society, our departure point into the Absolute Elsewhere, might seem to have been better placed in the first chapter, were it not that there is so little evidence for its influence over the activities of the Third Reich. In spite of this, it has come to occupy a central position in the dubious study of Nazi occult power and so demands a chapter of its own. But what was the strangely named Vril Society?

The first hint of the Vril Society's existence was discovered in a scene that would not have been out of place in one of Dennis Wheatley's occult thrillers. On 25 April 1945, so the story goes, a group of battle-weary Russian soldiers were making their cautious way through the shattered remnants of Berlin, mopping up the isolated pockets of German resistance that remained in the heart of the Third Reich. The soldiers moved carefully from one wrecked building to another, in a state of constant readiness against the threat of ambush.

In a ground-floor room of one blasted building, the soldiers made a surprising discovery. Lying in a circle on the floor were the bodies of six men, with a seventh corpse in the centre. All were dressed in German military uniforms, and the dead man in the centre of the group was wearing a pair of bright green gloves. The Russians' assumption that the bodies were those of soldiers was quickly dispelled when they realized that the dead men were all Orientals. One of the Russians, who was from Mongolia, identified the men as Tibetans. It was also evident to the Russian soldiers that the men had not died in battle but seemed to have committed suicide. Over the following week, hundreds more Tibetans were discovered in Berlin: some of them had clearly died in battle, while others had committed ritual suicide, like the ones discovered by the Russian unit. (2)

What were Tibetans doing in Nazi Germany towards the end of the Second World War? The answer to this question may be found in a curious novel entitled The Coming Race by Edward Bulwer-Lytton (1803-1873), first Baron Lytton. A prolific and very successful writer (his output included novels, plays, essays and poetry) Bulwer-Lytton was considered in his lifetime to be one of the greatest writers in the English language. Unfortunately, his reputation for vanity, ostentation and eccentricity attracted a good deal of hostility from the press and this has damaged his subsequent literary reputation to a disproportionate extent, with the result that today his books are extremely hard to find and his work is seldom—if at all—taught in universities in the English-speaking world. (3)

Throughout his career, Bulwer-Lytton wrote on many themes, including romance, politics, history, social satire, melodrama and the occult. It is perhaps unsurprising, therefore, that he should have turned to the subject of Utopian science fiction with The Coming Race, published in 1871. In this novel, the narrator, a traveller and adventurer of independent means, explores a mine in an unnamed location and discovers a vast subterranean world, inhabited by a superior race of humans called the Vril-ya. Once tenants of the Earth's outer surface, the Vril-ya were forced to retreat underground by a natural catastrophe similar to the biblical Flood many thousands of years ago. Their technology is far in advance of anything to be found in the world of ordinary humanity, and is based on the application of a force known as 'vril'. Befriended by a young female Vril-ya named Zee, the narrator asks about the nature of the vril force.

Therewith Zee began to enter into an explanation of which I understood very little, for there is no word in any language I know which is an exact synonym for vril. I should call it electricity, except that it comprehends in its manifold branches other forces of nature, to which, in our scientific nomenclature, differing names are assigned, such as magnetism, galvanism, &c. These people consider that in vril they have arrived at the unity in natural energetic agencies, which has been conjectured by many philosophers above ground, and which Faraday thus intimates under the more cautious term of correlation:

'I have long held an opinion,' says that illustrious experimentalist, 'almost amounting to a conviction, in common, I believe, with many other lovers of natural knowledge, that the various forms under which the forces of matter are made manifest have one common origin; or, in other words, are so directly related and mutually dependent, that they are convertible, as it were, into one another, and possess equivalents of power in their action.'

(4) According to Zee, all Vril-ya are trained in the application of vril, which can be used to control the physical world, including the minds and bodies of others, as well as to enhance the telepathic and telekinetic potentials of the human mind. The vril force is most often applied through the use of a device known as the Vril Staff which, like the vril force itself, requires many years to master. (The narrator is not allowed to hold one, 'for fear of some terrible accident occasioned by my ignorance of its use'.) The Vril Staff 'is hollow, and has in the handle several stops, keys, or springs by which its force can be altered, modified, or directed—so that by one process it destroys, by another it heals—by one it can rend the rock, by another disperse the vapour—by one it affects bodies, by another it can exercise a certain influence over minds'. (5)

During his protracted stay in the subterranean realm, the narrator learns of the system of government by which the Vril-ya live. They are ruled by a single supreme magistrate who abdicates the position at the first sign of advancing age.

Although their society is entirely free of crime or strife of any kind, they consider strength and force to be among the finest virtues, and the triumph of the strong over the weak to be in perfect accordance with Nature. Democracy and free institutions are, to them, merely the crude experiments of an immature culture.

The government of the tribe of Vril-ya ... was apparently very complicated, really very simple. It was based upon a principle recognized in theory, though little carried out in practice, above ground—viz., that the object of all systems of philosophical thought tends to the attainment of unity, or the ascent through all intervening labyrinths to the simplicity of a single first cause or principle. Thus in politics, even republican writers have agreed that a benevolent autocracy would insure the best administration, if there were any guarantees for its continuance, or against its gradual abuse of the powers accorded to it. There was ... in this society nothing to induce any of its members to covet the cares of office. No honors, no insignia of higher rank were assigned to it. The supreme magistrate was not distinguished from the rest by superior habitation or revenue. On the other hand, the duties awarded to him were marvelously light and easy, requiring no preponderant degree of energy or intelligence. (6)

After a number of adventures in the subterranean world—and a great many conversations with its denizens—the narrator comes to the following conclusion regarding the ultimate origins of the fantastic Vril-ya race:

[T]his people—though originally not only of our human race, but, as seems to me clear by the roots of their language, descended from the same ancestors as the great Aryan family, from which in varied streams has flowed the dominant civilization of the world; and having, according to their myths and their history, passed through phases of society familiar to ourselves,—had yet now developed into a distinct species with which it was impossible that any community in the upper world could amalgamate: And that if they ever emerged from these nether recesses into the light of day, they would, according to their own traditional persuasions of their ultimate destiny, destroy and replace our existent varieties of man. (7)

Although greatly impressed with the knowledge and accomplishments of the Vril-ya, the narrator is nevertheless terrified by their power and the ease with which they wield it, implying at one point that, should he have angered them at any time, they would have had no compunction in turning their Vril Staffs on him and reducing him to cinders. This uneasiness, coupled with his natural desire to return to the upper world and the life with which he is familiar, prompts the narrator to begin seeking a means of escape from the subterranean world of the Vril-ya. Aid comes in the unlikely form of Zee, who has fallen in love with him and has attempted to persuade him to stay, but who nevertheless understands that an unrequited love cannot result in happiness for either of them. It is she who leads him back to the mine shaft through which he first entered the realm of the Vrilya.

Upon his return home, the narrator begins to ponder the wonders he has beheld far below the surface of the Earth, and once again hints at the possible dreadful fate awaiting a blissfully unaware humanity at the hands of the 'Coming Race'. In the final chapter, we read:

[T]he more I think of a people calmly developing, in regions excluded from our sight and deemed uninhabitable by our sages, powers surpassing our most disciplined modes offeree, and virtues to which our life, social and political, becomes antagonistic in proportion as our civilization advances,—the more devoutly I pray that ages may yet elapse before there emerge into sunlight our inevitable destroyers. (8)

It is an assumption of many occultists that The Coming Race is fact disguised as fiction: that Bulwer-Lytton based his engaging novel on a genuine body of esoteric knowledge. He was greatly interested in the Rosicrucians, the powerful occult society which arose in the sixteenth century and which claimed to possess ancient wisdom, discovered in a secret underground chamber, regarding the ultimate secrets of the Universe. There is some evidence that Bulwer-Lytton believed in the possibility of a subterranean world, for he wrote to his friend Hargrave Jennings in 1854: 'So Rosenkreuz [the founder of the Rosicrucians] found his wisdom in a secret chamber. So will we all. There is much to be learned from the substrata of our planet.' (9)

Some writers, including Alec Maclellan, author of the fascinating book The Lost World of Agharti (1996), have suggested that The Coming Race revealed too much of the subterranean world, and was as a result suppressed in the years following Bulwer-Lytton's death in 1873. Indeed, he describes the book as 'one of the hardest to find of all books of mysticism', (10) and informs us of his own search for a copy, which for some years met with no success. While doubtless an intriguing piece of stage-setting on Maclellan's part, the rarity of the book can surely be accounted for by the unjust waning of Bulwer-Lytton's posthumous literary reputation (mentioned earlier). The present author searched for some months for a copy of The Coming Race, before finding an extremely affordable paperback edition in a high-street bookshop.

What is the connection between Bulwer-Lytton's strange novel and Nazi Germany? If there really was a large colony of Tibetan monks in Berlin in the 1940s, what were they doing there? It seems that the connection was none other than the Bavarian Karl Haushofer (1869-1946) whose theories of Geopolitics gave rise to the concept of Lebensraum (living space), which Hitler maintained would be necessary to the continued dominance of the superior Aryan race and which he intended to take, primarily, from the Soviet Union. Haushofer, along with Dietrich Eckart (1868-1923)—an anti-Semitic journalist and playwright who influenced Hitler's racial attitudes and introduced him to influential social circles after the First World War—is frequently described by believers in genuine Nazi occult power as a practicing black magician, and the 'Master Magician of the Nazi Party'. (11)

Haushofer excelled at Munich University, where he began to develop his lifelong interest in the Far East. After leaving university, he entered the German army, where his great intelligence ensured a rapid rise through the ranks. His knowledge of the Far East earned him a posting as military attache in Japan. The idea that Haushofer was an occult adept, with secret knowledge of powerful trans-human entities, was first suggested by Louis Pauwels and Jacques Bergier in their fascinating but historically unreliable book The Morning of the Magicians (which served as the model for a number of subsequent treatments of Nazi occultism in the 1960s and early 1970s).

According to Pauwels and Bergier:

[Haushofer] believed that the German people originated in Central Asia, and that it was the Indo-Germanic race which guaranteed the permanence, nobility and greatness of the world. While in Japan, Haushofer is said to have been initiated into one of the most important secret Buddhist societies and to have sworn, if he failed in his 'mission', to commit suicide in accordance with the time-honored ceremonial. (12)

Haushofer was also apparently a firm believer in the legend of Thule, the lost

OCCULT SECRETS OF THE THIRD REICH

Aryan homeland in the far north, which had once been the centre of an advanced civilization possessed of magical powers. Connecting this legend with the Thule Society, Pauwels and Bergier have this to say:

Beings intermediate between Man and other intelligent beings from Beyond would place at the disposal of the [Thule Society] Initiates a reservoir of forces which could be drawn on to enable Germany to dominate the world again and be the cradle of the coming race of Supermen which would result from the mutations of the human species. One day her legions would set out to annihilate everything that had stood in the way of the spiritual destiny of the Earth, and their leaders would be men who knew everything, deriving their strength from the very fountain-head of energy and guided by the Great Ones of the Ancient World ... It would seem that it was under the influence of Karl Haushofer that [the Thule Society] took on its true character of a society of Initiates in communion with the Invisible, and became the magic centre of the Nazi movement. (13)

Serious historians such as Nicholas Goodrick-Clarke take issue with the claims of Pauwels and Bergier and the later writers who reiterated them. Goodrick-Clarke, who has perhaps conducted more research into primary German sources than any other writer in this curious field, states that the claims regarding the secret guiding power of the Thule Society are 'entirely fallacious. The Thule Society was dissolved in 1925 when support had dwindled.' He goes on to assure us that 'there is no evidence at all to link Haushofer to the group l. (14) Nevertheless, Haushofer's alleged skill in the Black Arts has become an important link in the Nazi occult chain as described by writers on such fringe subjects.

After the end of the First World War, Haushofer returned to Munich, where he gained a doctorate from the university. He divided his time between teaching and writing and founded the Geopolitical Review in which he published his ideas on Lebensraum, which could 'both justify territorial conquest by evoking the colonizing of Slav lands by Teutonic knights in the Middle Ages and, emotively, conjure up notions of uniting in the Reich what came to be described as Volksdeutsche (ethnic Germans) scattered throughout eastern Europe'. (15)

While incarcerated in the fortress of Landsberg am Lech following the failure of the Munich Putsch in 1924, Adolf Hitler read and was influenced by Haushofer's books on geopolitics (he had already been introduced to Haushofer by the professor's student assistant, Rudolf Hess). There is no doubt that Hitler occupied his time in Landsberg judiciously, reading widely in several fields, though not for the sake of education so much as to confirm and clarify his own preconceptions. (He later said that Landsberg was his 'university paid for by the state'). (16)

According to Pauwels and Bergier and other fringe writers, Haushofer visited Hitler every day in Landsberg, where he explained his geopolitical theories and described his travels through India in the early years of the century. While in India, he had heard stories of a powerful civilization living beneath the Himalayas:

Thirty or forty centuries ago in the region of Gobi there was a highly developed civilization. As the result of a catastrophe, possibly of an atomic nature, Gobi was transformed into a desert, and the survivors emigrated, some going to the extreme North of Europe, and others towards the Caucasus. The Scandinavian god Thor is supposed to have been one of the heroes of this migration.

... Haushofer proclaimed the necessity of 'a return to the sources' of the human race—in other words, that it was necessary to conquer the whole of Eastern Europe, Turkestan, Pamir, Gobi and Thibet. These countries constituted, in his opinion, the central core, and whoever had control of them controlled the whole world. (17)

After the cataclysm that destroyed the Gobi civilization, the survivors migrated to a vast cavern system beneath the Himalayas where they split into two groups, one of which followed the path of spirituality, enlightenment and meditation while the other followed the path of violence and materialistic power. The first of these centers was called Agartha, the other Shambhala. (These names have many different spellings: for Agartha, I use the simplest; for Shambhala, the spelling favored by Orientalists.) We shall return for a closer look to the realms of Agartha and Shambhala in the next chapter.

According to Alec Maclellan, among the many books Hitler read while languishing in Landsberg was Bulwer-Lytton's The Coming Race, which, Haushofer informed him, was an essentially correct description of the race of Supermen living far beneath the surface of the Earth and corroborated much of what the professor had himself learned while traveling in Asia. Bulwer-Lytton's novel apparently galvanised Hitler's imagination, and he 'began to yearn for the day when he might establish for himself the actuality of the secret civilization beneath the snows of Tibet ...' (18)

In the following year, 1925, the Vril Society (also known as the Luminous Lodge) was formed by a group of Berlin Rosicrucians including Karl Haushofer. As Joscelyn Godwin informs us, there is only one primary source of information on the Vril Society: Willy Ley, a German rocket engineer who fled to the United States in 1933 and followed a successful career writing popular science books. In 1947, Ley published an article entitled 'Pseudoscience in Naziland'. Following a description of Ariosophy, Ley writes:

The next group was literally founded upon a novel. That group which I think called itself Wahrheitsgesellschaft -Society for Truth—and which was more or less localized in Berlin, devoted its spare time looking for Vril. Yes, their convictions were founded upon Bulwer-Lytton's 'The Coming Race'. They knew that the book was fiction, Bulwer-Lytton had used that device in order to be able to tell the truth about this 'power'. The subterranean humanity was nonsense, Vril was not. Possibly it had enabled the British, who kept it as a State secret, to amass their colonial empire. Surely the Romans had had it, inclosed [sic] in small metal balls, which guarded their homes and were referred to as lares. For reasons which I failed to penetrate, the secret of Vril could be found by contemplating the structure of an apple, sliced in halves. No, I am not joking, that is what I was told with great solemnity and secrecy. Such a group actually existed, they even got out the first issue of a magazine which was to proclaim their credo. (19)

Although they apparently interviewed Ley, Pauwels and Bergier could learn nothing more from him about this mysterious society; however, they later discovered that the group actually called itself the Vril Society, and that Karl Haushofer was intimately connected with it. (Joscelyn Godwin kindly reminds us of the unreliability of the splendid Pauwels and Bergier: although they cite Jack Fishman's The Seven Men of Spandau with regard to Haushofer's connection to the Vril Society, Fishman actually makes no such reference.) (20)

Pauwels and Bergier go on to inform us that, having failed in his mission, Haushofer committed suicide on 14 March 1946, in accordance with his pledge to his masters in the secret Japanese society into which he had been initiated. Once again, the truth is somewhat different: Haushofer did not commit ham kin but died from arsenic poisoning on 10 March. In addition, Ley's reference to 'contemplating the structure of an apple, sliced in halves' (thus revealing the five-pointed star at its centre) echoes Rudolf Steiner's suggestion in Knowledge of Higher Worlds and Its Attainment. Indeed, as Godwin reminds us, (21) the Theosophists were themselves interested in the concept of the vril force, which bears some resemblance to Reichenbach's Odic force, and to the Astral Light, also known as the Akashic Records: a subtle form of energy said to surround the Earth, in which is preserved a record of every thought and action that has ever occurred.

In spite of the sober research of writers like Goodrick-Clarke and Godwin, the idea of an immensely sinister and powerful Vril Society secretly controlling the Third Reich has lost nothing of its ability to fascinate. Many still maintain that Haushofer introduced Hitler to the leader of the group of Tibetan high lamas living in Berlin, a man known only as 'The Man with the Green Gloves', and that this man knew the locations of the hidden entrances to the subterranean realms of Agartha and Shambhala. (22)

These rumors doubtless gave rise to the famous legends about Hitler's obsessive search for the entrances to the inner world. According to Maclellan: 'The first expeditions were dispatched purely under the auspices of the Luminous Lodge, beginning in 1926, but later, after coming to power, Hitler took a more direct interest, overseeing the organization of the searches himself.' (23) Maclellan also states that Hitler believed unequivocally that 'certain representatives of the underground super-race were already abroad in the world', (24) citing Hermann Rauschning's famous book Hitler Speaks A Series of Political Conversations with Adolf Hitler on his Real Aims (1939). The conversations recorded by Rauschning have served as source material for many writers on the Third Reich, including serious ones. Proponents of genuine Nazi occult power have repeatedly pointed to the mystical elements in Hitler's conversations as relayed by Rauschning, who says that he repeatedly had the feeling that Hitler was a medium, possessed of supernatural powers. It seems that on one occasion, Hitler actually met one of the subterranean Supermen. Rauschning claims that Hitler confided to him: The new man is among us. He is here! Now are you satis-

OCCULT SECRETS OF THE THIRD REICH

fied? I will tell you a secret. I have seen the vision of the new man—fearless and formidable. I shrank from him.' (25)

To his credit, Maclellan states that this was more than likely a deranged fantasy on Hitler's part. However, Rauschning's very description should be treated with extreme caution: it should be noted that, in spite of the widespread interest it stimulated, Hitler Speaks has not stood the test of time as an accurate historical document. In fact, Ian Kershaw, one of the foremost authorities on Hitler and the author of Hitler 1889-1936: Hubris (1998), does not cite Rauschning's book anywhere in his monumental study, and states that it is 'a work now regarded to have so little authenticity that it is best to disregard it altogether'. (26)

As the story goes, Hitler ordered a number of expeditions into German, Swiss and Italian mines to search for the entrances to the cavern cities of the Supermen. He is even said to have ordered research to be conducted into the life of Bulwer-Lytton, in an effort to determine whether the author himself had visited the realm of the Vril-ya. While serious writers ignore these rumors, there is an interesting event on record that Maclellan quotes in his The Lost World of Agharti and that illustrates the frustrating nature of the 'twilight zone between fact and fiction' in which we find ourselves when discussing Nazi occultism.

Maclellan cites the testimony of one Antonin Horak, an expert speleologist and member of the Slovak Uprising, who accidentally discovered a strange tunnel in Czechoslovakia in October 1944. Dr. Horak kept quiet about the discovery until 1965, when he published an account in the National Speleological Society News. In his article, Dr. Horak stated that he and two other Resistance fighters found the tunnel near the villages of Plavince and Lubocna (he is quite specific about the location: 49.2 degrees north, 20.7 degrees east). Having just survived a skirmish with the Germans, the three men (one of whom was badly injured) asked a local peasant for help. He led them to an underground grotto where they could hide and rest. The peasant told the Resistance men that the cave contained pits, pockets of poison gas, and was also haunted, and warned them against venturing too far inside. This they had no intention of doing, such was their weariness. They attended to the wounds of their comrade and fell asleep.

The following day, Horak's curiosity got the better of him and, while he waited for the injured man to recover enough strength to travel again, he decided to do a little exploring inside the cave. Presently, he came to a section that was completely different from the rest of the cave. 'Lighting some torches, I saw that I was in a spacious, curved, black shaft formed by cliff-like walls. The floor in the incline was a solid lime pavement.' (27) The tunnel stretched interminably into the distance. Dr. Horak decided to take a sample of the wall, but was unable to make any impression with his pickaxe. He took his pistol and fired at the wall (surely an unwise thing to do, given the risk of a ricochet and with German soldiers possibly still in the vicinity).

'The bullet slammed into the substance of the walls with a deafening, fiery impact,' he wrote. 'Sparks flashed, there was a roaring sound, but not so much as a

191

OCCULT SECRETS OF THE THIRD REICH

splinter fell from the substance. Only a small welt appeared, about the length of half my finger, which gave off a pungent smell.'

Dr. Horak then returned to his comrades and told them about the apparently man-made tunnel. 'I sat there by the fire speculating. How far did it reach into the rocks? I wondered.

Who, or what, put it into the mountain? Was it man-made? And was it at last proof of the truth in legends—like Plato's—of long-lost civilizations with magic technologies which our rationale cannot grasp or believe?' (28) No one else, apparently, has explored this tunnel since Dr. Horak in 1944. The peasants who lived in the region obviously knew of its existence, but kept well away.

In addition to the stories of Nazi mine expeditions in Central and Eastern Europe during the Second World War, occult writers have frequently made reference to the Nazi Tibet Expeditions, allegedly an attempt to locate and make contact with a group of high lamas with access to fantastic power. Once again, Pauwels and Bergier have plenty to say on this subject, which is in itself enough to give pause to the cautious.

The American researcher Peter Levenda experienced a similar skepticism with regard to the supposed Nazi-Tibet connection, until he began to search for references in the microfilmed records in the Captured German Documents Section of the National Archives in Washington, DC. He discovered a wealth of material, running to many hundreds of pages, dealing with the work of Dr. Ernst Schafer of the Ahnenerbe. These documents included Dr. Schafer's personal notebooks, his correspondence, clippings from several German newspapers, and his SS file, which describes an expedition to East and Central Tibet from 1934-1936, and the official SS-Tibet Expedition of 1938-1939 under his leadership. (29)

As Levenda demonstrates, the expedition was not so much concerned with contacting Tibetan representatives of the subterranean super-race as with cataloguing the flora and fauna of the region (an activity of little military value to the Third Reich, which accounts for the difficulty Dr. Schafer occasionally had in securing funding for his trips).

Born in Cologne on 14 March 1910 into a wealthy industrialist family, Ernst Schafer attended school in Heidelberg and Gottingen, and embarked on his first expedition to Tibet in 1930 under the auspices of the Academy of Natural Sciences in Philadelphia when he was only twenty years old. The following year, he joined the American Brooke Dolan expedition to Siberia, China and Tibet. He became a member of the SS in mid1933, finally reaching the rank of Sturmbannfuhrer in 1942. In addition to being an SS officer, Dr. Schafer was also a respected scientist who published papers in various journals, such as the Proceedings of the Academy of Natural Sciences, Philadelphia. As Levenda wryly notes, Dr. Schafer was 'a man of many parts: one part SS officer and one part scholar, one part explorer and one part scientist: a Nazi Indiana Jones'. (30) Dr. Schafer was also deeply interested in the religious and cultural practices of the Tibetans, including their sexuality. (Indeed, the members of

192

the 1938-1939 expedition displayed a somewhat prurient fascination with intimate practices: the film-maker Ernst Krause, for instance, took great care to record his observation of a fifteen-year-old Lanchung girl masturbating on a bridge beam.) (31)

When not cataloguing flora and fauna (and spying on teenage girls), the members of the expedition managed to conduct other research, which included an exhaustive study of the physical attributes of the Tibetan people. Dr. Schafer noted height and weight, the shape of hands and feet, the color and shape of eyes, and even took plaster casts of Tibetans' faces. On 21 July 1939, Der Neue Tag published the following article:

SACRED TIBETAN SCRIPTURE ACQUIRED BY THE SCHAFER EXPEDITION ON NINE ANIMAL LOADS ACROSS THE HIGH-COUNTRY

The Tibet Expedition of Dr. Ernst Schafer, which during its expedition through Tibet stayed a long time in Lhasa and in the capital of the Panchen Lama, Shigatse, is presently on its return trip to Germany. Since the monsoons began unusually early, the return march of the expedition was hastened in order to secure the shipment of the precious collections. The expedition has singularly valuable scientific research results to inventory. In addition to outstanding accomplishments in the areas of geophysical and earth-magnetic research they succeeded in obtaining an extra-rich ethnological collection including, along with cult objects, many articles and tools of daily life.

With the help of the regent of Lhasa it was Dr. Schafer who also succeeded in obtaining the Kangschur, the extensive, 108-volume sacred script of the Tibetans, which required nine animal loads to transport. Also especially extensive are the zoological and botanical collections that the expedition has already shipped, in part, to Germany, the remainder of which they will bring themselves. The zoological collection includes the total bird-fauna of the research area. Dr. Schafer was also able, for the first time, to bag a Schapi, a hitherto unknown wild goat. About 50 live animals are on the way to Germany, while numerous other live animals are still with the expedition. An extensive herbarium of all existing plants is also on its way. Furthermore, valuable geographical and earth-historical accomplishments were made. Difficulties encountered due to political tensions with the English authorities were eliminated due to personal contact between Dr. Schafer and members of the British authorities in Shangtse, so that the unimpeded return of the expedition out of Tibet with its valuable collections was guaranteed. (32)

Levenda informs us that he was unable to discover the fate of the Kangschur, the 'core document' of Tibetan Buddhism, although he suspects that it was taken to Vienna. With regard to the expedition itself, while it must be conceded that it had very little to do with the occult or magical ambitions of the Third Reich, it is possible that the 'earth-magnetic' and 'geophysical' experiments had a firm foundation in a very shaky theory. Levenda suggests that the Tibet Expedition of 1938-1939 attempted to prove the pseudo-scientific World Ice Theory of Hans Horbiger. This bizarre theory will be discussed in detail in Chapter Seven. But for now, let us return to the concept embodied in the rumors about the Vril Society, with its alleged attempts to contact (and enlist the aid of) a mysterious group of vastly powerful Eastern adepts. To examine the origins of this idea, we must ourselves embark on a journey to Tibet, known in some quarters as 'the Phantom Kingdom'.

4—THE PHANTOM KINGDOM
THE NAZI-TIBET CONNECTION

At first sight, it might seem strange in the extreme that the architects of the Third Reich would be interested in a region that many consider to be the spiritual centre of the world; until, that is, we remember that, according to Thulean mythology, this centre was once the Aryan homeland in the Arctic, and was displaced with the fall of Atlantis around 10,800 BC (see Chapter Two). Since then, the spiritual centre, while remaining hidden from the vast majority of humanity who are unworthy of its secrets, has nevertheless been the primary force controlling the destiny of the planet. (1) The two hidden realms of Agartha and Shambhala constitute the double source of supernatural power emanating from Tibet, and have come to occupy an important place in twentieth-century occultism and fringe science.

Before we address the Third Reich's alleged interest in Agartha and Shambhala, it is essential that we pause for a (necessarily brief) examination of the role of Shambhala in Tibetan mysticism. In this way, we may chart the course of its warping and degradation as it was fitted into the Nazi scheme of crypto-history.

THE LAND OF THE IMMORTALS

The writer Andrew Tomas spent many years studying the myths and legends of the Far East, and his book Shambhala: Oasis of Light is an eloquent argument in favor of the realm's actual existence. In the book, Tomas cites the ancient writings of China, which refer to Nu and Kua, the 'Asiatic prototypes of Adam and Eve' and their birthplace in the Kun Lun Mountains of Central Asia. It is something of a mystery-why such a desolate, forbidding place should serve as the Chinese Garden of Eden rather than more hospitable regions such as the Yangtse Valley or the province of Shantung, and Tomas speculates that the Gobi Desert may at one time have been an inland sea with accompanying fertile land. (2) As we shall see later in this chapter, the Gobi is a prime candidate as a site for one of the ancient and unknown civilizing cultures whose wisdom has been passed down through the ages.

The Kun Lun Mountains hold a very important place in Chinese mythology, since it is in this range that the Immortals are believed to live, ruled by Hsi Wang Mu, the Queen Mother of the West. Hsi Wang Mu, who is also called Kuan Yin, the goddess of mercy, is said to live in a nine-storeyed palace of jade. Surrounding this palace is a vast garden in which grows the Peach Tree of Immortality. Only the most wise and virtuous of human beings are permitted to visit the garden and eat the fruit, which appears only once every 6,000 years. (3)

The Immortals who aid Hsi Wang Mu in her attempts to guide humanity towards wisdom and compassion possess perfect, ageless bodies, and are said to be able to travel anywhere in the Universe, and to live on the planets of other star systems. As Tomas notes, whether the ancient Chinese believed that the Immortals could travel in space in their physical bodies or by projecting their minds, this is still a remarkable concept to entertain, since it is based on an acceptance of the plurality of inhabited worlds in the Cosmos.

Ancient Chinese texts are replete with legends regarding the attempts of many people to cross the Gobi Desert to the Kun Lun Mountains. The most famous of these searchers is surely the great philosopher Lao Tzu (c. 6th century BC), author of the book of Taoist teaching Tao Te Ching, who is said to have made the journey across the Gobi towards the end of his life. The Vatican archives also contain many reports made by Catholic missionaries concerning deputations from the emperors of China to the spiritual beings living in the mountains. These beings possess bodies that are visible, but which are not made of flesh and blood: they are the 'mind-born' gods whose bodies are composed of elementary atomic matter, which allow them to live anywhere in the Universe, even at the centers of stars.

The people of India also believe in a place of wisdom and spiritual perfection; they call it Kalapa or Katapa, and it is said to lie in a region north of the Himalayas, in Tibet. According to Indian tradition, the Gobi Desert is the floor of what was once a great sea, which contained an island called Sweta-Dvipa (White Island). The great Yogis who once lived there are believed to live still in the high mountains and deep valleys that once formed the island of Sweta-Dvipa. This island has been identified by Orientalists with the Isle of Shambhala of Puranic literature, which is said to stand at the centre of a lake of nectar.

In the seventeenth century, two Jesuit missionaries, Stephen Cacella and John Cabral, recorded the existence of Chang Shambhala, as described to them by the lamas of Shigatse, where Cacella lived for 23 years until his death in 1650. (Chang Shambhala means Northern Shambhala, which differentiates the abode of the spiritual adepts from the town called Shamballa, north of Benares, India.) (4) Nearly 200 years later, a Hungarian philologist named Csoma de Koros, who lived for four years from 1827-30 in a Buddhist monastery in Tibet, claimed that Chang Shambhala lay between 45° and 50° north latitude, beyond the river Syr Daria. (5)

Legends of a hidden spiritual centre, a sacred zone whose inhabitants secretly guide the evolution of life on Earth, are widespread in the ancient cultures of the East. The writer Victoria Le Page describes this wondrous realm thus:

... [S]omewhere beyond Tibet, among the icy peaks and secluded valleys of Central Asia, there lies an inaccessible paradise, a place of universal wisdom and ineffable peace called Shambhala ... It is inhabited by adepts from every race and culture who form an inner circle of humanity secretly guiding its evolution. In that place, so the legends say, sages have existed since the beginning of human history in a valley of supreme beatitude that is sheltered from the icy arctic winds and where the climate is always warm and temperate, the sun always shines, the gentle airs are always beneficent and nature flowers luxuriantly. (6)

Only the purest of heart are allowed to find this place (others, less idealistically motivated, who search for it risk an icy grave) where want, evil, violence and injustice do not exist. The inhabitants possess both supernatural powers and a highly advanced technology; their bodies are perfect, and they devote their time to the study of the arts and sciences. The concept of the hidden spiritual centre of the world is to be found in Hinduism, Buddhism, Taoism, shamanism and other ancient traditions. In the Bon religion of pre-Buddhist Tibet, Shambhala is also called 'Olmolungring' and 'Dejong'. In Tibetan Buddhism, the Shambhalic tradition is enshrined within the Kalachakra texts, which are said to have been taught to the King of Shambhala by the Buddha before being returned to India. (7)

As might be expected with such a marvelous, legend-haunted place, there has been a great deal of speculation as to the exact whereabouts of Shambhala. (It is unlikely to be found at Koros's map coordinates.) While some esotericists believe that Shambhala is a real place with a concrete, physical presence in a secret location on Earth, others prefer to see it as existing on a higher spiritual plane, what might be called another dimension of space-time coterminous with our own. Alternatively, Shambhala might be considered as a state of mind, comparable to the terms in which some consider the Holy Grail. As with the Grail, Shambhala maybe a state within ourselves, in which we may gain an insight into the higher spirituality inherent in the Universe, as distinct from the mundane world of base matter in which we normally exist.

Having said this, it should be noted that there are certain cases on record in which Westerners have experienced visions of a place bearing a striking resemblance to the fabled Shambhala. Victoria Le Page cites a particularly intriguing case in her book Shambhala: The Fascinating Truth Behind the Myth of Shangri-la. The case was investigated by a Dr. Raynor Johnson who, in the 1960s, gathered together several hundred first-hand accounts of mystical experiences. It involved a young Australian woman who claimed to have psychic abilities, and who was referred to simply as L.C.W.

L.C.W. wrote that at the age of 21 she began to attend a place she came to know as 'Night-School'. At night she would fly in her sleep to this place, the location of which she had no idea. Once there she would join other people in dance exercises which she later recognized as being similar to the dervish exercises taught by George Gurdjieff. After several years, she graduated to a different class, where she was taught spiritual lessons from a great book of wisdom. It was only years later, when L.C.W. began to take an interest in mystical literature, that she realized the true location of Night-School must have been Shambhala. L.C.W. had other visions in which she saw what appeared to be a gigantic mast or antenna, extending from Earth deep into interstellar space. The base of this antenna was in the Pamirs or Tien Shan Mountains, regions which are traditionally associated with Shambhala. She was taken towards this antenna by an invisible guide, and saw that it was a pillar of energy whose branches were actually paths leading to other worlds, marked by geometrical figures such as circles, triangles and squares.

According to L.C.W., this 'antenna' was nothing less than a gateway to other times, other dimensions and other regions of this Universe. In addition to the antenna serving as a gateway for souls from Earth to travel to other times and places, 'she believed souls from other systems in space could enter the earth sphere by the same route, carrying their own spiritual influences with them'. (8) L.C.W. also maintained that the antenna could be controlled directly by the mind of the voyager, and would extend a branch or 'pseudopod' in response to a single thought. This branch then became a 'trajectory of light' along which the soul would travel; in her case, she found herself in China 30 years in the future. The spiritual being who was guiding her explained that the earth was in the process of being purified, and that a 'great rebirth' was about to occur. She also witnessed the apparent falling of a cluster of 'stars' that represented the arrival of 'high souls [that] were now coming down to help in the special event'. (9)

Our knowledge of the Shambhalic tradition in the West has come mainly from Orientalist scholars such as Helena Blavatsky, Rene Guenon, Louis Jacolliot, Saint-Yves d'Alveydre and Nicholas Roerich. Since we have already spent some time with Madame Blavatsky, we may turn our attention to the work of the others, notably Nicholas Roerich (1874-1947), poet, artist, mystic and humanist, and perhaps the most famous and respected of the esotericists who brought news of this fabulous realm to Westerners.

Born in St Petersburg, Russia in 1874, Nicholas Roerich came from a distinguished family whose ability to trace its origins to the Vikings of the tenth century inspired his early interest in archaeology. This interest led in turn to a lifelong fascination with art, through which, in the words of K. P. Tampy, who wrote a monograph on Roerich in 1935, he became 'possessed of a burning desire to get at the beautiful and make use of it for his brethren'. (10) After attending the St Petersburg Academy of Fine Art, Roerich went to Paris to continue his studies. In 1906, he won a prize for his design of a new church, and was also rewarded with the position of Director of the Academy for the Encouragement of Fine Arts in Russia. However, the Russian Revolution occurred while he was on a visit to America, and he found himself unable to return to his motherland.

Roerich's profound interest in Buddhist mysticism led to his proposing an expedition in 1923 that would explore India, Mongolia and Tibet. The Roerich Expedition of 1923-26 was made across the Gobi Desert to the Altai Mountains. It was during this expedition that Roerich's party had a most unusual experience—one of the many experiences that seem to offer strange and puzzling connections between apparently disparate elements of the paranormal and that make it such a complex and fascinating field of human enquiry. In the summer of 1926, Roerich had set up camp with his son, Dr. George Roerich, and several Mongolian guides in the Shara-gol valley near the Humboldt Mountains between Mongolia and Tibet. Roerich had just built a white stupa (or shrine), dedicated to Shambhala. The shrine was consecrated in August, with the ceremony witnessed by a number of invited lamas.

Two days later, the party watched as a large black bird wheeled through the sky above them. This, however, was not what astonished them, for far beyond the black bird, high up in the cloudless sky, they clearly saw a golden spheroidal object moving from the Altai Mountains to the north at tremendous speed. Veering sharply to the south-west, the golden sphere disappeared rapidly beyond the Humboldt Mountains. As the Mongolian guides shouted to one another in the utmost excitement, one of the lamas turned to Roerich and informed him that the fabulous golden orb was the sign of Shambhala, meaning that the lords of that realm approved of his mission of exploration.

Later, Roerich was asked by another lama if there had been a perfume on the air. When Roerich replied that there had been, the lama told him that he was guarded by the King of Shambhala, Rigden Jye-Po, that the black vulture was his enemy, but that he was protected by a 'Radiant form of Matter'. The lama added that anyone who saw the radiant sphere should follow the direction in which it flew, for in that direction lay Shambhala.

The exact purpose of this expedition (aside from exploration) was never made entirely clear by Roerich, but many writers on esoteric subjects have claimed that he was on a mission to return a certain sacred object to the King's Tower at the centre of Shambhala. According to Andrew Tomas, the sacred object was a fragment of the Chintamani stone, the great mass of which lies in the Tower. Astonishingly, the stone is said to have been brought to Earth originally by an extraterrestrial being.

According to tradition, a chest fell from the sky in AD 331; the chest contained four sacred objects, including the Chintamani stone. Many years after the casket was discovered, five strangers visited King Tho-tho-ri Nyan-tsan to explain the use of the sacred objects. The Chintamani stone is said to come from one of the star systems in the constellation of Orion, probably Sirius. The main body of the stone is always kept in the Tower of Shambhala, although small pieces are sometimes transferred to other parts of the world during times of great change.

It is rumored that the fragment of Chintamani which Roerich was returning to the Tower had been in the possession of the League of Nations, of which Roerich was a highly respected member.

THE CAVES BENEATH THE HIMALAYAS

The concept of a subterranean realm (which we will discuss in much greater detail in Chapter Seven) is common throughout the world's religions and mythologies. With regard to the present study, we can identify a powerful antecedent to the legends and rumors still extant today in the mythology of Tibet. In his 1930 book

Shambhala, Roerich describes his attempts to understand the origins of underworld legends 'to discover what memories were being cherished in the folk-memory'. (11) In commenting on the ubiquity of subterranean legends, he notes that the more one examines them, the greater the conviction that they are all 'but chapters from the one story'. (12) An examination of the folklores of 'Tibet, Mongolia, China, Turkestan, Kashmir, Persia, Altai, Siberia, the Ural, Caucasia, the Russian steppes, Lithuania, Poland, Hungary, Germany, France' (13) will yield tales of dwellers beneath the earth. In many places, the local people can even guide the curious traveller to cave entrances in isolated places, which are said to lead to the hidden world of the subterraneans.

Central Asia is home to legends of an underground race called the Agharti; the Altai Mountains are the dwelling place of the Chud. In Shambhala, Roerich states that the name 'Chud' in Russian has the same origin as the word 'wonder'. His guide through the Altai Mountains told him that the Chud were originally a powerful but peaceful tribe who flourished in the area in the distant past. However, they fell prey to marauding bands of warriors, and could only escape by leaving their fertile valley and departing into the earth to continue their civilization in subterranean realms.

Roerich's guide continued that at certain times the Chud could be heard singing in their underground temples. Elsewhere in the Altai Mountains, on the way to Khotan, Roerich reports that the hoofs of their horses sounded hollow upon the ground, as though they were riding over immense caves. Other members of the caravan called to Roerich: 'Do you hear what hollow subterranean passages we are crossing? Through these passages, people who are familiar with them can reach far-off countries.' (14) (The significance of this claim will become more apparent in Chapter Seven.) The caravaneers continued:

'Long ago people lived there; now they have gone inside; they have found a subterranean passage to the subterranean kingdom. Only rarely do some of them appear again on earth. At our bazaar such people come with strange, very ancient money, but nobody could even remember a time when such money was in usage here.' When Roerich asked if he, too, could see such people, his companions replied: 'Yes, if your thoughts are similarly high and in contact with these holy people, because only sinners are upon earth and the pure and courageous people pass on to something more beautiful.' (15)

In the region of Nijni Novgorod there is a legend of a subterranean city called Kerjenetz that sank into a lake. In Roerich's time, local people still held processions through the area, during which they would listen for the bells of invisible churches.

Roerich's party went on to discover four more groups of menhirs, and several tombs, taking the form of a square outlined by large stones. To the people of the Himalayas, those who built these monuments, although now departed, are not to be found anywhere on the Earth's surface: 'all which has disappeared, has departed underground'. (16)

Dr. Ferdinand Ossendowski, whom we shall meet again in a little while, was told by lamas in Mongolia of fabulous civilizations existing before recorded history. To Ossendowski's astonishment, the lamas claimed that when the homelands of these civilizations in the Atlantic and Pacific were destroyed by natural cataclysms some of their inhabitants survived in previously prepared subterranean shelters, illuminated by artificial light. Andrew Tomas speculates that the Celtic legend of 'the Lordly Ones in the hollow hills' is a folk memory of the survivors of the destruction of the Atlantic continent. (17)

In India, legends tell of a race of beings called the Nagas. Serpent-like and extremely intelligent, the Nagas live in vast caverns illuminated by precious stones. Although reptilian, the Nagas have human faces and are incredibly beautiful. Able to fly, they intermarried with kings and queens from the surface world, although they remain shy of surface dwellers and keep well away from all but the most spiritually advanced. Their capital city is called Bhogawati, and is said to be covered with rubies, emeralds and diamonds. (18)

Tomas writes that many Hindus and Tibetans have entered the caves of the Nagas, which stretch for hundreds of miles inside the mountains.

The inhabitants of this region speak of large lotus flowers floating on the surface of the Manasarawar Lake in the western part of the Tsang Po Valley. Radiant figures have also been seen near this extremely cold fresh-water lake.

THE REALM OF AGARTHA

Despite its inclusion in many popular books on Eastern mysticism, the name 'Agartha' is unknown in Asiatic mythology. In fact, one of the many variations on the name, 'Asgaard', was first used by the French writer Ernest Renan in the 1870s. Although clearly inspired by Nordic mythology, Renan placed his Asgaard in Central Asia, while another French writer, Louis Jacolliot (1837-1890), was writing at the same time about a city of Asgartha.

(19) A magistrate in Chandernagor, India, Jacolliot wrote a number of books on the relationship between Indian mythology and Christianity. He was allegedly told the legend of Asgartha by a group of local Brahmins, who allowed him to consult various sacred texts, such as the Book of Historical Zodiacs.

According to Jacolliot, Asgartha was a prehistoric 'City of the Sun', home of the Brahmatma, the visible manifestation of God on Earth. (20) Asgartha existed in India in 13,300 BC, where the Brahmatma lived in an immense palace; he was invisible, and only appeared to his subjects once a year. Interestingly, Jacolliot stated that this high prehistoric culture existed long before the Aryans, who conquered Asgartha around 10,000 BC. The priests of Asgartha then managed to form an alliance with the victorious Aryan Brahmins, which resulted in the formation of the warrior caste of Kshatriyas. About 5,000 years later, Asgartha was destroyed by the brothers Ioda and Skandah, who came from the Himalayas. Eventually driven out by the Brahmins, the brothers travelled north—and later gave their names to 'Odin' and 'Scandinavia'. (21)

Ferdinand Ossendowski (1876-1945) was another early writer on the legend of

OCCULT SECRETS OF THE THIRD REICH

Agartha. Although born in Vitebsk, Poland, he spent most of his early life in Russia, attending the University of St Petersburg. For much of the 1890s, he travelled extensively in Mongolia and Siberia, developing his interest in and knowledge of Buddhist mysticism. He returned to Europe in 1900 and gained a doctorate in Paris in 1903, before returning to Russia and working as a chemist for the Russian Army during the Russo-Japanese War of 1905. He then became president of the 'Revolutionary Government of the Russian Far East', before being taken prisoner by the Russian Government for his anti-Tsarist activities. (22)

After two years' imprisonment in Siberia, he taught physics and chemistry in the Siberian town of Omsk, until the Bolshevik Revolution forced him to flee Russia with a small group of fellow White Russians. Together they travelled across Siberia and into Mongolia, and he wrote of their adventures in his best-selling book Beasts, Men and Gods (1923). While in Mongolia, Ossendowski made the acquaintance of a fellow Russian, a priest named Tushegoun Lama who claimed to be a friend of the Dalai Lama. Tushegoun Lama told Ossendowski of the subterranean kingdom of Agartha, home of the King of the World. Intrigued by this reference, Ossendowski asked his friend for further information on this mysterious personage. 'Only one man knows his holy name. Only one man now living was ever in [Agartha]. That is I. This is the reason why the Most Holy Dalai Lama has honored me and why the Living Buddha in Urga fears me. But in vain, for I shall never sit on the Holy Throne of the highest priest in Lhasa nor reach that which has come down from Jenghis Khan to the Head of our Yellow Faith. I am no monk. I am a warrior and avenger.' (23)

Several months later, while continuing across Mongolia with some guides left behind by Tushegoun Lama (who had since gone his own way), Ossendowski was startled when his companions suddenly halted and dismounted from their camels, which immediately lay down. The Mongols began to pray, chanting: 'Om! Mani padme Hung!' Ossendowski waited until they had finished praying before asking them what was happening. One of the Mongol guides replied thus:

'Did you not see how our camels moved their ears in fear? How the herd of horses on the plain stood fixed in attention and how the herds of sheep and cattle lay crouched close to the ground? Did you notice that the birds did not fly, the marmots did not run and the dogs did not bark? The air trembled softly and bore from afar the music of a song which penetrated to the hearts of men, animals and birds alike. Earth and sky ceased breathing. The wind did not blow and the sun did not move. At such a moment the wolf that is stealing up on the sheep arrests his stealthy crawl; the frightened herd of antelopes suddenly checks its wild course; the knife of the shepherd cutting the sheep's throat falls from his hand; the rapacious ermine ceases to stalk the unsuspecting saiga. All living beings in fear are involuntarily thrown into prayer and waiting for their fate. So it was just now. Thus it has always been whenever the "King of the World" in his subterranean palace prays and searches out the destiny of all peoples on the earth.' (24)

Later, Ossendowski met an old Tibetan, Prince Chultun Beyli, living in exile in

Mongolia, who furnished him with more details of the subterranean realm of Agartha and the King of the World. Agartha, he said, extends throughout all the subterranean passageways of the world. The inhabitants owe allegiance to the 'King of the World'. They can cultivate crops due to a strange light that pervades the underground realm. Some of the inhabitants of these regions are extremely strange: one race has two tongues, enabling them to speak in two languages at the same time. There are also many fantastic animals, including tortoises with sixteen feet and one eye.

At this point, Ossendowski was approaching the Chinese border. It was his intention to take a train to Peking, from which he might find passage to the West. In the town of Urga he met an old lama, who provided him with yet more information on the King of the World. The King's influence on the activities of the world's apparent leaders was profound. If their plans were pleasing before God, then the King of the World would help them to realize them; but if they displeased God, then the King would surely destroy them. His power came from the 'mysterious science of "Om"', which is the name of an ancient Holyman who lived more than 300,000 years ago, the first man to know God.

When Ossendowski asked him if anyone had ever seen the King of the World, the old lama replied that during the solemn holidays of the ancient Buddhism in Siam and India the King appeared five times in a 'splendid car drawn by white elephants'. (25) He wore a white robe and a red tiara with strings of diamonds that hid his face. When he blessed the people with a golden apple surmounted by the figure of a lamb, the 'blind received their sight, the dumb spoke, the deaf heard, the crippled freely moved and the dead arose, wherever the eyes of the "King of the World" rested'. (26)

Ossendowski then asked the lama how many people had been to Agartha. He replied that very many had, but that they never spoke about what they had seen there. He continued that, when the Olets destroyed Lhasa, one of their detachments found its way into the outskirts of Agartha, where they learned some of the lesser mysterious sciences. This is the reason for the magical skills of the Olets and Kalmucks.

Another of Ossendowski's informants, a lama named Turgut, told him that the capital of Agartha is surrounded by the towns of the high priests and scientists, somewhat in the way that the Potala palace of the Dalai Lama in Lhasa is surrounded by monasteries and temples. The throne on which the King of the World sits is itself surrounded by millions of incarnated gods, the Holy Panditas. The King's palace is surrounded by the palaces of the Goro, who possess fantastic power, and who would easily be able to incinerate the entire surface of the Earth, should humankind be unwise enough to declare war on them. (As we shall see in Chapter Seven, the legend of the King of the World would serve as the inspiration for one of the most enduring technological myths of the twentieth century.)

The legend of Agartha was discussed at length by another writer, the self-educated Christian Hermeticist Saint-Yves d'Alveydre (1842-1909), whose marriage into money enabled him to indulge his yearning for mystical understanding. In 1885 he began to take lessons in Sanskrit from one Haji Sharif (1838-?), about whom very little is known save that he left India at the time of the Sepoy Revolt of 1857 and worked as a bird-seller at Le Havre. (27) The manuscripts of d'Alveydre's lessons are preserved in the library of the Sorbonne in Paris. In them, Sharif refers to the 'Great Agarthian School' and the 'Holy Land of Agarttha' (one of the many alternative spellings of the name).

Sharif claimed that the original language of humanity, called Vattan or Vattanian, derived from a 22-letter alphabet. Although he was unable physically to visit Agartha, d'Alveydre found an ingenious alternative: through disengaging his astral body, he was able to visit the fabulous realm in spirit form (see pages 108-110). His astral adventures resulted in a series of books (Mission des Souverains, Mission des Ouvriers, Mission des Juifs and Mission de l'Inde), which he published at his own expense. Interestingly, he destroyed the entire edition of the last work, Mission de l'Inde, for fear that he had revealed too many secrets of Agartha and might be made to pay for his transgression with his life. Only two copies survived: one that he kept himself and one that was hidden by the printer. (28)

He might well have been concerned, for Mission de l'Inde contains a detailed account of Agartha, which lies beneath the surface of the Earth somewhere in the East and is ruled over by an Ethiopian 'Sovereign Pontiff called the Brahmatma. The realm of Agartha was transferred underground at the beginning of the Kali-Yuga, about 3200 BC. The Agarthians possess technology that was impressive in d'Alveydre's day, including railways and air travel. They know everything about the surface-dwellers, and occasionally send emissaries. Agartha contains many libraries in which all the knowledge of Earth is recorded on stone tablets in Vattanian characters, including the means by which the living may communicate with the souls of the dead.

D'Alveydre states that, although many millions of students have tried to possess the secrets of Agartha, very few have ever succeeded in getting further than the outer circles of the realm.

Like Bulwer-Lytton, who wrote of the Vril-ya in his fictional work The Coming Race (discussed in the previous chapter), d'Alveydre speaks of the Agartthians as being superior to humanity in every respect, the true rulers of the world. A certain amount of controversy arose when Ossendowski published his Beasts, Men and Gods: it displayed such similarities to d'Alveydre's work that he was accused by some of plagiarism only imperfectly masked by an alteration in the spelling of Agartha. Ossendowski denied the charge vehemently, and claimed never to have heard of d'Alveydre before 1924. Rene Guenon defended Ossendowski, and claimed that there were many tales of subterranean realms told throughout Central Asia. In fact, Guenon's work would later be heavily criticized by his translator Marco Pallis, who called his book Le Roi du Monde (The King of the World) 'disastrous' in conversation with Joscelyn Godwin, on the grounds that Ossendowski's sources were unreliable, and Guenon had allowed himself to enter the realms of the sensational. (29)

OCCULT SECRETS OF THE THIRD REICH

THE NAZIS AND TIBETAN MYSTICISM

The legends surrounding the realms of Agartha and Shambhala are confusing to say the least, and their frequently contradictory nature does nothing to help in an understanding of their possible influence on the hideous philosophy of the Third Reich. As we have seen, some writers claim that Agartha and Shambhala are physical places, cities lying miles underground with houses, palaces, streets and millions of inhabitants. Others maintain that they are altogether more rarefied places, existing on some other level of reality but apparently coterminous with our physical world. With regard to their exact location, Childress offers a short summary of their many possible locations: 'Shambhala is sometimes said to be north of Lhasa, possibly in the Gobi Desert, and other times it is said to be somewhere in Mongolia, or else in northern Tibet, possibly in the Changtang Highlands. Agharta is said to be south of Lhasa, perhaps near the Shigatse Monastery, or even in Northeast Nepal beneath Mount Kanchenjunga. Occasionally it is said to be in Sri Lanka. Both have been located inside the hollow earth.' (30)

Adding to this confusion is the frequently made assertion that the two power centers are opposed to each other, with Agartha seen as following the right-hand path of goodness and light, and Shambhala following the left-hand path of evil and darkness (a dichotomy also expressed as spirituality versus materialism). There is, needless to say, an opposing view that holds that Agartha is a place of evil and Shambhala the abode of goodness.

There have been a number of rumors concerning practitioners of black magic operating in Tibet and referring to themselves as the Shambhala or the Agarthi. (31) Although apparently outlawed by Tibetan Buddhists, they are said to continue their activities in secret. One writer who claimed to have encountered them was a German named Theodore Illion who spent the mid-1930s traveling through Tibet. In his book *Darkness Over Tibet* (1937), he describes how he discovered a deep shaft in the countryside. Wishing to gauge its depth, he dropped several stones into it and waited for them to strike the bottom; he was rewarded only with silence. He was told by an initiate that the shaft was 'immeasurably deep' and that only the highest initiates knew where it ended. His companion added: 'Anyone who would find out where it leads to and what it is used for would have to die.' (32)

Illion claimed to have gained access to a subterranean city inhabited by monks, whom he later found to be 'black yogis' planning to control the world through telepathy and astral projection. When he discovered that the food he was being given contained human flesh, he decided to make a break for it and fled across Tibet with several of the monks after him. After several weeks on the run, he managed to escape from Tibet and returned to the West with his bizarre and frightening tale. (33)

There have also been persistent rumors that the Nazi interest in Tibet (itself a documented historical fact) was actually inspired by a desire to contact the black adepts of Shambhala and/or Agartha and to enlist their aid in the conquest of the world (see Chapter Three). One of the most vocal proponents of this idea was the

OCCULT SECRETS OF THE THIRD REICH

British occult writer Trevor Ravenscroft, whose claims we shall examine in greater detail in the next chapter. The schism between Shambhala and Agartha is described by Rene Guenon, who relates in Le Roi du Monde how the ancient civilization in the Gobi Desert was all but destroyed by a natural cataclysm, and the 'Sons of Intelligences of Beyond' retreated to the caverns beneath the Himalayas and re-established their civilization. There followed the formation of two groups: the Agarthi, who followed the way of spirituality, and the Shambhalists, who followed the way of violence and materialism.

Guenon claimed (as would Illion several years later) that the denizens of the subterranean world sought to influence the lives and actions of the surface dwellers through various occult means, including telepathic hypnosis and mediumship. Childress finds it intriguing that Hitler sent expeditions to Tibet in the late 1930s, soon after the publication of Illion's book Darkness Over Tibet, and suggests that their true objective was to make contact with the occult groups. (34)

This crypto-historical scenario continues with Hitler making the acquaintance of a mysterious Tibetan monk who told him that Germany could conquer the world by forging an alliance with the 'Lords of Creation'. While the victorious Russians were picking their way through the ruins of Berlin (and, according to some, discovering the bodies of several Tibetan monks, as we saw in Chapter Three), it is claimed by the crypto-historians that Hitler was flying out of the city's Tempelhof Airfield to a rendezvous with the U-boat (possibly U-977) that would take him either to Argentina or Antarctica. There is, however, a variation on this theme that has the Fuhrer escaping to Tibet to be hidden by those whose alliance he had sought. According to an article in the May 1950 issue of the pro-Nazi Tempo Der Welt, that magazine's publisher, Karl Heinz Kaerner, claimed to have met with Martin Bormann in Morocco the previous year. If the story is to be believed (which would be extremely unwise), Bormann informed Kaerner that Hitler was alive in a Tibetan monastery, and that one day he would be back in power in Germany!

In addressing the question of whether such black magicians really lived (or still live) in Tibet, Childress reminds us that in her book Initiations and Initiates in Tibet, the French writer, explorer and authority on Tibetan mysticism Alexandra David-Neel (1868-1969) describes an encounter with a man who could hypnotize and kill from a distance. Nicholas Roerich also mentions the occultists of the ancient Bon religion, who were at war with the Buddhists of Tibet.

As Childress notes:

Shambhala draws strong similarities to the Land of the Immortals (Hsi Wang Mu) in that it is said to be a wonderful, lush valley in the high mountains with a tall, ornate solid jade tower from which a brilliant light shines. Like in the Kun Lun Mountains, Agharta and Shambhala have a cache of fantastic inventions and artifacts from distant civilizations in the past.

In contrast to the Valley of the Immortals in the Kun Lun Mountains, the cave communities with their incredible sights were part illusion, say Illion and Ravenscroft.

206

At the Valley of the Immortals, perhaps there really were ancient artifacts of a time gone by watched over by Ancient Masters. Yet, it is unlikely that any person not chosen specifically by those who are the caretakers of this repository would be allowed inside Nor would those who had entered (such as possibly Nicholas Roerich) ever reveal the location or what they had seen there. (15)

While certainly intriguing, the claims of crypto-historians regarding Nazi involvement with the black magicians of Tibet suffer from a paucity of hard evidence in the form of documentation and testimony from surviving witnesses. (We have already noted that the much-quoted Hermann Rauschning is considered by some serious historians, such as Ian Kershaw, to be extremely unreliable.) As is so often the case in the field of occultism, the way is left open to those who are quite content to rely on spurious sources and hearsay in their creation of a tantalizing but incredible vision of history. One of the most famous of these crypto-historians is Trevor Ravenscroft, and it is to his claims that we now must turn.

OCCULT SECRETS OF THE THIRD REICH

5—TALISMAN OF CONQUEST
THE SPEAR OF LONGINUS

As we noted in the introduction, a number of writers on the occult have turned their attention over the years to the baffling catastrophe of Nazism and have added their own attempts to explain the terrifying mystery of its true origin by attempting to fit Nazi Germany into an occult context. Perhaps unsurprisingly, these writers have paid close attention to an intriguing statement Hitler is known to have made—'Shall we form a chosen band, made up of those who really know? An order: a brotherhood of the Knights of the Holy Grail, around the Holy Grail of Pure Blood'—and have attempted to use this statement as a point of connection between the Nazis and the occult. Although serious historians accept that occult and folkloric concepts played a significant role in the development of Nazi ideas and doctrine, it has been left largely to writers on 'fringe' subjects to push the envelope (wisely or otherwise) and claim that the Nazis were motivated by genuine occult forces: in other words, that there actually exist in the Universe malign, nonhuman intelligences that seek ways to influence the destiny of humanity for their own ends and that used the Nazis as conduits through which these influences might work. According to this scheme of history, the Nazis were, quite literally, practicing Satanists and black magicians. This is certainly an intriguing notion, but how useful is it as a means to explain the loathsome existence of Nazism?

THE HOLY LANCE AND ITS INFLUENCE ON NAZI OCCULTISM

In 1973 Trevor Ravenscroft, historian and veteran of the Second World War, published a book that would cause more controversy than any other dealing with the subject of Nazism and that is still the subject of heated debate today. Entitled The Spear of Destiny, the book chronicles the early career of the man who would stain the twentieth century with the blood of millions and whose name would become a synonym for cruelty of the most repulsive kind: Adolf Hitler. Hailed by some as a classic of occult history and derided by others as no more than a work of lurid fiction, The Spear of Destiny is still in print today and, whatever its merits or demerits, it remains one of the most important texts in the field of Nazi occultism. (It should be noted here that, such is the murky and bizarre nature of this field, to make such a claim for a book is by no means equivalent to defending its historical accuracy.)

Ravenscroft was a Commando in the Second World War, and spent four years in German POW camps after allegedly participating in an attempt to assassinate Field Marshal Rommel in North Africa in 1941. He made three escape attempts but was recaptured each time. While imprisoned, Ravenscroft claims to have experienced a sudden apprehension of 'higher levels of consciousness', which led him to study the legend of the Holy Grail 'and to research into the history of the Spear of Longinus and the legend of world destiny which had grown around it'. (1)

The spear in question is the one said to have been used by the Roman centurion Gaius Cassius to pierce the side of Christ during the crucifixion. Cassius suffered from cataracts in both eyes, which prevented him from battle service with his Legion, so he was sent to Jerusalem to report on events there. When the Nazarene was crucified, Cassius was present.

Isaiah had prophesied of the Messiah, 'A bone of Him shall not be broken.' Annas, the aged advisor to the Sanhedrin, and Caiaphas, the High Priest, were intent on mutilating the body of Christ to prove to the masses of the people that Jesus was not the Messiah, but merely a heretic and potential usurper of their own power.

The hours were passing and this presented the excuse they needed. For Annas was an authority on the Law, and the Jewish Law decreed that no man should be executed on the Sabbath Day. Straightaway, they petitioned Pontius Pilate for the authority to break the limbs of the crucified men so that they should die before dusk on that Friday afternoon. (2)

When the Temple Guard arrived to mutilate the bodies of Christ and the two thieves, Cassius decided to protect the Nazarene's body in the only way possible. He rode his horse towards the Cross and thrust his spear into Jesus's torso, between the fourth and fifth ribs. The flowing of the Saviour's blood completely restored the centurion's sight.

Gaius Cassius, who had performed a martial deed out of the compassionate motive to protect the body of Jesus Christ, became known as Longinus The Spearman. A convert to Christianity, he came to be revered as a great hero and saint by the first Christian community in Jerusalem, and a prime witness of the shedding of the Blood of the New Covenant for which the Spear became the symbol ...

The legend grew around it, gaining strength with the passing of the centuries, that whoever possessed it and understood the powers it served, held the destiny of the world in his hands for good or evil. (3)

Ravenscroft informs us that, by rights, the man who should have written The Spear of Destiny (and would surely have done so, had he not died in 1957) was a Viennese philosopher and wartime British secret agent named Walter Johannes Stein (b. 1891). An Austrian Jew, Stein had emigrated from Germany to Britain in 1933. His association with Ravenscroft came about as a result of a book Stein had written, entitled The Ninth Century World History in the Light of the Holy Grail (1928). Ravenscroft was greatly impressed by the book, which asserts that the medieval Grail Romances and their description of the quest for the Holy Grail Veiled a unique Western path to transcendent consciousness'. (4) It was clear to Ravenscroft that Dr. Stein had conducted his historical research along rather unorthodox lines, relying on occult methods of mind expansion to apprehend data rather than the more traditional means of consulting extant medieval texts. In view of his own experience of higher levels of consciousness, and his resulting fascination with the Grail legends, Ravenscroft decided to call on Stein at his home in Kensington.

During this meeting, Ravenscroft voiced his belief that Stein had utilized some transcendent faculty in his research for The Ninth Century, adding that he believed a similar faculty had inspired Wolfram von Eschenbach to write the great Grail romance Parsival (c. 1200). According to Stein, von Eschenbach based Parsival on the key figures of the ninth century, who served as models for the characters in the romance. The Grail king Anfortas corresponded to King Charles the Bald, grandson of Charlemagne; Cundrie, the sorceress and messenger of the Grail, was Ricilda the Bad; Parsival himself corresponded to Luitward of Vercelli, the Chancellor to the Frankish Court; and Klingsor, the fantastically evil magician who lived in the Castle of Wonders, was identified as Landulf II of Capua who had made a pact with Islam in Arab-occupied Sicily and whom Ravenscroft calls the most evil figure of the century. (5)

Stein had first read Parsival while taking a short, compulsory course on German literature at the University of Vienna. One night, he had a most unusual extra-sensory experience:

'He awoke ... to discover that he had been reciting whole tracts of the ... romantic verses in a sort of pictureless Dream!' (6) This happened three times in all. Stein wrote down the words he had been speaking and, on comparing them with von Eschenbach's romance, found them to be virtually identical. To Stein this strongly implied the existence of some preternatural mental faculty, a kind of 'higher memory' that could be accessed under certain circumstances.

His subsequent researches into the Grail Romances led to his discovery, one August morning in 1912 in a dingy bookshop in Vienna's old quarter, of a tattered, leather-bound copy of Parsival whose pages were covered with annotations in a minute script. Stein bought the book from the shop assistant and took it to Demel's Cafe in the Kohlmarkt, where he began to pore over its pages As he read, he became more and more uneasy at the nature of the annotations.

This was no ordinary commentary but the work of somebody who had achieved more than a working knowledge of the black arts! The unknown commentator had found the key to unveiling many of the deepest secrets of the Grail, yet obviously spurned the Christian ideals of the [Grail] Knights and delighted in the devious machinations of the Anti-Christ.

It suddenly dawned on him that he was reading the footnotes of Satan! (7)

Stein was repelled yet fascinated by the vulgar racial fanaticism displayed in the annotations, by the 'almost insane worship of Aryan blood lineage and Pan-Germanism'.

For instance, alongside the verses describing the Grail Procession and the Assembly of Knights at the High Mass in the Grail Castle, there appeared an entry written in large letters scrawled across the printed page: 'These men betrayed their pure Aryan Blood to the dirty superstitions of the Jew Jesus—superstitions as loathsome and ludicrous as the Yiddish rites of circumcision.' (8)

To Stein, the annotations represented the workings of a brilliant but utterly hideous mind, a mind that had inverted the traditional idea of the quest for the Grail as a gradual and immensely difficult awakening to wider spiritual reality, turning it into its antithesis: the opening of the human spirit, through the use of black magic, to the power and influence of Satan himself.

Shaken by what he had read in the annotated pages of the book, Stein glanced up for a moment through the cafe window and found himself looking into a disheveled, arrogant face with demoniacal eyes. The apparition was shabbily dressed and was holding several small watercolors that he was trying to sell to passers-by. When Stein left the cafe late that afternoon, he bought some watercolors from the down-and-out painter and hurried home. It was only then that he realized that the signature on the watercolors was the same as that on the copy of Parsival he had bought: Adolf Hitler.

According to Ravenscroft, by the time Stein found the annotated copy of Parsival Adolf Hitler had already paid many visits to the Weltliches Schatzkammer Museum (Habsburg Treasure House) in Vienna, which held the Lance of St Maurice (also known as Constantine's Lance) used as a symbol of the imperial power of Holy Roman emperors at their coronations. (9) Having failed to gain entry to the Vienna Academy of Fine Arts and the School of Architecture, and growing more and more embittered and consumed with an increasing sense of his own destiny as dominator of the world, Hitler had thrown himself into an intense study of Nordic and Teutonic mythology and folklore, German history, literature and philosophy. While sheltering from the rain in the Treasure House one day, he heard a tour guide explaining to a group of foreign politicians the legend associated with the Lance of St Maurice: that it was actually the spear that Gaius Cassius had used to pierce the side of Christ during the Crucifixion, and that whoever succeeded in understanding its secrets would hold the destiny of the world in his hands for good or evil.

'The Spear appeared to be some sort of magical medium of revelation for it brought the world of ideas into such close and living perspective that human imagination became more real than the world of sense.' (10)

Intent on meeting the man who had written so perceptively and frighteningly in the battered copy of Parsival, Stein returned to the dingy bookshop and this time encountered the owner, an extremely unsavory looking man named Ernst Pretzsche. Pretzsche told him that Hitler pawned many of his books in order to buy food, and redeemed them with money earned from selling his paintings. (Apparently, the shop assistant had made a mistake in selling Parsival to Stein.) Pretzsche showed Stein some of Hitler's other books, which included works by Hegel, Nietzsche and Houston S. Chamberlain, the British fascist and advocate of German racial superiority who frequently claimed to be chased by demons.

In the conversation that ensued, Pretzsche maintained that he was a master of black magic and had initiated Hitler into the dark arts. After inviting Stein to come

211

and consult him on esoteric matters at any time (which Stein had no intention of doing, such was the loathsomeness of the man), Pretzsche gave him Hitler's address in Meldemannstrasse.

Hitler was extremely irate when Stein walked up to him and told him of his interest in the annotations in the copy of Parsival he had bought. He cursed Pretzsche for selling one of the books he had pawned. However, once Stein had told him of his own researches into the Holy Grail and the Spear of Longinus, Hitler became more amicable, apparently regarding the young university student as a possible ally in the Pan-German cause. They decided to pay a visit to the Schatzkammer together to look at the Holy Lance. As they stood before the display, the two men responded to it in very different ways.

For some moments [Stein] was almost overcome by the powerful emotions which filled his breast and flowed like a river of healing warmth through his brain, evoking responses of reverence, humility and love. One message above all seemed to be inspired by the sight of this Spear which held within its central cavity one of the nails which had secured the body of Jesus to the Cross. It was a message of compassion which had been so wonderfully expressed in the motto of the Grail Knights: 'Durch Mitleid wissen.' A call from the Immortal Self of Man resounding in the darkness of confusion and doubt within the human soul: Through Compassion to Self-Knowledge. (11)

As Stein glanced at his companion, it seemed to him that Hitler was responding in a way which was diametrically opposite to his own.

Adolf Hitler stood beside him like a man in a trance, a man over whom some dreadful magic spell had been cast. His face was flushed and his brooding eyes shone with an alien emanation. He was swaying on his feet as though caught up in some totally inexplicable euphoria. The very space around him seemed enlivened with some subtle irradiation, a kind of ghostly ectoplasmic light. His whole physiognomy and stance appeared transformed as if some mighty Spirit now inhabited his very soul, creating within and around him a kind of evil transfiguration of its own nature and power. (12)

The inscrutable occult processes that were set in motion by Hitler's discovery of the Holy Lance were consolidated on 14 March 1938, when Hitler arrived in Vienna to complete the Anschluss of Austria. While the Viennese people cheered the German forces' arrival, the Jews and opponents of the Nazi regime faced a persecution that, while utterly appalling, was but a pale foreshadowing of the horrors to come. Seventy-six thousand people were arrested when the Nazis arrived, with a further 6,000 people dismissed from key ministries in the Austrian Government. (13) Jews of all ages, whether they were religious or not, were ordered to scrub anti-Nazi slogans from the streets; the water they were given was mixed with acid that burned their hands. Hitler's SS Death's Head squads and members of the Hitler Youth urinated on Jews and forced them to spit in each other's faces; others were forced to dance on Torah scrolls. In less than a month, the deportation of Jews to the concentration camps would begin. (14)

While these atrocities were being perpetrated, Hitler (according to Ravenscroft) went to the Habsburg Treasure House to claim the Holy Lance. With him were Heinrich Himmler and Wolfram Sievers, whom he ordered to leave him alone with the object of his diabolical desire.

Although ... the Spear of Longinus had been the inspiration of his whole life and the key to his meteoric rise to power, it was more than a quarter of a century since he had last seen it, and nearly thirty years since he first beheld it and heard of its unique legend.

Whatever Hitler's visions on this occasion, the scene of the German Fuhrer standing there before the ancient weapon must be regarded as the most critical moment of the twentieth century until the Americans claimed the Spear in Nuremberg in 1945, and, while holding it in their possession, inaugurated the Atomic Age by dropping their atom bombs on Hiroshima and Nagasaki. (15)

PROBLEMS WITH RAVENSCROFT'S ACCOUNT

Joscelyn Godwin has called The Spear of Destiny 'a bloodcurdling work of historical reinvention', (16) and in spite of the breathless praise it has received from occult writers and reviewers over the years, it is difficult to disagree with his judgement. This view is also taken by the Australian author and journalist Ken Anderson, whose book Hitler and the Occult (1995) is a powerful and well-argued critique of Ravenscroft, Stein and The Spear of Destiny. For the rest of this chapter, we must therefore turn our attention to the problems inherent in Ravenscroft's account, as he learned it from Stein, of Hitler's desire to claim this allegedly most powerful of magical talismans. To be sure, these problems are manifold and display clear inconsistencies both with what we know of the history of the Third Reich and the wider context of European history.

For instance, we are told in Spear that the Holy Lance had been prized by many great warriors through the centuries, including Napoleon Bonaparte, who had demanded the lance after the Battle of Austerlitz of December 1805. 'Just before the battle began, the lance had been smuggled out of Nuremberg and hidden in Vienna to keep it out of the French dictator's hands.' (17) However, as Anderson comments, it would have been a rather stupid decision to hide the lance in Vienna, since the French had already occupied the city the previous month. 'Why would anyone want to smuggle anything into an occupied city if the purpose in so doing was to keep it out of the hands of the head of the occupying force?' (18) Moreover, historical records prove that the lance was taken from Nuremberg to Vienna in 1800 and placed in the museum on full display. Had he wanted the lance, Napoleon could have acquired it at any time.

And what of the spear itself, which, claims Ravenscroft, was the very one used by the Roman centurion to pierce the side of Christ? We are told that Hitler found little difficulty in sorting out the merits of the various Spears, purporting to be the weapon of the Roman Centurion Longinus, which were scattered around the palaces, museums, cathedrals and churches of Europe . . . Adolf Hitler was excited to find one Spear which appeared to have been associated with a legend of world destiny throughout its entire history. This Spear, dating back to the Third Century, had apparently been traced by numerous historians right through to the tenth century to the reign of the Saxon King Heinrich I, the 'Fowler', where it was last mentioned in his hands at the famous battle of Unstrut in which the Saxon Cavalry conquered the marauding Magyars. (19) [Emphasis added.]

At this point, a question will doubtless have occurred to the reader: how could a weapon dating back only to the third century have been used to pierce the side of Christ? It is a question Ravenscroft does not answer. (20) The existence of a lance which was supposedly used to stab Christ is first recorded in the sixth century by the pilgrim St Antonius of Piacenza, who claims to have seen it in the Mount Zion Basilica in Jerusalem. When Jerusalem fell to the Persians in AD 615, the shaft of the lance was captured by the victors, while the lance-head was saved and taken to Constantinople where it was incorporated into an icon and kept in the Santa Sophia Church. More than six centuries later, the point found its way into the possession of the French King Louis and was taken to the Sainte-Chapelle in Paris. The lance-head disappeared (and was possibly destroyed) during the French Revolution. The shaft of the lance was sent to Jerusalem in about AD 670 by the Frankish pilgrim Arculf, and only reappears in history in the late ninth century, turning up in Constantinople. It was captured by the Turks in 1492, who sent it as a gift to Rome. It has remained in St Peter's since then, although its authenticity has never been established beyond doubt. (21)

However, archaeologists have established that this lance, first mentioned in the sixth century, is not the one Hitler found in the Habsburg Treasure House. This lance is known as the Lance of St Maurice, or Constantine's Lance, which was made in the eighth or ninth century. (22)

Anderson writes: 'It would take much research to examine each one of Ravenscroft's claims concerning the possessors of the Maurice Lance and its affect on them and on world history.' (23) And in fact, such a task lies well beyond the scope of this book also. He goes on:

Besides, we do not have the unique facility Ravenscroft had [i.e. techniques of psychic mind expansion] in tracing its owners where there is no written record, for example its progression from the time it left the hands of Heinrich I and turned up many years later in the possession of his son Otto the Great. Ravenscroft says Hitler's henchman SS head Heinrich Himmler put the finest scholars in Germany to work on bridging the gap but they were unable to do so. However, Ravenscroft's mentor, Dr. Walter Stein, 'by means of a unique method of historical research involving "Mind Expansion" was able to discover Heinrich had sent the lance to the English King Athelstan.' (Athelstan [895-940] was the grandson of Alfred the Great. Crowned King in 925, he was the first ruler of all England.) Stein 'found' that the lance was present at the Battle of Malmesbury in which the Danes were defeated on English soil. It was subsequently returned as a gift for Otto's wedding to Athelstan's sister Eadgita. (24)

OCCULT SECRETS OF THE THIRD REICH

Anderson spots a crucial mistake in this account of the lance (and one which certainly casts doubt on Stein's unorthodox methods of historical 'research'.) According to William of Malmesbury, the sword of Constantine the Great was sent by Hugh the Good, King of the Franks, to King Athelstan to persuade him to give his daughter's hand in marriage.

(25) It so happens that historical inaccuracies are also to be found in Ravenscroft's account of his own exploits in the Second World War, in which he claims to have been taken prisoner by the Germans after the attempted assassination of Rommel. Born in 1921, Ravenscroft attended Repton Public School and then Sandhurst Military College. Six months later, in December 1939, he received his commission in the Royal Scots Fusiliers. He then trained as a commando and joined the Special Services. (26) According to the cover blurb on various editions of The Spear of Destiny: 'He was captured on a raid which attempted to assassinate Field Marshal Rommel in North Africa and was a POW in Germany from 1944 to 1945, escaping three times but each time being recaptured.'

Although the raid on Rommel certainly took place on 13-14 November 1941 (with all but two of the party being captured), Ravenscroft is not mentioned in records as being present in the 28-man team who conducted the operation. Anderson reports that when he made enquiries of former Commando Sergeant Jack Terry, the ex-soldier insisted that Ravenscroft was not a member of the party. (27) 'In any case Ravenscroft's service record shows he was "missing at sea" on 24 October 1941, well before the raid. He was subsequently taken prisoner of war on an unspecified date.' (28)

There also appear to be inconsistencies in Ravenscroft's account of how he came to meet Walter Stein. A few years after the war, Ravenscroft read Stein's book World History in the Light of the Holy Grail and came to the conclusion that much of the material in the book had been accessed by Stein through occult means of mind expansion, perhaps similar to those he himself had employed while a prisoner of war. Paying Stein a visit in Kensington, London, Ravenscroft informed him of his belief, and also of his belief that Wolfram von Eschenbach had employed the same talents in composing his Grail romance Parsival in the twelfth century.

Ravenscroft quoted to Stein this extract from Eschenbach's work: 'If anyone requests me to [continue the story] let him not consider it as a book. I don't know a single letter of the alphabet.' Ravenscroft says that the reason Eschenbach was stressing that he did not know a letter of the alphabet was to make it clear that he had not gathered the material for the book from his contemporaries, traditional folklore, or any existing written work. Rather, he was saying his so-called Grail romance was an 'Initiation Document' of the highest order. (29)

Stein was impressed enough by his visitor's argument that he invited him to stay to lunch, and the two men remained friends and colleagues from then until Stein's death. Ravenscroft himself died of cancer in January 1989 in Torquay, England.

Anderson interviewed Ravenscroft's brother, Bill, in January 1995. A former

OCCULT SECRETS OF THE THIRD REICH

King's Own Borderers officer, Bill Ravenscroft stated that his brother met Walter Stein not by paying an unannounced visit to his Kensington home but rather through Stein's wife, Yopi, while Trevor Ravenscroft was teaching at the Rudolf Steiner school in East Grinstead, England just after the war. (30) According to Bill Ravenscroft, Trevor learned of Stein's impressive library through Yopi and was given permission by her to consult the books in the library in order to complete The Spear of Destiny. Trevor Ravenscroft makes no mention whatsoever of Yopi in his book. Anderson asks: why? 'Was Bill's memory of events incorrect? Was it because the symbiotic relationship that supposedly developed between Trevor and the man he claims was his mentor never happened?' (31)

If The Spear of Destiny is to be believed, the moment Hitler entered the Habsburg Treasure House upon the annexation of Austria in 1938 and stood before the holy artifact he had coveted for so long humanity in the twentieth century was lost, locked into an irrevocable collision course with disaster. And yet there are more problems with this pivotal point in the book. Ravenscroft writes: 'When Hitler was driven down the Ringstrasse to the Ring and on to the Heldenplatz to the reviewing stand in front of the Hofburg, the tumultuous jubilation of the crowds reached near-delirium. How could the citizens of Vienna have known that the ecstasy on the face of Adolf Hitler was the twisted ecstasy of revenge!' (32)

Joachim Fest, one of the greatest authorities on Hitler and the Third Reich offers a slightly different account of the Fuhrer's moment of triumph at the 'reunion' of Germany and Austria: 'All the aimlessness and impotence of those years were now vindicated, all his furious craving for compensation at last satisfied, when he stood on the balcony of the Hofburg and announced to hundreds of thousands in the Heldenplatz the "greatest report of a mission accomplished" in his life ...' (33) If Fest's academic credentials are insufficient, there are also photographs to prove that Hitler faced the Viennese crowds from the balcony of the Hofburg, not on a 'reviewing stand' in front of it.

Ravenscroft goes on to claim that after reviewing the Austrian SS and giving his permission for the founding of a new SS regiment, Hitler refused an invitation for a tour of the city. Instead, he 'left the Ring to drive directly to the Imperial Hotel where the most luxurious suite in the city awaited him'. (34) Arrangements for a civic dinner and reception were cancelled because Hitler was 'terrified that an attempt would be made to kill him' (35) and remained in his suite. Anderson asks a pertinent question: if Hitler was terrified that an attempt would be made on his life, why did he arrive in Vienna in an open car that passed through the cheering crowds, then stand in full view outside the Hofburg, and then go out onto the balcony of his hotel suite several times at the insistence of the Viennese people? (36)

In spite of this, Ravenscroft has Hitler leaving the Imperial Hotel 'long after midnight' to head for the Habsburg Treasure House and the Holy Lance. According to Anderson:

... Hitler arrived in Vienna at 5 p.m. on 14 March and the mass welcome in the

Heldenplatz took place the next day—the fifteenth. If Ravenscroft has meant us to understand that the rally in the square he speaks of was on the fifteenth, then there is a further problem: Hitler stayed in Vienna less than twenty-four hours! He was not there on the night of the fifteenth.

After attending a military parade at the Maria-Theresa monument at two o'clock that afternoon—the same parade which Ravenscroft says Hitler attended before going on to the Imperial—Hitler flew out in his Junkers aircraft as the twilight settled on an enervated Vienna. (37)

It is also difficult to imagine how Hitler could have left his hotel and gone to the Treasure House without being seen by anyone in the seething crowds that remained in the streets. It would surely have been easier for him to order the Holy Lance to be brought from the museum to his hotel suite. (38) On reflection, it must be said that the only things in the Habsburg Treasure House Hitler coveted were the Habsburg Crown Jewels (which were sent to Nuremberg immediately following the Anschluss), not to mention the Austrian gold and currency deposits that would aid a German economy stressed by preparations for war. Hitler was motivated more by financial than occult concerns, as the transfer of Austrian gold and currency reserves to Germany amply demonstrates. (39)

It will, one hopes, be apparent from this all too brief overview of the problems inherent in The Spear of Destiny that, while the book may be a fascinating—if somewhat lurid—read, in the Dennis Wheatley mould of occult ripping yarns, as a serious historical work it is completely unsatisfactory. It is, of course, conceivable that Trevor Ravenscroft was well aware that he was penning a work of almost total fiction; however, this is mere conjecture and is absolutely not proven. Even assuming that he wrote the book in good faith, believing its revelations regarding Hitler and the Holy Lance to be accurate, it is crippled by the research methods on which he appears to rely: namely, the use of occult techniques to enhance the powers of the mind and thus gain access to historical information that has not been preserved in any conventional way. In the final analysis, we must dismiss The Spear of Destiny on the grounds that when information gathered through psychic processes conflicts with what has been established through documentary evidence or the testimony of first-hand witnesses we have no serious alternative but to abandon it in favor of what can be verified by those who do not possess these psychic talents.

Before moving on, we must say a few words about the claims of many occult writers that Hitler was involved in black magic practices, having been initiated into the dark arts by Dietrich Eckart and Karl Haushofer. (Eckart, Alfred Rosenberg and Rudolf von Sebottendorff were said to have conducted horrific seances, in which a naked female medium exuded ectoplasm from her vagina and through whom contact was established with the seven Thulist hostages who had been murdered by the Communists in April 1919. The ghosts predicted that Hitler would claim the Holy Lance and lead Germany into global conflagration.) (40) There is no evidence whatsoever to link Hitler directly with black magic practices of any description. While it is of course beyond question that the Nazi Party arose out of the National Socialist German Workers' Party, which in turn began as the Thule Society (a group founded on occult and racist principles), there is no evidence that Hitler himself was an occultist—and considerable evidence that he wasn't.

Speer, for instance, recalls Hitler's contempt for the woolly-headed mysticism of Heinrich Himmler:

What nonsense! Here we have at last reached an age that has left all mysticism behind it, and now he wants to start all over again. We might just as well have stayed with the church. At least it had tradition. To think that I may some day be turned into an SS saint! Can you imagine it? I would turn over in my grave ... (41)

Hitler was also scornful of Himmler's attempts to establish archaeological links between modern Germans and the ancient Aryan descendants of Atlantis:

Why do we call the whole world's attention to the fact that we have no past? It isn't enough that the Romans were erecting great buildings when our forefathers were still living in mud huts; now Himmler is starting to dig up these villages of mud huts and enthusing over every potsherd and stone axe he finds. All we prove by that is that we were still throwing stone hatchets and crouching around open fires when Greece and Rome had already reached the highest stage of culture. We really should do our best to keep quiet about this past. Instead Himmler makes a great fuss about it all. The present-day Romans must be having a laugh at these revelations. (42)

In truth, those who subscribed to occultist or pseudo-religious notions were indeed something of a laughing stock in the high echelons of the Third Reich. Himmler's beliefs about the original prehistoric Germanic race were considered absurd by both Hitler and Goebbels, the propaganda minister. 'When, for example, the Japanese presented [Himmler] with a samurai sword, he at once discovered kinships between Japanese and Teutonic cults and called upon scientists to help him trace these similarities to a racial common denominator.' (43)

As for the belief that Hitler was deeply interested in astrology and kept in constant touch with astrologers who advised him on the various courses of action he should take, this too is completely fallacious. According to the former Office of Strategic Services (OSS) officer Walter Langer:

All of our informants who have known Hitler rather intimately discard the idea [of Hitler's belief] as absurd. They all agree that nothing is more foreign to Hitler's personality than to seek help from outside sources of this type.

The Fuhrer had never had his horoscope cast, but in an indicative move Hitler, some time before the war, forbade the practice of fortune-telling and star-reading in Germany. (44)

As we have just seen, while Hitler was contemptuous of mysticism and pseudoreligion, Himmler was another matter entirely, and it is to him that we must now turn our attention.

OCCULT SECRETS OF THE THIRD REICH

6. ORDINARY MADNESS
HEINRICH HIMMLER AND THE SS

Many writers on the occult have suggested that the notorious SS (Schutz Staffeln or Defense Squads) was actively engaged in black-magic rites designed to contact and enlist the aid of evil and immensely powerful transhuman powers, in order to secure the domination of the planet by the Third Reich. While conventional historians are contemptuous of this notion, it nevertheless holds some attraction for those struggling with the terrible mystery at the heart of Nazism, who have come to believe that only a supernatural explanation can possibly shed light on the movement's origins and deeds. Goodrick-Clarke, one of the very few serious historians to have explored the subject of the occult inspiration behind Nazism, stresses that although volkisch occultists such as Guido von List and Lanz von Liebenfels undoubtedly contributed to the 'mythological mood of the Nazi era' (with its bizarre notions of prehistoric Aryan superhumans inhabiting vanished continents), 'they cannot be said to have directly influenced the actions of persons in positions of political power and responsibility'. (1)

As Goodrick-Clarke concedes, however, the one exception is a man named Karl Maria Wiligut (1866-1946), who exerted a profound influence upon Reichsfuhrer-SS Heinrich Himmler. Before turning our attention to the SS itself, therefore, we must pause to examine the life and thought of Wiligut, and the reasons for his intellectual hold over the leader of the most powerful organization in the Third Reich.

THE MAN BEHIND HIMMLER

Wiligut was born in Vienna into a military family and followed his grandfather and father into the Austrian army, joining the 99th Infantry at Mostar, Herzegovina in late 1884 and reaching the rank of captain by the time he was 37. Throughout his years in the army, he maintained his interest in literature and folklore, writing poetry with a distinctly nationalistic flavor. In 1903, a book of his poems entitled Seyfrieds Runen was published by Friedrich Schalk, who had also published Guido von List. Although his studies in mythology had led him to join a quasi-Masonic lodge called the Schlarraffia in 1889, Wiligut does not seem to have been active in the volkisch or Pan-German nationalist movements at this time. (2)

During the First World War, Wiligut saw action against the Russians in the

Carpathians and was later transferred to the Italian front; by the summer of 1917, he had reached the rank of colonel. Decorated for bravery and highly thought of by his superiors, Wiligut was discharged from the army in January 1919, after nearly 35 years of exemplary service.

At around this time, the Viennese occult underground began to buzz with rumors concerning Wiligut and his alleged possession of an 'ancestral memory' that allowed him to recall the history of the Teutonic people all the way back to the year 228,000 BC.

According to Wiligut, his astonishing clairvoyant ability was the result of an uninterrupted family lineage extending thousands of years into the past. He claimed to have been initiated into the secrets of his family by his father in 1890. Goodrick-Clarke has identified the source of this information about Wiligut as Theodor Czepl, who knew of Wiligut through his occult connections in Vienna, which included Wiligut's cousin, Willy Thaler, and various members of the Order of the New Templars (ONT). Czepl paid several visits to Wiligut at his Salzburg home in the winter of 1920, and it was during these visits that Wiligut claimed that the Bible had been written in Germany, and that the Germanic god Krist had been appropriated by Christianity. (3)

According to Wiligut's view of prehistory, the Earth was originally lit by three suns and was inhabited by various mythological beings, including giants and dwarves. For many tens of thousands of years, the world was convulsed with warfare until Wiligut's ancestors, the Adler-Wiligoten, brought peace with the foundation of the 'second Boso culture' and the city of Arual-Joruvallas (Goslar, the chief shrine of ancient Germany) in 78,000 BC. The following millennia saw yet more conflicts involving various now-lost civilizations, until 12,500 BC, when the religion of Krist was established. Three thousand years later, an opposing group of Wotanists challenged this hitherto universal Germanic faith, and crucified the prophet of Krist, Baldur-Chrestos, who nevertheless managed to escape to Asia. The Wotanists destroyed Goslar in 1200 BC, forcing the followers of Krist to establish a new temple at Exsternsteine, near Detmold. (4)

The Wiligut family itself was originally the result of a mating between the gods of air and water, and in later centuries fled from persecution at the hands of Charlemagne, first to the Faroe Islands and then to Russia. Wiligut claimed that his family line included such heroic Germanic figures as Armin the Cherusker and Wittukind. As Goodrick-Clarke notes:

'It will be evident from this epic account of putative genealogy and family history that Wiligut's prehistorical speculations primarily served as a stage upon which he could project the experiences and importance of his own ancestors.' (5) In addition, Peter Levenda makes the salient point that Wiligut's 'cross-eyed thesis' was based on a spurious amalgamation of genuine cultural traditions (such as those described in the Eddas) and Theosophical belief systems that have little or no provenance in the actual history of mythology. (6)

OCCULT SECRETS OF THE THIRD REICH

In Wiligut's view, the victimization of his family that had been going on for tens of thousands of years was continuing at the hands of the Catholic Church, the Freemasons and the Jews, all of whom he held responsible for Germany's defeat in the First World War. His already somewhat precarious mental health was further undermined when his infant son died, thus destroying the male line of the family. This placed a great strain on his relationship with his wife, Malwine, who in any event was not particularly impressed with his claims of prehistoric greatness for his family. His home life continued to deteriorate, until his violence, threats to kill Malwine and bizarre occult interests resulted in his being committed to the mental asylum at Salzburg in November 1924. Certified insane, he was confined there until 1927.

In spite of this, Wiligut maintained contact with his colleagues in various occult circles, including the ONT and the Edda Society. Five years after his release from the asylum, Wiligut decided to move to Germany and settled in Munich. There he was feted by German occultists as a fount of priceless information on the remote and glorious history of the Germanic people.

Wiligut's introduction to Heinrich Himmler came about through the former's friend Richard Anders, who had contributed to the Edda Society's Hagal magazine and who was now an officer in the SS. Himmler was greatly impressed with the old man's ancestral memory, which implied a racial purity going back much further than 1750 (the year to which SS recruits had to be able to prove their Aryan family history). (7) Wiligut joined the SS in September 1933, using the name 'Karl Maria Weisthor'. He was made head of the Department for Pre- and Early History in the SS Race and Settlement Main Office in Munich, where he was charged with the task of recording on paper the events he clairvoyantly recalled. His work evidently met with the satisfaction of the Reichsfuhrer-SS, who promoted him to SS-Oberfuhrer (lieutenant-brigadier) in November 1934. (8)

As if his own ravings were not enough, Weisthor introduced Himmler to another occultist, a German crypto-historian and List Society member named Gunther Kirchhoff (18921975) who believed in the existence of energy lines crossing the face of the Earth. Weisthor took it upon himself to forward a number of Kirchhoff's essays and dissertations on ancient Germanic tradition to Himmler, who gave instructions to the Ahnenerbe (the SS Association for Research and Teaching on Heredity) to study them. One such dissertation concerned a detailed survey undertaken by Kirchhoff and Weisthor in the region of the Murg Valley near Baden-Baden in the Black Forest. After exhaustively examining 'old half-timbered houses, architectural ornament (including sculpture, coats-of-arms, runes, and other symbols), crosses, inscriptions, and natural and man-made rock formations in the forest', (9) the two occultists concluded that the region had been a prehistoric centre of the Krist religion.

Unfortunately for Kirchhoff, even the Ahnenerbe came to think of him as a crackpot who understood nothing of scholarly prehistorical research (quite an indictment, coming from that particular organization). When Kirchhoff accused them, along with the Catholic Church, of conspiring against him, the Ahnenerbe responded by describing his work as 'rubbish' and him as a 'fantasist of the worst kind'. (10) In spite of this, Himmler continued to instruct the Ahnenerbe to take seriously Kirchhoff's unscholarly rantings, until the outbreak of the Second World War forced him firmly into the background.

Weisthor, on the other hand, would make one further important contribution to Himmler's SS. While traveling through Westphalia during the Nazi electoral campaign of January 1933, Himmler was profoundly affected by the atmosphere of the region, with its romantic castles and the mist- (and myth-) shrouded Teutoburger Forest. After deciding to take over a castle for SS use, he returned to Westphalia in November and viewed the Wewelsburg castle, which he appropriated in August 1934 with the intention of turning it into an ideological-education college for SS officers. Although at first belonging to the Race and Settlement Main Office, the Wewelsburg castle was placed under the control of Himmler's Personal Staff in February 1935.

It is likely that Himmler's view of the Wewelsburg castle was influenced by Weisthor's assertion that it 'was destined to become a magical German strong point in a future conflict between Europe and Asia'. (11) Weisthor's inspiration for this prediction was a Westphalian legend regarding a titanic future battle between East and West. Himmler found this particularly interesting, in view of his own conviction that a major confrontation between East and West was inevitable -even if it were still a century or more in the future. In addition, it was Weisthor who influenced the development of SS ritual (which we shall examine later in this chapter) and who designed the SS Totenkopfring that symbolized membership of the order. The ring design was based on a death's head, and included a swastika, the double sig-rune of the SS and a hagall rune.

In 1935, Weisthor moved to Berlin, where he joined the Reichsfuhrer-SS Personal Staff and continued to advise Himmler on all aspects of his Germanic pseudo-history. Eyewitnesses recollect that this was a period of great activity, during which Weisthor travelled widely, corresponded extensively and oversaw numerous meetings. According to Goodrick-Clarke: 'Besides his involvement with the Wewelsburg castle and his land surveys in the Black Forest and elsewhere, Weisthor continued to produce examples of his family traditions such as the Halgarita mottoes, Germanic mantras designed to stimulate ancestral memory ... and the design for the SS Totenkopfring.' (12) In recognition of his work, Weisthor was promoted to SS-Brigadefuhrer (brigadier) in Himmler's Personal Staff in September 1936.

While in Berlin, Weisthor worked with the author and historian Otto Rahn (1904-1939), who had a profound interest in medieval Grail legends and the Cathar heresy. In 1933, Rahn published a romantic historical work entitled Kreuzzug gegen den Gral (Crusade Against the Grail), which was a study of the Albigensian Crusade, a war between the Roman Catholic Church and the Cathars (or Albigensians), an ascetic religious sect that flourished in southern France in the twelfth and thirteenth centuries. The Cathars believed that the teachings of Christ had been corrupted by the Church -and, indeed, that Christ was exclusively a being of spirit who had never been incarnated in human form. This belief arose from their conviction that all matter was the creation of an evil deity opposed to God. Thus they claimed that the dead would not be physically resurrected (since the body was made of matter and hence evil) and that procreation itself was evil, since it increased the amount of matter in the Universe and trapped souls in physicality. (13) The Cathars were eventually destroyed by Catholic armies on the orders of Pope Innocent III in the first decade of the thirteenth century.

As Levenda notes, Catharism held a particular fascination and attraction for Himmler and other leading Nazis. 'After all, the very word "Cathar" means "pure," and purity -particularly of the blood as the physical embodiment of spiritual "goodness"—was an issue of prime importance to the SS.' (14) Just as the Cathars had despised the materialism of the Catholic Church, so the Nazis despised Capitalism, which they equated with the 'excesses of the Jewish financiers that—they said—had brought the nation to ruin during the First World War and the depression that followed'. (15) The Cathar belief that the evil god who had created the material Universe was none other than Jehovah provided additional common ground with Nazi anti-Semitism.

Ritual suicide was also practiced by the Cathars. Known as the endura, it involved either starving oneself to death, self-poisoning or strangulation by one's fellow Cathars. Levenda makes another interesting point about the Nazi fascination with Catharism:

[T]he Cathars were fanatics, willing to die for their cause; sacrificing themselves to the Church's onslaught they enjoyed the always-enviable aura of spiritual underdogs. There was something madly beautiful in the way they were immolated on the stakes of the Inquisition, professing their faith and their hatred of Rome until the very end. The Nazis could identify with the Cathars: with their overall fanaticism, with their contempt for the way vital spiritual matters were commercialized (polluted) by the Establishment, and with their passion for 'purity'. It is perhaps inevitable that the Cathars should have made a sacrament out of suicide, for they must have known that their Quest was doomed to failure from the start. They must have wished for death as a release from a corrupt and insensitive world; and it's entirely possible that, at the root of Nazism, lay a similar death wish. Hitler was surrounded by the suicides of his mistresses and contemplated it himself on at least one occasion before he actually pulled the trigger in Berlin in 1945. Himmler and other captured Nazi leaders killed themselves rather than permit the Allies to do the honors for them. ... [L]ike the Cathars whom they admired, the Nazis saw in suicide that consolation and release from the world of Satanic matter promised by this most cynical of Cathar sacraments. (16)

The thesis of Rahn's book was that the Cathar heresy and Grail legends constituted an ancient Gothic Gnostic religion that had been suppressed by the Catholic Church, beginning with the persecution of the Cathars and ending with the destruction of the Knights Templar a century later. From 1933, Rahn lived in Berlin and his book and his continued researches into Germanic history came to the attention of

Himmler. In May 1935, Rahn joined Weisthor's staff, joining the SS less than a year later. In April 1936, he was promoted to the rank of SS-Unterscharfuhrer (NCO).

His second book, Luzifers Hofgesinde (Lucifer's Servants), which was an account of his research trip to Iceland for the SS, was published in 1937. This was followed by four months of military service with the SS-Death's Head Division 'Oberbayern' at Dachau concentration camp, after which he was allowed to pursue his writing and research full time. In February 1939, Rahn resigned from the SS for unknown reasons, and subsequently died from exposure the following month while walking on the mountains near Kufstein. (17)

As with Rahn's resignation from the SS, the reasons for Weisthor leaving the organization are uncertain. One possible reason is that his health was badly failing; although he was given powerful Drugs intended to maintain his mental faculties, they had serious side effects, including personality changes that resulted in heavy smoking and alcohol consumption. Also at this time his psychological history -including his committal for insanity—which had been a closely guarded secret became known, causing considerable embarrassment to Himmler. In February 1939, Weisthor's staff were informed that he had retired because of poor health, and that his office would be dissolved. (18) Although the old occultist was supported by the SS during the final years of his life, his influence on the Third Reich was at an end. He was given a home in Aufkirchen, but found it to be too far away from Berlin and he moved to Goslar in May 1940. When his accommodation was requisitioned for medical research in 1943, he moved again, this time to a small SS house in Carinthia where he spent the remainder of the war with his housekeeper, Elsa Baltrusch, a member of Himmler's Personal Staff. At the end of the war, he was sent by the British occupying forces to a refugee camp where he suffered a stroke. After their release, he and Baltrusch went first to his family home at Salzburg, and then to Baltrusch's family home at Arolsen. On 3 January 1946, his health finally gave out and he died in hospital. (19)

HEINRICH HIMMLER

The man who was so deeply impressed with the rantings of Wiligut, who would become most closely associated with the terror of the SS and an embodiment of evil second only to Adolf Hitler himself, was born in Munich on 7 October 1900. Himmler's father was the son of a police president and had been a tutor to the princes at the Bavarian court, and thus applied suitably authoritarian principles on his own family. (20) As Joachim Fest notes: 'No doubt it would be going too far to see in the son's early interest in Teutonic sagas, criminology and military affairs the beginnings of his later development, but the family milieu, with its combination of "officialdom, police work and teaching", manifestly had a lasting effect on him.' (21)

Himmler was not blessed with a robust physical constitution, and this hampered his family's initial intention that he should become a farmer. Nevertheless, the ideal of the noble peasant remained with him and heavily influenced his later ideology and plans for the SS. After serving very briefly at the end of the First World War, Himmler joined Hitler's NSDAP. In 1926 he met Margerete Boden, the daughter of a

West Prussian landowning family, and married her two years later. A fine example of the Germanic type (tall, fair-haired and blue-eyed), she was also seven years older than Himmler and is said to have inspired his interest in alternative medicine such as herbalism and homeopathy. (22)

Himmler was appointed head (Reichsfuhrer) of the SS on 6 January 1929. At that time the organization had barely 300 members, but such were Himmler's organizational skills that he increased its membership to over 50,000 in the next four years. In 1931 he established a special Security Service (SD) within the SS, which would oversee political intelligence. It was led by the psychopathic Reinhard Heydrich, 'the only top Nazi leader to fit the racial stereotype of being tall (six feet, three inches), blond, and blue-eyed'. (23) Himmler took control of the party's police functions in April 1934, and then took command of the Gestapo (Geheime Staatspolizei or Secret State Police). SS units were instrumental in Hitler's Blood Purge of 30 June 1934, which saw the end of the Sturmabteilung (SA), the brown-shirted and sadistic militia of the early Nazi Party, and its chief, Ernst Rohm.

Members of the SS were required to correspond to special racial criteria (tall, blond, blue-eyed) and had to be able to trace their Aryan ancestry at least as far back as the year 1750. Initially, the SS membership included approximately 44 per cent from the working class; however, as its status increased following the Nazi rise to power, it attracted more members from the upper class.

By 1937, the three major concentration camps in Germany were staffed by the SS Totenkopfverbande (Death's Head Units), and the following year saw the formation of the Verfugungstruppe (Action Groups), which numbered 200,000 and which later became the Waffen-SS (Military SS). By the end of 1938, SS membership had reached nearly 240,000, a figure that would later rise to approximately one million.

According to the historian Joachim C. Fest:

[T]he aims of the enormous SS apparatus were ... comprehensive and concerned not so much with controlling the state as with becoming a state itself. The occupants of the chief positions in the SS developed step by step into the holders of power in an authentic 'collateral state', which gradually penetrated existing institutions, undermined them, and finally began to dissolve them. Fundamentally there was no sphere of public life upon which the SS did not make its competing demands: the economic, ideological, military, scientific and technical spheres, as well as those of agrarian and population policies, legislation and general administration. This development found its most unmistakable expression in the hierarchy of the Senior SS and Police Commanders, especially in the Eastern zones; the considerable independence that Himmler's corps of leaders enjoyed vis-a-vis the civil or military administration was a working model for a shift of power planned for the whole area of the Greater German Reich after the war. This process received its initial impetus following the so-called Rohm Putsch, and it moved towards its completion after the attempted revolt of 20 July 1944. The SS now pushed its way into 'the centre of the organizational fabric of the Wehrmacht', and Himmler, who had meanwhile also become Reich Minister of the Interior, now in addition became chief of the Replacement Army. On top of his many other functions he was thus in charge 'of all military transport, military censorship, the intelligence service, surveillance of the troops, the supply of food, clothing and pay to the troops, and care of the wounded'. (24)

THE AHNENERBE AND THE RITUALS OF THE SS

It has been said of Himmler many times that his personality was a curious mixture of rationality and fantasy: that his capacity for rational planning, the following of orders and administrative detail existed alongside an idealist enthusiasm for utopianism, mysticism and the occult. This combination of the quotidian and the fantastic led to Himmler's conception of the ultimate role of the SS: 'his black-uniformed troops would provide both the bloodstock of the future Aryan master-race and the ideological elite of an ever-expanding Greater Germanic Reich'. (25)

From 1930, Himmler concentrated on the formulation of his plans for the SS, which included the establishment of the SS officers' college at the Wewelsburg castle in 1933. Two years later, he established the Ahnenerbe with the Nazi pagan ideologue Richard Walther Darre. The Ahnenerbe was the Ancestral Heritage Research and Teaching Society, and was initially an independent institute conducting research into Germanic prehistory, archaeology and occult mysticism. It was subsequently incorporated into the SS in April 1940, with its staff holding SS rank. Levenda thinks it likely that the inspiration for the Ahnenerbe came from a number of German intellectuals and occultists who had subscribed to the theories of the volkisch writers of the late nineteenth century, as well as from the adventures of a number of explorers and archaeologists, including the world-famous Swedish explorer Sven Hedin. (26)

Born in Stockholm in 1865, Hedin left Sweden at the age of twenty and sailed to Baku on the Caspian Sea. This was the first voyage of a man who would travel through most of Asia, and whose exploits would be recorded in the book My Life as an Explorer (1925). Hedin's voyages and tales of fabulous Asian cities did much to consolidate the European and American publics' fascination with the mysterious Orient—a fascination that had already been kindled by Madame Blavatsky and the Theosophical Society. (27)

Levenda writes:

There is evidence to suggest that the Ahnenerbe itself was formed as a private institution by several friends and admirers of Sven Hedin, including Wolfram Sievers (who would later find justice at the Nuremberg Trials) and Dr. Friedrich Hielscher who, according to the records of the Nuremberg Trial of November 1946, had been responsible for recruiting Sievers into the Ahnenerbe. In fact, there was a Sven Hedin Institute for Inner Asian Research in Munich that was part of the Ahnenerbe and as late as 1942 Hedin himself (then about seventy-seven years old) was in friendly communication with such important Ahnenerbe personnel as Dr. Ernst Schafer from his residence in Stockholm. Moreover, on January 16, 1943, the Sven Hedin Institute for Inner Asian (i.e. Mongolian) Research and Expeditions was formally inaugurated in Munich with 'great pomp,' a ceremony at which Hedin was in attendance as he was awarded with an honorary doctorate for the occasion.

(28) It is possible that Hedin may have met Karl Haushofer (whom we discussed in Chapter Three) while in the Far East, since Hedin was an occasional ambassador for the Swedish Government and Haushofer was a German military attache. 'Given Haushofer's excessive interest in political geography and his establishment of the Deutsche Akademie all over Asia (including China and India, Hedin's old stomping grounds), it would actually be odd if the two hadn't met.' (29) Indeed, the Deutsche Akademie and the Ahnenerbe, whose director was Wolfram Sievers, were run along very similar lines. Dr. Walther Wust, the Humanities chairman of the Ahnenerbe who carried the SS rank of Oberfuhrer, was also acting president of the Deutsche Akademie. Both organizations conducted field research at Dachau concentration camp. (30)

Himmler's vision of the SS required its transformation from Hitler's personal bodyguard to a pagan religious order with virtually complete autonomy, answerable only to the Fuhrer himself. As we have seen, Himmler chose as the headquarters for his order the castle of Wewelsburg, near Paderborn in Westphalia and close to the stone monument known as the Exsternsteine where the Teutonic hero Arminius was said to have battled the Romans.

The focal point of Wewelsburg, evidently owing much to the legend of King Arthur and the Knights of the Round Table, was a great dining hall with an oaken table to seat twelve picked from the senior Gruppenfuhrers. The walls were to be adorned with their coats of arms; although a high proportion lacked these -as of course did Himmler himself—they were assisted in the drafting of designs by Professor Diebitsch and experts from the Ahnenerbe. (31)

Beneath the dining hall was a circular room with a shallow depression reached by three stone steps (symbolizing the three Reichs). In this place of the dead, the coat of arms of the deceased 'Knight' of the SS would be ceremonially burned. Each member of Himmler's Inner Circle of Twelve had his own room, which was dedicated to an Aryan ancestor. Himmler's own quarters were dedicated to King Heinrich I, the Saxon king who had battled Hungarians and Slavs and of whom Himmler was convinced he was the reincarnation, (32) although he also claimed to have had conversations with Heinrich's ghost at night. (33)

Inside the dining hall, Himmler and his Inner Circle would perform various occult exercises, which included attempts to communicate with the spirits of dead Teutons and efforts to influence the mind of a person in the next room through the concentration of willpower.

There was no place for Christianity in the SS, and members were actively encouraged to break with the Church.

New religious ceremonies were developed to take the place of Christian ones; for instance, a winter solstice ceremony was designed to replace Christmas (starting in 1939 the word 'Christmas' was forbidden to appear in any official SS document), and another ceremony for the summer solstice. Gifts were to be given at the summer solstice ceremony rather than at the winter solstice ... (A possible, though by no means documented, cause for this switch of gift-giving to the summer solstice is the death of Hitler's mother on the winter solstice and all the grief and complex emotions this event represented for Hitler. It's understandable that Hitler—as the Fuhrer and at least nominally in charge of the direction the new state religion would take—would have wanted to remove every vestige of 'Christmas' from the pagan winter solstice festival. As a means of denying his grief? Or as an act of defiance against the god whose birth is celebrated on that day, a god who robbed Hitler of his beloved mother? It's worthwhile to note in this context that for a national 'Day of the German Mother' Hitler chose his own mother's birthday.) (34)

Besides Christmas, weddings and christenings were also replaced by pagan rituals, and pagan myths, as we saw earlier in this chapter, influenced Himmler's choice of Wewelsburg as the SS-order castle. The meticulous work of Peter Levenda in unearthing previously unpublished documents from the period allows us to consider the pagan world view of the Ahnenerbe and the SS. The files of the Ahnenerbe contained an article by A. E. Muller originally published in a monthly journal called Lower Saxony in 1903, which describes the celebration of the summer solstice at the Exsternsteine monument near the Wewelsburg in the mid-nineteenth century. [They are] like giants from a prehistoric world which, during the furious creation of the Earth, were placed there by God as eternal monuments ... Many of our Volk are known to have preserved the pagan belief and its rituals, and I remember that some sixty years ago, in my earliest childhood days ... the custom was to undertake a long, continuous journey that lasted for whole days and which only ended on St John's Day, to see those ancient 'Holy Stones' and to celebrate there, with the sunrise, the Festival of the Summer Solstice.

(35) The town of Paderborn itself also had considerable pagan significance, as demonstrated by a letter from a man named von Motz to the head of the Ahnenerbe, Wolfram Sievers, which is quoted in Levenda's hugely informative book Unholy Alliance:

I am sending to you now ... six photographs with explanatory text. Maybe these can appear in one of the next issues of [the official SS magazine] Schwarze Korps in order to show that it is to some extent a favored practice of the church on images of its saints and so forth to illustrate the defeat of adversaries by [having them] step on them.

The referenced essay also mentioned that there are depictions of the serpent's head, as the symbol of original sin, being stepped on [by the saints].

These depictions are quite uncommonly prevalent. It is always Mary who treads on original sin.

Now these pictures appear to me particularly interesting because the serpent refers to an ancient symbol of Germanic belief. At the Battle of Hastings the flag of the Saxons shows a golden serpent on a blue field ...

The Mary Statue at Paderborn was erected in the middle of the past century in the courtyard of the former Jesuit College. As professor Alois Fuchs related several times before in lectures concerning the Paderborn art monuments, the artist that created the Mary Statue must have been a Protestant. This is for me completely proven because the face in the moon-sickle in every case represents Luther.

It is well known that Rome and Judah, preferring thus to take advantage of their own victims, created victory monuments for them. (36)

As Levenda notes, these motifs are common in the volkisch underpinnings of Nazism, with the serpent, thought of as an archetype of evil in Christianity, considered sacred by the Aryans. In addition, '"Rome and Judah" shamelessly exploited the suffering of their own people by depicting them as heroes or as vanquishers of evil through their agonies (thus reinforcing weak, non-Aryan suicidal tendencies among the oppressed populations of Europe).' (37)

As we have noted, the Ahnenerbe received its official status within the SS in 1940, and while other occult-oriented groups such as the Freemasons, the Theosophists and the Hermetic Order of the Golden Dawn were being suppressed, the Ahnenerbe was given free rein to pursue its own line of mystical and occult enquiry, with the express purpose of proving the historical validity of Nazi paganism. Its more than 50 sections covered every aspect of occultism and paganism, including Celtic studies, the rituals surrounding the Externsteine monument, Scandinavian mythology, runic symbolism, the World Ice Theory of Hans Horbiger (which will be discussed in Chapter Seven), and an archaeological research group that attempted to prove the geographical ubiquity of the ancient Aryan civilization. In addition, at the door of the Ahnenerbe must lie the ineradicable iniquity of the medical experiments conducted at Dachau and other concentration camps, since it was this organization that commissioned the unbelievably hideous program of 'scientific research' on living human subjects.

The mental ambiguity of Heinrich Himmler—rational, obedient and totally desirous of security on the one hand; immersed in the spurious fantasy of Aryan destiny on the other—was demonstrated most powerfully in the final phase of the Nazi regime, when it became obvious that Germany would lose the war and the 'Thousand-year Reich' would become dust. From 1943 onward, Himmler maintained loose contacts with the Resistance Movement in Germany, and in the spring of 1945 he entered into secret negotiations with the World Jewish Congress. (By September 1944 he had already given orders for the murder of Jews to be halted, in order to offer a more 'presentable' face to the Allies, an order that was not followed). (38)

Himmler's actions at this time indicate what Fest calls 'an almost incredible divorce from reality', one example being his suggestion to a representative of the World Jewish Congress that 'it is time you Jews and we National Socialists buried the hatchet'. (39) He even assumed, in all seriousness, that he might lead a post-war Germany in an alliance with the West against the Soviet Union. When the reality of the Third Reich's defeat finally overwhelmed his fantasies and sent them to oblivion, and the idea of disguise and escape finally presented itself to him, Himmler adopted perhaps the worst false identity he could have chosen: the uniform of a sergeant-major of the Secret Military Police, a division of the Gestapo. Such was his 'divorce from reality', even then, that it did not occur to him that any Gestapo member would be arrested on sight by the Allies. This indeed occurred on 21 May 1945.

Like their master, many SS men took their own lives in 1945, appalled less at Himmler's betrayal of Hitler through his attempts to negotiate with the Allies than at his betrayal of the SS itself and of the ideals that had given meaning (at least to them) to the destruction they had wrought upon their six million victims. The collapse of this SS ideal 'left only a senseless, filthy, barbaric murder industry, for which there could be no defense'. (40)

OCCULT SECRETS OF THE THIRD REICH

7—THE SECRET AT THE HEART OF THE WORLD
NAZI COSMOLOGY AND BELIEF IN THE HOLLOW EARTH

For readers encountering the field of Nazi Occultism (and its unholy spawn, contemporary belief in genuine Nazi occult power) for the first time, the Hollow Earth Theory may well prompt a sigh of exasperation. We have already examined a number of esoteric concepts that may be more or less unpalatable to the modern mind; the realm we are about to enter, however, may be considered both the most ridiculous and the most sinister yet, since it constitutes both a synthesis and a further development of the strange ideas promulgated by the volkisch occultists and, later, by the philosophers and pseudoscientists of the Third Reich. As we shall see in this chapter, the concept of the hollow Earth -and the related notion of vast, inhabited caverns within a solid Earth—have come to occupy a central position in the fields of ufology, conspiracy theory, fringe science and Nazi-survival theories. Indeed, the relevance of these subjects to the belief systems that define late-twentieth-century popular occultism may come as a surprise to many readers.

THE PROVENANCE OF THE HOLLOW EARTH THEORY

Of all the strange and irrational beliefs held by the Nazis, the most bizarre is surely the idea that our planet is not a sphere floating in the emptiness of space, but rather is a hollow bubble, with everything—people, buildings, continents, oceans and even other planets and stars—existing on the inside. The origin of this curious notion, which would be developed and accepted in the twentieth century by people such as Peter Bender, Dr. Heinz Fisher and many members of the German Admiralty, can be traced back to the seventeenth century and the writings of the Jesuit Athanasius Kircher (1602-1680), who speculated on conditions beneath the surface of the Earth in a treatise written in 1665 entitled Mundus Subterraneus (The Subterranean World). In this work, Kircher draws on the theories and speculations of various medieval geographers about the unexplored north and south polar regions. As Joscelyn Godwin notes, Kircher paid particular attention to the thirteenth-century friar Bartholomew of England, who maintained that 'at the North Pole there is a black rock some 33 leagues in circumference, beneath which the ocean flows with incredible speed through four channels into the subpolar regions, and is absorbed by an immense whirlpool'. (1) Having entered this whirlpool, the waters then travel through a myriad 'recesses' and 'channels' inside the planet and finally emerge in the ocean at the South Pole (the continent of Antarctica had yet to be discovered).

OCCULT SECRETS OF THE THIRD REICH

Kircher's justification for his ideas was ingenious, if utterly flawed. He claimed that the polar vortices must exist, otherwise the northern and southern oceans would be still and would thus become stagnant, releasing noxious vapours that would prove lethal to life on Earth. In addition, he believed that the movement of water through the body of the Earth was analogous both to the recently discovered circulation of the blood and to the animal digestive system, with elements in sea water extracted for the production of metals and the waste voided at the South Pole. (2) This likening of the Earth to a single, living entity will doubtless call to mind certain New Age concepts, in particular the so-called 'Gaia Hypothesis'. (While New Ageism might appear to be nothing but benign, concerned as it is with the spiritual evolution of humanity, it does contain certain aspects that are more sinister and potentially dangerous.)

The seventeenth-century writer Thomas Burnet (1635?-1715) also suggested that water circulated through the body of the Earth, issuing from an opening at the North Pole. In 1768, this idea was further developed by Alexander Colcott, who added an interesting and portentous twist: Godwin suggests that he may have been the first to theorize that, once inside the Earth, the water joined a vast, concave ocean—in other words, that the Earth was actually a hollow globe. (3)

In the eighteenth century, the Hollow Earth Theory carried far more intellectual currency than it does now: even the illustrious Sir Edmund Halley (1656-1742), discoverer of the comet that carries his name, proposed in the Philosophical Transactions of the Royal Society of 1692 that the Earth was a hollow sphere containing two additional concentric spheres, at the centre of which was a hot core, a kind of central sun. The Swiss mathematician Leonhard Euler (1707-1783) concurred and, indeed, went somewhat further, stating that there 'was a center sun inside the Earth's interior, which provided daylight to a splendid subterranean civilization'. (4)

The apparent credibility of these theories resulted in a brand new subgenre of fantastic literature. Godwin provides a brief rundown, based on the work of the French author Michel Lamy, of the most significant of these tales:

While medieval theology, as celebrated in Dante's Divine Comedy, had found the interior of the earth to be a suitable location for Hell, later writers began to imagine quite the contrary. The universal philosopher Guillaume Postel, in his Compendium Cosmographicum (1561) and the topographer Georg Braun, in his Urbium praecipuarum totius mundi (1581), suggested that God had made the Earthly Paradise inaccessible to mankind by stowing it beneath the North Pole. Among the early novels on the theme of a Utopia beneath the surface of the earth are the Chevalier de Mouhy's Lamekis, ou les voyages extraordinaires d'un Egyptien dans la Terre interieure (Lamekis, or the extraordinary voyages of an Egyptian in the inner earth, 1737), and Ludvig Baron von Holberg's Nicholas Klim (1741), the latter much read in Holberg's native Denmark. Giovanni Jacopo Casanova, the adventurer and libertine, also situated Paradise inside the earth.

In Icosameron (1788), a work supposedly translated by him from the English, he describes the twenty-one years passed by his heroes Edward and Elizabeth among the 'megamicros,' the original inhabitants of the 'protocosm' in the interior of our globe. One way into this realm is through the labyrinthine caves near Lake Zirchnitz, a region of Transylvania. The megamicros issue from bottomless wells and assemble in temples, clad in red coats. Their gods are reptiles, with sharp teeth and a magnetic stare. (5) The literature of the Romantic era, needless to say, is rich in fantasies of polar mysteries and lands within the earth. The best known works are probably George Sand's Laura ou le voyage dans le crystal (Laura, or the voyage in the Crystal); Edgar Alien Poe's The Narrative of Arthur Gordon Pym; Alexander Dumas's Isaac Laquedem; Bulwer Lytton's The Coming Race [see Chapter Three]; Jules Verne's Voyage au centre de la terre (Voyage to the Centre of the Earth) and Le Sphinx des glaces (The Sphinx of the Ice). Novels by later and less distinguished authors include William Bradshaw's The Goddess of Atvatabar (1892), Robert Ames Bennet's Thyra, a Romance of the Polar Pit (1901), Willis George Emerson's The Smoky God (1908), and the Pellucidarian stories of Edgar Rice Burroughs, creator of Tarzan. (6)

In view of the exciting potential of the Hollow Earth Theory, not to mention the literary vogue for such romantic fictions, it was only a matter of time before someone had the bright idea of actually searching for the entrances to the mysterious world apparently lying beneath humanity's feet. Such a man was John Cleves Symmes (1780-1829), who spent a good portion of his life trying to convince the world not only that the Earth was hollow, but that it would be worthwhile to finance an expedition, under his leadership, to find a way inside.

'I Declare the Earth is Hollow ...'

A native of New Jersey, Symmes enlisted in the United States Army where he distinguished himself for bravery in the French and Indian Wars. Evidently a man of considerable personal integrity, he married a widow named Mary Anne Lockwood in 1808, and ensured that her inheritance from her husband was used to raise her five children (he had five of his own). In 1816, he retired with the rank of Captain and became a trader in St Louis. (7) Two years later, Symmes first announced his beliefs to the world, thus:

CIRCULAR Light gives light to discover—ad infinitum St Louis, Missouri Territory, North America April 10, AD 1818

To all the World:

I declare the earth is hollow and habitable within; containing a number of solid concentric spheres, one within the other, and that it is open at the poles twelve or sixteen degrees. I pledge my life in support of this truth, and am ready to explore the hollow, if the world will support and aid me in the undertaking.

Jno. Cleves Symmes Of Ohio, late Captain of Infantry.

N.B.—I have ready for the press a treatise on the principles of matter, wherein I show proofs of the above positions, account for various phenomena, and disclose Dr. Darwin's 'Golden Secret.' My terms are the patronage of THIS and the NEW WORLDS.

OCCULT SECRETS OF THE THIRD REICH

I dedicate to my wife and her ten children.

I select Dr. S.L. Mitchell, Sir H. Davy, and Baron Alexander Von Humboldt as my protectors.

I ask one hundred brave companions, well equipped, to start from Siberia, in the fall season, with reindeer and sleighs, on the ice of the frozen sea; I engage we will find a warm and rich land, stocked with thrifty vegetables and animals, if not men, on reaching one degree northward of latitude 82; we will return in the succeeding spring.

J.C.S. (8) Of all the academic societies in America and Europe to which Symmes sent his circular, only the French Academy of Sciences in Paris bothered to respond—and that was to say, in effect, that the theory of concentric spheres inside the Earth was nonsense. Undaunted by the total lack of academic interest in his ideas, Symmes spent the next ten years traveling around the United States, giving lectures and trying to raise sufficient funds to strike out for the interior of the planet. He petitioned Congress in 1822 and 1823 to finance his expedition, and even secured 25 votes the second time. (9) Ultimately, the strain of constant traveling and lecturing took its toll on Symmes's health. He died at Hamilton, Ohio on 29 May 1829. His grave in the Hamilton cemetery is marked by a stone model of the hollow Earth, placed there by his son, Americus.

Symmes's theory of the hollow Earth is described principally in two books: Symmes's Theory of Concentric Spheres (1826) by James McBride, and The Symmes Theory of Concentric Spheres (1878) by Americus Symmes. (10) (Symmes himself wrote a novel, under the pseudonym 'Captain Adam Seaborn', entitled Symzonia A Voyage of Discovery, published in 1820.) As Martin Gardner notes, in these books, 'Hundreds of reasons are given for believing the earth hollow—drawn from physics, astronomy, climatology, the migration habits of animals, and the reports of travelers. Moreover, a hollow planet, like the hollow bones of the body, would be a sturdy and economical way for the Creator to arrange things.' (11)

As we have noted, the Hollow Earth Theory attracted the attention of many writers of fiction. Aside from the best-known mentioned above, a number of minor authors explored the topic. In 1871, for instance, Professor William F. Lyon published The Hollow Globe, or the World's Agitator or Reconciler that included many bizarre speculations on open polar seas, the electro-magnetic origin of earthquakes (which were thought impossible unless the world were hollow) and the theory of gravitation (which needed considerable reworking in view of the drastically reduced mass of a hollow planet). The text of the book was apparently received during mediumistic trances by a Dr. Sherman and his wife, with Professor Lyon transcribing the material. Among the many curious revelations in this book is the 'great fact that this globe is a hollow or spherical shell with an interior as well as an exterior surface, and that it contains an inner concave as well as outer convex world, and that the inner is accessible by an extensive spirally formed aperture, provided with a deep and commodious channel suited to the purposes of navigation for the largest vessels that float, and that this aperture may be found in the unexplored open Polar Sea'. (12)

The Reverend William F. Warren, President of Boston University, published his book Paradise Found in 1885, in which he argued for the origin of the human race at the North Pole. While Warren did not claim that the Earth was hollow, his book nevertheless added to the speculation on the significance of the polar regions, and the idea that the solution to the mystery of humanity's origin might lie there. (13)

In 1896, John Uri Lloyd published his book Etidorhpa (the title is 'Aphrodite' reversed). One of the strangest books on the subject, Etidorhpa tells the story of one Llewellyn Drury, a Mason and seeker after mystery, who encounters a telepathic humanoid creature without a face. The creature takes Drury into a deep cave in Kentucky, and the two emerge on the inner surface of the Earth, where the adventurer is taught to levitate beneath the rays of the central sun. (14)

A SINGLE BUBBLE IN INFINITE NOTHINGNESS

In 1870, perhaps the strangest of all alternative cosmological theories was formulated by Cyrus Teed: the theory that not only is the Earth hollow but we are the ones living on the inside. Born in 1839 in Delaware County, New York, Teed received a Baptist upbringing. After a spell as a private with the United States Army, he attended the New York Eclectic Medical College in Utica, New York. (Eclecticism was an alternative form of medicine that relied on herbal treatments.) It seems that Teed was greatly troubled by the concept of infinite space, which he could not reconcile with the well-ordered Universe of the Scriptures. While he accepted that the Earth was round (he had little choice, since it had been circumnavigated), he found the notion of a ball of rock floating endlessly through an infinite void so unsettling that he set about attempting to formulate an alternative structure for the observable Cosmos.

The answer apparently came to him in a vision in his alchemical laboratory in Utica at midnight one night in 1869. A beautiful woman appeared before him, telling him of the previous lives he had lived, how he was destined to become a messiah, and about the true structure of the Universe. Under the pseudonym Koresh (the Hebrew for Cyrus), Teed published two works: The Illumination of Koresh: Marvellous Experience of the Great Alchemist at Utica, N.Y and The Cellular Cosmogony. In his splendid book Fads and Fallacies in the Name of Science, Martin Gardner summarizes the key points of Teed's outrageous cosmology:

The entire cosmos, Teed argued, is like an egg. We live on the inner surface of the shell, and inside the hollow are the sun, moon, stars, planets, and comets. What is outside? Absolutely nothing! The inside is all there is. You can't see across it because the atmosphere is too dense. The shell is 100 miles thick and made up of seventeen layers.

The inner five are geologic strata, under which are five mineral layers, and beneath that, seven metallic ones. A sun at the center of the open space is invisible, but a reflection of it is seen as our sun. The central sun is half light and half dark. Its rotation causes our illusory sun to rise and set. The moon is a reflection of the earth, and the planets are reflections of 'mercurial discs floating between the laminae of the metallic planes'. The heavenly bodies we see, therefore, are not material, but merely focal points of light, the nature of which Teed worked out in great detail by means of optical laws ...

The earth, it is true, seems to be convex, but according to Teed, it is all an illusion of optics. If you take the trouble to extend a horizontal line far enough, you will always encounter the earth's upward curvature. Such an experiment was actually carried out in 1897 by the Koreshan Geodetic Staff, on the Gulf Coast of Florida. There are photographs in later editions of the book showing this distinguished group of bearded scientists at work. Using a set of three double T-squares—Teed calls the device a 'rectilineator'—they extended a straight line for four miles along the coast only to have it plunge finally into the sea [thus proving the Earth to be a concave sphere]. Similar experiments had been conducted the previous year on the surface of the Old Illinois drainage Canal. (15)

As Gardner observes, Teed was undoubtedly a pseudo-scientist and displayed all the paranoia and obfuscation associated with that fascinating and infuriating group. His explanations of the structure of the Universe (the ways in which planets and comets are formed, for instance) were couched in impossible-to-understand terms such as 'cruosic force', 'coloric substance' and 'afferent and efferent fluxions of essence'. In addition, he bitterly attacked orthodox science, which sought to impose its erroneous view of reality on a 'credulous public'. He likened himself '(as does almost every pseudo-scientist) to the great innovators of the past who found it difficult to get their views accepted'. (16)

Teed's scientific pronouncements were combined with apocalyptic religious elements, as demonstrated in the following prophetic announcement:

We are now approaching a great biological conflagration. Thousands of people will dematerialize, through a biological electro-magnetic vibration. This will be brought about through the direction of one mind, the only one who has a knowledge of the law of this bioalchemical transmutation. The change will be accomplished through the formation of a biological battery, the laws of which are known only to one man. This man is Elijah the prophet, ordained of God, the Shepherd of the Gentiles and the central reincarnation of the ages. From this conflagration will spring the sons of God, the biune offspring of the Lord Jesus, the Christ and Son of God. (17)

Unfortunately for Teed, his revelations did not prove of any great interest to the natives of Utica, who took to calling him the 'crazy doctor' and sought their medical advice elsewhere. With his medical practice facing ruin and his wife already having left him, Teed decided to take to the road to spread his curious word. As a traveling orator, he was a spectacular success (he is said to have earned $60,000 in California alone). (18) He was particularly popular in Chicago, where he settled in 1886 and founded first the College of Life and later Koreshan Unity, a small communal society.

In the 1890s, Teed bought a small piece of land just south of Fort Meyers, Florida, and built a town called Estero. He referred to the town as 'the New Jerusalem', predicted that it would become the capital of the world, and told his followers to expect the arrival of eight million believers. The actual number who arrived was something of a disappointment, being closer to 200; nevertheless, the happy, efficient and hard-working community seems to have functioned extremely well. Their strange ideas notwithstanding, the members, male and female alike, were treated as equals, which is no bad thing. (19)

Teed died in 1908 after being beaten by the Marshal of Fort Meyers. He had claimed that after his death he would be taken up into Heaven with his followers. They dutifully held a prayer vigil over his body, awaiting the event that, unsurprisingly, did not take place. As Teed's body started to decompose, the county health officer arrived and ordered Teed's burial. He was finally interred in a concrete tomb on an island off the Gulf Coast. In 1921 a hurricane swept the tomb away: Teed's body was never found. (20)

As we shall see shortly, in Germany a theory comparable to Teed's was developed by an aviator named Peter Bender. Although Bender himself would die in a Nazi prison camp, his Hollow Earth Doctrine (Hohlweltlehre) found many followers in the Third Reich, including some naval leaders who thought that it might be possible to spy on British naval movements by pointing their radar beams up! As with the more conventional (!) Hollow Earth Theory, there are many people who still fervently believe that we are living on the inside of a hollow sphere.

THE HOLLOW EARTH IN THE TWENTIETH CENTURY

Instead of going the way of other strange notions about the nature of the Universe and collapsing in the face of empirical science, the Hollow Earth Theory survived the end of the nineteenth century, refusing to be banished to the realm of the defunct and disproved. Indeed, in spite of its utter erroneousness, its elegance, romance and air of fantastic mystery ensured it a place in the hearts of those who felt dismayed by the arrogance of orthodox science, not to mention the arrogance of the world's leaders. As we shall see, its very simplicity enabled (and still enables) believers to use it as a template for all manner of esoteric 'truths', conspiracy theories and 'proofs' of the secret nefarious activities of governments. This will become especially apparent when we examine the corollary to the Hollow Earth Theory which, for want of a better expression, we might term the Subterranean Cavern Theory. The idea that the planet is honeycombed with vast cave systems, many of which are inhabited by highly advanced beings and monstrous creatures, developed through the combination of Eastern mysticism (see Chapter Four) with Hollow Earth beliefs, and resulted in a frighteningly paranoid and bizarre scenario that includes the machinations of a secret, one-world government, clandestine alien occupation of our planet, and attempts to perfect mind-control of Earth's population. We will examine these subjects, together with the perceived involvement of the Nazis in their development, a little later; but for now, let us return to the status of the Hollow Earth Theory at the opening of the twentieth century.

The first important book of the twentieth century to deal with the theory was

The Phantom of the Poles by William Reed, published in 1906. This book was the first serious attempt to gather evidence for a hollow Earth, the 'phantom' of the title being a reference to the poles' existence only as locations in space, and not points on the Earth's surface. The only major alteration Reed made to earlier versions of the theory was to reduce the size of the openings at the North and South Poles to a few hundred miles instead of several thousand. The reason for this was that expeditions had been pushing further and further into the polar regions, without finding any evidence of vast openings into the Earth's interior. This refinement notwithstanding, Reed reiterated the beliefs of earlier theorists:

'The earth is hollow. The Poles, so long sought, are phantoms. There are openings at the northern and southern extremities. In the interior are vast continents, oceans, mountains and rivers. Vegetable and animal life are evident in the New World, and it is probably peopled by races unknown to dwellers on the Earth's surface.' (21)

In 1913, William Gardner published his book A Journey to the Earth's Interior or, Have the Poles Really Been Discovered? The book contained the now-famous illustration of the Earth with half of its northern hemisphere cut away to reveal the continents and oceans within. According to Gardner, the central sun was 600 miles in diameter, and its surface was 2,900 miles from the inner surface of the Earth. The polar openings were 1,400 miles wide, and the planetary shell was 800 miles thick. Like Reed and others before him, Gardner believed that conditions within the Earth were extremely pleasant, akin to some semi-tropical paradise. Like Symmes, he attempted to gather sufficient funds for an expedition, without success. At the end of A Journey to the Earth's Interior, Gardner wrote of his hope that one day, with the aid of airships, the openings would be proved to exist.

(22) Of course, the advent of routine manned flight proved his theory wrong, although, as we shall see later in this chapter, the words of one famous explorer who flew over the poles have been twisted by hollow Earth believers to imply things he never intended. Horbiger's World Ice Theory

While not proposing that the Earth is hollow, the World Ice Theory (Welteislehre, or WEL) of Hans Horbiger (1860-1931) amply demonstrates how outrageously inaccurate cosmological models can be used for political and propaganda purposes. Such was the case with Horbiger's Glazial-Kosmogonie, which the Viennese mining engineer wrote in collaboration with an amateur astronomer and which Martin Gardner calls 'one of the great classics in the history of crackpot science'. (23) Although ridiculed by astronomers in Germany—and by just about everyone else in the rest of the world—the World Ice Theory was to gain a fanatical following in Nazi Germany, where it was seen as a brilliant refutation of the orthodox materialistic science personified by the Jewish scientist Albert Einstein. Indeed, according to the rocket scientist Willy Ley (whom we have already met in Chapter Three and will meet again in the next chapter), supporters of this theory acted very much like a miniature political party, issuing leaflets, posters and circulars, and publishing a monthly journal, The Key to World Events. (24) Pauwels and Bergier offer a revealing snapshot of their behavior:

> [Horbiger] seemed to have considerable funds at his disposal, and operated like a party leader. He launched a campaign, with an information service, recruiting offices, membership subscriptions, and engaged propagandists and volunteers from among the Hitler Youth. The walls were covered with posters, the newspapers filled with announcements, tracts were distributed and meetings organized. When astronomers met in conference their meetings were interrupted by partisans shouting: 'Down with the orthodox scientists!' Professors were molested in the streets; the directors of scientific institutes were bombarded with leaflets: 'When we have won, you and your like will be begging in the gutter.' Businessmen and heads of firms before engaging an employee made him or her sign a declaration saying: 'I swear that I believe in the theory of eternal ice.' (25)

Horbiger was deeply fascinated by the origin and behavior of moons, believing that they held the key to the way in which the Universe functions. For example, our present moon, Luna, is not the only satellite that the Earth has had: there have been at least six others, all of which crashed into the Earth, causing massive geological upheavals, so Horbiger believed. According to Horbiger, too, space is not a vacuum but is filled with hydrogen, which has the effect of slowing down celestial bodies in their courses, causing them to spiral in gradually towards their parent body. This, he maintained, is the ultimate fate of the Solar System, with all of the planets falling into the Sun. As they head inexorably towards their parent star, smaller planets occasionally are captured by larger worlds, becoming temporary satellites.

The Austrian engineer's theories were taken up and developed after his death by a British mythologist named Hans Schindler Bellamy, who wrote a book entitled Moons, Myths and Man based on the World Ice Theory. (26) Martin Gardner provides us with an admirably condensed summary of his odd beliefs. Bellamy concentrated his research on the period in which the pre-Lunar moon orbited Earth: since humanity was present at this time, it was able to preserve a record of the moon's cataclysmic collision with the Earth in the form of myths and legends. Bellamy refers to this satellite as the 'tertiary moon'. As it spiraled closer and closer to the Earth, its gravitational field pulled the world's oceans into a 'girdle tide', a gigantic, raised belt of water rising up from the equator. Humanity was forced by the resulting planet-wide glaciation to live in mountainous regions on either side of the girdle tide. As the tertiary moon drew closer, its orbital velocity increased until it was circling the Earth six times every day, its scarred and pitted surface apparently giving rise to the legends of dragons and other flying monsters.

When the moon reached a certain distance from the Earth, the planet's stronger gravitational field tore the satellite apart The result was planet-wide rains and hail storms (all moons having thick coatings of ice on their surfaces), followed by bombardments of gigantic rocks and boulders as the moon finally disintegrated. With the moon gone, the girdle-tide of water collapsed, resulting in the Biblical Deluge.

Eventually, the Earth recovered from its titanic bruising, and this period of tran-

OCCULT SECRETS OF THE THIRD REICH

quillity gave rise to the legends of a Golden Age and earthly Paradise. However, with the arrival of the present moon, Luna, about 13,500 years ago, chaos reigned once again, with earthquakes, axial shifts and glaciation disfiguring the face of the planet. According to Bellamy, the Atlantean civilization was destroyed in this cataclysm. He also believed that the Book of Revelation is actually a historical account of the destruction of the tertiary moon, and Genesis a description of the Earth's recovery following the collision.

For his own part, Horbiger claimed that Luna is covered with a coating of ice 140 miles thick, and that ice also covers Mercury, Venus and Mars. In fact, the famous 'canals' on Mars (now known to be an optical illusion) are, in Horbiger's warped cosmology, cracks on the surface of a 250-mile-deep frozen sea on the Martian surface. The Universe, Horbiger maintained, was packed with gigantic blocks of ice, the action of which accounted for the majority of astronomical events. The Milky Way, for instance, was actually a ring of enormous blocks of ice, not hundreds of millions of stars as the doctored photographs of orthodox astronomy implied. Like moons, the blocks of ice also encounter resistance from the hydrogen with which space is filled, and also spiral into the Sun, causing sunspots when they hit.

Of course, the fact that a theory was idiotic was no barrier to its success in the Third Reich, and the World Ice Theory was eagerly embraced and disseminated by the Propaganda Ministry Willy Ley records some of the statements made by representatives of the cult of WEL in its literature:

Our Nordic ancestors grew strong in ice and snow; belief in the World Ice is consequently the natural heritage of Nordic Man.

Just as it needed a child of Austrian culture—Hitler! -to put the Jewish politicians in their place, so it needed an Austrian to cleanse the world of Jewish science.

The Fuhrer, by his very life, has proved how much a so-called 'amateur' can be superior to self-styled professionals; it needed another 'amateur' to give us complete understanding of the universe. (27)

Gardner, writing in the 1950s, ends his discussion of Horbiger with the amusing comment (from our present perspective) that 'the Cosmic Ice Theory will find disciples until the first spaceship lands on the cratered surface of an iceless moon'. (28) He was certainly correct, and Horbiger was certainly incorrect. However, it is difficult to resist the temptation to note the recent discovery of large ice deposits at the lunar poles, and the theory that they are the result of cometary impacts—comets being, of course, gigantic lumps of ice ...

THE PHANTOM UNIVERSE

The island of Rugen in the Baltic was the site of one of the most bizarre and misguided strategies of the Second World War. In April 1942, an expedition under the leadership of the infra-red ray specialist Dr.. Heinz Fisher and equipped with state-of-the-art radar sets landed on Rugen and began to make a series of observations. Fisher ordered the radar sets to be pointed at an angle of 45° into the sky, a position they maintained for several days. The reason for this peculiar experiment was to prove that the Earth is not a sphere floating in space but is actually a bubble set in an infinity of rock. With the radar pointed upwards at a 45° angle, it was hoped that the beams would be reflected back from objects at some distance along the internal surface of the bubble. It was also hoped that the radar would provide Fisher's team with an image of the British Fleet at Scapa Flow. (29)

According to Professor Gerard S. Kuiper of the Mount Palomar Observatory, who wrote several articles on the Hollow Earth Theory: 'High officials in the German Admiralty and Air Force believed in the theory of a hollow Earth. They thought this would be useful for locating the whereabouts of the British Fleet, because the concave curvature of the Earth would facilitate long-distance observation by means of infra-red rays, which are less curved than visible rays.' (30)

Although they are not the most reliable of sources, Pauwels and Bergier nevertheless make a good point in their occult classic The Morning of the Magicians when they note that if our modern civilization is unified by anything, it is by the fundamental agreement we reach over cosmology—in other words, we are at least able to agree that the Earth is a near-spherical object drifting in an immense void several billion light years in radius. It is one of the many indicators of the baffling and terrifying perversity of the Nazis that so many of them believed in this ridiculous inversion of reality:

The defenders of the Hollow Earth theory, who organized the famous parascientific expedition to the island of Rugen, believed that we are living inside a globe fixed into a mass of rock extending to infinity, adhering to its concave sides. The sky is in the middle of this globe; it is a mass of bluish gas, with points of brilliant light which we mistake for stars. There are only the Sun and the Moon—both infinitely smaller than the orthodox astronomers think. This is the entire Universe. We are all alone, surrounded by rock. (31)

The origin of this idea, as applied in Nazi Germany, can be traced to 1918 and a young German aviator, Peter Bender, who came upon some old copies of Cyrus Teed's periodical, The Sword of Fire. Bender developed and 'refined' the theory (if such a term can be used) into what he called the Hohlweltlehre (Hollow World Theory), also enlisting the strange ideas of Marshall B. Gardner who had claimed that the Sun is actually inside the Earth on whose surface we are kept not by gravity but by the pressure of sunlight. (32) Bender claimed that the hollow bubble of the Earth was the same size as we believe our spherical Earth to be, with solar radiation keeping everything pressed to the concave surface. Beneath our feet is an infinite mass of rock; above our heads the atmosphere stretches to 45 miles, beyond which there is a hard vacuum. At the centre of this vacuum there are three objects: the Sun, the Moon and the Phantom Universe, which is a globe of blue gas containing the shining points of light astronomers mistake for stars.

It is night over a part of this concave Earth when the blue mass passes in front of the Sun, and the shadow of this mass on the Moon produces eclipses ... This theory of Bender's became popular round about the 1930s. The rulers of Germany and officers of the Admiralty and Air Force High Command believed that the Earth is hollow. (33)

The Rugen experiment was, of course, a miserable failure. The Nazi hierarchy turned their backs on the Hohlweltlehre and on Peter Bender himself, who was sent to his death in a concentration camp. Horbiger's Welteislehre, with its equally ridiculous doctrine of the eternal conflict between ice and fire in an infinite Universe, won the day.

THE MUCH-ABUSED ADMIRAL BYRD

Few twentieth-century personalities have been more closely connected with the Hollow Earth Theory—not to mention the theory that UFOs are man-made and are based in Antarctica—than the great Arctic and Antarctic explorer Rear Admiral Richard E. Byrd. As we shall see in this section, and in the final chapter of this book, Admiral Byrd's exploits in the fastness of the South Polar regions have become the stuff of legend, not only in the history of the exploration of our world but also in the fields of ufology, crypto-history and paranoiac conspiracy theory.

Born into an illustrious family at Winchester, Virginia in 1888, Byrd enrolled at the United States Naval Academy at the age of twenty, and received his commission four years later, in 1912. He learned to fly in the First World War, and retained a love of and fascination with flight for the rest of his life. Following the war of 1914-1918, he conducted a number of experiments in flight over water and out of sight of land (and thus without any landmarks by which to navigate), using various scientific instruments such as bubble sextants and drift indicators. His pioneering work with this aspect of navigation led to his being appointed by the US Navy to plan the first transatlantic flight in 1919. The trip was made by the US Navy Flying Boats NC1, NC3 and NC4 (the NC4 being the first plane to complete the flight, via Newfoundland and the Azores, in May of that year). (34)

Seven years later, in 1926, Byrd and Floyd Bennett became the first men to fly over the North Pole. Byrd had been appointed navigator on the proposed transpolar flight from Alaska to Spitzbergen of the US Navy dirigible Shenandoah; but the flight was cancelled by President Coolidge. Upon their return to New York, Byrd was asked by Roald Amundsen what his next objective would be. His response was matter-of-fact: to fly over the South Pole.

Byrd's first Antarctic Expedition (1928-1930) was the first to utilise aircraft, aerial cameras and snowmobiles. With his three planes—a Ford Trimotor monoplane, a Fokker Universal and a Fairchild K3 monoplane—Byrd became the first explorer to combine aerial reconnaissance with ground surveys (making his expedition more important than that of Sir Hubert Wilkins, who had flown in Antarctica ten weeks previously).

The Second Byrd Antarctic Expedition (1933-1935) was, like the first, privately financed, thanks to the continuing American fascination with polar exploration. For most of the winter of 1934, Byrd remained alone in a meteorological hut some 120 miles into the Antarctic interior, conducting observations of the weather and aurora.

These observations were the first of their kind, and nearly cost Byrd his life: he was rescued from the hut by other expedition members when he fell victim to carbon monoxide poisoning.

The United States Antarctic Service Expedition (1939-1941) was led by Byrd, but financed by the US Government.

Its objectives were contained within an order from President Roosevelt in November 1939, which was received by Byrd five days later on board his ship, the North Star, in the Panama Canal Zone. Roosevelt wanted two bases to be established: East Base would be set up near Charcot Island or Alexander I Land; West Base would be built near King Edward VII Land or on the Bay of Whales. The principal objective of the expedition was the mapping of the Antarctic coastline between meridians 72°W and 148°W, with additional mapping to be undertaken on the west coast of the Weddell Sea between Cape Eielson and the Luitpold Coast.

The expedition was a great success, with most of the mapping (700 miles of coastline) being achieved, and the establishing of two bases 1,600 miles apart by air. In addition, numerous scientific observations were made on the summit of the Antarctic Peninsula, including seismic, cosmic ray, auroral, biological, tidal and magnetic surveys. The bases were evacuated with the outbreak of the Second World War, during which Byrd returned to active service as the Chief of Naval Operations.

In the early post-war years, Byrd contributed to the organization of the US Navy Antarctic Developments Project of 1946-1947, also known as 'Operation Highjump'. The project was one of the first military events of the Cold War, and was designed to offer US personnel experience of operating in polar conditions. Operation Highjump deployed 4,700 men, 33 aircraft, 13 ships and 10 caterpillar tractors, and also saw the first use of helicopters and icebreakers in Antarctica. Since Operation Highjump has become one of the most notorious and significant events in the crypto-history of post-war Nazi activities, we must leave an in-depth examination for the final chapter. For now, let us turn our attention to the reasons for Richard Byrd being so closely identified with the concept of a hollow Earth.

The blame can be laid firmly at the doors of three central figures in the Hollow Earth debate: Amadeo Giannini, Raymond Bernard and Ray Palmer. All three made astonishing claims regarding Rear Admiral Byrd's voyage over the North Pole in 1947—a voyage that did not, in fact, take place: we have already seen that he was not in the Arctic in 1947 but in Antarctica. (Giannini got around this inconvenient fact by claiming that Byrd made a secret trip to the Arctic in 1947.) Before we meet these three fascinating characters, we must pause to consider their claims that, regardless of their veracity, have become central in the argument for a hollow Earth and which are still cited by proponents of this bizarre theory.

The claims arise from certain comments made by Byrd about the North Polar regions. In February 1947, Byrd reportedly said: 'I'd like to see that land beyond the Pole. That area beyond the Pole is the centre of the great unknown.' This was followed by his mythical flight in that year, which took him 1,700 miles beyond the North

Pole. During this flight, he is said to have reported by radio that he saw vast areas of ice-free land with mountains, forests, lakes, rivers and lush vegetation. He even saw a large animal, resembling a mammoth, lumbering through the undergrowth! (35) Nine years later, in January 1956, Byrd is said to have made similarly monumental discoveries during a United States expedition to Antarctica, during which they 'accomplished a flight of 2,700 miles from the base at McMurdo Sound, which is 400 miles west of the South Pole, and penetrated a land extent of 2,300 miles beyond the Pole'. (36) Upon his return, Byrd stated that the expedition had 'opened up a vast new land'. Shortly before his death in 1957, Byrd referred to 'that enchanted continent in the sky, land of everlasting mystery'. (37)

For believers in the hollow Earth, these statements were a godsend: apparently corroborative testimony from a highly respected explorer. The interpretation was straightforward: the Earth really does have a vast opening at each Pole, leading to the hollow interior, and it was into these openings that Byrd had flown. The 'vast new land' was actually the lip of the South Polar opening, the curvature of which was so gradual that Byrd did not realize he was well on his way into the inner Earth. The 'enchanted continent in the sky' was none other than the fabulous Rainbow City, home of the hidden supercivilization that operated the UFOs. (38)

As the more responsible commentators on this subject state (often with noticeable relish), there is absolutely no evidence that the Earth is a hollow globe, and the statements attributed to Rear Admiral Byrd do not refer to journeys (witting or unwitting) into the Polar openings. As W.A. Harbinson and Joscelyn Godwin state, the 'great unknown' and the 'land beyond the Pole' are merely descriptions of those parts of Antarctica that had yet to be explored; the 'enchanted continent in the sky' was 'no more than a description of a phenomenon common in Antarctic conditions: the mirage-like reflection of the land below'. (39)

Harbinson continues with his sweeping away of the nonsense that has developed around Byrd's exploratory flights:

[W]hat, precisely, did Rear Admiral Byrd say? In extracts from his journal, published in the National Geographic magazine of October 1947, he wrote: 'As I write this, we are circling the South Pole ... The Pole is approximately 2500 feet [760 metres] below us. On the other side of the Pole we are looking into that vast unknown area we have struggled so hard to reach.'

Did Byrd claim to have flown 1,700 miles (2,750 kilometres) beyond the North Pole in February 1947? No. Describing his flight beyond the South Pole on 16 February 1947 he wrote: 'We flew to approximately latitude 88° 30' south, an estimated 100 miles [160 kilometres]. Then we made approximately a right-angle turn eastward until we reached the 45th east meridian, when we turned again, this time on the way back to Little America.'

Did Byrd report seeing on his journey, not ice and snow, but land areas consisting of mountains, forests, green vegetation, lakes and rivers: and, in the undergrowth, a strange animal that resembled a mammoth? No. According to his journal:

'Altogether we had surveyed nearly 10,000 square miles [25,900 square kilometres] of "the country beyond the Pole". As was to be expected, although it is somewhat disappointing to report, there was no observable feature of any significance beyond the Pole. There was only the rolling white desert from horizon to horizon.' (40)

It is a fundamental feature of 'paranormal' debate that believers will always find a way around skeptics' arguments, and also, of course, that skeptics will always find a way to rubbish the evidence provided by believers. The Hollow Earth theory is no exception, and Rear Admiral Byrd's voyages of Polar discovery continue to be presented as incontrovertible proof of the existence of the Polar openings and the fabulous lands and creatures within, in spite of the fact that those voyages, epoch-making as they were, revealed little more than ice. As we shall now see, Byrd's flights served as the inspiration for ever more elaborate variations on the basic Hollow Earth theme.

AMADEO GIANNINI AND THE PHYSICAL CONTINUITY OF THE UNIVERSE

The first writer to appropriate Rear Admiral Byrd's polar experiences (real or otherwise) in support of his own cosmological theories was Amadeo Giannini, who had had a kind of extrasensory revelation about the structure of the Earth and the surrounding Universe while walking through a forest in New England in October 1926. Like Symmes before him, Giannini spent many years attempting to gain both official recognition for his theory from orthodox scientists and astronomers and adequate funds to mount an expedition to the Polar regions to prove it. Again like Symmes, he was frustrated in both endeavors.

In 1959 he produced a book entitled Worlds Beyond the Poles that was published by the New York vanity publisher Vantage Press at a cost to Giannini of $3,000 and that set out, in confusing and badly written prose, his argument concerning what he called the 'Physical Continuity of the Universe'. The theory was bizarre even by the standards of the Hollow Earth thinking that had spawned Bender's Hohlweltlehre. According to Giannini, our belief that the Earth is a sphere floating in space is the result of an optical illusion: the Earth is actually physically connected to the rest of the Universe at the Poles.

In Giannini's view, Byrd, in flying beyond the Poles, had managed to reach the lands connecting this world to the next. Indeed, according to David Hatcher Childress, Giannini was the first to quote the great explorer's words about the 'land beyond the pole' and the 'great unknown'. Giannini stated: 'It must be conceded that the land beyond to which Admiral Byrd referred had to be land beyond and out of bounds of theoretic Earth extent. If it had been considered part of the mathematized Earth it would not have been referred to as the "center of the great unknown." (41) As we have already noted, it is a considerable leap of logic to take a poetic description of an unexplored land and claim that it connotes a hollow or infinitely extensive planet.

Ray Palmer, Richard Shaver and the Horror Beneath Our Feet

Anxious that his revolutionary theory should reach as wide an audience as possible, Giannini sent a copy of Worlds Beyond the Poles to the man most likely to give it a sympathetic reading: Raymond Palmer. Born in Milwaukee, Wisconsin in 1910, Palmer would become something of a Renaissance man in the fields of the bizarre and unusual, writing science fiction stories, editing pulp magazines and founding Fate, the world's longest-running journal of the paranormal.

It has to be said that life did not deal him the best of hands: at the age of seven he was run over by a truck and his back was broken; two years later, a failed spinal operation left him with a hunchback, and this, combined with a growth-hormone deficiency, resulted in an adult height of just four feet. Understandably enough, this led him to become something of a loner, with a voracious appetite for reading, particularly the fantastic romances that were becoming increasingly popular in the 1920s and 1930s. Palmer was also a great fan of Hugo Gernsback's pulp science fiction magazine Amazing Stones, the first of its kind. (The term 'pulp' comes from the low-grade paper on which these popular magazines were printed.) Palmer organized the first-ever science fiction fan club, the Science Correspondence Club, and founded the first SF fanzine, The Comet, in 1930. Over the next few years, he wrote a number of stories for the pulps before becoming editor of Amazing Stories in 1938. At that time, the magazine was in serious difficulties, but Palmer turned it around with an emphasis on romantic, suspenseful and picaresque adventures. Under his editorship, the magazine's circulation rose by several tens of thousands. (42)

The principal reason for the improvement in the fortunes of Amazing Stories was Palmer's knack of spotting what his reading public wanted and giving it to them, in spite of criticism from many of the 'hard' SF fans who later deserted him for John W. Campbell's Astounding Science Fiction, which published the technology-orientated fiction of people like Robert Heinlein, Isaac Asimov and A.E. van Vogt. However, the success or failure of magazines depends very much on their performance at the newsstands, and by that criterion Amazing was doing just fine. Palmer noticed that his readers seemed fascinated by the idea of lost civilizations -not to mention the paintings of nubile young women in skintight costumes that frequently graced the magazine's covers. This sexual imagery, combined with cosmic mysticism, seemed to Palmer a potentially lucrative mixture, and it did not escape his notice that Amazing always seemed to jump in circulation whenever it featured a story about Atlantis or Lemuria. This led Palmer to wonder how best he might capitalize on this curious interest among his readers. In late 1943, he found the answer in the form of a strange letter from a man named Richard Shaver.

Born in Berwick, Pennsylvania in 1907, Richard Sharpe Shaver was very fond of playing pranks on people, which earned him a somewhat dubious reputation. As a child, he had had two imaginary companions, one good, the other evil, who became more real to him than the living people around him. (43) After graduating from high school he worked for a meat packer and then a tree surgeon before moving to Detroit and enrolling in the Wicker School of Art. In 1930, Shaver joined a communist group called the John Reed Club (named after the American correspondent who had reported on the Russian Revolution).

(44) Like just about everyone else, Shaver fell on hard times with the arrival of the Depression, but managed to eke out a living as a part-time art instructor at the Wicker Art School, supplementing his meagre income by going to a park and selling sketches of passers-by for 25 cents each. In 1933, Shaver married a fellow art student named Sophie Gurivinch who had come originally from Kiev in the Ukraine. They had a daughter the same year, and Shaver took a job as a welder in Highland Park, Michigan. He continued in this job for about a year until he suffered heat stroke, lost the power of speech and was admitted to the Ypsilanti State Hospital for two weeks. In February 1934, Shaver's brother Tate, to whom he had been very close, died. His brother's death affected Shaver very badly and he became increasingly depressed and paranoid, claiming that people were following him. However, as Childress notes, (45) as a known communist, Shaver may well have been genuinely under surveillance.

Shaver received another blow when his wife Sophie died in a mysterious accident in her apartment (they were living separately at the time). While Shaver returned to his welding job, their daughter went to live with Sophie's parents (who apparently told her that her father, too, was dead). (46) For the next few years, Shaver travelled around North America, finding the odd job here and there and marrying again. The marriage was short-lived, his wife leaving him when she found papers indicating that he had been in a sanitarium. Shaver moved back to Pennsylvania and married for a third time.

In 1936, he came across an article in Science World magazine. Entitled 'The True Basis of Today's Alphabet' and written by a man named Albert F. Yeager, the article claimed that there were six letters in our alphabet that represented concepts in addition to sounds. These six letters could thus be used as a key to unlock the hidden meanings in words. In response to this article, Shaver wrote to Science World, claiming that he understood the hidden concepts behind all the letters of the alphabet. He called this conceptual language 'Mantong'.

After several years of work with the Mantong language, Shaver wrote the following letter to Amazing Stories in September 1943:

Sirs:

Am sending this in hopes you will insert it in an issue to keep it from dying with me. It would arouse a lot of discussion. Am sending you the language so that some time you can have it looked at by someone in the college or a friend who is a student of antique times. The language seems to me to be definite proof of the Atlantean legend.

A great number of our English words have come down intact as romantic—roman-tic—'science of man life patterning by control.' Trocadero—t ro see a dero - 'good one see a bad one'—applied now to theatre. This is perhaps the only copy of this language in existence and it represents my work over a long period of years. It is an immensely important find, suggesting the god legends have a base in some wiser race than modern man; but to understand it takes a good head as it contains multi-thoughts like many puns on the same subject. It is too deep for ordinary man—who thinks it is a mistake. A little study reveals ancient words in English occurring many times. It should be saved and placed in wise hands. I can't, will you? It really has an immense significance, and will perhaps put me right in your thoughts again if you will really understand this.

I need a little encouragement.

-R. S. Shaver, Barto, Pennsylvania (47)

Enclosed with this letter was the Roman alphabet together with its associated Mantong concepts, which Childress reprints in his excellent book Lost Continents and the Hollow Earth:

A—Animal (used AN for short) B—Be (to exist—often command) C—See D—(also used DE) Disintegrant energy; Detrimental (most important symbol in language) E—Energy (an all concept, including motion) F—Fecund (use FE as in female—fecund man) G—Generate (used GEN) H—Human (some doubt on this one) I—Self; Ego (same as our I) J—(see G) (same as generate) K—Kinetic (force of motion) L—Life M—Man N—Child; Spore; Seed O—Orifice (a source concept) P—Power Q—Quest (as question) R—(used as AR) Horror (symbol of dangerous quantity of dis force in the object) S—(SIS) (an important symbol of the sun) T—(used as TE) (the most important symbol; origin of the cross symbol) Integration; Force of growth (the intake of T is cause of gravity; the force is T; tic meant science of growth; remains as credit word) U- You V—Vital (used as VI) (the stuff Mesmer calls animal magnetism; sex appeal) W—Will X—Conflict (crossed force lines) Y—Why Z—Zero (a quantity of energy of T neutralized by an equal quantity of D) (48)

By applying these strange hidden meanings behind the letters of the alphabet, one can perceive even stranger hidden meanings behind various words. Childress supplies a number of examples, but we need only detain ourselves with a couple. The word BAD, for instance, can be interpreted as 'Be a de', to be a destructive force. LADY is interpreted as 'Lay de', a complimentary term meaning to allay depression. The reader will note that in both of these examples, the letter D (DE) is used, meaning unpleasant, destructive and detrimental. The letters D and T were of great importance to Shaver, as we shall see shortly.

At this point, it is worth noting a peculiar similarity between Shaver's strange interpretation of the alphabet and the spurious power and significance perceived by Rudolf John Gorsleben, the Edda Society and Karl-Maria Wiligut in the runes of Norse mythology (see Chapters One and Six). In each case, a hidden history of humanity was to be discovered by careful examination of the components of written language—with the aid, that is, of an overheated imagination. It must be added, however, that in Shaver's case the result was harmless, if somewhat lurid entertainment; while the historical and linguistic fantasizing of the Edda Society and its members became one of the motivators of racial hatred.

Shaver's letter landed on the desk of Amazing's, associate editor Howard

Browne. Perhaps unsurprisingly, he threw it into his waste basket as soon as he had finished reading it, dismissing Shaver as a crackpot. (49) Palmer, however, was intrigued and decided to publish both the letter and the accompanying alphabet in the December 1943 issue of *Amazing Stones*. Alongside Shaver's material was a caption that read: 'We present this interesting letter concerning an ancient language with no comment, except to say that we applied the letter-meaning to the individual letters of many old root words and proper names and got an amazing "sense" out of them. Perhaps if readers interested were to apply his formula to more of these root words, we will [sic] be able to discover if the formula applies ...' (50)

Palmer proved more perspicacious than his colleague Howard Browne: the December issue prompted hundreds of people to write in claiming that the Mantong alphabet really did release the hidden meanings of words. Encouraged by this response, Palmer wrote to Shaver asking for more information on the Mantong language and how his understanding of it had developed. Shaver responded by sending a 10,000-word manuscript evocatively entitled 'A Warning to Future Man'. Palmer felt that this was the circulation-booster he had been looking for: the article detailed the hidden history of the Earth, complete with ancient spacefaring civilizations, lost continents, sex, violence and high adventure. Shaver's writing style, however, was not as impressive as his subject matter, and Palmer decided to rewrite 'A Warning to Future Man', turning it into a 31,000-word story which he retitled 'I Remember Lemuria!' and published in the March 1945 issue of *Amazing Stones*. (51)

In this story and the many others that followed it (all of which were billed as true), Shaver painted a terrifying picture of a world honeycombed with vast caverns and tunnel systems containing enormous cities and advanced technology. Shaver's awareness of this world had begun while he was a welder in Highland Park in 1932. He realized that one of the welding guns was somehow allowing him to read the thoughts of his fellow workers in the factory. As if this were not bizarre enough, he also began to pick up the thoughts of evil creatures living far underground—creatures that apparently had the power to kidnap surface people and subject them to unthinkable tortures in their secret underground caverns. 'The voices came from beings I came to realize were not human; not normal modern men at all. They lived in great caves far beneath the surface. These alien minds I listened to seemed to know that they had great power, seemed conscious of the fact they were evil.' (52) This realization proved too much for Shaver: he quit his job and embarked on the aimless wanderings through North America mentioned earlier. During this time he was tormented by invisible, deleterious rays projected at him by the evil subterraneans. Eventually, however, he was contacted by a beautiful young woman named Nydia who was a member of another subterranean group opposed to the evil ones. Needless to say, they became lovers and with her help Shaver was able to gain entry into the underworld and access the 'thought records' that contained the fantastic history of the Earth.

According to the thought records, the Sun was originally a huge planet whose coal beds were ignited by a meteor strike, transforming it into a star. Since this star burned coal(!), it radiated clean, positive energy. The Earth was then colonized by two spacefaring civilizations, the Titans and the Atlans, who possessed marvelous technological devices such as the ben-ray, which broadcast healing energies; the stim-ray, which prolonged and heightened sexual pleasure; the telesolidograph, which could broadcast three-dimensional images; the penetray, used to observe events from vast distances; and the telepathic augmenter or telaug, which transmitted thought.' (53)

The Atlans and Titans called the Earth Lemuria, and lived in Utopian bliss until 20,000 years ago, when the Sun's outer shell was destroyed and it entered its current phase, producing harmful radiation, called d, de or dis. This disintegrant energy is the opposite of t or te, the integrative, formative energy in Shaver's dualistic world view. Their immortality under threat, the Atlans and Titans excavated gargantuan caverns and tunnels far below Lemuria/Earth's surface, in which they built fantastically huge cities, the largest of which would dwarf New York or London. These subterranean realms shielded the entire Titan and Atlan population, some 50 billion individuals. However, the underground cities did not prove a permanent solution and 12,000 years ago Lemuria/Earth was abandoned in favor of younger star systems. (54)

Many Lemurians had already fallen victim to the debilitating effects of the Sun's harmful radiation and were forced to remain on Earth. Some of them moved to the surface (the reader will not be surprised to learn that these were the ancestors of Homo sapiens), while the ones who remained in the subterranean realms degenerated into a race of disfigured, idiotic and very malicious beings known as the 'dero'. This word is a contraction of 'abandondero', and is based on the Mantong words 'de' (meaning negative or destructive) and 'ro' (meaning subservient). Hence the deros were, literally, controlled by negative forces. The group to which Shaver's exotic girlfriend belonged are known as the 'tero', or integrative ro, 'te' denoting positive or constructive energy. The tero, who somehow managed to avoid contamination by the Sun's radiation, are locked in a constant struggle with their unpleasant cousins.

According to Shaver, the fiendish, sadistic and perverted dero kidnap thousands of hapless surface-dwellers every year, and take them into their cavern cities where they are tortured, sexually abused, used as slave labour or eaten. Although fundamentally stupid and brutal, the dero nevertheless know how to use the fabulous machinery left behind by the Lemurians and are able to spread evil and destruction throughout the world by means of dis rays. As Bruce Lanier Wright wryly notes: 'If you doubt this, you may be suffering from brain damage. Vast numbers of surface worlders—you, me, and most certainly Richard Shaver—have been slyly lobotomized by rays projected from the caverns.' (55)

The response to 'I Remember Lemuria!' was astonishing. Not only did the March 1945 issue of Amazing sell out but Palmer received a torrent of mail, numbering thousands of letters, many of which were from people claiming to have had bizarre experiences with the denizens of the fabulous subterranean world. One letter, from an ex-Air Force captain, read in part:

> For heaven's sake drop the whole thing! You are playing with dynamite. My companion and I fought our way out of a cave with submachine guns. I have two 9-inch scars on my left arm ... [M]y friend has a hole the size of a dime in his right biceps. It was scarred inside. How we don't know. But we both believe we know more about The Shaver Mystery than any other pair ... [D]on't print our names. We are not cowards, but we are not crazy.

(56) While the above may or may not be true (Childress suggests that Palmer himself may have fabricated it), there is no doubt that many thousands of people were deeply affected by 'the Shaver Mystery', and wrote to Palmer to tell him so. Many had tales of encounters with strange people who may have been deros, while others complained that they, too, were hearing bizarre voices in their heads. Some even claimed to have visited the cavern-world itself.

By now, the phrase 'paranoid schizophrenia' will surely have suggested itself to the reader. To be sure, Shaver's claims sound very much like he was suffering from this condition: the voices in the head experienced in connection with a mechanical device (the welding gun) are classic symptoms, as is the belief that unpleasant influences are being projected at the victim through air ducts, pipes and so on. As Peebles notes, paranoid schizophrenics 'commonly believe a death ray is causing health problems, destroying their brain, or causing them to hear voices'. (57) This sounds remarkably like what the hapless Shaver was apparently going through, and yet it falls far short of explaining why the number of letters to Amazing Stories jumped from 50 per month before the Shaver Mystery to 2,500 per month during and after, virtually all of which maintained that something sinister and terrifying really was going on beneath the Earth's surface.

Palmer himself was reluctant to commit himself on the veracity of Shaver's claims. While he invariably supported Shaver, he also suggested that the dero caverns might not exist as physical locations in this dimension, but rather on the astral plane. However, Palmer did make the perhaps inevitable claim that he himself had heard the voices of the cavern dwellers while visiting Shaver and his last wife, Dorothy, at their Pennsylvania home.

Palmer claimed that he heard five disembodied voices discussing the dismemberment of a human being in a cavern four miles below. For his part, Shaver maintained that the deros and teros did not live on some astral plane but were solid, flesh-and-blood beings, and that the cavern world was a real place.

Despite its huge popularity with the readers of Amazing Stones, the Shaver Mystery prompted a powerful backlash among diverse groups, including hard science fiction fans who objected to a pornographic fantasy being marketed as truth (and who organized a campaign to boycott the magazine) and various occult groups who criticized Palmer for releasing information that would surely prove lethal to anyone inexperienced or foolish enough to attempt an exploration of the caverns. At the end of 1948, the Ziff-Davis Publishing Company, which published Amazing, decided that enough was enough, and the Shaver Mystery was dropped from the magazine, in spite of the fact that Shaver's 'revelations' had virtually doubled its readership and enabled it to move from quarterly to monthly publication. (58)

Palmer would later claim that the Shaver Mystery had been suppressed by a publisher 'too sedate' for material of this nature. However, Wright notes that Palmer's relations with Ziff-Davis had become rather strained, possibly as a result of his launching Fate magazine. (Palmer left Amazing in 1949 to concentrate on his new publication.) (59) According to Jim Probst in his book Shaver: The Early Years: 'The Queens Science Fiction League of New York passed a resolution that the Shaver stories endangered the sanity of their readers, and brought the resolution before the Society for the Suppression of Vice. A fan conference in Philadelphia was rocked by threats to draw up a petition to the Post Office, asking that Amazing Stories be banned from the mail.' (60)

This was not the end of the Shaver Mystery, however; it would later inspire a number of people to start their own publications. Richard Toronto published Shavertron between 1979 and 1985. Subtitled 'The Only Source of Post-Deluge Shaverania', the magazine reported on the continuing activities of the nefarious dero, such as the time they apparently interfered with Toronto's car while it was parked on a steep hillside and he was standing in front of it (Toronto barely managed to avoid being run over and killed). (61)

The Hollow Hassle was published by Mary Le Vesque between 1979 and 1983 and featured a regular column by the Rev Charles A. Marcoux, a fascinating and colorful character who claimed to have hunted the deros during his many cave explorations. In the August 1981 issue of The Hollow Hassle he wrote (in typically muddled syntax): 'My experiences in the cavern world began at a very young age with astral experiences in the caverns ever since my birth, and in other worlds from other dimensions too. I joined R. A. Palmer and R. S. Shaver's group in January of 1945, and I am one of the few original members left. I still "SEARCH FOR THE PORTALS," and as far as I know, am the only original member who does.' (62)

The Hollow Earth Insider ran for a few years in the early 1990s. Edited by Dennis Crenshaw, the journal included reprinted material by Shaver, in addition to news clippings and conspiracy theories, such as government (and dero) mind control. As Childress notes, the concept of mind control was central to the Shaver Mystery and adds the intriguing speculation that Shaver himself may well have been a victim. (We will take a closer look at the subject of mind control in the next chapter.)

Palmer made a last effort to perpetuate the Shaver Mystery in the early 1960s with The Hidden World, a trade paperback series that contained reprints of the original Shaver stories, together with yet more tales from people claiming to have encountered and been victimized by the fiendish deros. Unfortunately, The Hidden World was not particularly successful and publication ceased in 1964. Shaver himself claimed to have discovered pictorial records of the Titans and Atlans hidden within the rocks and stones of the Wisconsin prairies in the 1950s, and for the rest of his life tried in vain to persuade various scientists that they constituted final proof of the reality of the cavern world. He died of a heart attack in 1975. Palmer continued to publish journals, although none even approached the success of Amazing Stories and Fate. He died in 1977.

Before we continue, we must pause to examine what Palmer and many others considered to be the most impressive evidence for the Hollow Earth Theory, and which is still cited as proof that we are indeed living on the surface of a hollow sphere. In view of the ease with which this 'evidence' can be dismissed (and has been by a number of the more responsible commentators on this subject), it is surprising that so many writers still cling to it with such misguided tenacity.

In 1970, the Environmental Science Service Administration of the US Department of Commerce made public a collection of photographs taken by their weather satellite ESSA7 in November 1968. Several of these photographs contained, at first sight, an absolutely extraordinary image: an enormous dark area where the Earth's North Pole should have been. When Palmer saw the photographs, he had no hesitation in reproducing them in his magazine Flying Saucers, with an accompanying article stating that here, at last, was the proof—and from an official source—that there was indeed a gigantic opening at the North Pole, leading to the hollow interior of the planet.

The true reason for the dark area in the photographs was nowhere near as romantic and exciting as the Hollow Earthers would have their readers believe. The ESSA-7 photographs were actually photomosaics containing many hundreds of elements, rather than single exposures. Due to the satellite's orbital trajectory, the area at and immediately around the Pole had not been included in these photomosaics—they had simply not been photographed, and thus showed up as dark areas on the images. Unfortunately, this explanation has not dissuaded certain sensationalist writers from citing the ESSA-7 pictures, even to this day, as conclusive proof that the Earth is hollow. (63)

There is perhaps some truth in Peebles's assertion that the Shaver Mystery constituted, in effect, a modern mythology that served a number of functions, including escapism from post-war reality and the incipient threat of the Cold War; an answer to the question of why there was so much evil and suffering in the world; and, of course, an exciting corollary to the perceived menace of Communism: a new enemy whose very existence could be used to define the contrasting, positive attributes of the American Way. Palmer himself was a clever manipulator (if that is not too strong a word) of the public need both for escapism and for an explanation of the violence and evil that seemed to characterize life on Earth (it was all the fault of the deros). This was further illustrated by his reaction to the rise of the UFO mystery, which came to the world's attention with Kenneth Arnold's sighting of nine crescent-shaped objects over Mount Rainier in Washington State on 24 June 1947. Arnold's sighting was followed by a torrent of reports of strange objects flitting through the skies. In the pages of Fate magazine, Palmer instantly provided the answer to the puzzle: some of the UFOs were indeed alien spacecraft, but most were vessels piloted by the denizens of the cavern world. (We will look much more closely at the UFO mystery, which has become intimately connected to the idea of Nazi survival, in the next chapter.) Whatever the underlying truth (if any) of the claims of Shaver, Palmer and others about the strange and frightening drama constantly being played out beneath our feet, the Shaver Mystery has come to define the Hollow Earth Theory in the twentieth century and now occupies a central position in the complex network of rumors, speculations, cryptohistorical inferences, anomalous events and genuine government violations of public trust that constitutes modern conspiracy theory.

Raymond Bernard and the 'Greatest Geographical Discovery in History'

Perhaps the most famous of all books published on the subject of the hollow Earth is entitled (unsurprisingly) The Hollow Earth and is subtitled (unbelievably) 'The Greatest Geographical Discovery in History'. Its author was yet another colorful and far from trustworthy personality named Walter Siegmeister, although he also went under other names, for reasons that will become clear.

Siegmeister was born in New York in 1901. His father's occupation as a doctor perhaps had something to do with the boy's intense fascination with sexual reproduction and the male and female reproductive anatomy (he was particularly interested in menstruation).

(64) After completing his education at Columbia University and New York University (he gained a bachelor's degree from Columbia in 1924 and a master's degree and doctorate from NYU in 1930 and 1932), Siegmeister moved to Florida in 1933 where he published a newsletter entitled Diet and Health, through which he promulgated his opinions on the benefits of raw food and a healthy lifestyle.

After a disastrous business partnership with a confidence trickster named G.R. Clements, during which they sold useless, waterlogged land to people wishing to grow crops, Siegmeister fled the United States and the legal action with which he was threatened, and went to Ecuador in 1941. There he met a friend, John Wierlo, who had moved from America the previous year, and together they conceived the idea of creating a new Utopia and a 'super-race' somewhere in the jungles in the east of the country. The 'Adam' of this scheme would be Wierlo (by all accounts an impressive example of manhood); the 'Eve' would be a 24-year-old woman named Marian Windish, a hermit who had apparently lived for two years in the Ecuadorian jungle. (65) The new Utopia, however, was not to be: Wierlo later claimed that he had no intention of creating a super-race, and it also transpired that Marian Windish was already married. Wierlo also accused Siegmeister of faking an ability to walk on water by means of a series of supports just below the surface. So outlandish were Siegmeister's claims of miraculous powers and meetings with Tibetan masters on Ecuadorian mountains (many of which appeared in the American press) that he was forbidden from using the US Mail Service and deported by the Ecuadorian Immigration Department. (66)

OCCULT SECRETS OF THE THIRD REICH

Upon his return to the United States, Siegmeister, now using the name Dr. Robert Raymond, continued his promotion of a healthy diet by selling health foods and two books he had written, entitled Are You Being Poisoned lay the Food You Eat? and Super-Health thru Organic Super-Foods. He then began traveling again throughout South America, selling his books through mail order, now under the name Dr. Uriel Adriana, AB, MA, PhD. When his mother died in 1955, leaving him a substantial amount of money, he moved to Brazil and bought a large plot of land with the intention of continuing his efforts to create a super-race. In his 1955 book Escape From Destruction, which he again wrote under the pseudonym Raymond Bernard, he warned of a coming nuclear war, from which a few people would be saved by extraterrestrials who would take them to Mars. (67)

While in Brazil, Siegmeister came across an odd book entitled From the Subterranean World to the Sky by one O. C. Huguenin who seems to have held a high position in the Brazilian Theosophical Society. In common with Shaver, Huguenin claimed that the UFOs were the handiwork of an ancient civilization (Huguenin claimed they were the Atlanteans) that had built them 12,000 years ago, just before the destruction of their continent. Some Atlanteans escaped the cataclysm by taking their craft through the Polar openings and reestablishing their fabulous civilization in the inner Earth. The reason UFOs were being seen by so many surface dwellers was that the Atlanteans were concerned at humanity's use of nuclear energy (concerns that were also attributed to the so-called 'Space Brothers' by the American contactees of the 1950s—see Chapter Eight).

At this time, two Theosophist friends of Huguenin, Commander Paulo Strauss and Professor Henrique de Souza, were also actively promoting in Brazil the idea of the hollow Earth: Strauss by lecturing widely about a UFO base called Agharta, and de Souza by claiming that he was in contact with the Atlanteans. (68) Siegmeister also claimed to have met an Atlantean woman (who looked like an eighteen-year-old, but who was actually 70) at the Theosophical Society Headquarters in Sao Lourenco. At one of these meetings, de Souza told Siegmeister that Brazil contained a number of tunnels leading down to the inner Earth (Childress notes that one of the tunnels was supposed to be in the Roncador Mountains of the Matto Grosso, the region in which the famous explorer Colonel Percy Fawcett disappeared in 1925). (69) According to de Souza, Fawcett was still alive and well in an Atlantean city, although he was prevented from leaving in case the surface dwellers forced him to reveal its whereabouts. Although he claimed to have made many trips into the Roncador Mountains, Siegmeister never found any of the tunnel entrances.

When some friends in America sent him a copy of Ray Palmer's journal Flying Saucers, containing articles about Rear Admiral Byrd's flights and the Hollow Earth Theory, Siegmeister went into creative overdrive, writing Agharta, The Subterranean World and Flying Saucers from the Earth's Interior. At this time, 1960, Siegmeister received a letter from one Ottmar Kaub, who was a member of an organization called UFO World Research based in St Louis, Missouri. Kaub was writing on behalf of the organization's leader, Dr. George Marlo, who claimed to have visited the inner Earth on board a UFO, and who wished to live at Siegmeister's Brazilian colony. Dr. Marlo claimed to know two beings called Sol-Mar and Zola, who lived in a city called Masars II, underneath South Africa. Sol-Mar and Zola described the inner Earth as a paradise with a perfect climate, giant fruits, beautiful birds with 30-foot wingspans, and where the people grew to over 12 feet tall. (70)

For the next few years, Marlo tantalized Siegmeister with promises of a meeting with Sol-Mar and Zola—meetings that were always unavoidably postponed for various reasons. Eventually, Siegmeister realized that Marlo was lying about his contacts with the Inner Earthers and decided to continue his researches alone.

In 1964, he managed to find a New York publisher for his last book, The Hollow Earth, which was largely a rewrite of Flying Saucers from the Earth's Interior and also borrowed heavily from Reed, Gardner and Giannini. The book sold well, but unfortunately Siegmeister did not live to enjoy its success: he died of pneumonia in 1965. Although The Hollow Earth contains a great deal of material from earlier writers, it is distinguished by its lengthy treatment of the idea that the governments of the world are well aware of the 'fact' that UFOs are spacecraft, and that they come from the inner Earth (it was one of the first books to pay serious attention to this idea). In addition, Siegmeister was one of the first writers to suggest that the US and Soviet Governments were secret allies in the face of the potential threat posed by the Inner Earth civilization, a claim that has become an integral part of modern conspiracy theory. (71)

Siegmeister's greatest legacy, however, must be the identification of Brazil as the most significant location in the mythology of the hollow Earth. Not only is that country a hot spot for UFO activity and encounters with apparent 'aliens', it also contains possibly more subterranean tunnel networks and entrances to the inner Earth than any other country. Before moving on, we may cast a glance at some of the reports that have recently been coming out of Brazil concerning some rather unusual discoveries. For instance, the Brazilian organization Sociedade de Estudos Extraterrestres (SOCEX) has spent the last few years investigating claims that an elaborate tunnel network exists in the mountains of Santa Catarina and Parana States, particularly around the town of Joinville about 190 miles south-west of Sao Paulo (which, oddly enough, was Siegmeister's base of operations in Brazil). (72)

In another SOCEX report, two men entered a tunnel near the city of Ponta Grossa, 250 miles south-west of Sao Paulo, in which they discovered a staircase leading further underground. Descending the staircase, the men found themselves in a small underground city, where they remained for five days with its 50 inhabitants. Many people have reported UFOs in the area, and some say they have heard singing, the voices apparently coming from underground. (73)

While these stories may be taken with a large grain of salt (their protagonists are invariably referred to by pseudonyms or just initials), the claim that Brazil, and indeed the rest of South America, is an important centre of UFO activity and of the belief in powerful subterranean civilizations is of considerable significance to the present study. In South America we find the nexus of the ideas we shall be discussing in the last two chapters of this book: firstly, that by the end of the Second World War the Nazis had begun to develop aircraft and weapons systems radically in advance of anything in use elsewhere at the time; and secondly, that Nazism as a potent political force did not cease to exist with the defeat of the Third Reich but continues in one or more secret locations, still exerting a powerful influence on world events.

As with most aspects of what may broadly be termed 'the paranormal', the concepts of Nazi occultism and genuine Nazi occult power (the former a verifiable historical fact, the latter an unsafe extrapolation based on rumor and hearsay) have merged into one another to such a degree that a clear line of dichotomy between the two has become virtually impossible to define. This will become especially apparent as we conclude this chapter on the hollow Earth and subterranean civilizations with a look at the tunnel system that is said to exist beneath South America. While legends of tunnels beneath South America have existed ever since the Spanish conquest of the continent, referring to the mysterious places where the Incas were said to have hidden most of their gold, there is some evidence for their actual existence. Some modern explorers even claim to have visited them.

Chief among these is David Hatcher Childress, who has written many books on the more unorthodox aspects of archaeology and who offers an account of one such adventure he undertook in his fascinating and informative study of the Shaver Mystery and the Hollow Earth Theory, Lost Continents and the Hollow Earth. Childress describes how he followed a lead provided in a letter sent to him by one of his South American readers, named Marli, who described an opening leading to a tunnel system near the small mountain town of Sao Tome das Lettres, north of Sao Paulo.

Childress travelled to the town with Marli, and in a local restaurant they listened, together with about twenty others, to the owner as he told a strange story of a man-made tunnel extending far into the earth. Marli translated the restaurant owner's Portugese:

'The Brazilian army went into the tunnel one time to find out where it ends. After traveling for four days through the tunnel the team of Army explorers eventually came to a large room deep underground. This room had four openings to four tunnels, each going in a different direction. They had arrived in the room by one of the tunnels.

'They stayed in the room for some time, using it as their base, and attempted to explore each of the other three tunnels, but after following each for some time, turned back to the large room. Eventually they returned to the surface, here at Sao Tome das Lettres.

'... [T]here is a man here in town who claims to know the tunnel and claims that he has been many weeks inside the tunnel. This man claims that the tunnel goes all the way to Peru, to Machu Picchu in the Andes. This man claims that he went completely under South America, across Brazil and to Machu Picchu.' (74)

The restaurant owner went on to tell how he himself had encountered a strange man near the tunnel entrance one morning. The man was dressed in traditional Andean Indian clothes, and was extremely tall, approximately seven feet. As soon as he saw the restaurant owner, the man walked away without saying anything.

Childress goes on to report that the following morning he, Marli and a fellow explorer named Carl Hart went to the tunnel entrance with the intention of exploring as far as they could. He continues:

I was amazed at this ancient feat of engineering. We were descending down into the earth in a wide, gradually sloping tunnel that was dug into a red, clay-type dirt. It was not the smooth, laser-cut rock walls that Erich von Daniken had claimed to have seen in Ecuador in his book Gold of the Gods, but it was just as incredible.

It wouldn't have taken some space-age device to make this tunnel, just simple tools; yet, it was clearly a colossal undertaking. Why would anyone build such a tunnel? Was it an ancient mine that went deep into the earth, searching for an elusive vein of gold or merely red clay for the long-gone ceramic kilns? Was it an elaborate escape tunnel used in the horrific wars that were said to have been fought in South America—and around the world—in the distant past? Or was it some bizarre subterranean road that linked up with other tunnels in the Andes and ultimately could be used to journey safely to such places as Machu Picchu, Cuzco or the Atacama Desert? (75)

In the event, the answers to these questions evaded the small party: after an hour, they arrived at a point where the floor dropped approximately one metre, and decided that this was a convenient place to turn back, since the tunnel seemed to continue endlessly on, and they were not equipped for a lengthy exploration. Although the group did not encounter any fabulous wonders of the subterranean realm, the very existence of the tunnel proves that the legends associated with South America have some basis in fact.

8—THE CLOUD REICH
NAZI FLYING DISCS

So far in this book we have looked at some extremely strange notions, many of which were held by the Nazis themselves and many by certain writers who have, over the years, attempted to prove that the Third Reich was ruled by men who were, quite literally, practitioners of Black Magic. We now come to a subject that, at first sight, might seem somewhat out of place in our survey, and yet the suggestion has been frequently made that the UFOs (unidentified flying objects) first reported in the late 1940s were the products of experimental aircraft designs that were developed towards the end of the Second World War. Most (if not all) serious historians would throw up their hands in horror at the very mention of such a seemingly ludicrous idea, particularly when one considers the associated claims that, since sightings of UFOs are still reported today by thousands of people around the world, these radical aircraft designs must have been captured, copied and further developed by the victorious powers; and, what is more, that some UFOs may even be piloted by escaped Nazis operating out of one or more hidden bases.

As will surely be apparent from the material we have examined so far, the Nazi occultist idea is both bizarre and complicated, not least because it encompasses several additional fields of arcane knowledge and speculation. We have already seen how the Nazi elite were fascinated by the concepts of the Holy Grail and the Knights Templar, by Eastern mysticism and the Hollow Earth theory, by odd cosmological concepts and the hidden legacies of fabulous, long-vanished civilizations. In fact, the notion of the secret transmission of esoteric information through history (as discussed in Chapter Three, concerning the story of the Knights Templar following their suppression) can also be applied to the Nazis themselves and their awful legacy of racial hatred. While many would think that this legacy is confined to the demented ravings of a few groups of neo-fascists in Europe and America, there is some evidence to suggest that the truth may be far more sinister and frightening.

This evidence, which has been gathered and presented over the years by investigators of the UFO phenomenon, as well as by those with an interest in the more unusual German weapons designs of the Second World War, points to the possibility that some extremely advanced aircraft designs did actually reach the prototype stage in 1944 and 1945. Those researchers who have uncovered this evidence, and whom we shall meet in this chapter, have also taken the logical next step of suggesting that the Americans and Russians captured a number of designs at the end of the war and continued their development throughout the post-war years. In addition, they suggest that many leading Nazis (including, according to some accounts, Hitler himself) were able to escape the ruins of the Third Reich and continue their nefarious plans for world domination in the icy fastnesses of the Arctic and Antarctic.

Could there possibly be any truth to these incredible speculations? Could UFOs actually be man-made air- and spacecraft? Could some of them belong to a hidden 'Fourth Reich' that represents a cancer that was not, after all, cut from the body of humankind? To deal with these questions, we must, once again, enter the curious realm of crypto-history, where the line between reality and fantastic rumor becomes blurred and indistinct; in short, we must return to Pauwels's and Bergier's 'Absolute Elsewhere'. In this realm, science and occultism meet, as do theories of vast historical conspiracies and outrageous cosmological speculations. The claims about the survival of the Nazis are connected to all these fields, and depend to a great extent on the use of highly advanced technology and resources by secret forces.

THE MYSTERY OF THE UFOS

Although human beings have been seeing strange things in the skies since the dawn of history, the idea that some of them are actually technological devices (called by some 'X Devices', although that term is now obsolete) is relatively recent. The first person to suggest that mysterious objects and lights in the sky might be machines from another planet was probably the great American anomalist Charles Fort (1874-1932); however, it was not until the late 1940s that the idea began to gain a wider currency, following the famous sighting by pilot Kenneth Arnold over the Cascade Mountains in Washington State on 24 June 1947.

The UFO mystery has never gone away, and has certainly never been explained to universal satisfaction: indeed, it is now more deeply ingrained in the public consciousness than ever before, and the 'flying saucer' can truthfully be described as one of the great cultural icons of the twentieth century. While skeptics would argue that the reason for this is a mixture of wishful thinking, the misidentification of mundane phenomena and out-and-out hoaxes, the truth of the matter is more subtle and complex. It is certainly true that approximately 95 per cent of sightings can be attributed to stars, planets, meteorites, satellites, aircraft and so on; yet there remains the tantalizing five per cent that cannot be explained so easily.

In order to illustrate this fact, we can look very briefly at one of the classic UFO sightings from the early days of modern ufology. (Although there are many impressive sightings from the 1990s, they are still the subject of intense debate and I believe it is more prudent to choose a sighting that has stood the test of time and is still regarded as almost certainly genuine.) At about 7.45 on the evening of 11 May 1950, Mr and Mrs Paul Trent watched a large object fly over their farm near McMinnville, Oregon, USA. Mrs Trent had been out feeding their rabbits when she noticed the UFO. She called her husband, who was able to take two black-and-white photographs of it. The photographs show a circular object with a flat undersurface and a bevelled edge; extending from the upper surface of the object is a curious structure reminiscent of a submarine conning tower, which is offset slightly from the vertical axis.

The bright, silvery object was tilted slightly as it moved across the sky in absolute silence, and presently was lost to view. The Trents later said that they had felt a slight breeze from the underside of the UFO. The Trents sought no publicity following their sighting (in fact, they waited until they had used up the remainder of the camera's film before having the UFO photographs developed!); they mentioned the incident to only a few friends. However, news of the sighting quickly spread to a reporter from the local McMinnville Telephone Register who visited the Trents and found the photographic negatives under a writing desk where the Trent children had been playing with them. (1) A week later, the photographs appeared in Life magazine and became world-famous.

Seventeen years later, the McMinnville UFO sighting was investigated by William K. Hartmann and was included in the famous (and, in the UFO community, widely despised) Condon Report produced by the US Air Force-sponsored Colorado University Commission of Enquiry. The Condon Report (named after the enquiry's leader, the respected physicist Dr. Edward U. Condon) was dismissive of the UFO phenomenon, which it considered to be of no interest to science. However, the report contained a number of cases that it conceded were not amenable to any conventional explanation. One of these cases was the McMinnville sighting. The photographs were submitted to extremely rigorous scientific analysis, after which Hartmann concluded:

This is one of the few UFO reports in which all factors investigated, geometric, psychological, and physical, appear to be consistent with the assertion that an extraordinary flying object, silvery, metallic, disk-shaped, tens of meters in diameter, and evidently artificial, flew within sight of two witnesses. It cannot be said that the evidence positively rules out a fabrication, although there are some physical factors such as the accuracy of certain photometric measures of the original negatives which argue against a fabrication. (2)

In the 50 or so years since the Trents had their strange encounter, the photographs have been repeatedly subjected to more and more sophisticated analyses, and have passed every test. This case is just one of a large number of sightings of highly unusual, apparently intelligently guided objects, seen both in the skies and on the ground, that have been occurring for decades. There are, of course, various theories to account for these sightings, aside from the skeptical notion that all are, without exception, hoaxes, illusions or misidentifications of ordinary phenomena.

The most widely accepted theory is, of course, the Extraterrestrial Hypothesis (ETH), which holds that genuine UFOs are spacecraft piloted by explorers from another planet. This theory has the greatest currency in the United States. In Europe, more credence is given to an alternative theory known as the Psycho-social Hypothesis, which suggests that encounters with UFOs and 'aliens' may be due to subtle and ill-understood processes occurring within the mind of the percipient. Inspired by the Swiss psychoanalyst Carl G. Jung, who examined UFOs in his book Flying Saucers A Modern Myth of Things Seen in the Sky (1959), the psycho-sociologists see such encounters as similar to waking Dreams that fulfill an undefined psychic need. (To Jung, the circular shape of the UFO suggested a psychic need for wholeness and unity, represented by the mandala, a circular symbol identified by Jung as one of the archetypes residing in humanity's collective unconscious.)

There are a number of secondary theories for UFOs, including the idea that they are time machines from the future, that they are actually living beings indigenous to interplanetary space, that they originate in other dimensions of existence and so on, all of which are beyond the scope of this book. The idea that UFOs are man-made, and based on plans captured by the Allies in the ruins of Nazi Germany at the end of the Second World War, has been put forward by a number of writers and researchers. Outlandish as it may sound, it is actually well worth examining the evidence for 'Nazi flying saucers'.

THE FOO FIGHTERS

Although it set the stage for the drama of modern ufology, Kenneth Arnold's 1947 sighting of nine anomalous objects flitting between the peaks of the Cascade Mountains was not the first twentieth-century UFO encounter. In the closing stages of the Second World War, Allied pilots on night-time bombing raids over Europe frequently reported strange flying objects. These objects were christened Foo Fighters', after a catchphrase in the popular Smokey Stover comic strip. 'Where there's foo, there's fire.' ('Foo' was also a play on the French word feu, meaning fire.) The aircrews suspected that the objects might be some kind of German secret weapon. On 2 January 1945, the New York Herald Tribune carried the following brief Associated Press release:

Now, it seems, the Nazis have thrown something new into the night skies over Germany. It is the weird, mysterious Foo fighter' balls which race alongside the wings of Beaufighters flying intruder missions over Germany. Pilots have been encountering this eerie weapon for more than a month in their night flights. No one apparently knows what this sky weapon is. The 'balls of fire' appear suddenly and accompany the planes for miles. They seem to be radio-controlled from the ground, so official intelligence reports reveal. (3)

In their book Man-Made UFOs (1994), Renato Vesco (a pioneer of the Nazi-UFO hypothesis) and David Hatcher Childress cite the testimony of a former American flying officer who had worked for the intelligence section of the Eighth Air Force towards the end of the war. Wishing to remain anonymous, the officer said to the New York press:

'It is quite possible that the flying saucers are the latest development of a "psychological" anti-aircraft weapon that the Germans had already used. During night missions over western Germany I happened to see on several occasions shining discs or balls that followed our formations. It was well known that the German night fighters had powerful headlights in their noses or propeller hubs—lights that would suddenly catch the target, partly in order to give the German pilots better aim but mostly in order to blind the enemy tail gunners in their turrets. They caused frequent alarms and continual nervous tension among the crews, thereby lowering their efficiency. During the last year of the war the Germans also sent up a number of radio-controlled bright objects to interfere with the ignition systems of our engines or the operation of the on-board radar. In all probability American scientists picked up this invention and are now perfecting it so that it will be on a par with the new offensive and defensive air weapons.' (4)

Unfortunately, Vesco and Childress are not forthcoming with a detailed reference for this statement.

The British UFO investigators Peter Hough and Jenny Randles make the interesting point that the Second World War saw more people in the skies than any other prior period, and that it was therefore no great surprise that UFOs should have been spotted in abundance.

(5) Of course, this statement carries the implication of a likely nonhuman origin of the objects, which advocates of the Nazi-UFO hypothesis hotly dispute: for them, the large number of Foo Fighter sightings, coupled with the obvious interest the objects showed in Allied aircraft, strongly implies that they were built specifically to interact in some way with those aircraft. As is so often the case with the UFO mystery, genuine sightings generated various rumors of official interest in the phenomenon. For instance, there was, allegedly, a secret British government investigation into the Foo Fighter reports called the Massey Project. 'However,' write Hough and Randles, 'Air Chief Marshal Sir Victor Goddard—who was an outspoken believer in alien craft during the 1950s -flatly denied this and said that Treasury approval for such a minor exercise at a time when Britain was fighting for its survival would have been ludicrous.' (6)

Some encounters undoubtedly had mundane explanations. For example, during a bombing raid on a factory at Schweinfurt, Germany on 14 October 1943, flight crews of the American 384th Squadron observed a large cluster of discs, which were silver in color, one inch thick and about three inches in diameter. They were floating gently down through the air directly in the path of the American aircraft, and one pilot feared that his B17 Flying Fortress would be destroyed on contact with the objects. However, the bomber cut through the cluster of discs and continued on its way undamaged. It is quite possible that encounters such as this were actually with 'chaff, pieces of metal foil released by German Aphrodite balloons to confuse radar by returning false images. (7)

Nevertheless, many aircrews reported events that were not so easy to explain, including the harassment of their aircraft by small, glowing, disc-shaped and spherical objects that were highly maneuverable. On 23 November 1944, Lieutenant Edward Schlueter of the 415th US Night Fighter Squadron was flying a heavy night fighter from his base at Dijon towards Mainz. Twenty miles from Strasbourg, Lieutenant Fred Ringwald, an Air Force intelligence officer who was on the mission as an observer, glanced out of the cockpit and noticed about ten glowing red balls flying very fast in formation. Schlueter suggested that they might be stars, but this explanation was proved wrong when the objects approached the plane.

Schlueter radioed the American ground radar station, informing them that they were being chased by German night fighters, to which the station replied that nothing was showing on their scope. Schlueter's radar observer, Lieutenant Donald J. Meiers, checked his own scope, but could detect nothing unusual. Schlueter then decided to make for the objects at full throttle. The response from the Foo Fighters was instantaneous: their fiery red glow rapidly dimmed, until they were lost to sight. Less than two minutes later, however, they reappeared, although they seemed to have lost interest in the American aircraft and glided off into the night towards Germany. (8) Upon the objects' departure, the fighter's radar began to malfunction, forcing the crew to abandon their mission.

In an encounter of 27 November 1944 over Speyer, pilots Henry Giblin and Walter Cleary reported a large orange light flying at 250 mph about 1,500 feet above their fighter. The radar station in the sector replied that there was nothing else there. Nevertheless, a subsequent malfunction in the plane's radar system forced it to return to base. An official report was made—the first of its kind—which resulted in many jokes at the pilots' expense.

(9) After the 27 November encounter, pilots who saw the Foo Fighters decided not to include them in their flight reports. This self-imposed censorship was broken by two pilots named McFalls and Baker of the 415th, who submitted a flight report on their mission of 22 December 1944. In part, the report reads:

At 0600, near Hagenau, at 10,000 feet altitude, two very bright lights climbed toward us from the ground. They leveled off and stayed on the tail of our plane. They were huge bright orange lights. They stayed there for two minutes. On my tail all the time. They were under perfect control. Then they turned away from us, and the fire seemed to go out. (10)

The Foo Fighters were not only witnessed by air crews. Hough and Randles cite a report from a former prisoner of war at the Heydebreck camp in Upper Silesia, Poland.

At 3 p.m. on 22 January 1945 a number of men were being paraded by the Germans before being marched away to evade the liberating Russian Army. A bomber appeared overhead, flying at about 18,000 feet, and the men gazed in horror at what seemed to be fire pouring from its rear end. Then they thought it might be a flare caught up in the slipstream of the aircraft. Finally, they realized it was neither of these things: the object was a silvery ball hugging the bomber, which was desperately trying to evade it. The foo fighter was still right on the tail of the aircraft as both passed into the distance. (11)

On 1 January 1945, Howard W. Blakeslee, science editor of the Associated Press, claimed that the mysterious Foo Fighters were nothing more than St Elmo's Fire, spontaneous lights produced by an electrostatic discharge on the fuselages of the Allied aircraft. According to Blakeslee, this explanation also accounted for the fact that the Foo Fighters did not show up on radar. The pilots who actually encountered the objects were unimpressed with Blakeslee's solution: most of them had been flying for a number of years, and knew St Elmo's Fire when they saw it. The Foo Fighters were something entirely different: the light they produced went on and off at intervals that seemed to be related to their speed; their shape was often clearly discernible as either discoid or spherical; and they were frequently reported as spinning rapidly on their vertical axis. (12) No Allied aircraft were ever brought down by Foo Fighters (which seemed more content to pace them and interfere with their radar), and so it was considered likely that the objects were dangerous German secret weapons, perhaps a radical development of V-weapon technology. The V-1s were already causing carnage in London, and it was known that German scientists were desperately trying to develop a ballistic missile that could hit America.

According to Vesco and Childress, several Foo Fighter stories were leaked in December 1944 to the American Legion Magazine, which then published the personal opinions of several US Intelligence officers that the Foo Fighters were radio-controlled radar-jamming devices sent up by the Germans. (13) Vesco and Childress go on to cite the testimony of another (unnamed) B-17 pilot who decided to intercept a Foo Fighter and succeeded in getting within a few hundred yards of the shining sphere. He reported hearing 'a strange sound, like the "backwash of invisible planes"'. (14) The last reported encounter with Foo Fighters occurred in early May 1945, near the eastern edge of the Pfalzerwald. A pilot, once again from the 415th Squadron, saw five orange balls of light flying in a 'V formation in the distance. (15)

GHOST ROCKETS OVER SCANDINAVIA

In the two years between the end of the Second World War and the Kenneth Arnold sighting, strange unidentified aerial objects invaded the skies over Finland, Norway, Sweden and Denmark (and were later reported as far afield as Morocco and India). Nicknamed 'Ghost Rockets' because of their long, thin profile and occasional fiery exhaust, these objects were reported to perform astonishing maneuvers such as diving and climbing rapidly at enormous speeds. (16)

The British UFO investigator Timothy Good cites the following confidential Department of State telegram from the American Embassy in Stockholm, dated 11 July 1946:

For some weeks there have been numerous reports of strange rocket-like missiles being seen in Swedish and Finnish skies. During past few days reports of such objects being seen have greatly increased. Member of Legation saw one Tuesday afternoon. One landed on beach near Stockholm same afternoon without causing any damage and according to press fragments are now being studied by military authorities. Local scientist on first inspection stated it contained organic substance resembling carbide. Defense staff last night issued communique listing various places where missiles had been observed and urging public report all mysterious sound and light phenomena. Press this afternoon announces one such missile fell in

Stockholm suburb 2:30 this afternoon. Missile observed by member Legation made no sound and seemed to be falling rapidly to earth when observed. No sound of explosion followed however.

Military Attache is investigating through Swedish channels and has been promised results Swedish observations. Swedes profess ignorance as to origin, character or purpose of missiles but state definitely they are not launched by Swedes. Eyewitness reports state missiles came in from southerly direction proceeding to northwest. Six units Atlantic Fleet under Admiral Hewitt arrived Stockholm this morning. If missiles are of Soviet origin as generally believed (some reports say they are launched from Estonia), purpose might be political to intimidate Swedes in connection with Soviet pressure on Sweden being built up in connection with current loan negotiations or to offset supposed increase in our military pressure on Sweden resulting from the naval visit and recent Bikini [atomic] tests or both.

(17) The suspicion voiced in this telegram that the Soviets might be responsible for the Ghost Rocket sightings was natural enough, given that the Cold War was then just getting under way. Both the Americans and Russians, of course, captured German weapons technology at the end of the war, and it was assumed by many in authority that the Russians were experimenting with V-1 and V-2 rocket designs. (Actually, a German V-2 rocket had already crashed in Sweden in the summer of 1944.) The fact that both the United States and the Soviet Union carried out extensive experiments with captured Nazi technology will gain yet more significance as we examine the claims of the Nazi-UFO proponents.

A number of British scientists were sent to Sweden to examine the Ghost Rocket reports, among them Professor R. V. Jones, the then Director of Intelligence of Britain's Air Staff and scientific advisor to Section IV of MI6. In Most Secret War, his account of his involvement with British Scientific Intelligence between 1939 and 1949, Professor Jones writes of the fears that the rockets were Russian:

The general interpretation ... was that [the Ghost Rockets] were long-range flying bombs being flown by the Russians over Sweden as an act of intimidation. This interpretation was accepted by officers in our own Air Technical Intelligence, who worked out the performance of the bombs from the reported sightings in one of the incidents, where the object appeared to have dashed about at random over the whole of southern Sweden at speeds up to 2,000 mph. What the officers concerned failed to notice was that every observer, wherever he was, reported the object as well to the east. By far the most likely explanation was that it was a meteor, perhaps as far east as Finland, and the fantastic speeds that were reported were merely due to the fact that all observers had seen it more or less simultaneously, but that they had varying errors in their watches, so that any attempt to draw a track by linking up observations in a time sequence was unsound. (18)

Professor Jones considered it extremely unlikely that the Ghost Rockets could be Russian missiles based on German V-2 designs: he stated that the rockets seen over Scandinavia had more than twice the range of the V-2, an increase in performance that was too great given the short time since the capture of the German designs.

For myself, I simply asked two questions. First, what conceivable purpose could it serve the Russians, if they indeed had a controllable flying bomb, to fly it in great numbers over Sweden, without doing any more harm than to alert the West to the fact that they had such an impressive weapon? My second question followed from the first: how had the Russians succeeded in making a flying bomb of such fantastic reliability? The Germans had achieved no better than 90 per cent reliability in their flying bomb trials of 1944, at very much shorter range. Even if the Russians had achieved a reliability as high as 99 per cent over their much longer ranges, this still meant that one per cent of all sorties should have resulted in a bomb crashing on Swedish territory. Since there had been allegedly hundreds of sorties, there ought to be at least several crashed bombs already in Sweden, and yet nobody had ever picked up a fragment. I therefore said that I would not accept the theory that the apparitions were flying bombs from Russia until someone brought a piece into my office. (19)

Professor Jones goes on to relate an amusing incident that followed his challenge. When a substance that had allegedly fallen from a Ghost Rocket was collected and sent, via the Swedish General Staff and the British Air Staff, to the Royal Aircraft Establishment (RAE) at Farnborough, the scientists who analyzed the fragments claimed that over 98 per cent of their mass consisted of an unknown element. Jones had already seen the samples, and had quickly concluded that they were lumps of coke, 'four or five irregularly shaped solid lumps, none of which looked as if it had ever been associated with a mechanical device'.

(20) When he telephoned the head of chemistry at the RAE, enquiring whether they had thought to test for carbon, the chemist literally gasped. 'No one had stopped to look at the material, in an effort to get the analysis made quickly, and they had failed to test for carbon. The other lumps had similarly innocent explanations.' (21) Nevertheless, some Ghost Rocket sightings remained puzzling. One of the objects was photographed near Stockholm by a Swede named Erik Reuterswaerd. When the Swedish authorities examined the photograph, they concluded that the object's trail was not issuing from its rear but was actually enveloping it. The London Daily Telegraph, which published the photograph on 6 September 1946, opined that a new method of propulsion was being tested. (22)

For their part, the Swedish Government concluded in October 1946 that, of the 1,000 reports of Ghost Rockets they had received, 80 per cent could be attributed to 'celestial phenomena'; the remaining 20 per cent, they stated, could not be either natural phenomena or the products of imagination. (23)

RADICAL AIRCRAFT DESIGNS: FEUERBALL AND KUGELBLITZ

The conventional view of history is that, while the Germans possessed some remarkable and deadly weapons such as the V-1, the V-2 and the jet-engined Messerschmitt ME-262 fighter, their technological innovations did not extend much further than that. Indeed, serious historians treat claims of fantastic advances in Nazi technology with the utmost disdain. (We have already quoted Professor Jones's assertion that the Nazi flying bomb trials of 1944 were only 90 per cent reliable.) Nevertheless, we must ask the question: are they right to do so? Having looked briefly at the mystery of the Foo Fighters, Ghost Rockets and UFOs, which many professional scientists admit (however reluctantly and anonymously) constitute a puzzle worthy of serious investigation, we must now examine the claims of some UFO researchers that the wonderful devices seen so frequently flitting through the skies are actually machines based on Nazi designs for ultra-high-performance disc-shaped craft, capable of traveling not only through our atmosphere but also in outer space. The reader who baulks at this idea may well be further outraged by the claims made by some that the Nazis themselves succeeded in building prototypes of these machines. However, since we are already deep within the Absolute Elsewhere, we must press on through that weird realm, bearing in mind Pauwels's and Bergier's perceptive assertion that 'the historian maybe reasonable, but history is not'.

As we have already noted, Renato Vesco is a pioneer of the Nazi-UFO theory. A graduate of the University of Rome, he studied aeronautical engineering at the German Institute for Aerial Development and during the war was sent to work at Fiat's underground installation at Lake Garda in northern Italy. In the 1960s, Vesco investigated UFO sightings for the Italian Air Ministry. (24) In 1971, he published the seminal work on the theory of man-made flying saucers; entitled Intercettateh Senza Sparare (roughly translated as 'Intercept Without Firing'), the book examines in great detail the possible technology behind the UFOs and reaches the astonishing and highly controversial conclusion that UFO technology (seen in terms of the perceived flight characteristics of the objects) is well within the capabilities of human science—and was so even during the Second World War. Indeed, Vesco is quite certain that the origin of the UFOs still seen today by witnesses all over the world can be placed firmly in Nazi Germany in the early 1940s. In addition, the technological principles behind these craft were, he believes, divided between the United States and the Soviet Union at the end of the war, with both superpowers going on to develop and refine the designs for their own ends.

According to Vesco, Luftwaffe scientists in Oberammergau, Bavaria conducted extensive research into an electrical device capable of interfering with an aircraft engine up to a distance of about 100 feet. Through the generation of intense electromagnetic fields, this device could short-circuit the target aircraft's ignition system, causing total loss of power. This short range, however, was considered impractical for a successful weapon, so they attempted to increase it to 300 feet. These plans were still only on the drawing board by the end of the war, so the weapon was never put into production. Nevertheless, these researches yielded a by-product that was put to use by Albert Speer and the SS Technical General Staff. They produced a device capable of 'proximity radio interference' on the delicate radar systems of American night-fighters. (25)

Thus a highly original flying machine was born; it was circular and armored, more or less resembling the shell of a tortoise, and was powered by a special turbo-jet engine, also flat and circular, whose principles of operation recalled the well-known aeolipile of Hero, which generated a great halo of luminous flames. Hence it was named Feuerball (Fireball). It was unarmed and pilotless. Radio-controlled at the moment of take-off, it then automatically followed enemy aircraft, attracted by their exhaust flames, and approached close enough without collision to wreck their radar gear. (26)

The fiery halo around the craft's perimeter was generated by a combination of the rich fuel mixture and chemical additives causing the ionization of the atmosphere around the Feuerball. As it approached the target aircraft, this ionization would produce powerful electrostatic and electromagnetic fields that would interfere with its H2S radar. 'Since a metal arc carrying an oscillating current of the proper frequency -equal, that is, to the frequency used by the radar station—can cancel the blips (return signals from the target), the Feuerball was almost undetectable by the most powerful American radar of the time, despite its night-time visibility.' (27)

Vesco goes on to state that this night-time visibility had an additional advantage for the Feuerball: in the absence of daylight, the halo produced by the engine gave the impression of an enormous size, which had the effect of unnerving Allied pilots even more. As the Feuerballe approached, the pilots refrained from firing on them for fear of being caught in a gigantic explosion. (28) In fact, the devices did carry an explosive charge that would destroy them in the event of capture, in addition to an ingenious feature that would ensure a quick escape in the event of an attack by Allied aircraft. Underneath its armored outer shell, each Feuerball contained a thin sheet of electrically insulated aluminum. Should a bullet pierce the armor, contact would be made between it and the aluminum sheet, thus closing a circuit, activating a vertical maximum acceleration device and taking the craft out of weapons range in a matter of seconds. (29)

The Feuerballe were constructed at the Henschel-Rax aeronautical establishment at Wiener Neustadt. According to one (unnamed) witness who saw them being test-flown, in daylight the craft looked like shining discs spinning on their vertical axes, and at night like huge burning globes. Hermann Goering inspected the progress of the Feuerball project on a number of occasions, hoping that the mechanical principles could be applied to a much larger offensive saucer-shaped aircraft. His hopes were to be quickly realized.

Vesco calls the Kugelblitz (Ball Lightning) automatic fighter 'the second authentic antecedent [after the Feuerball] of the present-day flying saucers', and the first example of the 'jet-lift' aircraft. (30) In 1952, a former Luftwaffe engineer named Rudolph Schriever gave a series of interviews to the West German press in which he claimed to have designed an aircraft strikingly similar to Vesco's Kugelblitz. Schriever had been an engineer and test pilot for the Heinkel factory in Eger. In 1941, he began to toy with the idea of an aircraft that could take off vertically, thus eliminating the need for runways, which were vulnerable to enemy bombing.

By June the following year, he had built and test-flown a working model of his design, and work immediately began on a full-size fifteen-foot version. In mid-1944, Schriever was transferred to the BMW plant near Prague, Czechoslovakia, where he was joined by an engineer from the rocket site at Peenemunde named Walter Miethe, another engineer named Klaus Habermohl and an Italian physicist from the aeronautical complex at Riva del Garda, Dr. Giuseppe Belluzzo. Together, they built an even larger, piloted version of the disc, featuring a domed pilot's cabin sitting at the centre of a circular set of multiple wings driven by a turbine engine mounted on the disc's vertical axis.

The German disc program went under the title 'Project Saucer' (which W. A. Harbinson also took as the title for his excellent five-novel series inspired by the Nazi-UFO theory). According to the military historian Major Rudolph Lusar, Schriever's disc consisted of 'a wide-surface ring which rotated around a fixed, cupola-shaped cockpit'. The ring contained 'adjustable wing-discs which could be brought into appropriate position for the take-off or horizontal flight'. (31) The Model 3 flying disc had a diameter of 138 feet and a height of 105 feet.

According to Schriever, the finished disc was ready for test-flying early in 1944, but was destroyed by its builders to prevent it from falling into the hands of the advancing Allies. Schriever and his colleagues fled as the BMW plant was taken by Czechoslovakian patriots. In spite of Schriever's claim, Renato Vesco states that a highly advanced supersonic disc-shaped aircraft called the Kugelblitz was indeed test-flown near the Nordhausen underground rocket complex in February 1945. (32) Also known as the V-7, this machine was said to have climbed to a height of 37,600 feet in just three minutes, and reached a speed of 1,218 mph. This craft and the technicians who built it were apparently seized by the Russians and taken to Siberia, where the disc project continued under Soviet control.

While Vesco concedes that the hard evidence for a German flying-disc program is 'very tenuous', he notes that 'the senior official of a 1945 British technical mission revealed that he had discovered German plans for "entirely new and deadly developments in air warfare" '. Vesco continues:

These plans must obviously have gone beyond normal jet aircraft designs, as both sides already had jet-powered aircraft in production and operational service by the end of the war. Moreover, before Rudolf Schriever died some fifteen years after the war he had become convinced that the large numbers of post-war UFO sightings were evidence that his designs had been built and developed. (33)

On 2 May 1980, another man claimed to the German press that he had worked on Project Saucer. Heinrich Fleißner, then 76 years old, told Neue Presse magazine that he had been a technical consultant on a jet-propelled, disc-shaped aircraft that had been built at Peenemunde from parts manufactured in a number of other locations. Fleißner also claimed that Goering had been the patron of the project and planned to use the disc as a courier plane, but that the Wehrmacht had destroyed most of the plans in the face of the Allied advance. (34) Nevertheless, some material did reach both America and Russia. According to Harbinson, 'The notes and drawings for FleiBner's flying saucer, first registered in West Germany on 27 March 1954, were assigned to Trans-Oceanic, Los Angeles, California on 28 March the following year and registered with the United States Patent Office on 7 June 1960.' (35)

According to Vesco, the Austrian inventor Viktor Schauberger, after being kidnapped by the Nazis, designed a number of disc-shaped aircraft for the Third Reich between 1938 and 1945. The saucers were powered by what Schauberger called 'liquid vortex propulsion': 'If water or air is rotated into a twisting form of oscillation known as "colloidal",' he said, 'a build-up of energy results, which, with immense power, can cause levitation.'

(36) Whether this bizarre form of propulsion is workable is, of course, open to debate. Once again, however, the Americans seem to have taken many of Schauberger's documents at the end of the war, with the Russians taking what was left and blowing up his apartment when they had finished. Schauberger supposedly went to America in the 1950s to work on a top secret project in Texas for the US Government, although this unspecified project was apparently not particularly successful. Schauberger died in 1958, reportedly saying on his deathbed: 'They took everything from me. Everything. I don't even own myself.' (37) There is no doubt that radical aeroform designs were being tested at this time. For example, the Messerschmitt 163A was powered by a liquid-fuel Walter rocket, and was given its first powered flight in August 1941. It achieved speeds of over 600 mph, nearly twice as fast as the average speed of a fighter aircraft at that time. A second version, the Me 163B, was built with a more powerful motor. The design was not perfected, however, until mid-1944, when approximately 370 were built and deployed throughout Germany in a last-ditch attempt to thwart the Allied forces. The RAF and USAAF air crews who encountered them commented in their reports on how fast and dangerous these craft were: on many occasions, the Me 163s were so fast that the Allied air gunners had no chance to deal with them. However, the Me 163 could only remain in a combat situation for 25 minutes, for most of which time it was unpowered, and their relatively small number prevented them from having much success against the Allied advance. (38)

HANS KAMMLER

If the Germans did succeed in producing a piloted flying disc, what became of it? As several researchers have noted, the answer may lie with SS Obergruppenfuhrer Dr. Hans Kammler, who towards the end of the war had access to all areas of secret air-armaments projects. Kammler worked on the V-2 rocket project, along with Wernher von Braun (who would later head NASA's Apollo Moon program) and Luftwaffe Major General Walter Dornberger (who would later become vice-president of the Bell Aircraft Company in the United States). (39)

Heinrich Himmler planned to separate the SS from Nazi Party and state control through the establishment of a number of business and industrial fronts, making it independent of the state budget. Hitler approved this proposal early in 1944. (As Jim

Marrs notes, this strategy would subsequently be copied by the CIA in America.) (40)

By the end of the war, Hans Kammler had decided to use V-2 rocket technology and scientists as bargaining chips with the Allies. On 2 April 1945, 500 technicians and engineers were placed on a train along with 100 SS troops and sent to a secret Alpine location in Bavaria. Two days later, von Braun requested permission from Kammler to resume rocket research, to which Kammler replied that he was about to disappear for an indefinite length of time. This was the last anyone saw of Hans Kammler. (41) In view of the undoubted advantage he held when it came to negotiating for his life with the Allies, Kammler's disappearance is something of a puzzle, until we pause to consider the possibility that he possessed plans for a technology even more advanced than the V-2.

'Did the Reich, or an extension of it, have the capability to produce a UFO or the clout to deal from a position of strength with one of the Allied nations?' (42) Although it is assumed that Kammler committed suicide when about to be apprehended by the Czech resistance in Prague, there is no proof of this. What really happened to Kammler? In the final chapter, we will examine the theory that he, along with many other high-ranking Nazis, survived the end of the war and escaped to an unlikely location.

THE AVROCAR

The opinion of orthodox history is that, while many highly advanced weapons designs were on the drawing board, with some actually being put into limited production in the final months of the war, nothing with the design or performance characteristics of flying saucers was ever built in Nazi Germany. And yet, in 1953, only eight years after the end of the war, the Canadian Toronto Star announced that a flying saucer was being developed by the A. V. Roe company (AVRO-Canada) at its facilities near Malton, Ontario. According to the report, apparently leaked by a well-informed source within the company, the machine would have a top speed of 1,500 mph.

This understandably provoked a sudden and intense interest in the subject from other members of the press, who asked for clarification from the Canadian Government. A statement was released, declaring: 'The Defense authorities are examining all ideas, even revolutionary ones, that have been suggested for the development of new types of supersonic aircraft, also including flying discs. This, however, is still in the beginning phase of research and it will be a number of months before we are able to reach anything positive and seven or more years before we come to actual production.' (43)

On 16 February 1953, C.D. Howe, the Minister of Defense Production, told the Canadian House of Commons that the government was studying new fighter-aircraft concepts 'adding weight to reports that AVRO is even now working on a mock-up model of a "flying saucer" capable of flying 1500 miles per hour and climbing straight up in the air'. (44) Less than two weeks later, on 27 February, the AVRO President,

Crawford Gordon, Jr., wrote in the company's journal: 'One of our projects can be said to be quite revolutionary in concept and appearance. The prototype being built is so revolutionary that when it flies all other types of supersonic aircraft will become obsolescent. This is all that AVRO-Canada are going to say about this project.' (45)

This statement was followed by two months of silence, after which press interest was fired to an even greater degree by another revelation in the Toronto Star of 21 April:

Field Marshal Montgomery ... became one of a handful of people ever to see AVRO's mock-up of a 'flying saucer,' reputed to be capable of flying 1500 miles an hour. A guide who accompanied Montgomery quoted him as describing it as 'fantastic.' ... Security precautions surrounding this super-secret aircraft are so tight that two of Montgomery's escorts from Scotland Yard were barred from the forbidden, screened-off area of the AVRO plant.

(46) On 24 April, the Toronto Star added that the flying disc was constructed of metal, wood and plastics, and referred to it as a gyroscopic fighter, with a revolving gas turbine engine. Little more was written in the Canadian press until 1 November, when a brief report appeared stating: 'A mock-up of the Canadian flying saucer, the highly secret aircraft in whose existence few believe, was yesterday shown to a group of twenty-five American experts, including military officers and scientists.' (47) This $200 million-dollar prototype was also known as the AVRO Omega, probably because its shape was more like the Greek letter than a perfect circle.

The press claimed that the Canadian Government planned to deploy squadrons of flying saucers for the defense of the far north of the country, their VTOL (vertical take-off and landing) capabilities making them ideal for forested and snow-covered terrain. Once again, however, there followed a period of official and press silence on the matter, broken only by the revelation that the project's principal designer was the aeronautical engineer J.

C. M. Frost, and persistent rumors that the US military had become involved. Vesco quotes an unnamed press source, who stated enthusiastically: This is a ship that will be able to take off vertically, to hover in mid-air and to move at a speed of about 1850 mph. That is, it would be capable of performing all the maneuvers that flying discs are said to be capable of. This astonishing craft is the brain child of the English aeronautical engineer John Frost, who worked for the large de Havilland factory in England during the war and who later went on to A. V. Roe, in Malton, Canada. The aircraft that will be built for the U.S. Air Force is not, however, the first of this type that Frost has designed. Two years ago he had designed and submitted to American experts an aircraft which was called the Flying Manta because of its behavior on take-off. It more or less resembled the present disc, but it could not take off vertically. In addition, its top speed did not exceed 1430 mph. The Manta had interested the American General Staff, but in view of these operating deficiencies, it was decided not to build it. (48)

These high hopes for US-Canadian flying discs were dashed when, on 3 December 1954, the Canadian Defense Ministry suddenly announced that the project was to be abandoned on the grounds that the technology required to make it work was too expensive and speculative.

Nearly a year later, however, on 25 October 1955, US Air Force Secretary Donald Quarles made an intriguing statement through the Department of Defense press office.

We are now entering a period of aviation technology in which aircraft of unusual configuration and flight characteristics will begin to appear ... The Air Force will fly the first jet-powered vertical-rising airplane in a matter of days. We have another project under contract with AVRO Ltd., of Canada, which could result in disc-shaped aircraft somewhat similar to the popular concept of a flying saucer ... While some of these may take novel forms, such as the AVRO project, they are direct-line descendants of conventional aircraft and should not be regarded as supra-natural or mysterious ... Vertical-rising aircraft capable of transition to supersonic horizontal flight will be a new phenomenon in our skies, and under certain conditions could give the illusion of the so-called flying saucer. The Department of Defense will make every effort within the bounds of security to keep the public informed of these developments so they can be recognized for what they are ... I think we must recognize that other countries also have the capability of developing vertical-rising aircraft, perhaps of unconventional shapes. However, we are satisfied at this time that none of the sightings of so-called 'flying saucers' reported in this country were in fact aircraft of foreign origin. (49)

Quarles's surprising statement notwithstanding, the AVRO company was in fact going through something of a bad patch following the cancellation by the Canadian Government of the contract for the CF-105 Arrow heavy bomber, on the pretext of the diminished air threat from Russia which had only a limited number of intercontinental bombers. This decision resulted in 10,000 people being laid off, most of them specialists working on the saucer project, renamed the AVRO-Car.

It was not until August 1960 that American authorities decided to allow the press to see the prototype of the AVRO-Car. Its performance was less than impressive: it managed to do little more than hover a few feet above the ground, prompting an official statement that 'even for this type of VTOL plane ... the principal problem is low-speed stability. Tests with a full-scale model have been made at the large forty-by-eighty-foot wind tunnel at the Ames Research Center, belonging to NASA, but they were not completely successful. It became clear, however, that the various problems inherent in a circular aircraft of this type are not insurmountable.' (50)

Just over a year later, it was announced that the US Department of Defense would be withdrawing from the AVRO-Car project, on the grounds that it was unlikely that the design could ever be made to work successfully.

The lamentable story of the AVRO-Car (and its illustration of the problems besetting disc-shaped aircraft) has done nothing to dissuade Nazi-UFO proponents from maintaining that their basic thesis is correct. However, British ufologist Timothy Good quotes a CIA memorandum from W. E. Lexow, Chief of the Applied Science Division, Office of Scientific Intelligence, dated 19 October 1955, which may lend weight to this idea. According to the memorandum, John Frost, the designer of the AVRO-Car, 'is reported to have obtained his original idea for the flying machine from a group of Germans just after World War II. The Soviets may also have obtained information from this German group'. (51)

THE PROBLEM OF THE UFO OCCUPANTS

Any theory of the origin of UFOs must, of course, take into account all the available evidence, and this includes reported encounters with and descriptions of UFO occupants. Having looked at the idea that UFOs are man-made aircraft inspired by designs developed by Nazi scientists in the Second World War, we now find ourselves confronting material that would, at first sight, be sufficient to make the Nazi-UFO theory completely untenable. For as soon as the UFO lands and opens its hatches, we meet a variety of creatures that are anything but human. (To be sure, some UFO occupants are described as being completely human-looking but they seem to be very much in the minority.) This has naturally led the majority of UFO researchers and investigators to conclude that UFOs are extraterrestrial devices. Before dealing with this problem, let us illustrate it by examining briefly some of these alleged contacts with UFO occupants.

Over the decades since the modern era of ufology began with the Arnold sighting in 1947, people all over the world have claimed to have encountered an astonishing variety of creatures linked with UFOs on the ground. In the 1950s and 1960s these people were known as 'contactees' and, according to their testimony, humanity had nothing whatsoever to fear from the ufonauts. They were almost invariably described as being tall and strikingly attractive, with long, sandy-colored hair and blue eyes, a description which resulted in their being classified as 'Nordic' aliens. (In the present context, this description has obvious and sinister connotations but, as we shall see, is almost certainly coincidental.)

The most famous of the 1950s contactees was George Adamski who, on 20 November 1952, encountered a man claiming to come from Venus. Adamski, a self-styled philosopher and mystic, was running a hamburger stand a few miles from the Mount Palomar Observatory in California when he had his encounter. He was having lunch with several friends near Desert Center when they allegedly saw a gigantic cigar-shaped object in the sky. Telling his friends to remain behind, Adamski drove into the desert, where he witnessed the landing of a disc-shaped 'scout craft'. When the ship's single occupant appeared, Adamski was able to communicate with him through a combination of hand signals and telepathy and learned that the Venusians (together with other intelligent races throughout the Solar System) were deeply concerned at humanity's misuse of nuclear energy (a theme that would be repeated again and again by the contactees).

In common with the other contactees, Adamski's claims suffered from egregious scientific inaccuracies, not least of which was the utter inability of all the other planets in the Solar System to support intelligent humanoid life. In Adamski's case, this difficulty was somewhat compounded by a comment he made to two followers regarding Prohibition. During this period, he had secured a special licence from the government to make wine for religious purposes (he had founded a monastery in Laguna Beach), with the result that he claimed to have made 'enough wine for all of Southern California'. If it had not been for the repeal of Prohibition, he told his friends, 'I wouldn't have had to get into this saucer crap'. (52)

The contactee claims of the 1950s are rightly regarded as extremely dubious by most ufologists; however, in the decades since there have been a number of contact claims that demand more serious attention. Before proceeding, it is necessary for us to look briefly at some of the most impressive reports, since they form the backdrop to an increasingly popular conspiracy theory regarding Nazi activities in the post-war period.

When we examine reports of encounters with UFO occupants (particularly since the early 1960s), we see that the defining characteristic reveals itself to be what has come to be known as 'abduction', in which witnesses are taken from their normal environment against their will and are forced to interact in various ways with apparently non-human entities.

One of the most famous abduction cases occurred on 11 October 1973 on the shores of the Pascagoula River in Mississippi, USA. Charlie Hickson, 45, and Calvin Parker, 18, were fishing in the river when they witnessed the approach of a UFO. The following day, the United Press International news service carried the following report:

PASCAGOULA, Miss. Two shipyard workers who claimed they were hauled aboard a UFO and examined by silver-skinned creatures with big eyes and pointed ears were checked today at a military hospital and found to be free of radiation.

... Jackson County chief deputy Barney Mathis said the men told him they were fishing from an old pier on the west bank of the Pascagoula River about 7 p.m. Thursday when they noticed a strange craft about two miles away emitting a bluish haze.

They said it moved closer and then appeared to hover about three or four feet above the water, then 'three whatever-they-weres came out, either floating or walking, and carried us into the ship,' officers quoted Hickson as saying.

'The things had big eyes. They kept us about twenty minutes, photographed us, and then took us back to the pier. The only sound they made was a buzzing-humming sound. They left in a flash.'

'These are reliable people,' Sheriff Diamond said. 'They had no reason to say this if it had not been true. I know something did happen to them.'

The sheriff said the 'spacecraft' was described as fish-shaped, about ten feet long with an eight-foot ceiling. The occupants were said to have pale silvery skin, no hair, long pointed ears and noses, with an opening for a mouth and hands 'like crab claws.'

276

OCCULT SECRETS OF THE THIRD REICH

Inside the UFO, the two men were placed on a table and examined with a device that resembled a huge eye. They were later interviewed by Dr. J. Allen Hynek, the astronomer whose work as a consultant for the US Air Force's UFO investigation project, Blue Book, turned him from sceptic to cautious advocate of UFO reality. Hynek concluded that Hickson and Parker were in a state of genuine fright. Dr. James A. Harder, a consultant for the Aerial Phenomena Research Organization (APRO) who also investigated the case, described the UFO occupants as 'automata', or 'advanced robots', judging from the witnesses' descriptions.

Many people who are skeptical of UFO and alien abductions state, quite reasonably, that an advanced spacefaring civilization would not need to conduct the highly intrusive and traumatic experiments on human beings that their representatives are reported to conduct. The repeated taking of samples of blood, flesh, sperm and ova from unwilling subjects implies a curiously primitive medical technology for beings allegedly capable of building interstellar spacecraft. However, there is an intriguing correlation between the atrocities committed by 'aliens' on their human victims and those committed by Nazi 'doctors' (I use the term loosely) in the concentration camps during the Second World War. As we shall see later in this chapter, proponents of the Nazi-UFO Theory, such as W. A. Harbinson, have suggested that this may be due to an ongoing (and for the moment highly secret) Nazi plot to create a master-race from the raw material of humanity in its present form.

One of the most impressive and carefully investigated abduction cases occurred on 26 August 1976. Four art students, Charlie Foltz, Chuck Rak and brothers Jack and Jim Weiner were on a camping trip on the Allagash River in Maine, USA. While fishing in a boat on East Lake, they watched the approach of a large spherical light that frightened them considerably. The next thing they knew, they were standing on the shore of the lake, watching the object shoot up into the sky. There was nothing left of their blazing camp fire but a few glowing embers, implying that they had been away for several hours although they only remembered being on the lake for about twenty minutes.

Several years later, the case came to the attention of the respected UFO researcher Raymond E. Fowler, who investigated on behalf of the Mutual UFO Network (MUFON), the largest civilian UFO organization in the world. Fowler arranged for the four witnesses to undergo hypnotic regression to recover their lost memories of the evening. Each of the men (who had promised not to discuss with each other their individual hypnosis sessions) recalled being taken into the UFO through a beam of light. Once inside, they encountered several humanoid entities who forced them (apparently through some form of mind control) to undress and sit in a mist-filled room. Their bodies were examined and probed with various instruments, and samples of saliva, blood, skin, sperm, urine and faeces were taken. When the examination had been completed, the men were forced to walk through a circular doorway, whereupon they found themselves floating back down to their boat through the light beam.

Fowler later discovered that Jack Weiner had had an 'anomalous lump' surgically removed several years earlier. The pathologist who examined it had been somewhat mystified and had sent it on for analysis to the Center for Disease Control in Atlanta, Georgia. At Fowler's request, Jack Weiner asked for his medical records and discovered that the lump had been sent to the Armed Forces Institute of Pathology (AFIP) in Washington, D.C., instead of the Center for Disease Control. When Fowler telephoned the AFIP for an explanation, he was told by the public information officer that the AFIP occasionally assisted civilian doctors. 'When Jack asked why the lump was sent to the AFIP rather than the Center for Disease Control, he was told by his surgeon's secretary that it was less costly even though Jack was covered by insurance!' (53)

The Pascagoula and Allagash encounters display many of the hallmarks of the typical UFO abduction, the principal elements of which can be listed as follows: (1) the initial appearance of the entities and the taking of the percipient; (2) medical probing with various instruments; (3) machine examinations and mental testing; (4) sexual activity, in which the percipient is sometimes forced to 'mate' with other humans or even with the entities themselves; and (5) the returning of the percipient to his or her normal environment. (54) Although an extremely wide variety of 'alien' types has been encountered by people all over the world, one type in particular has become more and more commonly reported (particularly in the United States). The so-called 'Grey' is now regarded as the quintessential alien being and is one of the most immediately recognizable images in today's world.

In the unlikely event that the reader is unfamiliar with this image, we can briefly describe the Greys' physical characteristics as follows: they are usually described as approximately four feet tall (although some are as tall as eight feet), with extremely large craniums and enormous jet-black, almond-shaped eyes. They have no nose or ears to speak of, merely small holes where these should be; likewise, their mouths are usually described as no more than lipless slits. The torso and limbs are described as being very thin, almost sticklike, and more than one abductee has reported the impression that they seem to be made of an undifferentiated material, with no bone or muscular structure. Their hands are long and thin, sometimes with three fingers, sometimes with four. In addition, the Greys are frequently reported to be rather uncaring in their attitude towards humans, treating us much as we treat laboratory animals. Indeed, they have been described by some as militaristic and by others as hivelike in their demeanor, as if they had no individual consciousness of their own but were carrying out commands from some higher source.

It is clear that any claims of a Nazi origin of modern UFO encounters must take account of the bizarre creatures associated with the discs. This problem might seem insurmountable in view of the fact that, while we may not expect the UFO pilots to be strutting around in black leather trench coats and jackboots, they would surely nevertheless be recognizable as human beings. However, the research undertaken by W. A. Harbinson may offer a way around this apparent impasse, as well as providing us with some extremely unsettling food for thought.

OCCULT SECRETS OF THE THIRD REICH

NAZI CYBORGS?

Harbinson's thesis, that UFO occupants may well be cyborgs—biomedically engineered amalgamations of human and machine—is supported to a certain extent by medical research conducted since the 1960s. Although this research was at the time highly secret, the gruesome details have since come to light in the form of books and articles that describe not only the nature of the experiments conducted but also the frightening attitude of some members of the medical profession. According to David Fishlock: 'Even today there are people who believe that convicts, especially the criminal lunatic, and even conscientious objectors, should be compelled to lend themselves to science.' (55)

Referring to The People Shapers (1978) by Vance Packard, Harbinson reminds us of the direction in which medical research was heading more than 30 years ago.

[I]n the Cleveland Clinic's Department of Artificial Organs, not only medical specialists, but 'mechanical, electrical, chemical, and biomedical engineers, as well as biochemists and polymer chemists', were, in their busy operating theaters, enthusiastically engaged in 'surgery connected to the development of artificial substitutes for ... vital organs such as the liver, lungs, pancreas, and kidneys'. Conveniently within walking distance of the Cleveland Clinic's Department of Artificial Organs are the Neurosurgical Research

Laboratories of the Cleveland Metropolitan General Hospital, where great interest was being expressed, as far back as 1967, in the possibility of transferring the entire head of one human being to another. Switching human brains from one head to another would be complicated and costly, but, as Packard explains: 'By simply switching heads, on the other hand, only a few connections need to be severed and then re-established in the neck of the recipient body.' (56)

This procedure was successfully carried out on monkeys at the Cleveland Clinic, with each head apparently retaining its original mental characteristics when attached to its new body. In other words, if a monkey had been aggressive before the operation, it would remain so when its head was transplanted to another body. The eyes of the monkeys followed people as they walked past, implying that the heads retained some level of awareness. The unfortunate subjects of these procedures only lived for about one week.

Of course, the main problem in a procedure of this kind would be the regeneration of the severed spinal cord so that the brain could send nerve impulses to its new body; and yet even this feat seems not to be outside the bounds of possibility. In June 1976, a Soviet scientist named Levon A. Matinian 'reported from the fourth biennial conference on Regeneration of the Central Nervous System that he had succeeded in regrowing the spinal cords of rats'. (57) Harbinson suggests, almost certainly with some justification, that this area of research must have been continued 'behind closed doors' at military and scientific establishments since then. It is surely reasonable to suppose that, if this is the case, scientists have progressed well beyond the level of rats.

OCCULT SECRETS OF THE THIRD REICH

One can be forgiven for wondering what conceivable use such barbaric experiments could possibly have for humanity. While it is mercifully unlikely that head transplants will ever be in vogue, such research undoubtedly holds much potential for the enhancement of human beings who will eventually conduct routine work in hostile environments, such as the ocean floor and outer space. Fusion of a sort between human and machine has already been achieved, in the form of the so-called Cybernetic Anthropomorphous Machine System (CAMS), 'slave' machinery that mimics the movement of its human operators. According to Harbinson:

In an aerospace conference given in Boston in 1966, engineer William E. Bradley, who developed the idea of cable-less man-machine manipulator systems for the US Defense Department's Institute for Defense Analysis, stated his belief that man and machine would eventually be linked in such a way that by performing the maneuvers himself, the man would cause them to take place, through the machine, at a distance of thousands of miles. This concept soon led to the weapon-aiming system devised by the Philco Corporation for the US Air Force, in which the pilot's helmet is coupled with a servo-system that enables him to aim and fire his weapons automatically by merely swiveling his head until a camera located in his helmet shows the target. (58)

In addition, as early as 1967 US Air Force scientists had succeeded in transmitting thought impulses to a computer using a variation on Morse code composed of long and short bursts of alpha waves (59) (alpha waves are produced by the brain when it is at rest). This technology has developed to the point where today we have the potential for amputees to control their prosthetic limbs by means of nerve impulses directly from the brain.

In the field of organ transplantation, we have seen astonishing progress over the last 30 years and it is surely not rash to suggest that we will soon see artificial hearts and other organs routinely replacing those damaged through illness or accident. Likewise, in spite of concerns regarding the ethical implications of human cloning, we may also see the day when human organs are produced in the laboratory, ready for transplanting when the need arises. In view of the fact that research conducted under the aegis of national security is between ten and twenty years ahead of what is made public at any particular time (work on the Stealth fighter began in the mid-1970s, although the public were not made aware of its existence until the late 1980s), it is possible—perhaps likely—that advances in the field of medical and bioengineering research have already extended into the realm of what the public would consider science fiction.

Harbinson believes that what the public knows is merely the tip of the iceberg, and reminds us that 'the US Navy, Air Force, Army and government agencies such as NASA—all with top-secret research establishments in the White Sands Proving Ground and similar areas—have a particular need for advanced man-machine manipulations or cyborgs'. (60) He adds that the creatures seen in and around landed UFOs could be such cyborgs: human beings radically augmented by sophisticated mechanical prosthetics.

Theoretically, the lungs of such creatures would be partially collapsed and the blood in them artificially cooled. The cyborgs' respiration and other bodily functions would then be controlled cybernetically with artificial lungs and sensors which maintain constant temperature, metabolism and pressure, irrespective of external environmental fluctuations—thus, even if not protected by an antigravity (or gravitic) propulsion system, they would not be affected by the extraordinary accelerations and direction changes of their craft. The cyborgs would have no independent will, but could be remote-controlled, both physically and mentally, even across great distances, by computer-linked brain implants. Since this operation would render the mouth and nose superfluous, these would be sealed ... and completely non-functioning. (61) If we remember the basic description of the Greys noted earlier, with their slit-like and apparently useless mouths, vestigial noses and thin torsos, we can begin to see a frightening correspondence with the theoretical human-built cyborg, a nightmarish combination of genetically engineered human and highly sophisticated machine. To a startled, disorientated and terrified UFO witness, such a creature would surely look like nothing on earth ... would look, in fact, like an extraterrestrial alien.

Interestingly, many people claiming to have encountered UFO crews mention the presence of normal-looking humans alongside the bizarre entities. Some ufologists suggest that these human types are the Nordic aliens mentioned earlier, working alongside the Greys and perhaps forming part of some interplanetary federation; other, more conspiracy-minded researchers believe that the human types are just that: human beings who are in league with a hostile alien occupation force. There is, however, another possibility, based on the information we have just considered. It is conceivable that the humans seen on board UFOs are actually the controllers of the Greys/cyborgs. It is also conceivable that these humans are members of an ultra-secret group, existing completely independently of any nation on Earth, and perhaps hostile to all nations and all other humans.

Conceivable, yes—but true?

These suggestions, of course, raise a number of serious and difficult questions. If the controllers of the UFOs and their not-quite-human crew members really are from Earth, who are they? If they place their allegiance with no known nation, with whom does their allegiance lie? Why do they abduct what is apparently an enormous number of ordinary humans, some of whom are never returned? Such an organization or society could not operate without a well-supplied, protected and highly secret home base. Where is it?

In the final chapter of our survey, we will examine some of the theories that have been put forward to account for the origin and activities of this sinister group of humans. But first, we can attempt to answer one of the questions we have just posed. The answer, if true, is terrifying, and leads us inevitably to the final stage of our journey through the Absolute Elsewhere.

OCCULT SECRETS OF THE THIRD REICH

TELEMETRIC MIND CONTROL

What is the secret of so-called UFO abductions? Are hostile alien beings responsible, or is the solution to the mystery to be found right here on Earth? For a possible answer to these questions, we must look at the history of a subject that most people would assume lies firmly within the boundaries of science fiction and that has no place in the world of everyday experience. The subject is the control of the human mind from a distance and, as we shall now see, it is frighteningly practicable.

According to the US Air Force Scientific Advisory Board in its 1996 study of weapons technology, New World Vistas Air and Space Power for the 21st Century, it is possible to achieve the coupling of human and machine through what is known as Biological Process Control. 'One can envision the development of electromagnetic energy sources, the output of which can be pulsed, shaped, and focused, that can couple with the human body in a fashion that will allow one to prevent voluntary muscular movements, control emotions (and thus actions), produce sleep, transmit suggestions, interfere with both short-term and long-term memory, produce an experience set, and delete an experience set.' Researcher David Guyatt informs us that 'experience set' is jargon for one's life's memories: this technology is quite literally capable of deleting one's memories and replacing them with an entirely new set. (62)

Those who believe that such technology must still be decades away from perfection may be surprised to learn that Dr. Jose Delgado, a neurophysiologist at the Yale University School of Medicine, has been experimenting with Electronic Stimulation of the Brain (ESB) since the late 1940s. Perhaps his most impressive experiment was conducted in 1964, with the financial backing of the US Office of Naval Research. An electronic probe was implanted in the brain of a bull and a small radio receiver strapped to its head. The animal was then placed in a bullring, along with Dr. Delgado who was equipped with a remote-control handset. As the bull charged him, Delgado flipped a switch on the handset and the one-ton animal stopped dead in front of him, clearly in a state of confusion. This process was repeated several times. Guyatt writes: 'Speaking two years later, in 1966, Delgado stated that his experiments "support the distasteful conclusion that motion, emotion, and behavior can be directed by electrical [means] and that humans can be controlled like robots by push buttons".' (63) According to Delgado, this would eventually result in a 'psycho-civilized' society, whose citizens' brains would be computer-controlled through the use of implanted 'stimoceivers'. Guyatt informs us that in 1974 neurophysiologist Lawrence Pinneo of the Stanford Research Institute (SRI) developed a computer system capable of reading a person's mind by correlating brain waves on an electroencephalograph (EEC) with specific commands. (64)

Eighteen years earlier, in 1956, at the National Electronics Conference in Chicago, Curtiss Shafer, an electrical engineer for the Norden-Ketay Corporation, had stated that 'The ultimate achievement of biocontrol may be man himself. He continued: The controlled subjects would never be permitted to think as individuals. A few months after birth, a surgeon would equip each child with a socket mounted under the scalp and electrodes reaching selected areas of brain tissue'. The subject's 'sensory perceptions and muscular activity could be either modified or completely controlled by bioelectric signals radiating from state-controlled transmitters'. (65)

Among the horrors perpetrated at Auschwitz and Dachau concentration camps were frequently fatal experiments in mind control, conducted mainly with hypnosis and narcohypnosis, using drugs such as mescaline and various barbiturates. After the war, many Nazi scientists, doctors, engineers and intelligence personnel were secretly taken to the United States in the operation known as Project PAPERCLIP. Thirty-four Nazi scientists were sent to Randolph Air Force Base in San Antonio, Texas to continue their narcohypnosis experiments on non-volunteer subjects, including prisoners, mental patients and members of ethnic minorities. (66) The results of the narcohypnosis experiments suggested that the technique was unreliable (the main intention being to produce a programmable assassin), and greater emphasis was placed on electronic technology to erase a person's personality (a process known as 'depatterning') and replace it with a new personality devised by the experimenter (a technique called 'psychic driving'). (67)

As might be expected, the CIA has always been extremely interested in the concept of mind control. One of their experimental facilities was contained within the Allen Memorial Institute, the psychiatric division of McGill University in Montreal, Canada, directed by Dr. Ewen Cameron MD on a grant from the Rockefeller and Gerschickter Foundations. Cameron established a Radio Telemetry Laboratory in which experiments were conducted on non-volunteer subjects. Mind control researcher Alex Constantine provides us with a glimpse of the nature of these experiments, which included depatterning and psychic driving.

The psychotronic heart of the laboratory was the Grid Room, with its verticed, Amazing Tales interior. The subject was strapped into a chair involuntarily, by force, his head bristling with electrodes and transducers. Any resistance was met with a paralyzing dose of curare. The subject's brain waves were beamed to a nearby reception room crammed with voice analyzers, a wire recorder and radio receivers cobbled together by [Cameron's assistant] Rubenstein. The systematic annihilation, or 'depatterning' of a subject's mind and memory, was accomplished with overdoses of LSD, barbiturate sleep for 65 days at a stretch and ECT shocks at 75 times the recommended dosage. Psychic driving, the repetition of a recorded message for 16 hours a day, programmed the empty mind. (68)

The CIA has, over the years, established a number of secret projects to study and experiment with methods of mind control, using Drugs and various forms of electromagnetic (EM) radiation. The notorious MKULTRA behavior-control program is merely the best-known of these projects. The others include: Project CHATTER, a US Navy program aimed at the elimination of free will in subjects through the use of Drugs and psychology; Project BLUEBIRD, a CIA/Office of Scientific Intelligence program to develop behavioral Drugs for use in 'unconventional warfare'; and Project

OCCULT SECRETS OF THE THIRD REICH

PANDORA, which was established as a result of the Soviet bombardment of the US embassy in Moscow with low-intensity microwaves during the 1960s and 1970s. (69) PANDORA was set up to study the health effects of microwave radiation and experimented with the induction of hallucinations and heart seizures. According to Richard Cesaro, the director of the Defense Advanced Research Projects Agency (DARPA), the initial goal of PANDORA was to 'discover whether a carefully controlled microwave signal could control the mind'.

(70) According to Constantine, CIA researchers conducted further experiments with radio waves, which resulted in their subjects experiencing various emotions, sensations and visions. At the University of California at Los Angeles (UCLA), 'Dr. Ross Adey (who worked closely with emigreé Nazi technicians after WW II) rigged the brains of lab animals to transmit to a radio receiver, which shot signals back to a device that sparked any behavior desired by the researcher'. (71)

The use of electronic 'stimoceivers' inside the brains of subjects to control thought and behavior is paralleled by one of the most disturbing aspects of UFO abduction: the so-called 'alien implants' which, it is claimed, are inserted into the bodies of abductees for unknown purposes. Alien implants first came to widespread public attention with the publication of Communion (1987) by Whitley Strieber and Missing Time (1981) by Budd Hopkins. One of the defining characteristics of alien abduction is the introduction into the abductee's body of one or more small devices, frequently through the top of the nasal cavity and into the brain but also beneath the skin of arms, hands and legs. Some researchers speculate that the mysterious, so-called 'unknown bright objects' that occasionally show up on X-rays and CAT scans of the head are actually alien implants.

In the last few years, intensive efforts have been made by researchers and investigators to retrieve these objects from the body for scientific study. They have met with a good deal of success, with many alleged 'implants' having been surgically removed. The results of analysis, however, have been inconclusive, with no absolute proof of an extraterrestrial origin forthcoming to date. Indeed, the objects (which are typically two or three millimetres in length) have been shown to be composed of earthly materials such as carbon, silicon, oxygen and other trace elements. (Supporters of an extraterrestrial origin for implants state, quite reasonably, that these substances are common throughout the Universe and that this should not be taken as proof of their earthly origin. Nevertheless, one would expect a genuine alien artifact, even if constructed of materials found on Earth, to show utterly unusual combinations or methods of construction.)

While the exact purpose of the implants is unknown, it has been suggested by various researchers that they may be tracking devices, by which the 'aliens' can keep tabs on humans they wish to abduct (in much the same way as zoologists tag animals in the wild). Alternatively, they may function as monitors of metabolism and other physical processes within the body. Some investigators, fearful of a possible alien invasion of our planet, suggest that the implants are mind-control devices that will be activated if and when the aliens finally come out into the open, thus turning what may be millions of humans into a gigantic army of alien-controlled robots.

Although these ideas might seem rather paranoid and far-fetched, the last one raises the intriguing and extremely unsettling possibility that what are assumed by many to be alien implants are actually human implants—electromagnetic microwave devices giving the controllers direct access to the minds of the abductees. Naturally, in this scenario, the abductions themselves have nothing to do with alien activity: as the French-American ufologist Jacques Vallee has noted, (72) many apparent 'alien abductions' give every indication of being carefully engineered hoaxes—hoaxes, moreover, not perpetrated by the witnesses themselves but rather by a human agency with access to high technology and vast resources.

To illustrate this possibility, let us look at the case of an unfortunate man named Leonard Kille. A talented and successful electronics engineer, Kille was the co-inventor of the Land camera (named after Edwin Land of the Polaroid Corporation, who founded the Scientific Engineering Institute [SEI] on behalf of the CIA). (73) Alex Constantine writes: 'At South Vietnam's Bien Hoa Hospital ... an SEI team buried electrodes in the skulls of Vietcong POWs and attempted to spur them into violence by remote control. Upon completion of the experiments, the POWs were shot and cremated by a company of "America's best," the Green Berets.' (74)

In 1966, Kille suspected his wife of having an affair with a lodger. He did not believe her denials, and a psychiatrist interpreted his resultant anger as a 'personality pattern disturbance'. He was referred to CIA psychiatrists for neurological tests. They concluded that Kille was a paranoid and a mild psychomotor epileptic. Kille was admitted to the Massachusetts General Hospital and his wife threatened to divorce him if he did not submit to brain surgery. In fact, his wife had been conducting an affair with their lodger, and did divorce Kille after his surgery. (75)

The surgery conducted on Leonard Kille consisted of four electrical strands, each containing twenty electrodes, being implanted in his brain. The insertion of these stimoceivers totally disabled Kille and left him terrified that he would be operated on again. According to Constantine, 'in 1971 an attendant found him with a wastebasket on his head to "stop the microwaves"'. (76) When he was transferred to Boston's VA Hospital, his doctors were not informed that he had been implanted with electrode strands and therefore assumed that his claims were those of a delusional paranoiac. Kille's moods were controlled with electronic stimulation. 'The "haunting fear" left by Kille's ordeal, a psychiatrist wrote in the New England Journal of Medicine, is that "men may become slaves, perhaps, to an authoritarian state".' (77)

Constantine believes that UFO activity is conducted by human intelligence agencies: UFOs are strictly terrestrial, as one UFO abductee recognized. She phoned Julianne McKinney at the [Electronic] Surveillance Project in Washington to report her abduction, aware that it was government-directed. 'Her house is being shot at,' McKinney says, 'and they are harassing her viciously, the target of massive microwave assault.' The abuse of psychoactive technology is escalating, unbeknownst to the American public. Recurrent hypno-programed stalkers, ritual and 'alien' outrages and psychotronic forms of political persecution are on the upswing at the hands of the DIA [Defense Intelligence Agency], CIA, FBI, NSA [National Security Agency] and other covert branches of government. Hired guns in media, law enforcement and psychiatry protect them by discrediting the victims. In effect, an ambitious but meticulously concealed, undeclared war on American private citizens is in progress— a psywar. (78) [Original emphasis.]

More and more people in America are coming forward with complaints of psychotronic harassment. One of their greatest champions was Julianne McKinney (mentioned above), a CIA-trained military officer who decided to do something to help the victims and used her retirement bonus to finance the Electronic Surveillance Project (ESP), based in the offices of the Association of National Security Alumni in Washington, D.C. The running of the organization eventually drained all her savings, and in late 1995 McKinney left Washington. She has not been seen since, although she is rumored to be still alive. (79)

Microwave harassment and mind control experiments are not confined to the United States. Following a routine operation in a Stockholm hospital, Swede Robert Naeslund discovered that he had been implanted with a radio-hypnotic intracerebral control device and had become the target of directed microwave radiation. He subsequently claimed that he was unable to receive corrective treatment from any doctor in Sweden due to interference from SAPO, the Swedish security service. Naeslund travelled to Indonesia and succeeded in finding a surgeon willing to remove the implants; however, the operation was allegedly halted midway by the CIA. Although he has made numerous attempts to focus public awareness on his plight and that of others in his position, this has merely resulted in more electromagnetic harassment. (80)

In the United Kingdom, it has been claimed that the women who began protesting against the stationing of tactical nuclear weapons at the Greenham USAF base on Greenham Common in 1981 were also the victims of electromagnetic harassment. 'Protestors complained of severe headaches, temporary paralysis, nausea, palpitations and other classic symptoms of microwave poisoning. Tests revealed microwave radiation up to 100 times greater than background readings taken around the base.' (81)

In addition, targeted electromagnetic radiation has been implicated in the deaths of 25 British scientists who were working on secret electronic warfare projects for NATO, including the Strategic Defense Initiative ('Star Wars') in the mid-1980s. According to Alex Constantine:

A pattern to the killings in Great Britain begins with the fact that seven of the scientists worked for Marconi, a subsidiary of General Electric. At the time, Marconi was under investigation for bribing and defrauding ministers of government. But Britain's MoD found 'no evidence' linking the deaths. Blame for the sudden outbreak of suicides among Marconi engineers was laid on stress. (Another unlikely explanation was given for the 'hum' in Bristol, home of Marconi, a low-frequency noise ... blamed on 'frogs'.) Jonathan Walsh, a digital communications specialist at Marconi, was assigned to the secretive Martlesham Heath Research Laboratory under a General Electric contract. (GE has long led the field in the development of anti-personnel electronic weapons, an interest that gestated with participation in Project Comet, the Pentagon-based research program to explore the psychological effects of frequencies on the electromagnetic spectrum.) Walsh dropped from his hotel window in November 1985. (82)

It has been suggested that these scientists, one of whom killed himself by chewing on live electrical wires, were driven to their deaths through electromagnetic mind control.

Alex Constantine and other mind control researchers firmly believe that American and European intelligence services are to blame not only for barbaric mind control experiments but also for staging UFO sightings and 'alien' encounters as a cover for their activities. As we have seen, there is much evidence to support these assertions. However, we have also noted that there is evidence to suggest that modern UFOs are based on highly secret designs that were drawn up by Nazi engineers towards the end of the Second World War. Taken together, these claims have led some UFO researchers and conspiracy theorists to turn their backs on the concept of alien visitation and to suggest that innocent people throughout the world are being victimized and abused by a sinister, ultra-secret society—a society having little or nothing to do with the United States, Russia or any other country.

The outrageous suggestion put forward by these researchers is that this society is actually composed of Nazis who escaped from the ruins of Germany at the end of the Second World War, and who are continuing their pursuit of world domination from the icy fastness of Antarctica.

9—INVISIBLE EAGLE
RUMORS OF NAZI SURVIVAL TO THE PRESENT

There are, of course, a number of problems posed by the idea that the pattern of world events is being controlled by a secret colony of Nazis operating out of an impregnable fortress somewhere in Antarctica. The claims made by conspiracy theorists about ongoing Nazi activity in the present day sound at best like lurid and rather distasteful science fiction, at worst like the ravings of seriously unbalanced minds. Among the questions one feels obliged to ask are: how would such an operation be financed? How could such an elaborate colony remain hidden for the last 55 years? For that matter, how could it have been built in the first place? And what could be its ultimate aim? Given the enormous power and fantastic technology attributed to it by conspiratologists, what are its (doubtless nefarious) plans for the rest of humanity? In this final chapter, we will look at some of the claims concerning Antarctica's hidden residents, and at the evidence for the reality of this ultimate conspiracy.

OPERATION EAGLE FLIGHT

As we have just noted, one of the most important questions raised by the Nazis in Antarctica theory involves finance: how could a large, permanent base be constructed and maintained for more than half a century on the most inhospitable continent in the world? For an answer to this question, we must return to the closing months of the Second World War when it was becoming clear to Nazi officials that their 'Thousand-Year Reich' faced imminent destruction.

In August 1944, while an amphetamine-fuelled Adolf Hitler was venting his contempt for the German people whose incipient defeat had betrayed his vision ('If the German people was to be conquered in the struggle,' he said, 'then it had been too weak to face the test of history, and was fit only for destruction"), his deputy, Reichsleiter Martin Bormann, was at the Hotel Maison Rouge in Strasbourg planning the continuation of Nazi power and ideology. Addressing the meeting of Nazi Party officials and German business leaders, Bormann stated: 'German industry must realize that the war cannot now be won, and must take steps to prepare for a postwar commercial campaign which will in time ensure the economic resurgence of Germany.' (2)

These steps were implemented under the code name Aktion Adlerflug (Operation Eagle Flight) and resulted in the 'massive flight of money, gold, stocks, bonds, patents, copyrights, and even technical specialists from Germany'. (3) Along with the central Deutsche Bank and the chemical cartel I. G. Farben, one of the largest industrial organizations in Europe, Bormann succeeded in establishing 750 front corporations in Portugal, Spain, Sweden, Switzerland, Turkey and Argentina. Of course, Bormann would have been unable to achieve this without substantial help from both within and outside Germany. This came in the form of connections with banks and businesses dating back to before the war, (4) indeed to the financing of the Nazi Party itself following the elections of 1933. On 20 February of that year, 25 of the most prominent industrialists in Germany were invited by Hermann Goering to a meeting with Adolf Hitler, who stated: 'An impossible situation is created when one section of a people favors private property while another denies it. A struggle of that sort tears a people apart and the fight continues until one section emerges victorious ... It is not by accident that one man produces more than another; the concept of private property is rooted in this fact ... Human beings are anything but equal. As far as the economy is concerned, I have but one desire, namely, that it may enter upon a peaceful future ... There will, however, not be a domestic peace unless Marxism has been exterminated.' (5)

Another of these connections was with the American International Telephone & Telegraph Corporation (ITT), which continued to trade with Nazi Germany after America's entry into the war, selling communications and military equipment such as artillery fuses. Journalist Jim Marrs states that ITT's German chairman, Gerhardt Westrick, was 'a close associate of John Foster Dulles, who would become US secretary of state under President Dwight Eisenhower, and partner to Dr. Heinrich Albert, head of the Ford Motor Co. in Germany until 1945'. He adds: 'Two ITT directors were German banker Baron Kurt von Schroder and Walter Schellenberg, head of counter-intelligence for the Nazi Gestapo.' (6)

According to former New York Times writer Charles Higham, Standard Oil of New Jersey (ESSO) secretly sold gasoline to Germany and fascist Spain. 'The shipments to Spain indirectly assisted the Axis through Spanish transferences to Hamburg.' (7) By changing the country of registration for Standard's tanker fleet to Panama, company spokesmen could claim that the oil was coming not from the United States but the Caribbean. (8)

There were also numerous banking connections, one of which was the partnership established in 1936 between the J. Henry Schroder Bank of New York and several Rockefeller family members to form Schroder, Rockefeller and Company, Investment Bankers that provided economic support to the Rome-Berlin Axis. 'The partners in Schroder, Rockefeller and Company included Avery Rockefeller, nephew of John D., Baron Bruno von Schroder in London, and Kurt von Schroder [of the Bank of International Settlements] and the Gestapo in Cologne ... Standard Oil's Paris representatives were directors of the Banque de Paris et de Pays-Bas, which had intricate connections to the Nazis and to Chase [National Bank].' (9)

According to investigator Paul Manning, Hermann Schmitz, head of I.G. Farben, was president of Chase National Bank for seven years prior to the war, and later held as much stock in Standard Oil as did the Rockefellers. He held other shares in General Motors 'and other US blue chip industrial stocks, and the 700 secret companies controlled in his time by I. G. [Farben], as well as shares in the 750 corporations he helped Bormann establish during the last years of World War II'. Manning continues: 'The Bormann organization in South America utilizes the voting power of the Schmitz trust along with their own assets to guide the multinationals they control, as they keep steady the economic course of the Fatherland. The Bormann organization is not merely a group of ex-Nazis. It is a great economic power whose interests today supersede their ideology.' (10)

The financial relationship between the Nazis and the Swiss banks has been well documented. Through processes of investment and money laundering, approximately 15 billion Reichsmarks was moved through Switzerland, equivalent to three per cent of America's gross domestic product (GDP) in 1944. 'To put this into today's terms, three percent of America's GDP is $200 billion, which is more than the entire GDP of Switzerland. Allow for interest, compounded over 50 years, and the value of the Nazi cache that went through Switzerland moves into the region of a trillion dollars.' (11)

Over the years there has been considerable speculation on the fate of Martin Bormann, Hitler's deputy and the second most powerful man in the Third Reich. One of the main characteristics of the Nazi survival theory is, perhaps unsurprisingly, the idea that the Nazi leaders themselves managed to escape from Berlin during the Allies' final assault. Since Bormann played such a large part in planning the continuation of Nazi financial interests and power after the war, it is worth pausing briefly to note the findings of the internationally esteemed historian Hugh Trevor-Roper who, as a wartime intelligence officer, was charged with the task of establishing the ultimate fate of Hitler and his inner circle.

According to Trevor-Roper:

In 1945 the evidence [on Bormann's fate] was conflicting and uncertain. Several witnesses maintained that Bormann had been killed in a tank which exploded when hit by a Panzerfaust [bazooka] on the Weidendammer Bridge during the attempted breakthrough on the night of 1-2 May. On the other hand, all these witnesses have admitted that the scene was one of great confusion and none of them claims to have seen Bormann's body.

... Further, even in 1945 I had three witnesses who independently claimed to have accompanied Bormann in his attempted escape. One of these witnesses, Artur Axmann, claimed afterwards to have seen him dead. Whether we believe Axmann or not is entirely a matter of choice, for his word is unsupported by any other testimony. In his favor it can be said that his evidence on all other points has been vindicated. On the other hand, if he wished to protect Bormann against further search, his natural course would be to give false evidence of his death. This being so I came in 1945, to the only permissible conclusion, viz: that Bormann had certainly survived the tank explosion but had possibly, though by no means certainly, been killed later that night.

OCCULT SECRETS OF THE THIRD REICH

Such was the balance of evidence in 1945. (12)

Trevor-Roper adds that by 1956 the situation remained unchanged by new evidence. In 1953, a former SS major, Joachim Tibertius, made a statement to a Swiss newspaper, Der Bund, in which he claimed to have seen Bormann after the tank explosion, at the Hotel Atlas. According to Tibertius: 'He had by then changed into civilian clothes. We pushed on together towards the Schiffbauerdamm and the Albrechtstrasse. Then I finally lost sight of him. But he had as good a chance to escape as I had.' (13)

The absence of concrete evidence for Bormann's death in 1945 spawned a number of claims of his survival, including one that placed him in Bolivia. Another claim came from Reinhardt Gehlen, who had been an Abwehr officer during the war and had subsequently become head of the new West German intelligence service, the Bundesnachrichtendienst, 'thanks to his useful experience ... and the beginning of the Cold War'. (14) In 1971, Gehlen stated in his memoirs that during the war he had come to the conclusion that Bormann was actually a Soviet spy. Following the war, 'Bormann had sought and found protection in Moscow, where he had occasionally been seen by reliable witnesses and had recently died'. (15)

However, as Trevor-Roper informs us, Gehlen's claims were refuted in 1972 'when two human skeletons, which had been dug up in waste ground near the Lehrter Station in West Berlin—i.e. not far from the place where Axmann claimed to have seen the bodies were forensically examined and identified as those of Bormann and his companion in flight, Dr. [Ludwig] Stumpfegger', Hitler's surgeon. (16)

Although it has been established since 1972 that Bormann's attempt to escape from the ruins of the Third Reich ended in death, it is equally certain that his brainchild, Operation Eagle Flight, met with considerably greater success. According to conspiracy researcher Jim Keith, the Research and Analysis branch of the Office of Strategic Services (OSS), the forerunner of the CIA, stated in 1945 that 'Nazi Party members, German industrialists and the German military, realizing their victory can no longer be attained, are now developing postwar commercial projects, endeavoring to renew and cement friendships in foreign commercial circles and planning for renewals of pre-war cartel agreements'. (17) Keith goes on to quote the minutes of the secret meeting between Bormann and a group of German industrialists, mentioned earlier: 'The [Nazi] Party is ready to supply large amounts of money to those industrialists who contribute to the post-war organization abroad. In return, the Party demands all financial reserves which have already been transferred abroad or may be later transferred, so that after the defeat a strong new Reich can be built.' (18)

PROJECT PAPERCLIP

Those who subscribe to the idea of Nazi survival in the post-war period cite another documented historical fact in support of their theories. After the end of the war, both the Americans and the Russians began to search throughout occupied Germany for technical, intelligence, military and other scientific information. In September 1946, President Harry Truman authorized Project PAPERCLIP, a program to bring selected German scientists to America. Aside from expertise in their fields, the main requisite for their acceptance for residence in the United States was proof that they had not been active members of the Nazi Party, and had not displayed any allegiance to Hitler.

Background investigations of various German scientists were conducted by the Joint Intelligence Objectives Agency (JIOA), which found them all to have been enthusiastic Nazis. Nevertheless, it was decided that to send them back to Germany would probably result in their expertise being exploited by the Soviets and would thus constitute a greater threat to US security than any Nazi sympathies they might have had. Among these scientists was, of course, Wernher von Braun, who had been technical director of the Peenemunde rocket research centre, home of the dreaded V-2 missile that had caused such carnage in London and elsewhere. According to conspiratologists, OSS Director Allen Dulles ordered the scientists' dossiers to be cleansed of Nazi references, with the result that by 1955 more than 760 German scientists had been granted US citizenship. This was done without the knowledge of President Truman.

One of those who benefited from Project PAPERCLIP was the Abwehr officer Reinhardt Gehlen, whose insurance policy of microfilming a vast number of documents concerning Soviet intelligence came to the attention of Dulles. Gehlen and Dulles formulated an arrangement by which the Nazi and American intelligence apparatus would be combined, ostensibly on the basis of a common interest in a defense against communism. However, far from being committed exclusively to the protection of the United States and Western Europe, Gehlen's organization was committed exclusively to the security of the ODESSA (Organization of Veterans of the SS) and other 'rat lines' that had been set up to aid the escape of more than 5,000 Nazis— and to set up Nazi colonies throughout the world.

Jim Keith writes:

Once the Gehlen Organization] was in place, with an estimated 4,000 intelligence specialists in Germany and more than 4,000 undercover operatives in the Soviet bloc, the perceived threat to the United States by the Soviets was aggravated by Nazi intelligence, and the Cold War was inevitable. Gehlen and his cronies seemingly never admitted that Germany had lost the war and simply persisted with Nazi objectives, using different means to destroy the USSR, namely collaboration with the United States and the OSS/CIA. The Nazis may have, in addition, foreseen the devastating results of a Cold War between the US and the USSR. The Cold War provided a financial burden which has destroyed Russia and left the United States as the world's biggest debtor nation ... (19)

With secret control of hundreds of billions of dollars in financial and industrial assets, not to mention access to the intelligence agencies of the post-war superpowers and with hidden colonies throughout the world, this 'Nazi International' was in a position to reverse the failure of the Third Reich and finally achieve global domination. According to conspiratologists, the main headquarters of the Nazi International was—and is—in Antarctica.

THE MYSTERIOUS VOYAGE OF CAPTAIN SCHAEFFER

On 25 April 1945, the German submarine U-977 embarked on one of the most remarkable voyages of the Second World War. Commanded by Captain Hans Schaeffer, the submarine left Kiel Harbour in the Baltic, stopped briefly for fuel at Christiansand South the following day, and arrived at Mar del Plata, Argentina nearly four months later, on 17 August. (20) In his subsequent interrogation by the Allies, Schaeffer stated that he had heard over the radio that the war had ended several days after leaving Christiansand South, and had decided to make for Argentina rather than staying in Europe. He offered his crew the option of being put off the submarine on the Norwegian coast or continuing on with him.

Some of Schaeffer's crew opted to return to Germany, so the U-977 remained hidden in Norwegian waters until 10 May, when the departing crew members were put ashore near Bergen. Schaeffer and the rest of his crew 'then embarked upon what surely must have been one of the most remarkable naval feats of the war: a journey through the North Sea and English Channel, past Gibraltar and along the coast of Africa, to finally surface, all of sixty-six days later, in the middle of the South Atlantic Ocean'. (21) Over the next month, the U-977 evaded capture by diving, surfacing, and erecting imitation sails and funnel to make it look like a cargo steamer from a distance. (22)

On 17 August 1945, the U-977 put into Mar del Plata, in spite of Schaeffer having heard over the radio that the crew of another fleeing German submarine, the U-530, had been apprehended on the River Plate and handed over to the United States. During his initial interrogation by the Argentine authorities, Schaeffer was asked if he had carried anyone of 'political importance' on the voyage, to which he replied that he had not. Harbinson informs us that several weeks later Schaeffer was again interrogated, this time by a special Anglo-American commission composed of high-ranking officers. It seems that this commission wanted to explore the possibility that the U-977 had transported Hitler and Martin Bormann first to Argentina and then on to a secret Nazi base in Antarctica. (23)

The English and Americans apparently considered this to be a realistic possibility, for they subsequently flew both Schaeffer and Otto Wehrmut, the commander of the U-530, to Washington, D.C., where the interrogations continued for several more months. It is not clear what happened to Wehrmut at this point, but Schaeffer was taken to Antwerp, Belgium, where he was interrogated yet again. The U-977 itself was thoroughly searched and then taken to the United States where it was destroyed under orders from the US War Department. Schaeffer was then sent back to Germany, but decided to leave his country and return to Argentina. (24)

The testimony of Captain Schaeffer served as an early inspiration for the idea that high-ranking Nazis had escaped the destruction of the Third Reich and were continuing with their plans for world domination in one or more secret locations. Schaeffer's voyage suggested to some that the ultimate destination for escaping Nazis was Antarctica, via Argentina. The German Navy Admiral Karl Doenitz is reported to have stated in 1943: 'The German submarine fleet is proud of having built for the Fuhrer in another part of the world a Shangri-la on land, an impregnable fortress.' (25)

Where was this 'impregnable fortress'—if it existed? It is a matter of historical fact that Nazi Germany maintained an intense interest in the Antarctic continent throughout the war. As we shall now see, that beautiful, mysterious and hostile place also holds a prominent position in the thoughts of those who subscribe to the Nazi-survival theory.

OPERATION HIGHJUMP

Between 1946 and 1947, Rear Admiral Richard E. Byrd contributed to the US Navy Antarctic Developments Project, also known as Operation Highjump. This operation was ostensibly an exercise in polar combat, survival and exploration; however, conspiracy theorists have suggested another, far more sinister purpose. Operation Highjump began approximately one year after the arrival of the U-977 at Mar del Plata, Argentina. The vast resources placed at Byrd's disposal have suggested to many that the operation was intended as an actual assault force—but an assault against what, or whom?

The British author W. A. Harbinson has perhaps done more than any other writer to popularize the idea that the Nazis had developed extremely advanced aircraft designs by the end of the Second World War. In his novel sequence Projekt Saucer and his nonfiction study Project UFO, he also offers evidence of a secret flying-disc base in Antarctica. In his novel Genesis (1980) Harbinson includes a lengthy afterword, which was later reprinted as the introduction to Man-Mode UFOs 1944-1994- 50 Years of Suppression (1994) by Renato Vesco and David Hatcher Childress and which describes how, in May 1978, a single-issue tabloid paper called Brisant was being given away at Stand 111, in a scientific exhibition in the Hannover Messe Hall. This paper contained two articles: one on the scientific future of Antarctica, and the other on flying-disc technology at the end of the war.

In its article on Antarctica, Brisant asked why the Operation Highjump assault force docked near the German-claimed region of Neu Schwabenland on 27 January 1947, why it then divided into three separate task forces and, most importantly, why there had been so many foreign press reports that the operation had been a disaster. Harbinson writes:

That expedition became something of a mystery. Subsequent official reports stated that it had been an enormous success, revealing more about the Antarctic than had ever been known before. However, other, mainly foreign reports suggested that such in fact had not been the case: that many of Byrd's men were lost during the first day, that at least four of his airplanes inexplicably disappeared, and that while the expedition had gone provisioned for six to eight months, the men actually returned to America in February 1947, after only a few weeks. According to Brisant, Admiral Byrd later told a reporter (I could find no verification on this) that it was 'necessary for the USA to take defensive actions against enemy air fighters which come from the polar regions' and that in the case of a new war the USA would be 'attacked by fighters that are able to fly from one pole to the other with incredible speed.' Also, according to Brisant, shortly after his return from the Antarctic, Admiral Byrd was ordered to undergo a secret cross-examination—and the United States withdrew from the Antarctic for almost a decade. (26)

The article carried a serious and startling implication: that Operation Highjump had been a military invasion force disguised as a training and exploratory group, that it had intended to deal with a secret colony of Nazi survivors in an elaborate underground facility that had been constructed during the Second World War, and that this invasion force had met its match in the form of a squadron of Nazi-built flying discs based at the colony. The reason for the United States' temporary withdrawal from Antarctica was, allegedly, to allow itself time to develop its own flying discs, based upon designs captured at the end of the war. (27)

NAZI UFO BASES IN ANTARCTICA?

Most reasonable people would dismiss as fantastic nonsense the idea that many Nazis fled the ruins of the Third Reich and took up residence in a secret Antarctic colony, armed with a squadron of flying discs with which to protect themselves. However, the paranoid conspiracy theories that have proliferated in the second half of the twentieth century are based not so much on reason but rather on elaborate extrapolations of puzzling but inconclusive evidence. In the present case, this evidence centers on the undeniable interest the Third Reich maintained in Antarctica throughout the war: German ships and U-boats constantly patrolled the South Atlantic between South Africa and the region of Antarctica containing Neu Schwabenland, and it is certainly possible that many of these voyages could have included shipments of personnel and supplies for the construction of heavily fortified facilities. When we add to this the testimony of the captain of the U-977, Hans Schaeffer (which admittedly may well be false), the claims of the neo-Nazi publication Brisant that such trips included the transfer of flying-disc research teams and disc components, and the rumors regarding the disastrous failure of Byrd's Operation Highjump, we have the ingredients of a powerful and enduring modern myth, in which the evils of Nazism did not meet destruction at the hands of the victorious Allies in 1945 but continue to exert a terrible influence over human affairs to this day.

Indeed, it is somewhat ironic that the political system that identified the Jews as its scapegoat and moved with such barbarism against them should now be chosen by many conspiracy theorists as the scapegoat responsible for the machinations of a putative 'New World Order'. It is quite possible that the concept of Nazi survival itself has survived to the present day because of the very extremity of the crimes perpetrated by the Third Reich. While it may be argued that our continuing interest in Nazi Germany constitutes an unhealthy fascination with the suffering and terror of an ultimate inhumanity, there is also a case for saying that this interest is born of a deep and despairing bafflement (see the Introduction). I believe it is not going too far to suggest that the elaborate conspiracy theory involving Nazi survival is born of a deeply ingrained suspicion that such wickedness could not have been completely defeated at the war's end; this suspicion may well have been reinforced by the fact that the volkisch and Pan-German forerunners of the Nazi Party were influenced by occult and mythological belief systems, combined with the more generalized occult revival occurring throughout Europe in the post-war years.

Of course, conspiracy theories cannot survive without conspiratologists to conceive and propagate them. We shall now, therefore, turn our attention to the means by which the theory of Nazi survival has been developed.

THE BLACK ORDER

Throughout the post-war period, material has been added constantly to the sinister mythological system built around the idea that the Third Reich continues its activities in a hidden location. This cabal of surviving Nazis is sometimes referred to as the Fourth Reich but more often as the 'Black Order'. Those who contend that such a concept can have no place in a rational person's world view are underestimating the subtle power exerted by the strange concepts contained within the field of popular occultism. The British writer Joscelyn Godwin has produced a splendid, highly informative study of this field in his book Arktos The Polar Myth in Science, Symbolism, and Nazi Survival, in which he maintains an admirably skeptical standpoint while acknowledging that the notions embodied in popular occultism must be treated with respect, if only for their powerful influence over the public mind. He also includes a pertinent quote from the German Pastor Ekkehard Hieronimus regarding popular beliefs:

What is going on in the lower reaches of society is probably very much more potent and effective than what happens in intellectual circles. We think, of course, that it is the intellectuals—now in the broadest sense of the term, in which I include the scientists -who define our life. But lately the intellectuals have been rather like a film of oil on a great puddle of water: it shines mischievously and thinks that it is the whole thing, but it is only one molecule thick. I can see quite definite things coming towards us. The things going on in the so-called cultural underground, or the so-called subculture, are very strange. (28)

Godwin then wryly offers an example of a product of this 'subculture', a report from the 16 April 1991 issue of the London newspaper the Sun, that claims that the ruins of Atlantis have been discovered in the Arctic by a joint French-Soviet research expedition. The 'proof is a photomontage of some Doric columns rising from an icy landscape. While the vast majority of people seeing this would probably think it interesting but almost certainly spurious, the idea is nevertheless firmly embedded in their unconscious. As Godwin notes (and as we have discussed in earlier chapters), uncritical belief in the literal reality of certain occult concepts aided in no small degree the rise of National Socialism. 'One has to be thankful that our tabloids are not proclaiming Aryan supremacy or describing Jewish ritual murder; but one may well ask what collective attitudes are being formed by the currents in the "great puddle" of popular occultism.' (29)

It is one thing for a collective attitude to admit the possibility of visitation by alien spacecraft, or the existence of ghosts or relict hominids such as Bigfoot, the Yeti and so on; it is quite another to admit of the undying—perhaps supernatural—power of an ideology that has already irreparably demeaned humanity and could quite conceivably wreak havoc once again.

'GOTZEN GEGEN THULE'

In 1971, Wilhelm Landig published a strange novel entitled Gotzen gegen Thule (Godlets Against Thule). In an echo of the nineteenth-century vogue for presenting fantasy as a 'true story', Landig subtitles his novel 'a fiction full of facts' and claims that it contains accurate information on the radical advances in aviation and weapons technology made in the years since the end of the war. Gotzen gegen Thule is fundamentally an adventure story that follows the exploits of two German airmen, Recke and Reimer (which Godwin translates as 'Brave Warrior' and 'Poet' respectively) (30), who are sent to a secret German base in the far north of Canada towards the end of the Second World War. This base, known as Point 103, is a large underground facility possessing highly advanced technology and supplied by powerful allies in the United States. Its occupants constitute a force opposed to the Third Reich, which is seen as a Satanic force.

Point 103 is, in fact, solidly anti-racist, as evidenced by one scene in which a conference there is attended by 'a Tibetan lama, Japanese, Chinese, and American officers, Indians, a Black Ethiopian, Arabs, Persians, a Brazilian officer, a Venezuelan, a Siamese, and a full-blooded Mexican Indian'. (31) Travel to and from this remote and ultra-secret facility is by a highly advanced aircraft called the V7, which is shaped like a sphere with a rotating circular wing containing jet turbines. Interestingly enough, even the responsible and skeptical Godwin is willing to concede that this part of Landig's novel may well have a basis in fact (see Chapter Eight).

The two airmen are sent on a mission to Prague to prevent the disc-plane technology from falling into Allied hands; following the end of the war and the defeat of Nazi Germany, Point 103 declares itself independent and continues with its pursuit of Thulean ideals. These ideals are explained by another character, an ex-Waffen-SS officer named Gutmann ('Good man'). Godwin provides a summary of the Thulean philosophy:

The light of Thule comes not from the East but from the North. Its tradition is 'Uranian,' being derived from Uranos, lord of the cosmic world order and of the primordial Paradise of the Aryan Race, situated at the North Pole. It was Uranos's usurping son Saturn who brought upon this originally happy and unified humanity the dubious gift of the egoic state. The temptations consequent upon this change in the human constitution lead to the loss of primeval unity and, eventually, the destruction of Saturn's realm, Atlantis. Thereupon the warm climate of the secret island of the Hyperboreans was suddenly replaced by bitter winter. The primordial races of the Arctic and of the Nordic Atlantis both lost their homes, and were forced to migrate southwards. Wherever they settled—in Europe, Persia, India, and elsewhere—they tried to remake their lost Paradise, and in their myths and legends cherished the memory of it. (32)

As Godwin notes, Uranos and Saturn seem to be personifications of events in remote antiquity; however, the Thulean religion included an unmanifested God beyond space and time, and a Son through whom the will of the Father operates and who is identified with the laws of nature. Landig himself identifies the legend of Thule (which in geographical terms is located close to Point 103) with that of the spiritual centre of the world, sometimes called Shambhala. The reader will recall Nicholas Roerich's encounter with a golden flying disc, described in Chapter Four, and how his guide stated that the UFO represented the beneficent influence of Rigden-Jyepo, the King of the World, who was watching over them. Through another character, a French collaborator named Belisse ('from Belisane, sun god of the Gauls'), (33) Landig describes in elaborate detail the nature of this phenomenon, which he calls 'Manisolas'. They are living, intelligent bio-mechanical entities with a complex life cycle that begins as a circle of light and continues through a metallic form before reaching the reproductive stage. Through a regenerative process, a new Manisola grows within the womb of the adult.

The regenerated part is expelled by the remaining mother-nucleus as a new energetic circle of light, corresponding to a birthing technique. This new circle enters on the same seven developmental stages, while the expelling maternal element rolls itself into a ball, which then explodes. The metallic remains contain particles of copper. The optical impressions that eyewitnesses of these Manisolas have had up to now are basically quite uniform. In the daytime they display an extremely bright gold or silver luminescence, sometimes with traces of rose-colored smoke which then often condense into grayish-white trails. At night the disks shine in glowing or glossy colors, showing on occasion long flames at the edges and red and blue sparks, which can grow so strong as to wreathe them in fire. Most remarkable is their power of reaction against pursuers, like that of a rational creature, far exceeding any possible electronic self-steering or radio control. (34)

Landig goes on to describe how, throughout the ages, all mythologies refer in one way or another to the Manisolas, which are seen as symbols of spiritual potency, unity and love. Although Point 103 is claimed to be a non-racist society, the Thuleans nevertheless consider Israel to be in eternal opposition to their ideals, and remember the time when their ancestors, the Nordic Atlanteans, were held in slavery by Semitic sorcerers.

Perhaps unsurprisingly, the Ark of the Covenant is brought into this bizarre occult adventure and is described as a kind of battery for astral energy to be used in magical operations. This energy is the fertilizing 'force-field of the Aryans', which is stolen by Hebrew magicians and stored in the Ark for their own anti-Aryan purposes. The international conspiracy against the Aryans is further defined when the characters travel to Tibet and meet another German, Juncker ('Aristocrat'), (35) who tells them that the Asiatic peoples are waiting for a great warrior who will come from the subterranean realm of Agartha and lead them to domination of the world. We then learn of the nature of 'Shambala' and 'Agartha', which is another perversion of Buddhist teaching, similar to that suggested by Ravenscroft in The Spear of Destiny (see Chapter Five). The central point of Gotzen gegen Thule is that the Third Reich arose with the assistance of the twin power centers of Agartha and Shambhala and was defeated when it succumbed to the materialistic attractions of Shambhala, thus destroying the balance between the two. We can look again to Godwin for a good translation of Landig's original:

The source of material energies of the left hand, which have their seat in Shambala, is the upper-earth city of power and might, which is ruled by a great King of Fear. But it is the same seat of Shambala that a part of the western secret brotherhoods and lodges regards as their point of origin, from which come the promises and warnings of a Lord of the World. This Shambala is a searchlight of our will! Then there is the second source: Agartha, the inner, underworld realm of contemplation and its energies. There too is a Lord and King of the World, who promises his domination. At the proper moment, this center will lead good men against the evil ones; and it is firmly connected with Brahytma, that is, God. And that is the king to serve, the one who will set up our empire and rule over the others ... [T]he men in [the Third] Reich ... joined themselves with the energies of Shambala, of pure force, and in their secret way worked against the other men of [the] Reich ... And behind these energies which manifest themselves in Shambala stands the Caucasian, Stalin-Dugaschvili! He knew everything, he knew the men of the circle in [the] Reich and he played his own cards with them as if they were their own. Stalin-Dugaschvili had the support of the Lord of Fear and Power against [the] Reich! (36)

In the final stages of the novel, the heroes leave Tibet but are captured in India by the British, who place them in a prisoner-of-war camp. When they finally return to Germany, it becomes clear that they will probably never rejoin Point 103, which 'seems to have forgotten them: they ruefully admit ... that if it still exists, it has probably had to isolate itself completely from the world of today'.

All that remains to [the Thuleans] is to constitute a 'Fourth Reich in exile,' patiently waiting for the Age of Pisces to reach its inevitable end. And as the Fish Age passes, so St Peter's religious tyranny in Rome will crumble ... and the Jewish Ark will lose its potency. Then, says Landig, the ... banner of the Aryans will fly again ... (37)

Added to the weird flights of fancy, Gotzen gegen Thule contains several statements that mark it out as a work of pernicious historical revisionism, such as Juncker's claim that the bodies in the liberated concentration camps were actually those of Germans killed in Allied air raids on Munich. (38) Aside from this, the novel manages to weave together a wide variety of myths, all of which have come to be associated with the concept of Nazi survival: Nordic mythology, UFOs as man-made aircraft, the subterranean realms of Shambhala and Agartha, the Hollow Earth, the Holy Grail, and the international conspiracy to inaugurate a secret One-World Government. While it might be expected that such a ridiculous and (in its attempt at historical revisionism) morally reprehensible tale would sink into a merciful literary oblivion, it did nothing of the kind; instead, it entered the murky realm of the cultural underground, where it was discovered by certain interested parties who saw in it an opportunity to further their own agendas.

ERNST ZUNDEL AND 'SAMISDAT'

The articles in the neo-Nazi publication Brisant did not carry by-lines. Intrigued and unsettled by the strange information they contained, W. A. Harbinson embarked on a little detective work, checking the origins of the magazine and discovering that it had been published in West Germany by a company that had since disappeared, Lintec GmbH of Hamburg. According to Harbinson, the 'company was not listed with any of the West German press organizations, nor with any public relations bureau'. (39) Nevertheless, he realized that the information contained in the Brisant articles had been culled from two books: UFOs. Nazi Secret Weapons? by Mattern Friedrich and Secret Nazi Polar Expeditions by Christof Friedrich. Both books were published by a company called Samisdat Publishers Limited of Toronto, Canada.

As Harbinson notes, 'Mattern Friedrich' and 'Christof Friedrich' are actually pseudonyms for Ernst Zundel, a Canadian resident but German citizen and one of the most outspoken and active of those who deny that the Holocaust occurred. Through his many apparent links with surviving Nazis in South America and elsewhere, Zundel 'now runs Samisdat Publishers Limited as a mouthpiece of neo-Nazi propaganda and commercial enterprise, specializing in the sale of Nazi books, record albums, tape recordings, photographs, medals and other Nazi memorabilia'. (40) Zundel maintains in his books that UFOs are actually Nazi secret weapons, launched from their hidden base at or near the South Pole. He also is an advocate (apparently) of the Hollow Earth Theory, and in his Samisdat newsletter in 1978 advertised an expedition by chartered jet to the South Pole where, he claimed, the passengers would discover not only Hitler's Antarctic UFO base but also the entrance to the interior of the planet. A ticket for the chartered flight would cost $9,999.

The following selection from the Samisdat article will enable the reader to gain some idea of the nature of Zundel's claims:

ACHTUNG! SAMISDAT NEWS BULLETIN SAMISDAT HOLLOW EARTH EXPEDITION $9999.00 IN SEARCH OF HOLES IN THE POLES SEARCH FOR HITLER'S ANTARCTIC U.F.O. BASES ...

Your response to our most recent mailout and activities has been most encouraging! We have received orders and enquiries from as far away as Noumea in the South Pacific, Easter Island, Chile, Argentina, Brazil, Venezuela, Panama, Mexico, Soviet Satellite countries, China, South Africa, Persia, the Congo, Australia, Japan, as well as from every country in Western Europe and almost every state in the U.S.A. Not only is this response extensive, it is massive—a clear indication on the part of knowledgeable UFO researchers and members of the public that they are tired of the 'Junk food' being served up by old-line UFO groups and publications who expound the official CIA-KGB alibi that all UFOs are extraterrestrial. What the UFO-watching world wants now is the real meat of the matter—a serious investigation of UFOs whose origins are terrestrial.

SAMISDAT is the only organization making such an effort, but we are not alone, for we have thousands of supporters like yourself who want to know the truth which the saucer-charlatans have for 30 years tried to cover up with fairy-tale fantasies of 'little green men'. It is people like yourself who have made SAMISDAT the most active UFO Organization and publisher on Planet Earth! ...

Our discoveries have led us into the production of a number of currently suppressed and sometimes vilified books which are now underground bestsellers. "UFOs -NAZI SECRET WEAPON?" was our first title, now sold out in 5 complete editions. Our second book, "SECRET NAZI POLAR EXPEDITIONS", is coming up fast and has sold out 2 full editions. Foreign-language translations of these books are selling briskly, and it is becoming obvious to everyone that the media-enforced blockade of the truth has now been broken. Three additional books are currently under production and these will round out our Phase I Publishing Program: "THE CIA-KGB-UFO COVERUP", "THE ANTARCTICA THEORY" and "THE LAST BATTALION".

We have also been able to establish research teams in Canada, the U.S.A. and in particular, Germany, whose task it is to rediscover basic wingless flight which brought the original Nazi UFOs into being. Already, these teams have designed and constructed small scale models, some using conventional power and others which have propulsion systems unprecedented in today's aerospace technology. With additional research, we hope to make available several different models in kit form for hobby-builders. Any contributions to these research projects, whether of ideas or money, will be very much appreciated. Checks should be made out to SAMISDAT with the notation "For SAMPROJ R-1" ...

For the truly dedicated UFO researcher, SAMISDAT is embarking upon a magnificent and awe-inspiring experience! We are negotiating with several international airlines and chartered air carriers in regard to our planned investigation of the "Inner Earth Theory" coupled with our search for "Hitler's Flying Saucer Bases in Antarctica." Our 'launching pad' for which we are also negotiating will be located in Rio de Janeiro or Buenos Aires. This site will be the gathering place for an International UFO Convention which is scheduled to take place some time in 1979 or 1980. From this convention site, those who are interested and financially able may join Christof Friedrich and members of a specially-selected SAMISDAT research team on the Antarctic Expedition who will not only search for Hitler's Saucer Bases in German Antarctica, but who will further attempt to settle the controversy about Admiral Byrd's "Flight into the Polar Opening" by actually flying over the South Pole! Our tentative flight path is here shown. It is anticipated that a specially-prepared, long-range jet will be available for the Antarctic Expedition's polar flight ...

SAMISDAT's Antarctic Expedition in Search of Hitler's Flying Saucer Bases and the South Polar Opening into Inner Earth will be the unique event of a lifetime. As only a very limited number of people can be accommodated, our selection standards are of necessity rigorous. The approximate cost per person on this expedition may be as high as $9,999.00. However, the cost could be reduced considerably, provided we are able to raise money from our SAMISDAT SERIES of lectures, tapes, conventions, UFO models and book sales in this interim period. You can help to realize this Dream of a lifetime in several ways:

(1) You can become one of our book distributors by buying SAMISDAT books and other items at wholesale dealers' prices and then retailing them to friends, colleagues, UFO conventioneers, and visitors to county fairs, psychic fairs and flea markets. By purchasing SAMISDAT titles in bulk, you could easily realize almost a 100% profit on each item sold. This money you could then apply toward your share in the Expedition or use as you see fit. (2) You can organize a UFO club and hold your own UFO conventions on a profit-sharing basis with SAMISDAT. (3) You can help us find sponsors for the Expedition. (4) If you are rich and conscientious, you can underwrite the whole or part of the Expedition and realize our goal of a lifetime much, much faster. But empty promises and other hot-air products from windbags and do-nothings, however well off, will not serve to waft the Expedition to Antarctica and back. The only thing capable of doing that is cold, hard cash up front. If you've got what it takes and want to put your money to work right away, then please contact us! (5) You can set up your own fund-raising campaign for the Expedition. For details and assistance in regard to these and other ideas, do not hesitate to contact us. These are but a few of the ways in which we can hasten that glorious day when we board our sleek, silvery aircraft and wing our way to Antarctica and beyond—to our rendezvous with history. When we return, we shall have unearthed Inner Earth and/or found evidence of Hitler's UFO Bases—or we shall have gone a long way toward dispelling two of the most tenaciously persistent mysteries of our Scientific Era. (41)

The reader will note that Zimdel's apparent intention to launch an expedition to Antarctica could only be realized if readers of Samisdat bought his products 'in bulk' (needless to say, the charter flight to the Antarctic never took place). Zundel's apparently nonsensical claims regarding Nazi UFOs, secret bases at the South Pole and the Hollow Earth hide an altogether more sinister revisionist agenda.

In fact, Zundel himself has admitted as much. According to Frank Miele, a member of the Skeptics Society in the United States, who wrote an article on Holocaust revisionism for that society's magazine in 1994, Zundel told him that his book UFOs: Nazi Secret Weapons? (which became an underground bestseller, going through seven printings) was nothing more than a ploy to attract readers. Said Zundel in a telephone conversation with Miele: 'I realized that North Americans were not interested in being educated. They want to be entertained. The book was for fun. With a picture of the Fuhrer on the cover and flying saucers coming out of Antarctica it was a chance to get on radio and TV talk shows. For about 15 minutes of an hour program I'd talk about that esoteric stuff. Then I would start talking about all those Jewish scientists in concentration camps, working on these secret weapons. And that was my chance to talk about what I wanted to talk about.' (42)

As one might expect (and hope), Zundel's Holocaust revisionism has landed him in hot water with the Canadian authorities. In 1984, criminal proceedings were initiated against him by the Canadian Government, based on a private complaint made by a Holocaust survivor named Sabrina Citron. Zundel was charged under Section 177 of the Criminal Code of Canada, which makes it a criminal offence to publish willfully a statement one knows is false and that causes, or is likely to cause, injury to the public interest. Zundel had published two books by other authors: The West, War, and Islam and Did Six Million Really Die? He was convicted for publishing the latter title and sentenced to fifteen months in jail. The conviction, however, was overturned on appeal and a second trial was ordered.

The second trial received massive coverage in the Canadian media, with Zundel calling other leading revisionists as expert witnesses. He was again convicted, but the case was taken to the Canadian Supreme Court, which found that the statute on false statements was an unconstitutional violation of free speech. As Miele ironically remarks, Zundel the Holocaust revisionist found himself 'a civil libertarian hero of Canada'. (43) Notwithstanding this, several Canadian Jewish groups have initiated proceedings against him under Canadian anti-hate laws.

MIGUEL SERRANO AND THE GLORIFICATION OF HITLER

The strange and esoteric notions that seem so often to go hand in hand with Holocaust revisionism are most strikingly exemplified by the Chilean diplomat Miguel Serrano (b. 1917), who was Ambassador to India (1953-62), Yugoslavia (1962-64) and Austria (196470). (44) The possessor of a formidable intellect, Serrano wrote on a number of arcane subjects including Yoga, Tantra and other areas of mysticism, as well as a book on his friendships with Carl Jung and Hermann Hesse. He also travelled widely in search of wisdom in India, South America and Antarctica. In 1984 he published a long explication of his mystical and philosophical thought, entitled Adolf Hitler, el Ultimo Avatara (Adolf Hitler, the Last Avatar), which he dedicates To the glory of the Fuhrer, Adolf Hitler'. (45)

According to Godwin:

We are to understand the title quite literally: Serrano means that Hitler is the Tenth Avatar of Vishnu, the Kalki Avatar, who has incarnated to bring about the end of the Kali Yuga and usher in a New Age. In the terminology of Buddhism, Hitler is a Tulku or a Bodhisattva, who having previously emancipated himself from bondage to the circles of this world has taken on voluntary birth for the sake of mankind. Therefore he is beyond criticism. (46)

Serrano believes that Hitler himself is still alive, having escaped from the ruins of Berlin in one of the Nazi disc-planes, and is continuing to direct an Esoteric War from the safety of a secret realm at the South Pole. The background to this scenario involves, once again, the legendary land of Hyperborea and its fabulous inhabitants, with further variations on the theme we have already discussed (see Chapter Two). According to Serrano, the Hyperboreans were originally from beyond our galaxy, arriving on Earth in remote antiquity. Their existence has been suppressed by a monumental conspiracy, which also seeks to misrepresent them as physical 'aliens'; in fact, we only perceive them as 'flying saucers' because we lack the perception to see them as they really are. They founded the First Hyperborea here on Earth, a realm that was not composed of mundane matter but which extended beyond the physical plane of existence created and controlled by the Demiurge, an inferior god whose first experiments in the creation of intelligent life resulted in Neanderthal Man. (47)

The Demiurge instituted a cosmic regime by which all creatures would take the Way of the Ancestors—in other words, they would be reincarnated on Earth indefinitely. This was unacceptable to the Hyperboreans who preferred to take the Way of the Gods, only being reincarnated if they chose. The Hyperboreans possessed the power of Vril (see Chapter Three), which they wielded in their battles with the mechanistic Demiurge. (48) The war between the Hyperboreans and the Demiurge resulted in the founding of a Second Hyperborea at the North Pole, taking the form of a physical, circular continent from which the Hyperboreans began to organize the spiritualization of the Earth. This would be achieved through the instilling of a single particle of immortality in the Neanderthals and other proto-humans, which would raise them out of their semi-animal state.

The Hyperboreans' plans seemed to be going well enough, until they made the mistake of having sexual intercourse with the creations of the Demiurge. This miscegenation was associated with a catastrophic cometary impact that caused the North and South Poles to change position. From that moment on, the Earth became 'the battleground between the Demiurge and the Hyperboreans, the latter always in danger of diluting their blood'. (49) Godwin quotes Serrano thus: 'There is nothing more mysterious than blood. Paracelsus considered it a condensation of light. I believe that the Aryan, Hyperborean blood is that—but not the light of the Golden Sun, not of a galactic sun, but of the light of the Black Sun ...', (50) the Black Sun being a symbol not only of the void inside the Hollow Earth but also of the ultimate void from which all creation flows.

Serrano claims to have met a certain Master who told him that at a certain point in the practice of Yoga one is able to leave one's body and go through mystical death to reach the Black Sun, the realm occupied by the Hyperboreans beyond the physical universe. However, such a spiritual voyage is not within the capabilities of all humanity—only those 'whose blood preserves the memory of the ancient White, Hyperborean race'. (51)

The Jewish people are seen by Serrano as the instruments of the Demiurge (whom he identifies with Jehovah). They constitute an 'anti-race' that is engaged in a gigantic conspiracy involving all the world's institutions, the undeclared enemies of Hyperborean ideals. These ideals gave rise to the Thule Society, which Serrano claims had links with the Hermetic Order of the Golden Dawn but 'was perverted by the degeneracy of Aleister Crowley and the Jewish Bergsons'. (52)

During the earlier part of Hitler's campaigns, according to Serrano, his intention had simply been to reconquer the ancient territories of the Aryans or Hyperboreans. Rudolf Hess's flight to England in 1941 was the last stage of this effort, intended through renewed contacts with the Golden Dawn to unite Germany with her Aryan cousins, the British, and encourage them also to purify their race. But after the apparent failure of this mission, Hitler took up his avataric destiny of total war on all fronts against international Jewry and the Demiurge, attacking them in their most powerful creation, the Communist Soviet Union. (53)

As with other revisionists, Serrano denies that the Holocaust took place (he calls it the 'Myth of the Six Million') on the grounds that the German is heroic but not cruel (cruelty being an attribute of mixed blood). Indeed, during the Second World War, the Nazis were allegedly concentrating on the perfection of 'magical realism', including the development of disc-planes, establishing contact with ascended Masters in Tibet and dematerialization. Hitler himself did not commit suicide but escaped through an underground passage, designed by Albert Speer, connecting the Bunker with Tempelhof Airfield where he boarded one of the disc-planes and left the ruins of the Third Reich behind. (54)

As Godwin notes, quoting the Chilean writer thus, Serrano here enters realms usually identified with the bizarre fringes of ufology and cosmology:

Had the German submarines discovered at the North Pole or in John Dee's Greenland the exact point through which one penetrates, as through a black funnel, going to connect with the Other Pole, emerging in that paradisal land and sea that are no longer here, yet exist? An impregnable paradise, from which one can continue the war and win it—for when this war is lost, the other is won. The Golden Age, Ultima Thule, Hyperborea, the other side of things; so easy and so difficult to attain. The inner earth, the Other Earth, the counter-earth, the astral earth, to which one passes as it were with a 'click'; a bilocation, or trilocation of space. (55)

Serrano believes that the Hollow Earth is still inhabited by the First Hyperboreans and that the Nazis found a way through to their realm via the South Pole, a belief shared (apparently) by the French writer Jean Robin—although it must be added that Robin is no denier of the Holocaust. In 1989, Robin published his Operation Orth, which offers the account, supposedly given to Robin by a friend, of a journey to a subterranean complex made aboard a flying saucer that could pass through solid rock. The underground city was near the Chilean coastal city of Valparaiso, north of Santiago; it had a population of some 350,000, all of whom were members of the Black Order and some of whom were Jews who blamed 'their fellows for their "refusal to collaborate" with the evolutionary process'.

(56) Robin's story differs from other Nazi-survival myths in that Hitler died in this new Agartha in 1953 and his body was placed in a transparent, hexagonal casket. Rather astonishingly, this casket also contained the body of the Swedish diplomat Raoul Wallenberg, who saved thousands of Jews from the concentration camps and who mysteriously disappeared at the end of the war. Godwin is justifiably nonplussed by this: Operation Orth poses every manner of problem ... to the reader, who can

only wonder what prompted Jean Robin to present the shocking images of Hitler and Wallenberg reconciled, and the casual dismissal of the Holocaust by the Jews of the Black Order. In the context of Guenonian attitudes, which are nothing if not respectful of the Jewish people and their tradition, there is nothing to be said, unless it be that Robin actually accepts his friend's account, and is warning us of the [evolutionary process's] final obscenity. (57)

ALTERNATIVE 3

Anyone familiar with the above phrase will surely be wondering what possible significance it can have to the present study. I have decided to discuss it for two reasons: firstly, the terrifying conspiracy-to-end-all-conspiracies known as 'Alternative 3' has been implicated by more than one writer in the ongoing saga of ultra-secret Nazi activities; and secondly because, since Alternative 3 was actually nothing more than a cleverly engineered hoax, it offers us a salutary lesson in how the public can be manipulated by fantasy and propaganda masquerading as fact. Since many readers may be unfamiliar with Alternative 3, we must review its principal elements before turning our attention to the Nazi connection and the reasons why, even today, it is still believed by many to be essentially true.

The tale begins on 20 June 1977, when the UK Independent Television Company Anglia transmitted a documentary program in its highly regarded Science Report series. The program was entitled Alternative 3, and the British TV guide TV Times had this to say about it: 'What this program shows may be considered unethical, but this film is transmitted ... as a challenge to those who know the answers to the questions raised to tell the truth.' (58) The program finished at 10 P. M., and from then until midnight and throughout the following day Anglia Television was swamped with telephone calls (10,000, according to one estimate), some from people who had enjoyed the program and wanted to know if there was any truth in it but many from viewers who were genuinely frightened by its 'revelations' and who wanted to know what was being done about them. Anglia hastily issued a statement assuring its viewers that Alternative 3 had, in fact, originally been meant as an April Fool's Day joke—as evidenced by the closing credits, which included the copyright caption: 'Anglia Television—April 1, 1977'.

Shortly before the transmission, Anglia had issued a press release, stating:

A team of journalists investigating, among other topical subjects, the drought of 1976, and the changes in the world's atmospheric conditions, and also a disturbing rise in the statistics of disappearing people, follow a trail of information and scientific research through England and America.

A Cambridge scientist and an ex-astronaut living in unpublicised retirement following a nervous breakdown, are among the links in their investigations, which come together finally in some strange discoveries about the future of life on Earth and elsewhere in the Solar System.

As a result of our private screenings a few weeks ago, this program has been acquired for simultaneous transmission in Australia, New Zealand, Canada, Denmark and Iceland and will be seen eventually in the majority of European and Asian markets.

The program's theme may seem extraordinary, but it is scientifically possible. The question is, how far does it mirror the truth?

On the day of the transmission, journalist Kenneth Hughes, who had gained access to some of the material to be presented, wrote an article in the London Daily Mirror entitled 'WHAT ON EARTH IS GOING ON?'

A science program is likely to keep millions of Britons glued to their armchairs.

ALTERNATIVE 3 ... is an investigation into the disappearance of several scientists. They seem simply to have vanished from the face of the Earth. Chilling news is read by former ITV newscaster Simon Butler who gives a gloomy report on the future. The program will be screened in several other countries—but not in America. Network bosses there want to assess its effect on British viewers.

The program's structure centered on a series of interviews with one Dr. Carl Gerstein, who described the hideous nature of Alternative 3. Dr. Gerstein claimed to have attended a secret conference in Huntsville, Alabama in 1957, at which it was agreed that industrial pollution and the accompanying greenhouse effect (caused by high levels of carbon dioxide trapping heat within the atmosphere) was destroying the Earth's biosphere, and that the decline in air quality was irreversible, so that by the year 2000 the Earth would undergo a complete environmental collapse, wiping out most life (including humanity).

Three alternatives for survival were suggested. Alternative 1 called for the deployment of a large number of nuclear bombs in the upper atmosphere. It was suggested that their detonation would blow holes in the carbon dioxide envelope, allowing the excess heat in the atmosphere to escape into space. This idea was rejected on the grounds that it would have replaced one problem with another—a massive amount of radiation in the atmosphere. Gerstein's description of Alternative 2 takes us right back to the subterranean realms discussed elsewhere. In the book version of Alternative 3, Gerstein is quoted thus:

'Alternative 2, in my view, was even crazier than Alternative 1. I recognize, of course, that there is enough atmosphere locked in the soil to support life but ... no, this was the most unrealistic of all the alternatives.

'There is good reason to believe that this world was once more civilised and far more scientifically advanced than it is today. Our really distant ancestors, living millennia before what we call Prehistoric Man, had progressed far beyond our present state of knowledge.

'Then, it is argued, there was some cataclysmic disaster—maybe one comparable with that facing us now—and these highly sophisticated people built completely new civilizations deep beneath the surface of the earth ...

'There is evidence, quite considerable evidence, to suggest that there were once whole cities—linked by an elaborate complex of tunnels—far below the surface. Remains of them have been found under many parts of the world. Under South America ... China ... Russia ... oh, all over the place. And in this subterranean world, so it is said, there is a green luminescence which replaces the sun as a source of energy—and which makes it possible for crops to be grown ...

'Maybe there's some historical truth in the Biblical story of the great Flood. Maybe the disaster which drove them there in the first place was followed by the Flood—and they were all trapped and drowned down there. Maybe that's how their civilizations ended.

'And it could follow that the people we think of as prehistoric Men were merely the descendants of a handful of survivors—the real children of Noah, if you accept the Bible version—who had to start from scratch in a world which had been utterly devastated. Is that why they took so naturally—instinctively, if you like -to living in caves? Then the agonizingly slow process of rebuilding the world started all over again until now we find ourselves in a similar position ...' (59)

Thus, Alternative 2 called for the evacuation of the world's elites (the rest would have to take their chances on the surface) into these abandoned cities. However, this alternative was also discarded, since the heat from the greenhouse effect would eventually permeate down through the Earth's crust, making life equally impossible for those living underground.

The only option left was Alternative 3, which called for the evacuation (of the elites, once again) from Earth to Mars. Gerstein reiterated the theory that the Red Planet was once inhabited, and that its atmosphere might still be locked away in the soil. He added that in 1959 a Russian rocket had exploded on the launch pad, killing a large number of people and devastating the surrounding area. The implication was that the rocket had been carrying a nuclear device whose detonation would have unlocked the atmosphere on Mars and transformed it into a habitable planet once again. Gerstein went on to suggest that another rocket might have been sent to Mars, and that this mission might have been successful.

The Alternative 3 program also contained some footage of an alleged top secret unmanned mission to Mars, undertaken by the United States and the Soviet Union in 1962. The film showed the rocky landscape of Mars, seen from the approaching probe, accompanied by Russian and American voices. Near the end of the footage, an American voice said: 'That's it! We got it ... we got it! Boy, if they ever take the wraps off this thing, it's going to be the biggest date in history! May 22, 1962. We're on the planet Mars—and we have air!' The presenter of the program, Tim Brinton, commented that there must have been a very good reason why the true conditions on Mars were kept from the public, and why the mission had been jointly undertaken by the US and the USSR. The implication was of an ultra-secret interplanetary project which, Brinton claimed, could well be Gerstein's Alternative 3. (60)

By way of corroborative 'evidence', the makers of Alternative 3 pointed to the large numbers of people who go missing throughout the world each year, suggesting that many are actually being abducted by the Alternative 3 controllers and transformed, through surgical and chemical means, into mindless slave laborers who are then transported as 'Batch Consignments' to the colony on Mars. These hapless victims are referred to as 'superfluous people' by the controllers, who see their barbaric treatment as perfectly acceptable.

The controllers were also interested in recruiting scientists and academics from a wide range of disciplines. These personnel were called 'Designated Movers', and apparently accounted for the so-called 'brain drain' of the 1960s and 1970s whereby many scientists left Britain, ostensibly to take up better-paid posts overseas. (It was claimed that an investigation of the brain drain had been the original impetus behind the Science Report program.) The entire operation was headquartered in Geneva and was also controlled, in typical James Bond fashion, by a fleet of nuclear submarines stationed underneath the North Polar ice cap. Here the controllers ensured the conspiracy's continued secrecy by arranging 'hot jobs' (remote-controlled spontaneous human combustion) for those investigators who got too close to the truth.

The ingenious makers of Alternative 3 also brought in the NASA Moon flights as more evidence of the conspiracy. The reader may be aware that the Apollo program is a firm favorite of conspiratologists, some of whom maintain that NASA is hiding the discovery of derelict alien cities on the Moon, while others claim that all of the Moon landings were actually hoaxed, with the astronauts bouncing around a sound stage somewhere in Nevada or California. In Alternative 3, it was suggested that the Apollo astronauts did not stumble upon a derelict alien city but a fully functioning man-made way station for flights en route to the Martian colony. The following transcript of a conversation between Mission Control in Houston, Texas and an astronaut named Bob Grodin was presented in the book:

MISSION CONTROL: Could you take a look out over that flat area there? Do you see anything beyond?

GRODIN: There's a kind of a ridge with a pretty spectacular ... oh, my God! What is that there? That's all I want to know! What the hell is that?

MISSION CONTROL: Roger. Interesting. Go Tango ... immediately ... go Tango.

GRODIN: There's a kind of a light now ...

MISSION CONTROL (hurriedly): Roger. We've got it, we've marked it. Lose a little communication, huh? Bravo Tango ... Bravo Tango ... select Jezebel, Jezebel...

GRODIN: Yeah ... yeah ... but this is unbelievable ... recorder off ... (61)

Another transcript, this time between astronauts Scott and Irwin and Mission Control during their Moonwalk in August 1971, runs thus:

SCOTT: Arrowhead really runs east to west.

MISSION CONTROL: Roger, we copy.

IRWIN: Tracks here as we go down slope.

MISSION CONTROL: Just follow the tracks, huh?

IRWIN: Right ... we're (garble) ... we know that's a fairly good run. We're bearing 320, hitting range for 413 ... I can't get over those lineations, that layering on

Mount Hadley.

    SCOTT: I can't either. That's really spectacular.

    IRWIN: They sure look beautiful.

    SCOTT: Talk about organization!

    IRWIN: That's the most organized structure I've ever seen!

    SCOTT: It's (garble) ... so uniform in width . . .

    IRWIN: Nothing we've seen before this has shown such uniform thickness from the top of the tracks to the bottom. (62)

The book version of Alternative 3 also contains an episode described by an inside source calling himself 'Trojan'. The events occurred in a base inside the crater Archimedes, which lies on the western border of the Mare Imbrium. The Archimedes Base is allegedly a large transit camp beneath a hermetically sealed transparent dome. Here one of the Designated Movers, a marine biologist named Matt Anderson, secretly visited a segregated area where the Batch Consignments of slaves were housed. In this slave village, Anderson encountered a childhood friend. Having yet to undergo the psychological conditioning that enabled the Designated Movers to accept the concept of slavery, Anderson was appalled and decided to escape with as many slaves as possible and expose the horror of Alternative 3.

Teaming up with a NASA-trained aerospace technician named Cowers, Anderson managed to get 84 slaves aboard a Moon ship and headed for one of the gigantic airlocks in the dome. However, a technician in the main control room saw what was happening and raised the alarm. The airlock was sealed shut and Gowers, who was flying the ship, panicked and lost control, sending it crashing into the dome. The resulting explosion tore a hole in the protective shell and the resultant cataclysmic depressurization killed almost everyone at the base. As a result of this disaster, an earlier base in the crater Cassini was redeveloped, and Alternative 3 is going ahead as planned.

As mentioned, the huge number of telephone calls from concerned viewers resulted in a speedy statement from Anglia Television that Alternative 3 had been an April Fool's Day jape and nothing more. Indeed, the participation of several quite well-known actors (one of whom appeared in a dog food commercial before the beginning of the program!) could mean little else. In spite of this, Alternative 3 has taken on a life of its own, offering a kind of template for the suspicions of other writers and conspiracy researchers.

Most notable among these is the American conspiratologist Jim Keith (who sadly died in September 1999). In his Casebook on Alternative 3 (1994), he lists more than 30 scientists connected with the Strategic Defense Initiative (SDI) 'Star Wars' anti-missile project who either committed suicide, disappeared or otherwise died in mysterious circumstances. This parallel with the missing scientists in the Alternative 3 scenario is an example of Keith's case as presented in his book. When the conspiracy is examined closely, its principal elements become recognizable aspects of other conspiracy theories. It is as if the creators of the Anglia Television program had pre-empted the protagonists of Umberto Eco's novel Foucault's Pendulum, in which a small group of bored intellectuals working for a publisher of esoteric texts take all the information they can find on secret societies and historical conspiracies, and feed it into a computer nicknamed 'Abulafia' (after the Cabalist). The computer then links all of the snippets it has been given into a cogent and internally consistent (although completely fictitious) scenario in which all the secret societies in history have handed down to each other the elements of a fantastic Secret that will give the holder incredible power. Through indiscretion, word of the protagonists' discovery spreads through the international network of contemporary secret occult groups, who then hound the intellectuals (literally) to death, thinking that they have the Secret. The book's hero, Casaubon, meets his death at the hands of occultists who wish the Secret to remain a secret.

With Alternative 3, we can see a similar process at work. The basic template of a secret power elite making plans to abandon a dying Earth and colonize Mars offers the basis for a wider and more elaborate scenario. It begins with the rise of human civilization, which from its very inception contained the roots of a powerful and totally unscrupulous elite that has secretly directed the course of history for thousands of years. In the twentieth century (with which we are primarily concerned in this chapter), the most extreme and barbaric example of this power elite at work was Nazi ideology.

Jim Keith makes the interesting point that Hitler himself conceived of four 'alternatives' to deal with the coming world of scarcity that he envisaged. In Mein Kampf Hitler wrote:

A clear examination of the premises for foreign activity on the part of German statecraft inevitably led to the following conviction:

Germany has an annual increase in population of nearly nine hundred thousand souls. The difficulty of feeding this army of new citizens must grow greater from year to year and ultimately end in catastrophe, unless ways and means are found to forestall the danger of starvation and misery in time.

There were four ways of avoiding so terrible a development for the future:

1. Following the French example, the increase of births could be artificially restricted, thus meeting the problem of over-population ... 2. A second way would be one which today we, time and time again, see proposed and recommended: internal colonization ... 3. Either new soil could be acquired and the superfluous millions sent off each year, thus keeping the nation on a self-sustaining basis; or we could 4. Produce for foreign needs through industry and commerce, and defray the cost of living from the proceeds. (63) Hitler rejected the first of these options on the grounds that the self-limitation of a population through birth control would necessarily result in a weakening of that population, since the natural laws of Darwinian survival of the fittest would be circumvented. 'For as soon as procreation as such is limited and the number of births diminished, the natural struggle for existence which leaves only the

strongest and healthiest alive is obviously replaced by the obvious desire to 'save' even the weakest and most sickly at any price, and this plants the seed of a future generation which must inevitably grow more and more deplorable the longer this mockery of Nature and her will continues.' (64)

The second option—of 'internal colonization' and the increase of resource-yield within Germany—he rejected on the grounds that it could not be sustained indefinitely: 'Without doubt the productivity of the soil can be increased up to a certain limit. But only up to a certain limit, and not continuously without end. For a certain time it will be possible to compensate for the increase of the German people without having to think of hunger, by increasing the productivity of our soil. But beside this, we must face the fact that our demands on life ordinarily rise even more rapidly than the number of the population.' (65)

The third option refers, of course, to the concept of Lebensraum:

The acquisition of new soil for the settlement of the excess population possesses an infinite number of advantages, particularly if we turn from the present to the future. ... We must ... coolly and objectively adopt the standpoint that it can certainly not be the intention of Heaven to give one people fifty times as much land and soil in this world as another. In this case we must not let political boundaries obscure for us the boundaries of eternal justice. If this earth really has room for all to live in, let us be given the soil we need for our livelihood.

True, they will not willingly do this. But then the law of self-preservation goes into effect; and what is refused to amicable methods, it is up to the fist to take. (66)

The fourth option, which relied on German interdependence with other nations through international commerce, Hitler rejected on the grounds that the survival of the Aryan race would necessarily depend on the activities of other nation states:

If ... Germany took this road, she should at least have clearly recognized that this development would some day ... end in struggle. Only children could have thought that they could get their bananas in the 'peaceful contest of nations', by friendly and moral conduct and constant emphasis on their peaceful intentions, as they so high-soundingly and unctuously babbled; in other words, without ever having to take up arms. (67)

Having made the interesting but rather tenuous connection between Hitler's alternatives and the possible options stated in Alternative 3 (the former referring to Hitler's perception of the problems facing the German people; the latter referring to the problems facing humanity as a whole), Keith then quotes a passage from Mein Kampf in which Hitler writes:

[T]he folkish philosophy finds the importance of mankind in its basic racial elements. In the state it sees on principle only a means to an end and construes its end as the preservation of the racial existence of man. ... And so the folkish philosophy of life corresponds to the innermost will of Nature, since it restores that free play of forces which must lead to a continuous mutual higher breeding, until at last the best of humanity, having achieved possession of this earth, will have a free path for activity in domains which will be partly above it and partly outside it. (68) [Keith's emphasis.]

Keith considers it highly significant that Hitler should have mentioned domains lying above and outside the Earth, in view of the events following the defeat of the Third Reich. He continues:

Summing up ideas that seem to add up to ... Alternative 3, we are familiar with the advanced disk aircraft designs perfected by the Nazis during World War II, and also know that the American space program was run by prominent Nazis, or at least ex-Nazis. Nazi interests have also been entwined, since the emergence of the philosophy, with other totalitarian control mechanisms of the world, with the intelligence, police, and psychiatric establishments, with eugenics and genetic research, as well as with the plans of monied elites whose philosophies might better be defined in parapolitical, rather than political terms. (69)

We have already examined the theory of German flying discs in Chapter Eight, and noted at the beginning of this chapter that many prominent Nazis were transferred to the United States at the end of the war, under Project PAPERCLIP—including Wernher von Braun, who designed much of the hardware for NASA's Apollo program. With regard to the continuation of Nazi objectives in the post-war years, mentioned earlier in this chapter, Keith offers the following quote from the Research and Analysis branch of the OSS from 1945:

The Nazi regime in Germany has developed well-arranged plans for the perpetuation of Nazi doctrines after the war. Some of these plans have already been put into operation and others are ready to be launched on a widespread scale immediately upon termination of hostilities in Europe . . . Nazi party members, German industrialists and the German military, realizing that victory can no longer be attained, are now developing post-war commercial projects, endeavoring to renew and cement friendships in foreign commercial circles and planning for renewals of pre-war cartel agreements. German technicians, cultural experts and undercover agents have well-laid plans to infiltrate into foreign countries with the object of developing economic, cultural and political ties. German technicians and scientific research experts will be made available at low cost to industrial firms and technical schools in foreign countries. German capital and plans for the construction of ultra-modern technical schools and research laboratories will be offered at extremely favorable terms since they will afford the Germans an excellent opportunity to design and perfect new weapons. (70)

For conspiratologists such as Keith, the fabric of Alternative 3 can be unwoven to reveal its component strands, all of which seem to be supported by evidence of varying quality. As Keith himself states: 'One of the difficulties in researching Alternative 3 was that the evidence kept leading me in a direction I wasn't particularly happy to go in: toward the Nazis. ... A possibility, which I admit is wild speculation, yet at the same time comprises a startling alignment of facts, is that Alternative 3 is an expression of Nazi occult doctrine and that there is a long term elitist program to abandon Earth and to implement another step in Hitler's "Final Solution".' (71)

The component strands of Keith's vision of Alternative 3 can be summarized as follows: Towards the end of the Second World War, the Nazis developed radical aircraft designs, including the Foo Fighters and larger, manned flying discs. The plans for these machines, along with a number of components and scientific personnel, were transferred to a hidden colony in Neu Schwabenland, Antarctica in the closing stages of the war. The two operations known as 'Eagle Flight' and 'Paperclip' ensured that Nazi financial interests and espionage respectively were maintained after the war's end. Given that colonies of Nazis continue to exist in Antarctica and South America, it is probable that their own aerospace research has continued unabated, to the point where they have made manned space flight safe and routine. The discovery that life on Earth is doomed as a result of pollution and overpopulation led to the formulation of Alternative 3, whereby the monied elites of the world would effectively jump ship and establish a human colony on Mars. Far from being mortal enemies, the United States and the Soviet Union were actually the closest of allies: the Cold War was a monumental con on the rest of humanity, which unwittingly supplied the slave labour required for the gigantic construction projects. The Nazi survivors, one of the main players in this scenario of secret world history, saw this as a perfect opportunity to continue with the creation of a master race, with their Lebensraum relocated to Mars. Keith continues:

My belief is that the Nazis have been major, but far from the only players in the game of world domination since the end of World War II: one among many heads of the Hydra. Influential Nazis (possibly including Hitler) have been behind the scenes since the end of the war, creating and implementing schemes for the ultimate triumph of Die Neuordnung [New Order]. Almost all of Hitler's cohorts survived Nuremberg and may have been involved in manipulations including international terrorism and the establishment of drug and arms markets, as well as in collaboration with other more 'respectable' networks of world influence.

While I cannot state with certainty that Nazis are creating the 'real' domination of Alternative 3, that they have constructed or are constructing bases on Mars or the moon to carry the ancient Grail of Aryan racial purity away from what they conceive as a cataclysm-doomed Earth, I do have to wonder at the logic and symmetry of detail. (72)

The complex, interconnected system of rumors -paranormal, historical and political—that has grown up around Alternative 3 is perhaps the most extreme expression of the postwar Nazi-survival idea. Indeed, its very extremeness provides a perfect example of the way in which seemingly unconnected mysteries, truths and half-truths can take on an independent life that quickly rages beyond control, spawning fantastically baroque conspiracy theories that bear scant resemblance to the components from which they arose.

CONCLUSION: THE MYTH MACHINE
THE REALITY AND FANTASY OF NAZI OCCULTISM

Occultism is a curious and fecund beast. Beliefs, and the events to which they give rise, have a frequently unfortunate habit of generating additional beliefs. If, as in the case of Nazi occultism, the initial beliefs were little more than crypto-historical idiocies, there can be little hope of improvement in their ideological progeny. This book has been as much a history of belief about Nazi occultism as about Nazi occultism itself, and there is little doubt that the principal driving force behind the development of this belief is an attempt to explain the dreadful aberration that was the Third Reich.

Given that human beings have always been fascinated with the occult and the supernatural, precisely because they promise so much in offering the prospect of a higher meaning to the vagaries of existence, and given also our quest for an answer to the problem of evil, it is only to be expected that many should seek to explain Nazism in terms that transcend the merely human. We noted in the Introduction that some serious orthodox historians place Hitler outside the spectrum of human behavior—a spectrum that includes the most barbarous of crimes. Hitler is seen by them as uniquely evil, wicked beyond even the human capacity for wickedness. Others, who are inclined to accept the reality of a cosmic evil originating beyond humanity, in some Outer Darkness eternally forsaken by God, see Hitler and the Nazis as examples of how, given the right circumstances, this Darkness can enter humanity, an 'eruption of demonism into history'.

Nevertheless, the demonic can easily be confused with insanity: one shudders to think of the number of unfortunates throughout history whose madness was mistaken by their fellows for possession by the forces of Darkness. We have seen that the origins of National Socialism can be traced to volkisch occultists who believed wholeheartedly not only in the existence of a prehistoric Germanic race of superhumans but also that their very superiority had been transmitted through the ages to modern Germans by means of a magically active, pure Aryan blood. The bizarre occult statements of Theosophists such as Madame Blavatsky, Rudolf Steiner and others seemed to offer evidence of the existence of a fabulous Aryan race that established great civilizations on the lost continents of Atlantis, Lemuria and the mythical island of Thule in the incredibly remote past.

OCCULT SECRETS OF THE THIRD REICH

The idea of genuine Nazi occult power (as opposed to Nazi belief in that power) seems to have arisen out of our own continuing fascination with the legends in which the volkisch and Pan-German occultists believed so fervently. Belief in all aspects of the paranormal is extremely prevalent, whether it be belief in alien visitation, the spirits of the dead, dark and demonic forces from beyond the realm of humanity, or technologically advanced prehistoric civilizations such as those of Atlantis and Lemuria; and it seems to me that this belief lies at the core of the mythological development of Nazi occultism that has occurred in the second half of the twentieth century. For if the supernatural really exists, might not the Nazis have discovered a way to harness its power to further their dreadful ambitions?

The answer to this question must be negative: we have already seen that the evidence for Hitler's initiation into the mysteries of the black arts is non-existent, while the evidence for his utter contempt for mysticism of any kind (particularly that practiced by Himmler in Wewelsburg, his sick joke of a Grail castle) is documented time and again. Indeed, such was Hitler's lack of interest in these matters that he never deigned even to visit Wewelsburg. What of Himmler, then? Did he not practice dark rites with his SS Gruppenfuhrers in their Order Castle, attempting to contact the souls of long-departed Teutons? The answer to this question is, of course, yes. However, occult-orientated writers have, over the years, continually made the same mistake in claiming that, because Himmler attempted to contact supernatural forces, those forces exist to be contacted. I consider myself a sceptic, rather than an incredulous doubter, [*] and so I cannot say that supernatural forces do not exist, any more than I can say that they do exist. In truth, no one can. But we must not allow ourselves to make any connection whatsoever between Himmler's ideas on the supernatural and the veracity of the supernatural itself.

Ken Anderson makes an interesting point in his Hitler and the Occult:

From early in their rise to power Hitler and his Nazis were enveloped in an aura of mysticism almost despite themselves. This aura appears closer to the experience of occultism than any other major movement in the twentieth century. Hitler came to personify the invisible structure which became the occult myth dealt with here.

With the help of contemporary occult writers, the illusion is today more pervasive. We find no such occult mystique surrounding other aberrations of civilization.

To this we might add that the aura of mysticism surrounding the Nazis was enhanced and disseminated throughout German society by means of photography and cinema, notably Leni Riefenstahl's virulently propagandist films, which include Triumph of the Will and Olympia, and which glorify German-ness and emphasize the inherent superiority of the Aryan race. The Nazis were nothing if not masters of self-promotion.

Just as the early volkisch occultists took various elements of prehistoric mythology to construct a totally spurious history for the Germanic 'master race', so many occult-orientated writers have taken the image of the Nazi black magician and his

316

diabolical allies and with it have attempted to create an equally spurious history of the Third Reich. The insubstantial edifice of their wild speculations is 'supported' by the incorporation of Eastern mysticism, with its tales of hidden cities inhabited by ascended masters who are the real controllers of humanity's destiny on Earth. Whatever their veracity, these myths are exquisitely beautiful and elaborate, and it is something of a tragedy that they should have been hijacked by Western writers in their quest to connect Nazism with a putative source of genuine occult power in the East.

We have also seen how Nazi cosmology, with its utterly insane notions of 'World Ice' and the Earth as a bubble in an infinity of rock, arose from the grandiose but untenable cosmological theories of previous centuries. Moreover, after the end of the Second World War they became part of the twentieth-century fascination with alternative cosmologies, including the Hollow Earth theory, which has stubbornly persisted to this day.

Another example of how the Third Reich generated strange rumors can be seen in the concept of the Nazi flying discs, which arose partly from admittedly intriguing (but still inconclusive) evidence, and partly from the unassailable evidence that Nazi scientists were indeed experimenting with radical aircraft designs and weapons systems. Thanks to clever manipulators of public opinion such as Ray Palmer, the quite possibly genuine mystery of the UFOs was 'explained' in terms of the rumors that the Nazis had actually perfected high-performance disc-shaped aircraft.

As we have seen, this in turn gave rise to the idea that these disc-planes were used by high-ranking Nazis to escape from the Allies during the fall of Berlin. Once again, it is clear that the various outlandish claims of Nazi hideouts in Antarctica owe their inception to genuinely puzzling events such as Admiral Byrd's apparently disastrous Operation Highjump, in addition to the indisputable fact that many Nazi war criminals did indeed escape from the ruins of the Third Reich to take up residence in various South American countries. All of this provides conspiracy theorists with a heady mixture of components with which to construct their nightmarish scenario of hideous clandestine forces maliciously pulling the strings on which we all dance. At the risk of offering a cliche, what we have here is a classic example of putting two and two together and getting five.

As we noted in the Introduction, with the passage of time and the deaths of important firsthand witnesses any chance of finding an adequate explanation of Nazism and the horrors it unleashed has now almost certainly been lost. We are left with the awful question that will continue to haunt us for as long as we remain human: why? The question is made more awful by the likelihood that the answer lies not in Outer Darkness, not in the 'Absolute Elsewhere', but much closer, in that most frightening and ill-explored of realms: the human mind.

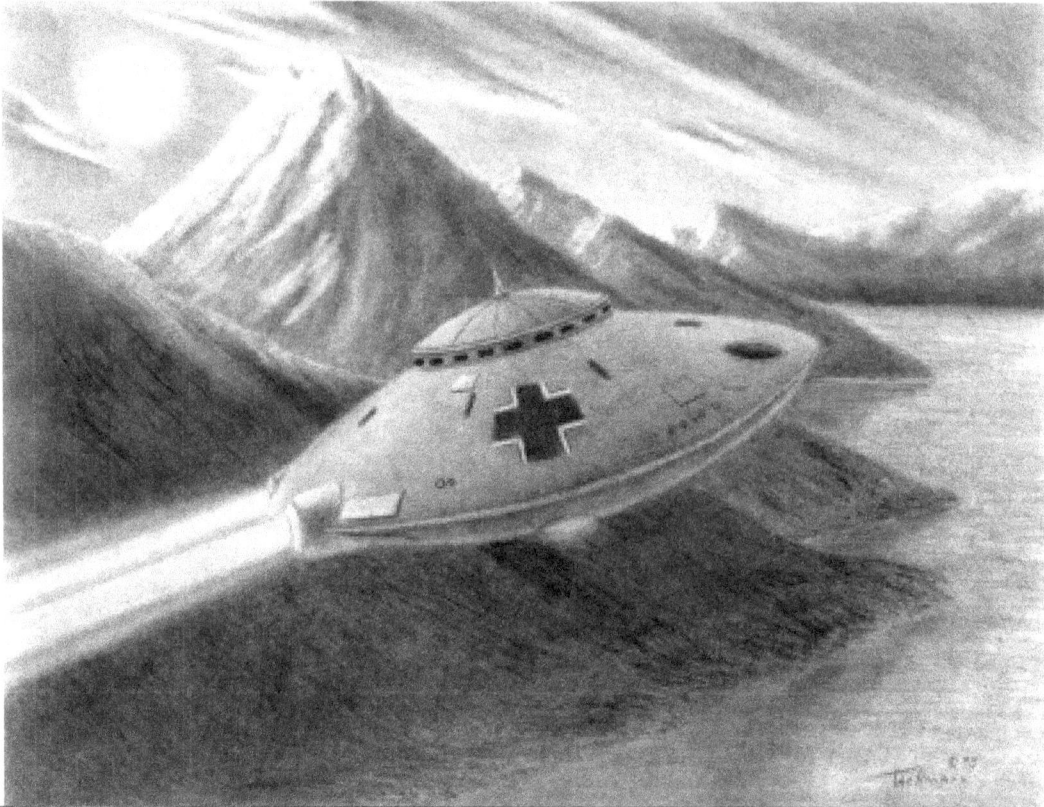

Artist rendering of German saucers, based on eye-witness accounts.

320

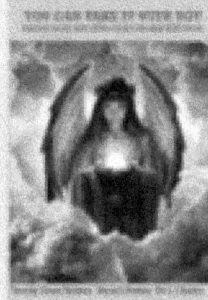

323

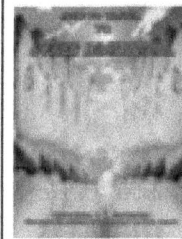

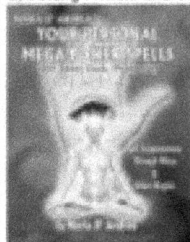

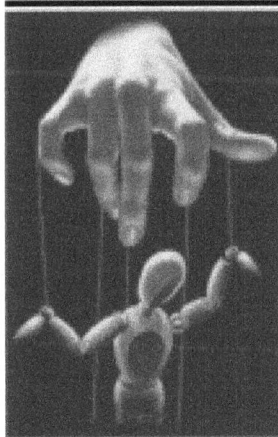

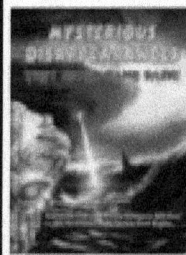

332